Secrets

of the Fascist Era

How Uncle Sam Obtained
Some of the Top-Level Documents
of Mussolini's Period

Howard McGaw Smyth

SOUTHERN ILLINOIS UNIVERSITY PRESS
Carbondale and Edwardsville

Feffer & Simons, Inc.
London and Amsterdam

Library of Congress Cataloging in Publication Data

Smyth, Howard McGaw.
  Secrets of the Fascist era; how . . .

  Bibliography: p. 277-290
  Includes index.
  1. Italy—History—1922–1945—Sources. 2. Ciano,
Galeazzo, conte, 1903–1944. 3. Mussolini, Benito,
1883–1945. 4. World War, 1939–1945—Secret service—
United States. I. Title.
DG571.A2S63   945.091   74-31340
ISBN 0-8093-0696-4

Contents

Illustrations

Preface

Some years ago the late E. Taylor Parks, my colleague in the Historical Office of the Department of State, served as Head of the Advisory and Review Branch. Although my assigned work was with the captured German Foreign Office records, he would, from time to time, refer inquiries about Italian documentary materials to me. I had a background in modern Italian history. Furthermore I had got acquainted with some of the collections of Italian documents that the United States government had seized during World War II in the course of my service in various official positions since coming to Washington in 1942: in the OSS, in the Division of Territorial Studies and in the Division of Southern European Affairs of the Department of State, and in the Office of the Chief of Military History (now termed Center of Military History), Department of the Army. Several times Dr. Parks urged that I write up the stories of the acquisition of these collections lest, with the passing of time, the knowledge become lost or so eroded that future retrieval or reconstruction would present great difficulties. Thus I began the project which resulted in this book. Initially I thought that I might achieve my goal in a couple of articles but my perspective soon changed. When I began putting a few notes in order and sorting out some records that I had kept I did not realize that the requisite materials for my project would be so scattered and difficult to track down.

Fortunately, during the course of my researches, I was able to draw on the help of many friends whom I had met in government service and in the historical profession, in this country and abroad. Others who kindly responded to my inquiries are persons whom I have not met personally and who might at best be described as pen pals in the profession. Foremost I express my gratitude toward two men, students during that bygone era when I offered a course in Modern Italy at Berkeley. Professor George A. Carbone of Portland State University was in Rome for a part of the time of my search for materials. He ordered books for me, sent me microfilmed copies of various items, joyfully responded to numerous queries. Mr. Raymond Rocca, who served with the OSS in Italy during the war, gave me several invaluable leads and introduced me to the late

ix

Allen W. Dulles who graciously granted me the use of some files that he kept when he headed the OSS in Switzerland.

In the Historical Office and elsewhere in the department there were many who gave me suggestions and criticisms. My former coworkers in the German Documents Branch, Dr. George O. Kent, now Professor of History at the University of Maryland, and Dr. Arthur G. Kogan, who succeeded E. Taylor Parks in the job of providing visiting scholars with advice and review, gave me help with many phases of my work. Valuable leads came from the late G. Bernard Noble, former Director of the Historical Office, and important help and useful criticism from his successor, Dr. William M. Franklin. Dr. Fredrick Aandahl, now Chief of the Foreign Relations Division, supplied me with useful clues. Dr. Marvin W. Kranz, formerly with the Historical Office but now with the Library of Congress, assisted me in many of my searches for materials there. Mrs. G. M. Richardson Dougall, wife of the deputy director, offered some very relevant information.

The library of the Department of State has an excellent collection of governmental publications, of materials in international relations and in the fields of modern history and government. The staff members were always helpful with my requests. If some published work that I wanted was not there, Mr. Ernest Halton obligingly secured it for me through interlibrary loan.

The successful completion of my undertaking would not have been possible without the aid of some devoted and very knowledgeable public servants at the National Archives. Mr. Robert Wolfe, Chief of the Captured Records Branch, Military Archives Division, answered countless inquiries on my part. Mrs. Patricia Dowling assisted me on many occasions in locating files, reels of microfilm, and documents. Others, now or formerly with the National Archives and Records Service, who gave me help with some puzzling problem or search for detail were Philip G. Brower, Richard Bauer, Hermann Goldbeck, Kenneth Munden, Wilbur J. Nigh, and Donald E. Spencer.

In the Office of the Chief of Military History (OCMH) Mr. Detmar Finke, Mr. Charles F. Romanus, and Mrs. Magna E. Bauer gladly offered me aid and advice. I am grateful for help given me by several professional historians, Professor Gerhard Weinberg, and Professor Emeritus Howard M. Ehrmann of the University of Michigan, Professor Charles F. Delzell of Vanderbilt University, and Oron J. Hale, Professor Emeritus of the University of Virginia.

In England Miss Margaret Lambert, British Editor in Chief of the *Documents on German Foreign Policy, 1918–1945*, wrote me numerous letters in response to my queries. Mr. Brian Melland of the Historical Section of the Cabinet Office, whom I met when I was stationed in England, was most helpful and Professor Hugh Trevor-Roper of Oxford supplied me with very useful information in response to transatlantic requests. Peter Tompkins, journalist, author, quondam "Spy in Rome," got several items for me as did Miss Lisa Sergio, journalist, lecturer, and onetime member of the staff of the Ministry of Popular Culture. Mr. John Marshall, recently retired, was with the Rockefeller Foundation at the Villa Serbelloni at Bellagio during my researches and very kindly sent me books and copies of articles after my meeting him by mail. Professor Reginald Aaragon of Reed College was intermediary. Mrs. Florence W. Lehman, Alumni Director at Reed, was most responsive to the inquiries that I addressed to her.

My daughter, AnnaLee, now Mrs. Abidin Atabay, skillfully read my longhand, penciled drafts and typed most of the manuscript. This was in one copy only. My younger son, H. Edward Smyth, gladly made the requisite, additional copies with the Xerox machine whose use was offered by C. L. McCabe & Son, Inc., of Selbyville, Delaware. Most of all I acknowledge the help given me by my wife. She patiently listened to my various drafts; with her sensitive ear she caught the rough passages that needed smoothing out; she quickly detected the sentences or paragraphs that were not clearly written; and she saw me through all stages of the work.

Bethany Beach, Delaware   HOWARD MCGAW SMYTH

February 1974

Introduction

There are in our national capital some half-dozen collections of Italian official documents or state papers, most of them now in microfilm form, and on deposit for the use of scholars at the National Archives. These collections of top-level records of the Fascist era, which came to Washington in consequence of our involvement against Mussolini's Italy in World War II are as follows:

1) The Lisbon Papers, letters, telegrams, and memoranda of conversations which emanated from the office of Count Ciano as Italian foreign minister (Microcopy, or Microfilm Publication T-816);

2) A much smaller collection of German translations of papers from Ciano's office, a collection known as the Ciano Papers: Rose Garden (one roll of microfilm in Microfilm Publication T-120);

3) Transcripts, made by an Anglo-American team, of documents seized in Rome in the files of the Fascist Ministry of Popular Culture;

4) A very large and thoroughly indexed collection of Italian military documents which were initially seized by the Germans after Italy surrendered to the Allies in 1943 and were later captured in Germany by the United States Army (Microfilm Publication T-821);

5) Mussolini's Private Papers, documents which fell into Anglo-American hands after the collapse of the neofascist regime in April 1945 (Microfilm Publication T-586);

6) A small, rather miscellaneous collection of Italian materials at the Library of Congress.

These collections of Italian documentary materials offer a sharp contrast to our American holdings of Nazi German records. The Italian collections are few, whereas there is a plethora of German materials. Sheer chance played a large part in the discovery, seizure, and microfilming of the Italian collections, whereas the collecting of German National Socialist documents was a matter of deliberate policy.[1]

1. The Nazi records for the most part fall into three great groups as follows: (1) Documents and testimony gathered in preparation for or during the Nuremberg trials, portions of which were published in *Trial of the Major War Criminals before the International Military Tribunal Nuremberg 14 November 1945–1 October 1946*, 42 vols. (Nuremberg 1947–49); (2) The

Finally there is a strong contrast between the German and Italian records available in Washington as regards publicity and public knowledge. Compared to the seized German documents, so carefully indexed and with their systematic descriptions of parentage, the few, stray collections of filmed Italian official papers have seemed like orphans without any records of lineage. The first general description of these documents embodying so many secrets of the Fascist era was my paper which was delivered at the National Archives in November 1968.[2]

Prior to any evaluation of the contents of a document, it must be established that the text is authentic, that the document is what it purports to be. On the other hand, to continue to doubt, or to discount the testimony of a document or of a collection of papers when it has passed the tests establishing authenticity is intellectually as much in error as is gullible acceptance of the fact statements of a spurious text.[3]

German Foreign Office records which were held in Anglo-American custody 1945–58, selections from which were published in the series *Documents on German Foreign Policy, 1918–1945,* 18 volumes issued by the Department of State and the British Foreign Office. Some three million pages or "frames" were microfilmed, forming a collection designated Microfilm Publication T-120 at the National Archives. There is an excellent guide to the documents for the early period issued by the American Historical Association, Committee for the Study of War Documents, *A Catalogue of Files and Microfilms of the German Foreign Ministry Archives 1867–1920* (Oxford: Oxford University Press, 1959). For the later period the Department of State and the Hoover Institution on War, Revolution and Peace have issued *A Catalog of Files and Microfilms of the German Foreign Ministry Archives 1920–1945,* comp. and ed. George O. Kent, 4 vols. (Stanford, Calif.: Hoover Institution Press, 1962–72). (3) Many tons of records of the German armed forces, of a number of the executive departments of the Nazi regime, of business firms and even of some individuals were seized by the U.S. Army with the cooperation of the British at the end of World War II and were shipped to Alexandria, Virginia. Having completed its own exploitation of these documents for intelligence purposes, the Department of Defense planned to ship them back to the German Federal Republic without microfilming. In September 1955 the American Committee for the Study of War Documents was launched and the next year the group became a Committee of the American Historical Association which got funds for the microfilming project from various foundations and which enjoyed the cooperation of the Department of Defense. In the years 1958–64 the committee issued 40 catalogues or guides to German records microfilmed under its direction. Since that time the work has been continued by the National Archives and Records Service (NARS). As of this writing there has been a total of 66 numbered *Guides to German Records Microfilmed at Alexandria, Va.*

2. "Italian Civil and Military Records on Microfilm," to be published by the National Archives along with the other papers of that conference; Robert Wolfe, editor.

3. The late Ruggero Zangrandi wrote the most exhaustive study in the Italian language regarding Italy's surrender to the Allies, *1943: 25 luglio–8 settembre* (Milan: Feltrinelli, 1964). On p. 486, n. 37 he suggests that the documents used by F. W. Deakin at St. Antony's College, Oxford, might have been fabricated and planted so as to be picked up by the Allies in the course of the Italian campaign. These are Mussolini's Private Papers and most certainly are genuine as will be developed in chap. 5.

In regard to any official document the first question is where is it from, in what office or bureau did it originate. Or if a state paper, or even a so-called private letter from one official to another has been received, read, circulated and acted upon, in what file or collection was it retired. In other words, the first problem is to determine provenance.

In case a document, or the alleged text of a document turns up in an odd place, the critic wants to know how it got there. With microfilmed copies of documents the problem is compounded. The critic will want the answers to further, unavoidable questions: where and how the microfilms were made; and what became of the originals. In many cases the documents themselves offer some answers, but often, when files or films have repeatedly changed hands, the face of a document reveals no more about its travels than does a five-dollar bill.

Washington, D.C. is not a natural repository of Italian state papers; it is not the place where one would normally expect to find documents or photographic copies of documents of the Fascist era. For each of the six collections of Italian records in Washington with their secrets of Mussolini's period I propose to discuss the provenance of the documents, the voyages and vicissitudes of the collections in Italy and beyond if such movements took place, to describe precisely who did the filming, where and how it took place, and finally to account for the originals.

I am not discussing the revelations of these documents, not evaluating the testimony which they offer regarding Italy under Mussolini. My attention is focused strictly on the problem of authenticity: The chapters which follow are, then, a series of essays in external criticism. In each narrative I have begun with that period in time which is the point of departure for the story of that documentary collection. Consequently I have gone over some of the same ground more than once, and I have viewed and reviewed some events but from different angles. Lest this back and forth movement lead to confusion in the mind of the reader, I have provided for reference, the chronology which immediately follows this introduction.

Chronology

October 28, 1922. The "March on Rome" leading to the appointment on October 30 of Mussolini as prime minister and the beginnings of the Fascist regime.

October 3, 1935–May 9, 1936. Italian invasion and annexation of Ethiopia.

June 9, 1936. Count Ciano named Minister of Foreign Affairs.

November 6, 1937. Italian adherence to the Anti-Comintern Pact initially concluded between Germany and Japan.

May 22, 1939. Signature of the Italo-German alliance, the "Pact of Steel."

September 1, 1939. German invasion of Poland.

September 3, 1939. France and Great Britain declared war on Germany.

December 7–8, 1939. First meeting of the Grand Council of Fascism since the outbreak of the war; an order of the day confirmed Italy's policy of "non-belligerency."

June 10, 1940. Italian declaration of war on France and Great Britain.

June 24, 1940. Armistice between France and Italy (two days after the Franco-German armistice).

September 27, 1940. Tripartite Pact of Japan, Germany and Italy.

October 28, 1940. Italian attack on Greece.

November 12, 1940. The British Royal Air Force attacked the Italian fleet at Taranto severely damaging three battleships.

December 6, 1940. Marshal Badoglio resigned as Chief of the Armed Forces General Staff (*Comando Supremo*); Gen. Ugo Cavallero was named his successor.

December 10–11, 1940. Disastrous defeat by the British of the Italian forces in Libya under Marshal Graziani.

June 22, 1941. Germany invaded Soviet Russia; Mussolini prepared to send an army corps to assist the Germans.

December 7, 1941. Japanese attack at Pearl Harbor.

December 11, 1941. Germany and Italy declared war on the United States.

1942

October 22–November 5, 1942. Battle of El Alamein, decisive defeat of the German-Italian forces by the British Eighth Army.

November 7–8, 1942. American and British forces landed in French North Africa (Operation Torch).

December 18–20, 1942. Conference of Ciano and General Cavallero with Hitler at German headquarters in Russia.

1943

January 14–25, 1943. Casablanca Conference; Roosevelt and Churchill announced the demand for the unconditional surrender of Germany, Japan and Italy.

January 30, 1943. Gen. Vittorio Ambrosio succeeded Cavallero as Chief of the *Comando Supremo*.

February 5, 1943. Mussolini's last "change of the Guard"; Ciano removed from the Ministry of Foreign Affairs and named Ambassador to the Holy See; Mussolini took over the ministry with Bastianini as Undersecretary.

May 12–25, 1943. Trident Conference in Washington.

May 13, 1943. Surrender of the German-Italian forces in North Africa.

July 10, 1943. Allied invasion of Sicily (Operation Husky); occupation of the island completed August 17.

July 19, 1943. Conference of Mussolini and Hitler at Feltre.

July 24–25, 1943. Meeting of the Grand Council of Fascism which voted a resolution against Mussolini.

July 26, 1943. King Victor Emmanuel III appointed Badoglio as Head of the Government; beginning of the "forty-five days of Badoglio" (to September 8); beginning of Mussolini's imprisonment in Rome, Gaeta, Ventotene, Ponza, La Maddalena, and on the Gran Sasso.

August 1, 1943. Formulation of the German plan *"Achse"* for the occupation of North Italy and the elimination of Italy's armed forces; Lanza d'Ajeta's mission to Lisbon to make contact with the Allies.

August 17, 1943. Allies completed the conquest of Sicily; the Germans completed the withdrawal to the Italian mainland of three and a half divisions and their equipment.

August 27, 1943. Flight of Ciano and his family to Germany.

September 3, 1943. Secret signature of the "Short Terms" of Armistice between Italy and the Allies at Cassibile in Sicily.

September 8, 1943. Announcement of the Armistice; launching of the Allied attack at Salerno (Operation Avalanche); beginning of the execution of Plan *Achse*.

September 9, 1943. Secret departure of the royal family, of Badoglio, and of the Italian high command from Rome to seek safety behind the Allied lines.

September 10, 1943. Capitulation of the Italian forces guarding Rome; German occupation of the city.

September 12, 1943. Mussolini was liberated from the Gran Sasso and flown to Germany; beginning of the "six hundred days of Mussolini" (actually 595 to April 28, 1945).

September 15, 1943. Mussolini in Germany proclaimed his headship of the Republican Fascist party with the task of supporting the German armed forces.

September 23, 1943. Announcement of the Italian Social Republic (*Repubblica Sociale Italiana*); its capital was later established at Salò near the German lines of communication; Marshal Graziani was named commander of the new armed forces and Minister of Defense.

September 29, 1943. Signature of the "Long Terms" of Armistice by Badoglio at Malta.

October 1, 1943. The Allied armies entered Naples.

October 13, 1943. The Royal Italian government declared war on Germany and was recognized by the Allies as a "cobelligerent."

November 10, 1943. General Eisenhower announced the establishment of the Allied Control Commission for Italy with the duty of carrying out the terms of the Armistice.

1944

January 8–10, 1944. The Verona trials of the Grand Councillors who had voted against Mussolini; all were found guilty of treason; (only Ciano and five others had been apprehended).

January 11, 1944. Ciano and four others were shot; Tullio Cianetti was sentenced to thirty years in prison.

April 22, 1944. Badoglio formed a broad-based ministry including representatives of the Communist party and their Socialist allies.

June 4, 1944. The Allies occupied Rome; the German Tenth Army successfully withdrew and formed a new line of defense northward of the capital.

June 24–July 18, 1944. Serial publication in the *Corriere della Sera* of Mussolini's *Storia di un anno*, issued in November in book form with the title *Il tempo del bastone e della carota*.

October 26, 1944. Announcement that the United States would resume diplomatic relations with Italy.

November 1, 1944. The Allied Control Commission was redesignated the Allied Commission.

December 7, 1944. The United States Senate confirmed the nomination of Alexander C. Kirk as Ambassador to Italy.

1945

February 24, 1945. Allied aide-mémoire to the Italian government providing for considerable relaxation of control by the Allied Commission.

April 18, 1945. Mussolini moved his capital from Salò to Milan.

April 25, 1945. Mussolini conferred with Resistance leaders in Milan; he and some of his followers then moved on to Como.

April 27, 1945. Mussolini and a group of his followers were captured at Dongo.

April 28, 1945. Mussolini and his mistress were shot at Giulino di Mezzegra; a group of Fascist leaders were shot at Dongo.

April 29, 1945. Signature of the surrender of the German forces in Italy at Allied Headquarters at Caserta (effective May 2).

April 30, 1945. Hitler's suicide in Berlin.

December 31, 1945. Termination of Allied military government in Italy (except for the area around Trieste).

1945–1946. Negotiation by the United States, the Soviet Union, Great Britain and France of the Treaty of Peace with Italy.

1946

May 9, 1946. Abdication of Victor Emmanuel III in favor of his son, Humbert II.

June 2, 1946. Simultaneous plebiscite and election in Italy. The plebiscite decided that Italy would be a republic; the election determined the membership of the Constituent Assembly to draft the new constitution.

1947

February 10, 1947. Treaty of Peace with Italy signed at Paris.

February 16, 1947. Abolition of the Allied Commission for Italy.

May 31, 1947. De Gasperi formed a ministry excluding the Communists and Socialists.

July 31, 1947. The Constituent Assembly ratified the Treaty of Peace.

September 15, 1947. The Treaty of Peace became effective with the deposit of the instruments of ratification at Paris.

September 17, 1947. Allied Force Headquarters (AFHQ) was abolished.

December 22, 1947. Adoption of the new constitution by the Constituent Assembly.

December 1947. Withdrawal of the last units of American forces from Italy (except for the Free Territory of Trieste which was separated from Italy by the Treaty).

1948

January 31, 1948. Dissolution of the Constituent Assembly.

April 18 and 20, 1948. Election of the Legislative Assembly under the new constitution.

1949

April 4, 1949. Italy signed the North Atlantic Treaty.

Secrets of the Fascist Era

1 / The Lisbon Papers

The Ministerial Cabinet and the Cabinet Archives

The Italian Ministry of Foreign Affairs, like the other executive departments or ministries of that government, had a ministerial cabinet. It was headed by a *Capo di Gabinetto* whose office and functions were closely comparable to those of the *Chef de Cabinet* in the French *Ministère des Affaires Étrangères*. Traditionally the *Gabinetto* had been a kind of personal secretariat of the minister of foreign affairs, its head, the *Capo di Gabinetto*, a kind of personal secretary.[1]

After Mussolini in June 1936 appointed his son-in-law, Count Galeazzo Ciano, to the post of minister of foreign affairs, the operations of the ministerial cabinet were greatly enlarged. Ciano used the cabinet to carry out his policy of fascistization of the Foreign Ministry. Hitherto most of the work of the ministry had fallen on the three principal political bureaux (*direzione generale*): the Bureau for European and Mediterranean Affairs; the Bureau for Overseas Affairs; and the Bureau for General Affairs. Each was headed by an experienced, professional member of the Italian diplomatic service.[2]

1. For the development of the ministerial cabinet and the office of its chief since 1853, see Luigi Vittorio Ferraris, *L'amministrazione centrale del Ministero degli Esteri italiano nel suo sviluppo storico (1848–1954)* (Florence: Biblioteca della "Rivista di studi politici," 1955) passim.

Cf. Ernst Posner, "The Administration of Current Records in Italian Public Agencies," National Archives, *Records Administration Circular* no. 5 (November 1943), p. 3.

2. For the table of organization of the Ministry of Foreign Affairs at the outbreak of

During Mussolini's first period as minister of foreign affairs (1922–29) he had carried on a struggle against the professionals and the traditional spirit in the Palazzo Chigi. He appointed Dino Grandi, one of the Fascist bully boys, as undersecretary. But the outcome was not the fascistization of Italy's diplomatic corps: what happened was that the career men took Grandi into their fraternity.[3]

Count Ciano concentrated the business of conducting foreign policy in the ministerial cabinet. He reduced the regular structure of the Foreign Ministry, as indicated by its table of organization, to an empty shell. The old professionals found it peculiarly galling to be lorded over by Ciano's young favorites. The cabinet took control of the distribution of information; its officials decided whether incoming telegrams and despatches should be passed to the directors of the bureaux for action or placed directly on Ciano's desk. This withholding of information naturally became a subject of bitter complaint by career men, and a source of considerable confusion and error in the conduct of business.[4] But it meant also that the Cabinet Archives (*Archivio di Gabinetto*) in the Fascist era assumed a peculiar importance. The editors of the Italian diplomatic documents have offered this official explanation of the significance of the Cabinet Archives:

With the custom gradually becoming established, particularly after 1927, of concentrating in the Cabinet the handling of all the more important questions, the Cabinet Archives undoubtedly represent the principal source. Here one finds: the originals of the confidential communications coming from foreign personalities and from the representatives accredited to the Quirinal; the memoranda relating to the conversations of the Head of the Government; of the Minister and of the Chief of the Cabinet with foreign diplomats and personalities; copies of each of the principal secret telegrams which were not circulated, both those sent and received; the more important secret reports of our chief of mission (sometimes in a single copy, sometimes in two or three copies for the most restricted distribution within the Cabinet); the personal correspondence of the Minister with the various Italian diplomats abroad; the memoranda for the Minister from the Chief of the Cabinet and from the Directors General; copies of the

World War II see: Ministero degli Affari Esteri, Commissione per la pubblicazione dei documenti diplomatici, *I documenti diplomatici italiani*, 8th ser., 1935–39 (Rome: Libreria dello stato, 1953), vol. 13, August 12–September 3, 1939, appendix 8, pp. 455–60.

Like most foreign offices the Italian ministry issued annually a personnel list, the *Elenchi del personale*, with the dates of appointment and service of its officials.

3. Alan Cassels, *Mussolini's Early Diplomacy* (Princeton: Princeton University Press, 1970), pp. viii–ix, 260–61, 386–87; H. Stuart Hughes, "The Early Diplomacy of Italian Fascism," *The Diplomats*, ed. Gordon A. Craig and Felix Gilbert (Princeton: Princeton University Press, 1953), pp. 217–19, 226, 230–31.

4. Felix Gilbert, "Ciano and His Ambassadors," *The Diplomats*, pp. 517–19.

unclassified telegrams relating to matters handled by the Cabinet; and a series of files or volumes containing the material regarding specific problems (e.g. the Tripartite Alliance, Alto Adige, etc.) or particular countries (e.g. Germany, Albania, etc.).[5]

Transfer of Selected Papers to Lisbon

When Mussolini was overthrown in July 1943, Raffaele Guariglia was appointed minister of foreign affairs in the regime which was headed by Marshal Badoglio. Guariglia's first thought, on getting back to Rome from Turkey where he had been Italian ambassador, was to make contact with the Western Allies. After trying in vain to establish contact through the Vatican, Guariglia on August 1 decided to employ Blasco Lanza d'Ajeta by naming him counselor of legation in Portugal. Lanza d'Ajeta had been private secretary (*Capo di Gabinetto*) to Count Ciano, and on the other side he was son-in-law of Sumner Welles, United States undersecretary of state, and thus very well suited to initiate peace feelers.

Guariglia saw to it that the principal part of the Cabinet Archives was hidden in the cellars of the Palazzo dei Principi Lancellotti at the time of the Armistice and thus escaped seizure by the Germans during their occupation of Rome. These materials were recuperated after ratification of the Treaty of Peace, but many documents were badly damaged and needed to be recopied in preparation for publication in the official series of Italian diplomatic documents.[6]

But there was a small portion of the documents of the Cabinet Archives of the period when Ciano was minister of foreign affairs which Guariglia was very anxious to preserve from seizure by either the Germans or the Anglo-Americans. These were packed in a large suitcase which Lanza d'Ajeta bore with him on his flight to Lisbon. By this time the Italian government was half paralyzed with fear of a German stroke against Rome, the stroke which Hitler in fact was planning in order to liberate Mussolini, grab the Italian government and possibly the pope and restore fascism.[7] The greatest secrecy was observed regarding Lanza d'Ajeta's mission. He had scarcely taken off, however, when gossip in

---

5. *I documenti diplomatici italiani*, p. ix.

6. Ibid.

7. Albert N. Garland and Howard McGaw Smyth, *Sicily and the Surrender of Italy* (Washington, D.C.: Office of the Chief of Military History, Department of the Army, 1965), pp. 283, 287–88: Frederick W. Deakin, *The Brutal Friendship: Mussolini, Hitler and the Fall of Italian Fascism* (New York and Evanston: Harper & Row, 1962), pp. 490–502.

polite Roman circles had it that his errand was to transport the Ciano jewels to safety.[8]

At the Italian legation in Lisbon the small but critically important portion of the Cabinet Archives was delivered to Renato Prunas, the Italian minister. Apparently no catalogue of these documents had been made in Rome, but some time after their delivery in Portugal, on instruction from the Ministry of Foreign Affairs in the Italian capital, an index was made. Each package with its list enclosed was then sealed in the presence of Secretaries Assettati and Silj. Apparently no copies or reproductions of these documents were made in Lisbon.[9] They remained hidden and secure in the safe of the Italian legation until well after the end of the war in Europe.

The Americans Learn of the Papers at Lisbon

Within the Department of State there had been established in 1940 the Division of Foreign Activity Correlation, "charged with the conduct and correlation of such foreign activities and operations as the Secretary of State may direct, and with such other functions as shall be assigned to it by the Secretary of State." The new division was given the symbol designation: FC.[10]

As the war drew to a close the department developed its "Safehaven" program which was designed "to prevent German economic power from evading Allied controls by going into hiding or achieving legalistic sanctuary in areas governed by non-United Nations sovereignties." The areas where German economic power might find a safe haven were indicated as principally "the European neutrals and Argentina, and the chief

8. Raffaele Guariglia, *Ricordi 1922–1946* (Naples: Edizioni scientifici italiani, 1950), p. 587. Cf. *Documenti diplomatici italiani*, p. x.

Lanza d'Ajeta himself in his testimony and documentation presented to the Council of State in its epuration proceedings makes no mention of his role in transporting the documents, although he gives a rather full account, marred only by some chronological inaccuracies, of his part in attempting to establish contact with the Western Allies. See Consiglio di Stato, Sezione speciale per l'epurazione, *Memoria a svolgimento del recorso del Consigliere di Legazione Blasco Lanza d'Ajeta contro la decisione 4 gennaio 1946 della Commissione per l'epurazione del personale dipendente dal Ministero degli Affari Esteri* (Rome: Tipografia Ferraiola, 1946), passim; and *Documenti prodotti a corredo della memoria del Consigliere di Legazione Blasco Lanza d'Ajeta* (Rome: Tipografia Ferraiola, 1946), passim.

9. Statement by Prunas to the American chargé d'affaires, Key, Rome telegram no. 1314, March 11, 1946 (862.20235/3-1146); Lisbon telegram no. 268, March 13, 1946 (862.20235/3-146), Central Files, Department of State. When retired to the National Archives, these files constitute Record Group 59. Cf. note 39 below.

10. Departmental order no. 915-A, November 2, 1940 (111.017/409 1/2), Central Files, Department of State.

problem . . . to equate Allied security objectives with the sovereignty of these countries." The chief forms of enemy economic power to be searched for were "property looted by the Germans in occupied countries, German liquid assets fleeing Germany, and long-standing German investments in neutral countries." [11] The execution of the Safehaven program involved an intense search for enemy documents and this task, as far as the Department of State's participation was concerned, devolved primarily on FC.[12]

The trail of the Lisbon documents was first picked up in June 1945. Ambassador Kirk [13] wired the department on June 1 that Col. Henry H. Cuming, assistant chief of staff, G-2, of Headquarters, Peninsular Base Section,[14] had learned of a "considerable amount of secret diplomatic correspondence dealing mainly with Italo-German and Hispano-German affairs" which had been sent to the Italian legation in Lisbon. This most promising trail was lost the next month. On July 10 the department received the sad news that Colonel Cuming had died that morning of infantile paralysis.[15] The quest for the Lisbon documents lapsed.

11. Covey T. Oliver, "Information Memorandum for the Secretary of State, The Safehaven Project," March 7, 1945, (800.515/3-745), Central Files, Department of State.

12. Interview with Herbert J. Cummings, June 4, 1964. Cummings in 1945–46 was assistant chief of FC.

It may be noted that the teams of experts who followed the Allied armies into Germany and gathered up the German Foreign Office records and began their microfilming, operated, on the American side, under the direction of the Division of Foreign Activity Correlation.

13. Alexander Comstock Kirk. On March 31, 1944, he was appointed United States representative, with the rank of ambassador, on the Advisory Council for Italy, and on December 8, 1944, was officially named ambassador to Italy.

14. Like many others in the American intelligence services in World War II, Henry Hartford Cuming, Jr. (1905–45) came from academic life. As an undergraduate he was one of the greatest sprinters of all time of the University of Virginia, twice captain of the track team, and was a member of the American Olympic team of 1923. After serving on the United Press staff in Paris for a couple of years he returned to Virginia for graduate study in 1932 and a year later was invited to join the political science faculty. He spent the years 1936–38 in study and travel abroad, gathering material for his monograph on *Franco-British Rivalry in the Post-War Near East.*

Cuming entered the army as a reserve major in September 1941, was sent to England for further training, and in February 1942 was assigned to the War Department General Staff, G-2. In November he went into North Africa as a lieutenant colonel and thence to Italy as assistant chief of staff, G-2, at Fifth Army Base Section which later was designated Peninsula Base Section. In April 1945 he was promoted to colonel.

In 1944 Cuming had had an important role in the American acquisition of the Ciano diaries. Cf. notes 15 and 85, chap. 2.

15. Caserta telegram no. 2445, June 1, 1945 (840.414/6-145); departmental telegram to Caserta no. 553, June 6, 1945 (840.414/6-145); departmental telegram to Caserta no. 579, June 13, 1945 (840.414/6-745); Caserta telegram no. 2779, June 27, 1945 (840.414/6-2745); Caserta telegram no. 2916, July 10, 1945 (840.414/7-1045), Central Files, Department of State.

But not for long. After a couple of months G-2 of AFHQ passed certain intelligence to Ambassador Kirk who relayed to Washington the information that "Duke Blasco D'Ajeta" had certain very important documents in his personal possession; that he was still in Lisbon awaiting a more favorable time for returning to Italy.[16] After Lanza d'Ajeta returned to Rome he was interviewed by members of the staff of the American embassy. Between the lines of the solid documentary evidence it appears that there was some Italian who well knew the story, who had a grudge against Lanza d'Ajeta, and saw to it that the Americans learned about his action with the documents in 1943. Lanza d'Ajeta, on being questioned, admitted something about the documents, but he denied that they related—as was suspected in the department—to action by Germany, Italy, and Spain in South America. It emerged that the documents were still in Lisbon and the American ambassador there [17] was alerted that he might be instructed to ask for them.[18]

On January 11, 1946, Carmel Offie [19] and a member of the staff of the American embassy called on Prunas to ask about the documents. The man who had received them when they were brought secretly to Lisbon was now secretary general in the Ministry of Foreign Affairs. Prunas tended to play down the importance of the documents: he declared that he himself had not seen them; that so far as he was aware what was in Lisbon was correspondence of Mussolini and Hitler; and this, he mentioned, had already been published in the Italian and American press.[20] He agreed, however, to instruct the Italian legation in Lisbon to make the documents which had been delivered there in 1943 available to the American embassy.[21]

16. Caserta telegram no. 3519, September 6, 1945 (840.414/9-645), Central Files, Department of State.

17. Herman B. Baruch.

18. Departmental telegram to Rome, no. 2305, December 10, 1945 (862.20235/12-1045); to Lisbon, no. 1942, December 21, 1945 (862.20235/12-2145), Central Files, Department of State.

Cf. Mario Toscano, *The History of Treaties and International Politics vol. 1* (Baltimore: The Johns Hopkins Press, 1966), 1:252–53.

19. A foreign service officer. He had been detailed to the Navy Department on July 1, 1942; on March 17, 1944 was appointed to the staff of the United States member of the Advisory Council for Italy and of the Allied Control Commission; on June 23, 1944 he was assigned to the office of the United States Political Adviser, staff of the Supreme Allied Commander, Mediterranean Theater. In October 1944 he followed Ambassador Murphy north of the Alps serving him in his role as United States political adviser on German affairs. He was thus familiar with the search for Italian as well as German documents.

20. Cf. chap. 5. Although the book, *Hitler e Mussolini: Lettere e documenti* (Milan and Rome, Rizzoli, 1946) was not published until June 10, several of the letters had already been printed in whole or in part by Italian newspapers. See the introduction to that book, p. ix.

21. Rome telegram no. 172, January 12, 1946 (862.20235/1-1246), Central Files, Department of State.

The Department of State Demands Surrender of the Lisbon Documents

Four days later the department directed the ambassador in Lisbon to approach the Italian legation there, to obtain the documents, and to forward them to Washington by the quickest means. The ambassador was warned to be on guard lest any of the documents be concealed or removed.[22] In Rome, however, Prunas did not instruct the legation in Portugal as he had promised to do. Instead he wrote a letter to the American ambassador explaining: that the little collection of documents sent to Lisbon for safekeeping was composed exclusively of anti-German reports; that it was certain that the collection contained no material relating to Argentina or to South America in general; and confidentially he mentioned that it was the intention of the Italian government officially to publish the documents in order to show the real nature of the wartime relationship of Italy with Germany. Prunas concluded by stating that he had authorized the mission in Lisbon to reply to Ambassador Baruch that the documents would be sent to Rome where the Italian Foreign Ministry would provide the American embassy with any information which it might wish regarding them.[23]

The department refused to accept Prunas's proposal for return of the documents to Rome and insisted on their delivery into American hands. Prunas thereupon countermanded his own instructions to Lisbon and on February 5, 1946, the Italian chargé d'affaires at Lisbon confirmed the existence in the legation's safe of three sealed packages which were assumed to be the documents. He promised that they would be made available on return of the minister, Rossi Longhi, the next day.[24]

On the night of February 6, Ambassador Baruch received from the Italian minister in Lisbon three packages which he described as follows: [25]

Package No. 1. 6 bound volumes of copies entitled in translation "Conversations with Foreign Diplomatic Representatives in Rome" and four bound volumes "Letters from the Fuehrer to the Duce and from the Duce to the Fuehrer."

22. Departmental telegram to Lisbon, no. 47, January 15, 1946 (862.20235/1-1246), Central Files, Department of State.

23. Rome telegram no. 399, January 25, 1946 (862.20235/1-2546), Central Files, Department of State.

24. Departmental telegram to Rome, no. 121, January 18, 1946 (862.20235/1-1746); to Rome no. 206, January 28, 1946 (862.20235/1-2846); Rome telegram no. 584, February 4, 1946 (862.20235/2-446); Lisbon telegram no. 130, February 5, 1946 (862.20235/2-546), Central Files, Department of State.

25. Lisbon telegram no. 133, February 7, 1946 (862.20235/2-746), Central Files, Department of State.

Package No. 2. 5 bound volumes entitled "Resignation of Mr. Eden February 20, 1938"; "Czechoslovak Crisis, Meeting at Monaco [Munich] September 29, 1938," "Conference at Vienna November 2, 1938"; "Alto Adige"; "Albania April 7–12, 1939," "Italo-German Arbitration of Vienna, August 20, 1940." Also a folder containing "Documents which refer to the arbitration of Vienna November 2, 1938."

Package No. 3. 5 folders containing a total of 39 items covering exchanges of conversations, memoranda, etc., dealing with England, Germany, Rumania, Hungary, and the Russian front. Also three folders containing a total of 189 items dealing exclusively with events leading up to the conflict and dated August–September 1939.

Edward S. Crocker, the American counselor of embassy, signed a receipt for the documents.[26]

Transfer of the Lisbon Documents to Washington: Their Filming by FC

The three bundles of papers were not, however, immediately expedited to Washington for there were diverse views as to the next course. Within the Department of State, the Division of Foreign Activity Correlation was hot on the trail of the displaced documents, suspicious of the Italians who had secreted them, and rather convinced that they would reveal the Nazi-Fascist tie-up with Argentina, a matter in which Spruille Braden [27] was greatly interested. The officers of FC proposed that the Italian staff at Lisbon "should be thoroughly, if diplomatically interrogated by us with respect to the opening of the packages, the extraction or substitution of documents, and the possibility that other documents exist elsewhere." [28] They were ready to insist to the full on American rights under the Armistice.[29]

The officers of the Division of Southern European Affairs (SE) held a very different attitude. They were not looking at past Fascist sins: they were intent on bolstering the democratic forces within Italy, on aiding

26. See note 37 below.
27. Served as assistant secretary of state for American Republic Affairs from August 25, 1945 until his resignation June 6, 1947. Cf. note 33 below.
28. Memorandum, Klaus to Cummings, February 8, 1946 (740.00119 EW/2-846); departmental telegram to Rome, no. 357, February 13, 1946 (840.414/9-645), Central Files, Department of State.
29. Article 35 of the Long Terms of Armistice, signed at Malta September 29, 1943, specified: "The Italian Government will supply all information and provide all documents required by the United Nations. There shall be no destruction or concealment of archives, records, plans or any other documents or information."

the economic revival of the country, and on seeing that the peace treaty would be one which would enable a democratic regime to survive.[30] Ambassador Kirk was a key instrument in this policy. Prunas felt sure of his man in complaining in a personal letter of the procedure which the American government had followed in getting possession of the documents. He mentioned that "the circumstances and the methods used have embittered them; that collaboration between Italy and PW [psychological warfare] which is beyond doubt, is not involved in this affair." Prunas's remarks were relayed, not unsympathetically, to the department by Ambassador Kirk.[31]

Director General Prunas knew considerably more about the documents than he had originally let on, and he was worried. He had received a telegram from Lisbon, he explained to Ambassador Kirk on February 12, which indicated that among the papers turned over to the Americans was a series of intercepts of British communications of 1939 and some material relating to Eden's resignation in 1938. The British government, he felt sure, would not be pleased if it were to learn that such documents had been turned over to a third power. He felt that the Italian government should itself inform the British of the existence of these intercepts.[32]

Our embassy in Lisbon, promptly provided with information copies of the exchanges between Washington and Rome, asked that it be immediately informed should Prunas instruct Rossi Longhi to explain the matter to his British colleague in Lisbon. In any case Ambassador Baruch was now ready to return the documents to the Italian legation for transmission to Rome by Italian channels. The American charges against Argentina [33] had been published, he noted, and whatever purpose the

30. Personal recollection of the author who at the time was attached to the Italian desk as "Country Specialist."

31. Rome telegram no. 709 February 9, 1946 (862.20235/2-946), Central Files, Department of State.

32. Rome telegram no. 752, February 12, 1946 (862.20235/2-1246), Central Files, Department of State.

See the interesting entry in Ciano's diary for April 16, 1938: "At 6.30 p.m. the Pact with England was signed. Lord Perth was moved. He said to me: You know how much I have wanted this moment to come.' It is true. Perth has been a friend. Witness dozens of his reports which are in our hands." *Ciano's Hidden Diary 1937–1938* (New York: E. P. Dutton & Co., 1953), p. 102.

See also *The Ciano Diaries 1939–1943* (Garden City, New York: Doubleday & Co., 1946), p. 239 (entry for April 26, 1940).

33. *Consultation among the American Republics with Respect to the Argentine Situation: Memorandum of the United States Government, February 1946* (Washington: Government Printing Office, 1946, Department of State Publication 2473). The preface states: "This

documents might serve, it was too late to use them in that indictment.[34]

In Rome on February 17 Ambassador Kirk telegraphed the department that he had carried out his instructions to insist on the delivery of the Lisbon documents into American hands. Yet he expressed his personal view "that correct procedure is for original documents to be returned to Italian Government. They could be microfilmed by the Joint Diplomatic Research Agency [35] and copies sent Washington for Department's perusal." The Italian minister in Lisbon was being instructed to inform his British colleague regarding the documents, Kirk reported, and Prunas had also assured him that the Italian government itself would question Lanza d'Ajeta regarding any possible tampering with the documents.[36]

But FC had its way. The instruction that the documents be sent to Washington was not reversed. On February 19 Ambassador Baruch telegraphed that they would go forward with the next courier on February 22. In despatch no. 750 of February 20 he included a complete listing of the documents in each of the three packages, and a statement-receipt of their transfer which in translation read as follows:

> The Minister, Rossi Longhi, hereby declares terminated his custody of all the pertinent documents of the Ministry of Foreign Affairs which were in safekeeping in this Legation and were delivered to him at the time of his assumption of duties in Lisbon, by the Chargé d'Affaires ad interim, Assettati, in three sealed packages.
>
> The Counselor of Embassy of the United States, Mr. Edward S. Crocker, in taking over the same documents, confirms that they will all be returned by the Embassy of the United States in Lisbon to the Italian Legation in Lisbon, immediately after they have been examined and photostatic copies made.
>
> Lisbon, February 6, 1946
>
> A. Rossi Longhi   Edward S. Crocker
> Minister of Italy   Counselor of the Embassy
>   of the United States [37]

memorandum was delivered on February 11, 1946 to representatives of the other American Republics engaged in the consultation."

The pamphlet was prepared when Spruille Braden was assistant secretary of state for American Republic Affairs.

34. Lisbon telegram no. 161, February 14, 1946 (862.20235/2-1446), Central Files, Department of State.

35. For the Joint Diplomatic Research Agency, see chap. 5 (Establishment of the Joint Allied Intelligence Agency).

36. Rome telegram no. 863, February 17, 1946 (862.20235/2-1746), Central Files, Department of State.

37. Lisbon telegram no. 181, February 19, 1946 (862.20235/2-1946); Lisbon despatch no. 750, February 20, 1946 (862.20235/2-2046), Central Files, Department of State.

In despatch no. 777 of March 6 Crocker forwarded a list of nine errata in the index accompanying the shipment.[38]

There was nothing now for the Italian Foreign Office to do but put the best face on the matter and prepare to accept the situation which Guariglia in the summer of 1943 had been most anxious to preclude, that is American-British possession of the very cream of the Cabinet Archives of Count Ciano. On or about March 11 Prunas had a discussion of the matter with the American chargé, Key, a discussion marked by considerably more candor than Prunas had hitherto displayed. He explained that the documents had been removed from the Ministry of Foreign Affairs before the Armistice and emphasized that they had been transferred to Lisbon to avoid the danger of their falling into German hands in Italy. The papers had been collected in haste and packed into a suitcase (*valigia*) and they had not been sealed. Unfortunately the secretary who had performed the task had subsequently been shot by the Germans in the Ardeatine Caves massacre of hostages. It was only after the delivery of the documents in Lisbon and on orders from Rome that lists had been prepared and the packages had been sealed by Assettati and Silj. He felt certain that no documents had been removed at that time. Prunas now repeated to Key what he had told Kirk in confidence in January: "the Minister of Foreign Affairs who had complete responsibility for documents intended to proceed with an officially documented publication of this material." [39]

In Washington the Division of Foreign Activity Correlation proceeded with the microfilming of the documents with the intentions of restoring them promptly to Lisbon. In response to the request of the British embassy in Washington that it be permitted to examine the documents in leisure (it was explained that in Lisbon the British had been able to make only a superficial examination) the department on April 8 delivered one roll of microfilm of these documents to the second secretary of the British embassy, Mr. Peter Solly-Flood.[40]

38. (862.20235/3-646,), Central Files, Department of State.

39. Rome telegram no. 1314, March 11, 1946 (862.20235/3-1146), Central Files, Department of State. Cf. note 32 above.

40. Departmental telegram to Rome no. 605, March 15, 1946 (862.20235/3-1146); note of the British ambassador to the secretary of state, no. 169, March 21, 1946 (840.414/3-2146); memorandum of J. W. Amshey, FC, April 8, 1946, (740.00119 EW/4-846), Central Files, Department of State.

Restitution of the Lisbon Documents to the Italian Government: Transfer of the Microfilms to the National Archives

In London the British proceeded to examine the documents given them in microfilm form. Meanwhile the Italian government began pressing our embassy in Rome for the return of its documents in accordance with the assurances given in Lisbon. Not until May 8 was word received in Washington that the British government had completed its examination of the microfilm copies of the documents and that the department should feel free, as far as the Foreign Office was concerned, to return the originals to the Italian government.[41]

On May 23 the American chargé d'affaires at Rome reported that the archives from the Italian legation at Lisbon had arrived in four packages and these had been delivered intact to the Italian foreign minister. The Italians quickly checked over the contents of the packages. Five documents, it appeared, were missing, which were described and listed. These were rather quickly located in Washington as well as three others whose absence had not been noted in Rome. On June 18, Key was able to report that these missing documents had also been returned to the Italian Foreign Ministry "which now informs Embassy that this completes set of archives originally made available by Italian Legation at Lisbon." [42]

In Washington the Lisbon Papers were initially embodied in two very long rolls of microfilms. Within the Department of State they were turned over by the Division of Foreign Activity Correlation to the Historical Division (then known as the Division of Historical Policy Research). There they remained for some time in the immediate custody of the German Documents Branch which was responsible for custody of the microfilms of the documents of the former German Foreign Office and the editing of the *Documents on German Foreign Policy, 1918–1945*. A portion of the microfilms were "blown up" by the branch where they were officially

41. Rome telegram no. 2090, April 20, 1946 (862.20235/4-2046); memorandum, J. W. Amshey to Herbert J. Cummings, April 29, 1946 (740.0019 EW/4-2946); departmental telegram to Rome, no. 967, April 30, 1946, repeated to Lisbon as no. 430, (865.414/4-3046); memorandum of telephone conversation, Mr. J. W. Amshey, FC, and Mr. Peter Solly-Flood, second secretary, British embassy, May 8, 1946 (865.414/5-846), Central Files, Department of State.

42. Rome telegram no. 2566, May 23, 1946 (865.414/5-2346); departmental telegram to Rome, no. 1167, May 28, 1946 (repeated to Lisbon as no. 538), (865.414/5-2346); departmental instruction to Rome, no. 1288, May 29, 1946 (865.414/5-2346); Rome airgram A-638, June 18, 1946 (865.414/6-1846), Central Files, Department of State.

The Italian government acknowledged the restitution of its papers. See *Documenti diplomatici italiani*, 8th ser. vol. 13, p. x.

used in the publication, particularly in supplementing the German copies of the correspondence of Hitler and Mussolini.[43]

After completing the official use of the Lisbon documents the Historical Office transferred the microfilms to the National Archives where they were accessioned on December 19, 1962. There the collection is designated, microcopy T-816. The listing of the documents made by the Italians, and which was forwarded when the documents were sent from Lisbon to Washington, is at hand in copy in the National Archives as a guide.

Analysis of the Collection

Microfilm publication (or microcopy) T-816, "The Lisbon Papers," consists of three rolls of film, reels 1, 2, and 3, formerly reels 2196, 2197, and 2197A of the Whaddon Hall collection, T-120. The frames are not numbered. Each reel, however, is made up of several Italian files or groups of related documents, which thus constitute a unit within the reel. These groups or items usually have numbered pages, and by designating the reel, the group, and the page number within it, almost any document of microcopy T-816 can be precisely located on the film.

I have given arbitrary designations of these groups by letter, designations which do not appear on the film but are suggested merely for convenience: letters A to G for roll 1 (or reel 2196); letters H to S for roll 2 (former reel 2197); and X, Y, and Z for reel 3 (reel 2197A). The British have used *items* and have broken down the whole collection into twenty-one numbered items. The twenty-one groups or items are as follows with their titles as they appear on the film and by which each can be identified.

Reel 1 (Reel 2196) with 1304 Frames

2196 Group A [item 12]. "I, Colloqui con uomini di stato stranieri; II, Colloqui con rappresentanti diplomatici esteri a Roma; III, Lettere." (June 1941 to December 1942, 11 records of conversations and 7 letters; 94 numbered pages.)

---

43. See vol. 9 of series D, no. 68, pp. 104–5 and fn. 1, p. 104, and appendix, p. 706; no. 138, pp. 200–205 and fn. 1, p. 200; no. 212, pp. 299–300 and fn. 1, p. 299; vol. 11, no. 452, pp. 789–91 and fn. 1, p. 789; vol. 13, no. 156, pp. 220–22 and fn. 2, p. 220; no. 242, pp. 383–88, and fn. 1, p. 383.

A portion at least of these Lisbon Papers were used by Deakin (see *Brutal Friendship*, p. 820). A set of blow ups of the Lisbon Papers was donated by the Historical Office to the Hoover Institution but that set, as transferred in 1958, lacked the copies used by the German Documents Branch.

2196 Group B [item 13]. "Impostazione; II Preparazione; III Realizzazione; IV Compimento; V Communicazione alle Potenze; VI Documentazione." (Papers relating to the occupation of Albania, May 1938 to April 1939; 93 documents in 242 pages.)

2196 Group C [item 14]. "Colloqui con rappresentanti diplomatici esteri a Roma (Argentina, Austria, Francia, Germania, Giappone, Gran Bretagna, Jugoslavia, Haiti, Messico, Polonia, Romania, Spagna, Svizzera, Turchia, Ungheria); Vari; Incontri con. uomini di stato stranieri." (1936 and 1937; 62 documents in 251 pages.)

2196 Group D [item 15]. "Colloqui con rappresentanti diplomatici esteri a Roma; Colloqui con uomini di stato stranieri (Brasile, Germania, Giappone, Gran Bretagna, Jugoslavia, Polonia, Spagna, Ungheria, U.R.S.S., Stati Uniti)." (1937 and 1938, 42 documents in 199 pages.)

2196 Group E [item 16]. "Colloqui con rappresentanti esteri a Roma: Colloqui con uomini di stato stranieri. (Francia, Stati Uniti d'America, Germania, Romania, Spagna, Stati Uniti d'America, Ungheria); Lettere (Germania, Gran Bretagna, Spagna, Ungheria)." (1939–40; 24 documents [16 records of conversation; 8 letters] 181 pages.)

2196 Group F [item 17]. "Colloqui con uomini di stato stranieri; colloqui con rappresentanti diplomatici esteri a Roma (Germania, Romania, Spagna, Germania) Lettere (Albania, Croazia, Germania, Spagna, Ungheria)." (1940–41; 36 documents [20 records of conversation; 16 letters] 169 pages.)

2196 Group G [item 18]. "Colloqui con rappresentanti diplomatici esteri a Roma; Colloqui con uomini stranieri (Bulgaria, Francia, Germania, Jugoslavia, Gran Bretagna, Romania, Turchia- Ungheria, Germania, Gran Bretagna, Jugoslavia, Polonia, Ungheria) Lettere." (1938–39; 35 documents [31 records of conversation; 4 letters] 170 pages.)

Reel 2 (Reel 2197) with 1663 Frames

2197 Group H [item 1]. "Alto Adige: Documenti" Letter Hitler to Mussolini, March 11, 1938: Letter Ciano to Magistrati, April 18, 1938; Letter Magistrati to Ciano, April 21, 1938; Toast by Hitler at the Palazzo Venezia, May 7, 1938. (Four documents as listed, 25 pages.)

2197 Group I [item 2]. "Arbitrato Italo-Germanico di Vienna (30 agosto 1940 XVIII) Per le revendicazioni territoriali Ungheresi verso la Romania." (July 15–August 30, 1940; 14 documents [letters, records of discussion, protocols] listed by index; 42 pages plus maps.)

2197 Group J [item 3]. "Lettere del Führer al Duce e del Duce al Führer" I. (March 1938–June 9, 1940, a total of 34 letters in 176 pages. The letters are listed in 5 groups and are indexed by pages, 170 pages in arabic numbers plus pages 1–VI.)

2197 Group K [item 4]. "Lettere del Führer al Duce e del Duce al Führer" II. (June 1940–April 1941, a total of 21 letters in 112 pages. These are indexed in 3 groups: June–October 1940; October 1940–March 1941; March–April 1941. The texts are followed by a subject and name index of contents of the letters, pp. 113–29.)

2197 Group L [item 5]. "Lettere del Führer al Duce e del Duce al Führer III Campagna di Russia." (June 21, 1941–January 23, 1942, in 123 pages. There is an index but it fails to list the last letter.)

2197 Group M [item 6], "Lettere del Führer al Duce e del Duce al Führer," IV (June 23, 1942–May 19, 1943, 14 letters, 122 pages, listed in sequence.)

2197 Group N [item 7]. "Varie." (A total of 57 items of which five are duplicates and one a translation, not listed or indexed, in 192 pages. Of the 51 documents: 45 are of the spring and summer of 1943; four from September to October 1939; one of January 6–7, 1940; and one of January 15–18, 1942.)

2197 Group O [item 8]. "R. Ministero degli Affair Esteri—Archivio del Gabinetto di S.E. il Ministro—Germania III Titolo 72. I precedenti immediati del conflitto agosto-settembre 1939: Dall'incontro di Salisburgo allo scoppio della guerra." (A bound volume with 143 documents, many of them signed originals, August 11 to September 18, 1939 in 418 pages. An introductory note, p. 1, indicates that these highly classified documents were selected with a view toward a possible "green book" which would also include some less restricted materials. Page numbers at the bottom of sheets. Seven subseries are indicated by letters in the upper right corner: 72a–72z; 72ba–72bz; 72ca–72cz; 72da–72dv; 72eb–72ez; 72fa–72fz; and 72ga–gn.)

2197 Group P [item 9]. "R. Ministero degli Affari Esteri-Archivio del Gabinetto di S.E. il Ministro—Germania III, Titolo 73 and 74. (This item consists of two parts or groups: *Titolo 73* "Scambio di lettere Duce Führer" August 25–September 3, 1939; 12 documents, pp. 1–78. Many of the letters in several copies, some with translations and with longhand drafts. The letters have an archival enumeration 73a–73m.)

2197 Group Q [item 9]. *Titolo 74* "Communicazioni dell'Ambasciata Britannica," (August 20–September 2, 1939; 36 documents, all except two from the British embassy in Rome; usually the original and a translation, pp. 1–229. The archival listing is 34, giving no number to a reply by Ciano and no number to a memo by the embassy. There is an archival enumeration 74a–74z and 74ba–74bn. There is no 74bk.)

2197 Group R [item 10]. "Titolo 75. Cronologia dei Principali Av-

venimenti Precedenti lo Scoppio della Guerra—maggio–settembre 1939"
(a chronology in 51 pages).

2197 Group S [item 11]. "Titolo 73." (A duplication, the same as the
first part of 2197 Group P above, "Scambio di lettere Duce-Führer," pp.
1–78.)

Reel 3 (Reel 2197A) with 247 Frames

2197A Group X [item 19]. "Ministero degli Affari Esteri-Gabinetto
'Dimissione del Signor Eden (20 febbraio 1938-XVI) Documenti.' " (A
series of 13 indexed documents: no. 1, Ciano to Grandi, June 20, 1937;
the others from February 15 to February 23, 1938. A variety of documents: letters, telegrams, telephone messages; pages 1–146.)

2197A Group Y [item 20]. "Ministero degli Affari Esteri-Gabinetto
'Crisi Cecoslovacca-Convegno di Monaco- 29 settembre 1938-XVI; Convegno di Vienna- 2 novembre 1938-XVII-Documenti.' " (A series of 29
indexed documents of which two are memoranda of conversations, May
1938, and 27 documents from April to November 1938; 4 maps.)

2197A Group Z [item 21] "Arbitrato di Vienna." (A series of 10 miscellaneous items including four telegrams of November 1938, in 27 unnumbered pages plus 14 maps.)

Publication of Ciano's Diplomatic Papers

In January 1948 there appeared in Italy under copyright by Arnoldo
Mondadori a most interesting book entitled: *L'Europa verso la catastrofe.*
French and English translations of the work with identical selections of
documents promptly followed.[44] The English edition is entitled *Ciano's
Diplomatic Papers,* and the subtitle reads: "being a record of nearly 200
conversations held during the years 1936–1942 with Hitler, Mussolini,
Franco, Goering, Ribbentrop, Chamberlain, Eden, Sumner Welles,
Schuschnigg, Lord Perth, François-Poncet, and many other world diplo-
matic and political figures, together with important memoranda, letters,
telegrams, etc."

Regretfully we must note that the texts of several of the documents
published in the Italian version, *L'Europa verso la catastrofe,* have not
been printed with complete integrity. Those which differ from the photocopies of the originals, now available in the National Archives in

44. *Les archives secrètes du comte Ciano 1936–1942,* traduction de Maurice Vaussard
(Paris: Librarie Plon, 1948); *Ciano's Diplomatic Papers,* ed. Malcolm Muggeridge (Long Acre,
London: Odhams Press, Ltd., 1948).

Washington and also in London, are indicated, each with an asterisk, in the Appendix.

The English edition, we must add with even greater regret, does not, at least for one document, fully reflect in translation the Italian published text. In the Italian work on pages 249–78 we have Dino Grandi's famous report of February 19, 1938 regarding his meeting with Chamberlain. For some reason the Italian version gives the incorrect date of February 13. This is corrected in the English version. But in the Italian text Sir Joseph Ball, secretary of the Conservative party, is mentioned as Chamberlain's secret link with the Italian ambassador. The Italian text reads in full translation:

There came to me on Thursday afternoon Sir Joseph Ball, General Secretary of the Conservative Party, the confidential agent of Chamberlain and who, since the month of October last year, has been functioning as a direct and "secret" link between me and Chamberlain. Sir Joseph Ball with whom I have been in contact, one may say almost daily since January 15.

The published English version reads:

there came to me on Thursday afternoon the confidential agent of Chamberlain, who, since the month of October last year, has been functioning as a direct and "secret" link between myself and Chamberlain. This agent, with whom one may say I have been in almost daily contact since the 15th January.

Professor Trevor-Roper spotted the discrepancy between the two versions soon after the British edition was issued. He reviewed the Italian publication for the *Economist* but his reference to the role of Sir Joseph Ball was omitted. He also reviewed *Ciano's Diplomatic Papers* for the *Observer* and drew attention to the divergence between the Italian original and the English translation. The sentence with this reference was deleted before publication. But when the *New Statesman* wondered who the secret link might be, Trevor-Roper drafted a letter pointing out the name given in the Italian original text.

Professor Trevor-Roper later learned that Ball had threatened a libel suit if the British publishers mentioned his name. Apparently the publishing house would have been willing to meet a libel suit, but such legal action would have so delayed publication as to destroy the commercial value of the English edition. The name was deleted.[45]

---

45. Letter of Professor Hugh Trevor-Roper to the author, July 18, 1968.
The passage quoted in translation from the Italian version is from p. 251; that from the English edition is from p. 165. The corresponding passage in the French edition, which is an accurate translation giving the name of Sir Joseph Ball, is on p. 148.
A rather garbled account of this episode, referring to the Ciano diaries rather than to the diplomatic papers of Ciano, is to be found in the work by Bruce Page, David Leitch,

Where did the texts of these most interesting documents come from? There is no indication in the book itself regarding their provenance. It is not completely excluded by such explanations as have been offered regarding the archival origins of the *Documenti diplomatici italiani* that copies of these papers were among those which were hidden in the cellars of the Palazzo dei Principi Lancellotti.[46] But the original editor in chief of that whole series did not indicate such an origin. He suggested or hinted rather that the texts in *L'Europa verso la catastrofe* were from Ciano's own selections and which fell into the hands of the Germans during the final phase of the war.[47] We shall deal with this explanation in the next chapter. It is not valid. The evidence is overwhelming that the Italian texts of Ciano's own selections of supporting papers were destroyed, and that what survives of his copies is in German translation only and possibly incomplete.

The Nazis hated and despised Ciano, particularly for his skepticism, which was apparent as early as 1941, regarding their promises of victory. They ransacked Rome after the Armistice in search of proof of Italian "treason" to the Axis, looking particularly for the records of Ciano's attitudes and activities. The Germans seized a good part of the Italian Foreign Office records of the Fascist era, the so-called archives of the Palazzo Chigi.[48] These files were taken to Berlin and at Ribbentrop's direction were carefully studied. They have not been recovered. Apparently they were destroyed by fire in the German capital.[49] We can exclude the Palazzo Chigi's archives as a possible source for the texts in *Ciano's Diplomatic Papers.*

Philip Knightly, *The Philby Conspiracy* (Garden City, N.Y.: Doubleday & Co., 1968), pp. 73–74.

Cf. The Memoirs of Anthony Eden, Earl of Avon, *Facing the Dictators* (Boston: Houghton Mifflin Co., 1962), pp. 706–8; (London: *Cassell & Co.*, Ltd., 1962), pp. 619–22.

46. See note 6 above.

47. "After September 8, 1943, the Germans were able to acquire a copy of the collection containing Ciano's minutes, and they took it to Germany to be copied and translated. Perhaps the publication referred to here is based on one of these copies which went astray during the last days of the war." Toscano, *History of Treaties and International Politics,* 1:289.

48. During Mussolini's first year in office he moved the Ministry of Foreign Affairs from the Palazzo della Consulta to the Palazzo Chigi, a change symbolizing fascism's break with the past.

49. The records of the German seizure and exploitation of the Palazzo Chigi archives are contained in the files of the *Auswärtiges Amt* which are now at Bonn, and in microfilm form in Washington and London. There is a thorough discussion of the problem in the appendix of Deakin's *Brutal Friendship,* pp. 827–37, "The German Authorities and the Italian Foreign Archives (1943–44)." The late Professor Toscano covered the same ground in his article, "Le vicende degli archivi di Palazzo Chigi e dei diari di prigionia di Mussolini catturati dai Nazisti dopo l'armistizio," originally published in the *Nuova Antologia* of March

The Italian publisher of *L'Europa verso la catastrofe* offers no indication of how the documents were acquired or even who the individual was who prepared them for publication. In default of such explanation I suggest that it was the Italian government itself which published these papers and from the originals which had been sent to Lisbon. The publication is selective. It does not, by any means, comprise all of the documents which were secreted at Lisbon. But there is no text included in *Ciano's Diplomatic Papers* which is not to be found among the Lisbon Papers.[50] I suggest that it was the Italian government which, realizing that copies of these most revealing documents were already in the hands of the American and British governments, decided to forestall any possible embarrassment of foreign publication by bringing out the papers itself. It did precisely what Renato Prunas in January 1946 had confidentially informed Ambassador Kirk, and had repeated to Chargé d'Affaires Key in March, that it would do.

Historians the world over owe a debt of gratitude to the Italian republic for the provision of so much sound evidence of the real nature of Axis diplomacy, no matter what the constraining factors were in leading to the publication. Historians should also be grateful to those zealous officers of the Division of Foreign Activity Correlation in the Department of State. They may not have found what they were searching for in Lisbon; they did not get the evidence which they hoped for of a Nazi-Fascist-Argentine conspiracy. But they did get some of the most critically important documents of World War II.

1961, and reprinted as chap. 9, pp. 249–81, *Pagine di storia diplomatica contemporanea*, vol. 2, *Origini e vicende della seconda guerra mondiale* (Milan: Dott. A. Giuffrè, 1963).

The relevant documents on this problem were discovered by the staff of the German war Documents Project in their screening of the files while they were in Anglo-American custody at Whaddon Hall, near Bletchley, Bucks, England, 1948–58. In preparation for possible future publication, these documents were reproduced on what was termed the "Whaddon Special Film."

These selections made by the Whaddon staff plus a few others were made available in London to Professor Deakin during the course of his researches. Somewhat later these same selections were made available to Professor Toscano. (Letter of the Honorable Margaret Lambert to the author, August 10, 1966.) Professor Toscano expressed his thanks to Miss Lambert and specifically refers to the group of documents made available by her (Toscano, p. 250). Professor Deakin offers no clue as to how he obtained these documents.

50. See Appendix.

2 / The Ciano Papers: Rose Garden

Count Galeazzo Ciano: His Diary and Supporting Papers

Galeazzo Ciano, dei conti di Cortellazzo, was born on March 18, 1903 at Leghorn, the son of Admiral Costanzo Ciano, an Italian hero of World War I and an early supporter of Mussolini. After gaining his degree young Ciano dabbled for a time in journalism and then in 1925 entered the Italian diplomatic service. He served briefly at Rio de Janeiro, Peking, and the Holy See. On April 24, 1930 he married Edda, the daughter of Mussolini. Thereafter his promotions were very rapid indeed. After a brief period serving as consul general at Shanghai, Ciano was named minister to China and in 1932 served as presiding officer of the League of Nations' Commission of Inquiry on the Sino-Japanese conflict. In August 1933, Mussolini named his son-in-law chief of his press office, which in September of the next year was upgraded and renamed the Office of Press and Propaganda with Ciano as its undersecretary. In June of 1935 the office was transformed into a full-fledged ministry with Ciano as its head.

Ciano volunteered for the Ethiopian War and served in command of a bomber squadron. He was decorated by Marshal Badoglio for military valor in that war. Then on June 9, 1936, at the age of thirty-three he was appointed minister of foreign affairs, an office which he filled until February 1943. Young Ciano was even accorded, retroactively it would seem, that great Fascist honor of having taken part in the "March on Rome" (1922).[1]

---

1. At least it is so stated in the *Enciclopedia italiana,* appendix 1, p. 412. See, however: Duilio Susmel, *Vita sbagliata di Galeazzo Ciano* (Milan: Aldo Palazzi, 1962), p. 56.

Countess Edda Ciano liked to speak of herself as half Russian, ascribing her moodiness and weak lungs to her Russian blood. Mussolini's wife dismissed such talk as mere gossip: Edda was born to us on September 1, 1910, she writes, but Benito and she were not yet regularly married; hence the stupid insinuation that Angelica Balabanoff was the mother of Edda.[2]

The Cianos had three children: the older son, baptized Fabrizio Benito Costanzo, born October 1, 1931; the daughter, Raimonda, born December 21, 1933; and Marzio, the younger son, born December 18, 1937. But the marriage was not a happy one: It was common knowledge that each spouse had numerous affairs. Edda was headstrong and violent in her feelings, something which seemed to endear her to her father.[3]

Ciano was minister of foreign affairs during the period of the British acceptance of Italy's conquest of Ethiopia, of the Italian intervention in the Spanish Civil War, of Italy's rapprochement and subsequent alliance with Nazi Germany, and of the Second World War until February 1943. It was in the course of the Italian intervention in the Spanish Civil War that Ciano instigated the murder of the Rosselli brothers, Carlo and Nello, founders of the movement Giustizia e Libertà.[4] He met and spoke with practically all the important European leaders of the time and kept a diary or diaries during all or most of the period of his ministry. The larger portion of these diaries was first published in English translation in the American edition of January 1946.[5] An earlier portion of the diaries was first published in Italian in 1948. The English translation followed in 1953.[6] These diaries are unquestionably, incomparably, the

---

2. Rachele Mussolini, *La mia vita con Benito* (Milan: Arnoldo Mondadori, 1948), p. 31.

3. Roman Dombrowski, *Mussolini: Twilight and Fall* (New York: Roy Publishers, 1956), p. 114.

Susmel, *Vita sbagliata*, p. 58, relates that when Edda returned from her trip to Germany in 1937 where she had been shown great attention by Hitler and the Nazi bigwigs, Galeazzo asked her directly if she had ever betrayed him. She answered "No," and Susmel assures us that this was the truth.

The statements to the contrary are too numerous to be listed.

4. Charles F. Delzell, *Mussolini's Enemies: The Italian Anti-Fascist Reistance* (Princeton: Princeton University Press, 1961), pp. 159–60; Susmel, *Vita sbagliata*, pp. 74–75.

Cf. Massimo Salvadori *The Labour and the Wounds, A Personal Chronicle of One Man's Fight for Freedom* (London: Pall Mall Press, 1958), pp. 118–19.

5. *The Ciano Diaries 1939–1943: The Complete, Unabridged Diaries of Count Galeazzo Ciano, Italian Minister for Foreign Affairs, 1936–1943*, ed. Hugh Gibson, Introduction by Sumner Welles (Garden City, N.Y.: Doubleday & Co., 1946).

6. Galeazzo Ciano, *1937–1938 diario* (Bologna: Cappelli, 1948); *Ciano's Hidden Diary 1937–1938*, translation and notes by Andreas Mayor, with an Introduction by Malcolm Muggeridge (New York: E. P. Dutton & Co., 1953.)

most interesting and important Italian memoir material regarding World War II.[7]

Closely associated with Ciano's private and often highly subjective notations in the booklets of his diary were the supporting papers. In the American edition of the diaries one encounters such interpolations as these:

January 12, 1939 (p. 10): "I shall let Mackensen read yesterday's record."

July 19, 1939 (p. 110): "I have set down my impressions of Spain in a notebook."

October 1, 1939 (p. 154): "As usual I have summarized in a memorandum in my conference book the official account of my contacts with Hitler and other high officials of the Reich."[8]

In the diaries for 1937–38, English edition, one finds such references as these:

November 5, 1937 (p. 29): "An extremely interesting conversation. I have summarized it in a minute."

January 3, 1938 (p. 58): "Conversation with Perth, of which I have made a minute."

January 5, 1938 (p. 60): "The first [conversation of the Duce] of which I have made a minute, was with Count Bethlen."

These supporting papers of Count Ciano, in the form which they had taken when they reached Washington, came to be known as "The Ciano Papers: Rose Garden." Our primary aim in this chapter is to narrate how they got here. But this story cannot be told by itself. To make it intelligible we must at the same time unravel the story of the diaries. But even before the diary and supporting papers begin their movements from Rome, a few things should be noted.

The diary was not very secret. Parts of it had been shown or read to: Dino Alfieri, ambassador to Germany; Filippo Anfuso, Ciano's secretary and later ambassador to Hungary; Zenone Benini, a lifelong friend of Ciano's, undersecretary in the Ministry of Foreign Affairs in 1939, and minister of public works in Mussolini's last cabinet before the overthrow of July 1943. Benini later told the Americans about the diary. It was known also to: Felice Guarneri, undersecretary in the Ministry for Cur-

---

7. Mario Toscano, *The History of Treaties and International Politics*, pt. 1, "An Introduction to the History of Treaties and International Politics: The Documentary and Memoir Sources" (Baltimore: The Johns Hopkins Press, 1966), pp. 454–55.

Cf. Lewis Bernstein Namier, *Diplomatic Prelude 1938–1939* (London: Macmillan & Co. 1948), p. 494.

8. Other such references are to be found on pp. 175, 212, 219, 223, 255, 274, 277, 293, 305, 306, 419, 436, 470, 477, 552, 556.

rency and Foreign Exchange; to Giorgio Nelson Page and to Orio Vergagni, also friends of many years.[9] Sumner Welles recorded: "He showed it *[the diary]* to me and read me excerpts from it in my first conversation with him." [10]

Mussolini was thoroughly aware that his son-in-law was keeping a diary; he knew of Ciano's dislike and suspicion of the Germans; and that the diary and selection of supporting papers reflected this attitude. In the entry for July 6, 1941, Ciano noted Mussolini's irritation over German activity in the Alto Adige (or the South Tyrol as the Austrians call it). "Note it down in your diary," Mussolini said, "that I foresee an unavoidable conflict arising between Italy and Germany." For November 6, 1942, it is recorded: "Mussolini asked me if I was keeping my diary up to date. When I answered affirmatively, he said that it will serve to prove how the Germans, both in military and political fields, have always acted without his knowledge." On February 8, 1943, three days after Mussolini had told Ciano that he was being transferred from the Ministry of Foreign Affairs to the embassy to the Vatican, the Duce "asked me if I had all my documents in order." Ciano assured him that they were in order, and that he could document all the treacheries perpetrated on Italy by the Germans.[11]

The diary entries were recorded by Ciano in calendar notebooks issued by the Italian Red Cross, page by page, usually one page for one day. These sheets were about eight inches by ten inches. The notations were in longhand in ink. Now and then, when much was recorded for a given day, extra sheets had been pasted in. At other places the handwriting was extremely cramped in order to compress one day's material on one sheet. One booklet was used for each year. The booklets were kept in the little safe in Ciano's office.[12]

The published volume for 1937–38 at the second entry, that for August 23, 1937 reads: "From today I mean to resume a regular diary."

9. Susmel, *Vita sbagliata*, pp. 76–77.

10. *The Ciano Diaries, 1939–1943*, p. xxvii. Cf. p. 212, entry for February 26, 1940.

11. Ibid., pp. 374, 539, and 580.

12. Interview with Mr. Allen W. Dulles, January 17, 1966; telegram, Bern to Washington (Dulles to OSS), January 11, 1945, item 58L, file "Edda Ciano Diaries," personal files of Allen Dulles.

This file, which the late Allen Dulles was kind enough to lend me, is a manila folder with a series of documents, copies or originals, arranged in reverse chronological order, and clipped to each side, seventy-one to the right side and sixty-two to the left. References are to the items by number, with R indicating right and L indicating left. See also Susmel, *Vita sbagliata*, p. 76.

The *Ciano Diaries 1939–1943*, pp. 1, 189, 329, 429, and 563 reproduce the covers of the Red Cross notebooks used by Ciano. The *1937–1938 diario*, between p. xvii and p. 1, provides a facsimile of the entry for August 22, 1937.

This implies or suggests strongly that there were other, antecedent diary notations. This recording, however, should be read in conjunction with the entry for August 22: "My writer's vanity makes me beg that, if one day publicity is given to these notes, it will be remembered that they were thrown on to the paper by me, in bits and pieces, between an interview and a telephone call." [13] The wording may mean that there was at some time some sort of systematic set of notations by Ciano for 1936, a notebook which did not survive the vicissitudes we are about to relate. Susmel insists that the Ciano diaries originally consisted of eight notebooks, one for each of the years 1936 to 1943. [14] The author has found positive evidence of only seven booklets in the various movements of the diaries from 1943 onward. The notation for August 22, 1937, may merely indicate that Ciano experimented from time to time with diary notations prior to that date, but kept a systematic record only thereafter.

In 1944 when American intelligence officers first picked up the trail of the diaries and papers, Zenone Benini, who seems not to have drawn a clear distinction between diary and papers, mentioned additional people to whom the diary was known: Blasco Lanza d'Ajeta, Duke Marcello del Drago, and the writer Curzio Malaparte. Benini felt sure that the German embassy knew of the diary. According to Benini, Curzio Malaparte stated that as early as May, 1942, Ciano had been advised by a friend to resign and seek refuge in some foreign country but had replied: " 'The publication of my Diary will be sufficient not only to protect me from all political vengeance and persecution, but will rehabilitate me even in the eyes of my adversaries.' Ciano stated on several occasions to his friends that he intended to publish this document abroad, perhaps in America or in England." [15]

The Cianos "Escape" to Germany

Count Ciano, whom Mussolini had relieved of his position as minister of foreign affairs on February 5, 1943, was one of the ringleaders of the revolt against the Duce in the Grand Council of Fascism. In his new position as ambassador to the Holy See, Ciano worked assiduously for Italy's withdrawal from the war, with Mussolini if possible, without him

13. *1937–1938 diario*, p. 5: but placed separate in the English edition (*Hidden Diary*, p. vi) and labeled "Ciano's Foreword."

14. *Vita sbagliata*, pp. 57, 336, 370.

15. Headquarters Peninsula Base Section, memorandum (by Lt. Col. Henry H. Cuming) for A.C. of S., G-2, AFHQ, 16 August 1944, subject: Count Ciano's Diary, enclosure 2, despatch no. 703, Robert D. Murphy to the secretary of state, August 25, 1944, item 63R, file "Edda Ciano Diaries," personal files of Allen Dulles.

and even against him if necessary. He cooperated closely with Bottai and Grandi in preparing for the meeting of the Grand Council on July 24–25, and in lining up a majority of the councillors to vote for Grandi's resolution. Throughout Ciano's speech Mussolini glowered at him in contempt and indignation. The revolt within the Grand Council gave the king the opportunity to dismiss Mussolini and to appoint Marshal Badoglio as his successor.[16]

Prior to the meeting of the Grand Council, Ciano seems to have had high hopes that he would play a leading part in the new government, that he and Grandi would steer the Italian ship of state into the harbor of a separate peace with the Western Powers. The king's ideas were utterly different. It was the government headed by Badoglio, assisted by a cabinet of technicians, which took over after Mussolini, a regime which was launched with the slogan that "the war continues." Ciano then reverted to the idea of a withdrawal into private life. He decided to resign as ambassador to the Vatican, and through Ambrosio, whom he had supported as successor to Cavallero as chief of the *Comando Supremo*, Ciano asked for passports so that he and his family might seek exile in Spain.[17] But the days turned into weeks and the passports were not forthcoming. Not only that, but the Badoglio government created a commission to investigate into the matter of illicit personal gains by members of the Fascist hierarchy and a press campaign was launched against Ciano charging him with financial corruption. Ciano was placed under house arrest and he began to fear for his personal safety if he remained in Italy.[18]

In these circumstances Edda Ciano got in touch with Eugen Dollmann and through him arrangements were made for the German *Sicherheitsdienst* to transport Galeazzo, Edda, and the three children to Ger-

16. There were no stenographic minutes of this last meeting of the grand council but some of the participants made their own records: Benito Mussolini, *Il tempo del bastone e della carota: Storia di un anno* (ottobre 1942–settembre 1943) supplemento del "Corriere della Sera" no. 190 del 9–8–1944, pp. 16–18; Dino Grandi, "Count Dino Grandi Explains," *Life* (February 26, 1945), pp. 21ff.; Giuseppe Bottai, *Vent' anni e un giorno* (Milan: Garzanti, 1949), pp. 295–318; Dino Alfieri, *Due dittatori di fronte* (Milan: Rizzoli, 1948), pp. 320ff.

The fullest secondary account in English is that by Frederick W. Deakin, *The Brutal Friendship: Mussolini, Hitler and the Fall of Italian Fascism* (New York and Evanston: Harper & Row, 1962), pp. 438–56. See also Ivone Kirkpatrick, *Mussolini: A Study in Power* (New York: Hawthorne Books, Inc., 1964), pp. 545–67. There are very full accounts in the Italian works, Giorgio Pini and Duilio Susmel, *Mussolini, l'uomo e l'opera*, 4 vols., vol. 4 *Dall' impero alla repubblica, 1938–1945* (Florence: La Fenice, 1955), pp. 244–55; Ruggero Zangrandi, *1943: 25 luglio–8 settembre* (Milan: Feltrinelli, 1964), pp. 108–42.

17. It is said that Ciano and Serrano Suñer had a pact of mutual assistance that each would help the other in case of need for refuge outside his own country. Ermanno Amicucci, *I 600 giorni di Mussolini* (Rome: Editrice "Faro," 1948), p. 19.

18. Susmel, *Vita sbagliata*, pp. 289–93.

many. The escape, as Count Ciano and the countess regarded their departure, went off according to plan on August 27. Edda and the children in one car eluded the Italian police; Ciano took a different car and a different route. They were each picked up later by a German military truck and taken to Ciampino airfield. There they were put on board a Junker 52 plane which flew them to Munich, and from there they went by auto to Oberallmannshausen. The man who made these arrangements was Wilhelm Hoettl.[19]

A word may be in order here about the organization and the persons involved in the German Security Service (*Sicherheitsdienst* or SD) in Germany and in Italy in 1943. The head of all of the Nazi police forces was Heinrich Himmler. Back in 1929 when the National Socialists were merely a party contending for leadership in the German state, Himmler was simply the head of Hitler's private body guard (the *Schutz Staffel* or SS) who at that time numbered possibly three hundred men. By 1933 this elite corps of the Nazi party had grown to fifty-two thousand.

Within the SS a Security Service had been organized as early as 1931. In the summer of 1934 the SD under Reinhard Heydrich, Himmler's chief lieutenant, was recognized as the sole intelligence and counterintelligence agency of the Nazi party. Himmler also managed to take control of the Prussian police away from Goering in 1934. Himmler's lieutenant, Reinhard Heydrich, brought all the police forces together under one central office, the Main Security Office (*Reichssicherheitshauptamt*) which was generally known by its initials, the R.S.H.A. After Heydrich's assassination he was succeeded by Ernst Kaltenbrunner who bore the title of *Obergruppenführer*, a rank in the SS equivalent to lieutenant general in the regular army. As head of the Main Security Office, Kaltenbrunner was second only to Himmler in the control of the police, in the operation of that principal instrument of terror of the Nazi regime. These were the men who organized the wholesale slaughter of the Jews of Europe. After Germany's defeat and the dawn of the day of reckoning, Himmler committed suicide (May 23, 1945). Kaltenbrunner was tried before the International Military Tribunal of Nuremberg; was sentenced to death on October 1, and hanged on October 17, 1946.[20]

19. Ibid., pp. 292–93. Later in the year Ciano told his friend Benini that the Germans tricked him and broke a promise to let him get out to Spain. Zenone Benini, *Vigilia a Verona* (Milan: Garzanti, 1949), pp. 44–45. Hoettl denies any such promise at this time. Susmel, *Vita sbagliata*, p. 293.

The pilot of the plane was Capt. Erich Priebke, whom Peter Tompkins later met in Rome in rather unusual circumstances. Peter Tompkins, *A Spy in Rome* (New York: Published by arrangement with Simon and Schuster, 1962), p. 171.

20. *History of the United Nations War Crimes Commission and the Development of the Laws of War* (London: H. M. Stationery Office, 1948), pp. 520–21.

The Main Security Office (R.S.H.A.) was divided into seven subordinate offices (*Ämter*) such as Amt III, which dealt with intelligence work in Germany and the occupied countries; or Amt IV, the old Secret State Police (*Geheime Staats Polizei*, or *Gestapo*) whose task was to ferret out opposition to the state. Amt VI dealt with foreign intelligence. In June 1941, Schellenberg took over Amt VI and reorganized the Foreign Intelligence Service.[21]

Until the end of 1942, there had been no German secret service in Italy because Hitler, out of deference to Mussolini, had forbidden it. The foundations of a very modest service were laid in the early part of 1943, and apparently without Hitler's direct knowledge. In February Wilhelm Hoettl was made head of the section of Amt VI which dealt with Italy. In April the Security Service submitted a report which delineated the growing opposition to Mussolini within Fascist Italy, the physical and psychic decline of the Duce, and something of the moves by Ciano, Grandi, and Bottai. Hitler merely acknowledged the report and Schellenberg thereupon determined to organize a thorough service in Italy. In a sense it was too late. The Grand Council meeting of July 25 and the king's dismissal and arrest of Mussolini took Hitler quite by surprise.[22]

The German search for Mussolini in the summer of 1943, the enticement of Ciano into Germany, and, as we shall see, the search for Ciano's diaries and papers were the work of the SD and particularly of Hoettl as *Referent* for Italy in Amt VI of the R.S.H.A.

To anticipate the story somewhat, there is one more character whom we should introduce in the SD in Italy, SS *Gruppenführer* (General) Wilhelm Harster. From 1940 to 1943 Harster had served in the SD in the Netherlands where he was instrumental in rounding up the Dutch Jews and sending them on for others to exterminate. On September 9, 1943, General Harster came to Italy and set up his headquarters in Verona. He headed the whole of the SD in Italy ranking just below Kaltenbrunner.[23]

21. See the introduction by Alan Bullock to *The Labyrinth: Memoirs of Walter Schellenberg* (New York: Harper & Brother, 1956), pp. ix–xiii; or Hildegard v. Kotze, "Hitlers Sicherheitsdienst im Ausland," *Die politische Meinung*, August 1963, pp. 75–80.

22. Wilhelm Hoettl, *The Secret Front: The Story of Nazi Political Espionage*, with an Introduction by Ian Colvin; trans. R. H. Stevens, 2d ed. (London: Weidenfeld & Nicholson, 1954), pp. 221–23. This English edition is much superior to Hoettl's first account which was published under the pseudonym of Walter Hagen, *Die geheime Front: Organisation. Personen und Aktionen des deutschen Geheimdienst*, 2d ed. (Linz and Vienna: Nibelungen Verlag, 1950).

23. See Allen Dulles, *The Secret Surrender* (New York, Evanston, and London: Harper & Row, 1966), pp. 58–59. Harster in 1949 was sentenced by the government of the Netherlands to a term of twelve years for his part in the deportation of some eighty thousand Dutch Jews. In January 1967 he was again tried, in Munich, and on February 24 was sen-

Throughout the summer of 1943 Hitler had spurred the *Sicherheits-dienst* to the greatest efforts to locate Mussolini. On September 12, four days after the Allied attack at Salerno and the simultaneous announcement of Italy's surrender to the Allies, Hitler was successful. Otto Skorzeny had learned that Mussolini was held in the ski lodge on the Gran Sasso, highest peak in the Apennines. He and a small group of paratroopers made a daring drop on the mountaintop, seized Mussolini, flew him to Rome and then north to Vienna. On the next day Edda Ciano met her father. She vigorously defended her husband's actions in the Grand Council meeting. The next day, September 14, Mussolini was flown to Hitler's headquarters in East Prussia.

Ever since learning of the Grand Council meeting, Hitler had had the plan of restoring Mussolini and of reconstituting the Fascist regime. In his eyes the Grand Councillors who had voted against Mussolini were guilty of treason, and he felt it essential that a revived Fascist government punish such traitors with death. But at the meeting with Hitler, Mussolini appears to have defended Ciano's conduct. On September 19 the ex-Duce returned to Bavaria and spoke with his son-in-law. He assured him on this occasion that he had told the Führer "that he would guarantee with his own head the correctness of the attitude of Count Ciano." [24]

Mussolini's attitude toward Ciano, and his lack of desire for vengeance, left the Germans quite puzzled. They began to write Mussolini off, even though they were determined to re-install him as chief of the government of Italy. They thought that Edda's hold on her father was the knowledge that Mussolini himself had had the idea of deserting Germany. [25]

When Ciano realized that he would not be permitted simply to fly out to Madrid, he approached Hoettl with a proposition. In exchange for facilitating his transfer to Spain with Edda and the children, he offered his diaries. Hoettl soon became convinced that these materials were of great political and historical value. He persuaded Kaltenbrunner that Ciano's diaries and supporting papers could be used to discredit Ribbentrop, the German foreign minister, a man whom Himmler and Kaltenbrunner loathed. It appears that arrangements were practically completed for the Ciano family to fly to Spain. Hoettl had even prepared false passports to take the family to South America. But against Hoettl's ad-

tenced to imprisonment for complicity in the murder of those Jews whose deportation he had arranged (Washington *Post,* February 25, 1967).

24. Giuseppe Silvestri, *Albergo agli Scalzi* (Milan: Garzanti, 1946), p. 77.

25. *The Goebbels Diaries 1942–1943,* ed. and trans. Louis P. Lochner (Garden City, N. Y.: Doubleday & Co., 1948), pp. 468–69, 471, 480–81.

vice, Edda insisted on asking for the Führer's permission. Hitler would have none of it, and the plan fell through.[26] Ciano remained in German custody. The diaries and supporting papers remained where Ciano had secreted them in Italy.

We may note in passing that this notion of using Ciano's diaries to discredit the German foreign minister was by no means fantastic. Some of the notations by Ciano were used in 1946 to confound and confute Ribbentrop, but not in the fashion and circumstances which Himmler and Kaltenbrunner would in 1943 have imagined, for extracts from the diary were produced in evidence at Nuremberg in refuting Ribbentrop's testimony,[27] the same tribunal which condemned Kaltenbrunner to hanging.

The Cianos Return to Italy

On September 27, Edda Ciano returned to Italy alone on a slow military train. She had come to appreciate, somewhat earlier than did her husband, the extreme danger which threatened him. First she went to Ponte a Moriano where she met her mother-in-law, Carolina Ciano, who turned over to her the notebooks which constituted the diary of Galeazzo. The widow of the Admiral Costanzo Ciano is said to have remarked on this occasion that these were worth the life of her son.[28]

It is said that Edda then went to Rocca delle Caminate, Mussolini's onetime summer residence, and now the temporary capital of the neofascist puppet state, the Italian Social Republic as it came to be called, in which Mussolini was being reinstated in power by Hitler. Whatever function it performed for the Italians, it spared the Germans the burden of having to administer by means of military government the four-fifths of the Italian peninsula which they occupied. Here Edda came to realize how much her husband was hated by her countrymen who were loyal to

26. Hoettl, *Secret Front*, pp. 274–75; *The Goebbels Diaries*, pp. 479–81. Cf. Susmel, *Vita sbagliata*, pp. 296–97.

27. Extracts from the diary were submitted in evidence as document 2987-PS (Exhibit U.S.A.-166), *Trial of the Major War Criminals before the International Military Tribunal, Nuremberg 14 November 1945–1 October 1946*, English edition, vol. 31, pp. 434–38; comment by Sir David Maxwell-Fyffe, January 8, 1946, vol. 4, pp. 567–68.

Cf. the introduction to the French edition by S. Stelling-Michaud, Comte Galeazzo Ciano, *Journal politique 1939–1943*, 2 vols. (Neuchatel and Paris, 1948) 1; vi; and Eugene Davidson, *The Trial of the Germans* (New York: Macmillan Co., 1966), pp. 153–54. (The citations here in fnn. 9 and 10 should be to *The Ciano Diaries 1939–1943*.)

28. Susmel, *Vita sbagliata*, p. 302. Susmel asserts that there were *eight* booklets of the diary which were transferred, and which constituted the whole. I have not found confirmation of this number. There seem to have been only seven.

her father. She persisted in defending her husband's actions and integrity. She told Mussolini that Galeazzo wished to return to Italy. He seems to have been persuaded, for a time at least, that he might have a position in the neofascist government.

Edda had been under great strain and this was apparent to her father who suggested to her that she go to a clinic for rest. This she did, entering the clinic operated by the Melocchi brothers at Ramiola near Parma. But before entering the rest home she made a trip to Rome where she gathered up her wardrobe. It is said that on this occasion she also carefully hid the diary in a secure place there. It was October 10 when she entered the clinic.[29]

The author of the diaries, Count Ciano remained at Oberallmannshausen, a "guest" of the German government. Although the first attempt to barter his diaries for his freedom had failed when Hitler refused permission for the Cianos to fly to Spain, Ciano recurred to this scheme. He knew that within the seemingly monolithic structure of the Nazi dictatorship there was an incessant struggle for power among the chieftains surrounding the Führer. He too had an intense dislike for Von Ribbentrop, and he knew that this antipathy—perhaps even hatred is not too strong a word—was shared by Himmler and Kaltenbrunner, who, as we have remarked, were particularly anxious to get hold of Ciano's diaries and supporting papers in order to use them to discredit Von Ribbentrop and bring about his replacement. Ribbentrop, on the other hand, was equally determined to see that Ciano was punished and eliminated for his "treason" to the Axis and that his diaries and papers were suppressed.

Whether Ciano would be able to trade his diaries for his freedom remained to be seen, but of the German interest in the diaries there can be no doubt. Himmler and Kaltenbrunner would have been quite happy to get the diaries without any bargain, if only they could find them. Doubtlessly at the urging of his superiors, Hoettl now provided Ciano with an interpreter, whose real task was to find out the location of the diaries and supporting papers. This was a pretty, highly intelligent, sensitive, and sweet-natured woman known as "La Burkhardt," or Frau Beetz, or "Felicitas" Beetz. Her husband was an officer in the Luft-

29. Ibid., pp. 302–3, whose account here is apparently based on "Il carnet d'oro della duchessa di Sermoneta" which appeared in ten installments in *L'Europeo,* June 26–September 28, 1949.

Ciano's diary, that is the seven or eight booklets, may have been hidden at this time, but not in Rome. But the supporting papers, that is the records of Ciano's conversations, were concealed in Rome along with some other materials. These were retrieved on January 4, 1944. See note 47 below.

waffe.[30] Ciano recognized her for what she was, someone set to spy on him, but nevertheless he found her very attractive, *simpatica*. She was not a professional spy; this was her first assignment as an agent; and she found herself strongly attracted to Count Ciano. Frau Beetz was destined to play an extraordinary role in the final chapter of the Ciano's life and in the rescue of his diary and supporting papers for posterity.[31]

On October 17 Hoettl appeared at Oberallmannshausen and informed Ciano that he was to be returned to Italy. Ciano had meanwhile had an operation on his ear and on returning to the castle learned that his children had been brought to their grandmother, Rachele Mussolini. The children for the time being remained north of the Alps. Ciano was flown back to Italy on October 19 along with Frau Beetz and some SS men. When the plane landed at Verona he was promptly arrested by both German and Italian police.[32]

Meanwhile, Mussolini had established himself in the Villa Feltrinelli at Gargnano on the shore of Lake Garda. Donna Rachele rejoined him there and the three Ciano children were also brought back to Italy by their uncle, Vittorio Mussolini. Edda Ciano demanded the return of her children to her own custody and in this demand she was successful. She now began to see the full picture of her husband's plight and how difficult it might be to save him. As Dombrowski has phrased it: "It was a public secret in Italy that the Ciano couple were not a good match and their married life was unhappy. They each went their own way, and nobody thought she had any depth of feeling for him. Yet in the face of this threat she determined to make every effort to save him." [33] Edda Ciano's extraordinary efforts to save her husband, and when that failed, to revenge him and to vindicate his memory, are crucial parts of the story of

30. Frau Beetz, born Hildegard Burkhardt, at Obernissa near Weimar in 1919; finished secondary school in 1938; then attended a private interpreters' school in Leipzig. In 1939 she entered the *Sicherheitsdienst,* served in Weimar until March 1940 when she was transferred to Amt VI of the R.S.H.A. and worked as an interpreter and translator of Italian in the Rome and Berlin offices. In Rome during the spring of 1943 she met Hoettl who at the time was *Referent* for Italy and Hungary. She returned to Germany, then was back in Rome in July in the staff of the German embassy. In August she was evacuated to the Reich along with the other female employees of the embassy and thus was at hand when Hoettl determined to employ her as an agent. Her husband, Capt. (later Maj.) Gerhardt Beetz, was an acquaintance of the Cianos. In 1951 she married Dr. Karl Heinz Purwin.

31. Benini, *Vigilia a Verona*, p. 29, records that when he first met her in the Scalzi prison, he wondered if she really were German, for her Italian was almost perfect.

He records further that when he spoke to her shortly before Christmas, she said there was no hope for Ciano; he would be shot. She wept when she said it, and Benini knew that this could not have been pretence (p. 93).

32. Rachele Mussolini, *Vita con Benito*, pp. 222–23; Susmel, *Vita sbagliata*, pp. 303–4.

33. Dombrowski, *Mussolini: Twilight and Fall*, p. 114.

his diary and supporting papers. Apparently it was through Frau Beetz that Edda Ciano learned that her husband was actually under arrest.[34]

In late October of 1943 the Council of Ministers of the Italian Social Republic set up a court to investigate and try those who had scuttled the Fascist ship by voting against Mussolini in the Grand Council on July 25. Ciano and the other disloyal Grand Councillors who had been caught were transferred to the Verona prison in early November. Frau Beetz had meanwhile presented herself to General Harster, head of the *Sicherheitsdienst* in Italy, and he had granted her free rein. She came and went to and from Ciano's cell. But Edda was forbidden to see her husband. Frau Beetz came to serve as intermediary between the two.

Edda had begun to fear that even her children, Mussolini's grandchildren, were not safe in this puppet neofascist regime. Her friends had been legion before July 25; now she found almost none. But there was one friend of former days of the Cianos whose loyalties were undiminished, Lieutenant Pucci of the Italian air force.[35] With Pucci's help, Edda Ciano managed to get her children across the border into neutral Switzerland, out of the reach of Nazi or Fascist vengeance. This action apparently took place on December 12. Pucci and Countess Edda took the children by auto from Ramiola to Milan where they were transferred to

34. See report of Pucci to Allen Dulles, May 24, 1945, item 18R, file "Edda Ciano Diaries," personal files of Allen Dulles. This item, 17 double-spaced, typewritten folio pages, is cited hereafter simply as *Pucci Report.*

A considerable portion of this report is quoted in the article by Andrea Niccoletti, "The Decline and Fall of Edda Ciano," *Colliers,* April 20 and April 27, 1946. "Fräulein Ilse" is substituted in this printing for the name of Frau Beetz. The article is based on the documents assembled by Mr. Dulles in the file "Edda Ciano Diaries." Further citations to this article will read: Niccoletti, *Colliers,* date and page. Cf. Susmel, *Vita sbagliata,* p. 305.

35. Emilio Pucci di Barsento, born in Naples, November 20, 1914, scion of an ancient Florentine family but with some blending of foreign blood, for his paternal great grandmother was a niece of Catherine II of Russia. A real part of Pucci's education was in the United States. He studied agriculture at the University of Georgia, and then political science at Reed College under Professor G. Bernard Noble; received the M.A. degree in 1937. At Reed he was very popular with students and faculty alike, despite his vigorous defense of the Fascist regime, the government of his native land. A man of strong loyalties: to his country, to his college, to his friends. Pucci was endowed by nature with superb physical coordination, an extraordinarily graceful dancer, a natural sportsman. At Reed, Pucci served for a time as a ski instructor (it is a scant sixty miles from the center of Portland to the slopes of Mt. Hood) and apparently during this period he began designing ski costumes, exhibiting the talent that later won him world acclaim.

Pucci returned to Italy in 1937; received his doctorate (*laurea*) at Florence, but his hopes of entering the Italian diplomatic service were frustrated by Italy's entrance into World War II. He joined the Royal Italian Air Force in 1938, served for more than a decade; was decorated for valor. Since the war Pucci has become one of the world's leading fashion designers. In August 1963 he became a deputy in the Italian Parliament, taking his seat with the Liberal group.

friends of Pucci's who got them across the border. At this time Pucci urged that Edda herself also flee to Switzerland, taking the "documents" with her, but she insisted on remaining in Italy and exhausting every possibility of freeing her husband.[36] German agents observed and reported the movement of Ciano's children across the frontier.[37]

About the middle of December the preliminary investigation of the treason trials of Verona began with Ciano himself as the first. Edda now appealed to her father for her husband. There were strong words and hot tears from each, but Mussolini would not relent. He had a document, he said, that was proof of Ciano's betrayal and he thought that Edda herself would some day appreciate this.[38]

36. "Relazione Pucci," *Libera Stampa*, September 6, 1945. In 1945, shortly after returning to Italy from Switzerland, Pucci himself published an account of his relationship to Edda Ciano and of his aid in getting the diaries into Switzerland. This account appeared in ten numbered installments in the *Libera Stampa* of Rome, issues of September 6–16, save for September 10. The heading of each installment was "Il marchese Pucci racconta" but the narrative was also referred to as the "Relazione Pucci." By arrangement with the *Libera Stampa* which held copyright, the "Relazione Pucci" was also published by the *Giornale di Sicilia* of Palermo in installments September 6–22 under the title "Le memorie del marchese Pucci."

Apparently the "Relazione Pucci," as it will be cited here, was composed soon after the *Pucci Report*, for it is dated Lausanne, June 20, 1945. (*Libera Stampa*, September 16, p. 2) In the introductory statement by the newspaper it is explained that publication was authorized by the Allied authorities with whom Pucci had collaborated. He himself stated that it was his military duty which prompted his publication, not the wish for monetary gain. "I have," he wrote, "an absolutely tranquil conscience and I am convinced that I acted in conformity with my duty" (*Libera Stampa*, September 6, p. 1).

There are some details in the "Relazione Pucci" which are not found in the *Pucci Report*, and there are some minor discrepancies between the two accounts, but the *Report*, which was not intended for publication, is much the better source. At the time of publishing the "Relazione," Pucci did not know the fate of Frau Beetz and chivalrously avoided any mention of her name or even precise identification. She is referred to only as "Signor X" (*Libera Stampa*, September 6, 7, 8, 9, 11 and 13). In the "Relazione," Pucci also avoided naming Allen Dulles and certain other actors in the drama.

Dombrowski, *Twilight and Fall*, bases his whole account at this point, chap. 6, "To Save One Life," pp. 114–25, on Pucci's "Relazione," but he suspected, as did others, that "Signor X" was really a woman.

"When Edda Ciano returned to Italy she was repeatedly asked to reveal the true name of 'Mr. X.' She always replied that as Pucci had kept it secret there must be good reason for it, and she felt bound to follow his example." But Edda did know that the Allies knew the correct name (p. 125). Cf. note 128 below.

37. Kaltenbrunner, in reporting to Ribbentrop regarding the crossing of the Swiss frontier by Edda Ciano on January 9, 1944, from the Hotel Madonnina stated: "In this same locality the children of Frau R [i.e. Countess Edda] were brought across the border by a pastor who was discovered at that time" (my translation). File Inland II geheim, "Geheime Reichssachen" 1944, vol. 15 (box 3) as filmed in microcopy T-120, National Archives (712/262452–53). Cf. note 60 below.

38. The encounter took place December 18. Rachele Mussolini, *Vita con Benito*, p. 233.

Operation Conte: Its Veto by Hitler

On the night before Christmas Eve—Thursday—Ciano came to realize that he would be found guilty and executed. In his cell he wrote out
three documents, a preface for his diary, a letter to King Victor Emmanuel III, and a letter to the British prime minister, Churchill. Frau
Beetz again served as messenger and delivered these three items to Edda.
Each was a denial by Ciano of his guilt and a bitter accusation against
his father-in-law. The first, intended as a preface, became the final entry
of the diary as printed in America. It contains not one word of recognition of his own gigantic mistakes. It blames the Germans only, and particularly Ribbentrop, for the war. Damning Mussolini for the death
awaiting him, he wrote:

> Within a few days a sham tribunal will make public a sentence which has al-
> ready been decided by Mussolini under the influence of that circle of prostitutes
> and white slavers which for some years have plagued Italian political life and
> brought our country to the brink of the abyss. I accept calmly what is to be my
> infamous destiny.[39]

Countess Edda apparently sent the letters for the king and for Churchill to her husband's brother-in-law, Massimo Magistrati, Italian minister in Bern.[40] Victor Emmanuel III received the letter addressed to him
and had it authenticated by a notary, believing it would help the cause of
the House of Savoy. Ciano mentioned in that letter: "I have arranged
that as soon as possible after my death my diary and some documents
will be published which will shed much true light on many facts hitherto
unknown." [41]

On Christmas Day 1943 Lieutenant Pucci drove Edda Ciano to
Verona but she was forbidden to see her husband. It was her father who
had so ordered. Through Frau Beetz, Edda and Pucci learned that the
trial was now set for December 28 and that the outcome was a foregone
conclusion: Ciano would be executed. Edda was terribly depressed on
hearing that her husband would die, and that her father insisted on his
execution. Pucci now urged Edda that she escape into Switzerland and
during the next day or so this loyal friend, who had made the Cianos's

---

39. *The Ciano Diaries 1939–1943*, pp. 583–84.

40. Emilio Settimelli, *Edda contro Benito: Indagine sulla personalità del Duce attraverso un
memoriale autografo di Edda Ciano Mussolini, qui riprodotto* (Rome: Corso, 1952), pp. 26, 53.

41. The letter to the king is published in Attilio Tamaro, *Due anni di storia, 1943–1945*
(Rome: Tosi, 1948–50), no. 41, pp. 363–64. Cf. Pini and Susmel, *Mussolini,* vol. 4, pp.
379–81.

Edda later told Pucci in Switzerland that Churchill made no acknowledgment of the letter addressed to him (*Pucci Report,* p. 15).

cause his own, made a series of preparations to get the countess over the border with the diary in her possession in order to be able to make good Ciano's threats. The booklets containing the diary were carefully hidden in Milan on the day after Christmas. Lieutenant Pucci then accompanied Edda back to Ramiola and made arrangements so that she would be able to make contact with certain people in Como and from there cross the border into Switzerland on December 27, the day before the scheduled opening of the trial. The plan at this stage was that, once safe in Switzerland, Edda would threaten vengeance by publishing her husband's diary if her father would not relent. Pucci would himself come back with the letter threatening revenge against Mussolini. The arrangements were almost finished, and on the morning of December 27 Pucci and Edda drove off from Ramiola, heading for Como by way of Verona where they had arranged to meet Frau Beetz.

The three met at midday, December 27. La Burkhardt, this German interpreter, agent, and go-between, now came forward with the scheme that came to be known as "Operation Conte." She told Edda to return to Ramiola, and there she would receive a proposal from the German authorities that Count Ciano would be freed despite the wishes of the government of Salò, if Ciano's documents were turned over to the Germans. The proposal by Frau Beetz was confirmed by a letter from Count Ciano himself.[42]

The next day, December 28, Frau Beetz came to General Harster in his office, greatly disturbed. She explained that it was Ciano's fate to be condemned and shot, but in that case his diary and other documents would be published in America and England. Only if his life were traded for these materials, she indicated, could such publication be prevented. General Harster immediately got in touch with his superior, Kaltenbrunner, who agreed to such an exchange. Kaltenbrunner in turn got the consent of Himmler, the leading contender for power in the group immediately surrounding Hitler. These two, as we have noted, were extremely anxious to get hold of Ciano's papers, believing that they would provide the means for discrediting Von Ribbentrop. They planned to act without informing Hitler in advance, to confront him with an accomplished fact. The scheme was to employ a couple of SS men disguised as Fascists. They would abduct Ciano from his cell, and speed him on his way with Edda over Switzerland to Hungary. When she got confirmation of Ciano's release she was expected to turn over the diary and the supporting papers.[43]

42. *Pucci Report*, pp. 3–4; "Relazione Pucci," *Libera Stampa*, September 8, 1945. Cf. Niccoletti, *Colliers*, April 20, 1946, p. 53. See also Susmel, *Vita sbagliata*, pp. 323–25.

43. Susmel, *Vita sbagliata*, pp. 328–30. Susmel's account here is based on testimony given him after the war by Harster.

Kaltenbrunner approved the plan but he wished a written agreement with Count Ciano regarding the surrender of the diaries and papers, and he summoned General Harster for a discussion at Innsbruck.

On January 2, 1944 there was a regular conference of Kaltenbrunner with Harster, Hoettl, and Frau Beetz. The proposed deal with Ciano, the scheme known as Operation Conte, was now written out in detail in four steps.

Step 1. Ciano was to reveal the hiding place of his Foreign Office records in Rome so that the SD could take them over.

Step 2. Ciano was to be "sprung" from his cell, and quickly taken to Switzerland with Edda, with the children, and with Frau Beetz.[44]

Step 3. Ciano, safe in Switzerland, was to turn his diaries over to Frau Beetz.

Step 4. She in turn would return to Italy to deliver them to General Harster. Apparently some stipulation was also made to give Ciano some funds so that he could live in Switzerland.[45]

The "springing" of Count Ciano was set for January 7 in accordance with the postponement of his trial, which was now scheduled for January 8. Lieutenant Pucci, who had heard nothing from "La Burkhardt" since December 27, had meanwhile gone to Florence on New Year's to be with his family. Late in the afternoon of January 3 he returned to Ramiola. Frau Beetz had come there that same day, a few hours before him, with the complete details of Operation Conte. These were embodied in oral instructions and in two letters which Ciano gave to Frau Beetz for delivery to his wife.

Edda was to drive to Rome in a car which was to be provided by the Gestapo and there she was to pick up two groups of documents which were to be used as part payment for Galeazzo's life. The two letters elaborated the oral instructions. In the first, which Ciano wrote with the knowledge that it would be read by the Germans, it was explained that Ciano was to be freed if the documents were turned over to German agents. The first group of documents, which have been hitherto referred to as the supporting papers, were the *colloqui,* that is the records of conversations to which one finds reference from time to time in the diary. These documents were to be turned over directly to the Germans.

The second group of documents was a parcel labeled "Germania." In

44. Frau Beetz at this time was aware that the children were already in Switzerland, but made no mention of it.

45. See Susmel, *Vita sbagliata,* p. 330, who bases his account at this point on postwar statements made to him by General Harster. Note that the *documents* (or supporting papers) were to be turned over in advance. The *diaries* were to be surrendered only after Ciano was free on Swiss soil.

the second letter, intended for Edda's eyes only, Galeazzo directed that the parcel be retrieved in Rome, and taken north. But Edda was to keep it in her possession so that in case the Germans reneged on their promise to release him, she might deliver the parcel to the Allies.[46]

When Frau Beetz explained the plans to Edda, the countess did not like it. She did not trust the Germans; she thought it was dirty business. Lieutenant Pucci argued with her till far into the night (actually the early morning hours of the next day, January 4). He finally convinced her that it was the only chance to save her husband from Nazi-Fascist vengeance at Verona.

But Edda by this time was quite worn out, and in no condition to undertake the hurried trip to Rome by automobile. Lieutenant Pucci now volunteered to go in her stead, to retrieve Count Ciano's supporting papers, and to deliver them over to the Germans in fulfillment of the first step of the agreement for Operation Conte.

At 3:30 A.M. of January 4 Lieutenant Pucci left Ramiola and at 4:00 A.M., a few miles out of Parma, he met the car with the Gestapo agents.

They were an odd bunch. There were two Gestapo agents, Pucci records, an officer and a petty officer, Frau Beetz, and he himself in place of Edda. The officer had come from Holland especially for the operation. He had the knack of killing a man with one blow in the face before the victim could utter a sound, and his part was expected to be to deal with the Fascist guards. This was the Dutchman named Johanssen, Harster recalled, and the other was SS Lieutenant Johan Thito, a confidential agent of Harster's. The party drove on to Rome for ten hours without stopping.

In Rome, Pucci and Frau Beetz left the automobile at Gestapo headquarters and took another car to meet a friend of Ciano's. He then took them to a part of the city with which they were quite unfamiliar and to the apartment where the documents were hidden. They had been nicely concealed by being built into a wall over a doorway. These papers were: (1) five volumes bound in green leather and marked "Conversations" (colloqui); (2) a large package labeled "Germania"; and (3) Ciano's political testament. Pucci took the first two items but left the will. Privately he opened up one of the volumes of conversations and on the first page

---

46. *Pucci Report*, p. 4; Susmel, *Vita sbagliata*, p. 330. At this point of his narrative Susmel draws on postwar statements by Harster who incorrectly stated that the diaries as well as the other papers were in Rome. Pucci's knowledge was firsthand; Harster's was not. The earlier collaborative work by Susmel is more accurate on this point. Pini and Susmel, *Mussolini*, vol. 4, p. 382 where the reference is to Silvestri, *Albergo agli Scalzi*, pp. 147–49 and to the Italian translation of Walter Hagen's German monograph. Cf. Niccoletti, *Colliers*, April 20, 1946, p. 53.

under the title was the notation: "Personal copy of His Excellency, the Minister" (*Copia personale dell' Ecc. il Ministro*).[47]

It was sometime after midnight (Janaury 4–5) that the foursome started its return trip north. Apparently Pucci turned over to Frau Beetz the volumes of the memoranda of conversations, but he kept the package marked "Germania" concealed under his air force overcoat.[48] Not far from Rome the car got stuck in the snow: The engine conked out completely. Pucci remembered and recorded that he spent the next eighteen hours walking knee-deep in snow, trying to get another car for the return trip; that by January 5 they managed to get the car started again, and only on the evening of January 6 did they reach Verona.[49]

But it was probably on the evening of January 5 that they reached Verona, and here certain of the materials which had been recovered at Rome were turned over by Frau Beetz to General Harster. These were apparently the conversations (*colloqui*) or a good part of them.[50] Pucci now turned back to Ramiola. The first step in Operation Conte had been carried out. Edda Ciano had arranged for the delivery of Count Ciano's papers, or at least a good part of them, to the Germans. And it was Frau Beetz who had brought General Harster into possession of these coveted papers. At this point the story of the diaries diverges from the story of the supporting papers.

On receiving the five or six volumes of records of conversation, Gen-

47. This episode in Rome is more fully described in installment 3 of the "Relazione Pucci," *Libera Stampa,* September 8, 1945, than in the *Pucci Report,* pp. 4–5.

Susmel, *Vita sbagliata,* pp. 331–32, states that Marchese Pucci retrieved all of the Ciano materials in Rome: the diary in eight volumes; the records of conversations in sixteen volumes; the package labeled "Germania"; and the papers regarding Ciano's last mission as foreign minister. The primary evidence for Susmel's account here is not clear. In any case the diary was not in Rome, and Susmel's various references to the number of volumes of conversations are not consistent. For some obscure reason Susmel overlooked or omitted reference to the "Relazione Pucci" in writing his life of Ciano.

Cf. Dombrowski, *Twilight and Fall,* pp. 117–19; Niccoletti, *Colliers,* April 20, 1946, p. 53.

48. In the *Report,* p. 5, Pucci states that he took the volumes of the *colloqui* in his own hands. In the "Relazione Pucci" (*Libera Stampa,* September 8, 1945) it is stated that these volumes were turned over to "Signor X" [Frau Beetz] directly after their retrieval in Rome.

49. *Pucci Report,* p. 5; "Relazione Pucci," *Libera Stampa,* September 8, 1945; Niccoletti, *Colliers,* April 20, 1946, p. 53.

50. At this point the evidence is not clear or consistent. Pucci (*Report,* p. 5) does not mention delivery of the volumes of the "colloqui," but states merely that he later went on to Ramiola, and still had the parcel of documents with him, i.e. the package marked "Germania."

Susmel, *Vita sbagliata,* p. 332, states that six volumes of the conversations were turned over by Frau Beetz to General Harster, and that the remainder were taken to Edda at Ramiola. (If sixteen were recovered at Rome, then the remainder should be ten, but Susmel is not consistent with his numbers.)

eral Harster consigned them to a young SS lieutenant, Walter Segna, a South Tyrolese who was attached to the SD headquarters in Verona. Segna after the war told Susmel that he remembered these volumes as rather large, each bound in green leather. He remembered also that what he saw related to the whole period, 1938–43. Some of the documents were typewritten, some were stenciled. At the order of General Harster all the volumes of the conversations were filmed by Segna who was assisted by a Lt. Fritz von Aufschneiter of Bolzano. The pair also translated a few selected documents into German and prepared a general summary. They worked against time, right through the night, and then turned everything back to General Harster.[51]

Harster locked the photographic copies of the documents and the general summary in his safe. He commanded Lieutenant Segna to take the original papers, that is the five or six volumes of the records of conversations, by air directly to Berlin and to deliver them personally to Kaltenbrunner. On receiving this portion of the Ciano materials, Kaltenbrunner telegraphed Harster to go ahead with Operation Conte.[52] Harster in turn notified La Burkhardt who was able to let Edda Ciano know of the next step: She was to be on the road Verona-Brescia at a point ten kilometers from Verona at 9:00 P.M. of January 7. Edda was asked to bring plenty of money with her, apparently for living expenses once they made their way through Switzerland into Hungary. The expectation was that at the appointed rendezvous Edda would meet her husband, and once over the border she would deliver the diary, and possibly the remainder of the papers and other materials, as the balance of the payment due for Galeazzo's life.[53]

Everything was going according to plan and everything was set for carrying out Operation Conte. The SS agents, the husky Dutchman Johanssen and his teammate were on hand. They were prepared to disguise themselves as Fascists, to overpower the guards and liberate Count Ciano. The guards at the key points of the prison, the marshals Krutsch and Guck, had been instructed in their roles: to aid the SS men, but to pretend opposition and act as if they had been overcome. Frau Beetz had carried out her assignment beautifully. She had achieved the delivery of Ciano's papers and had arranged that Harster, Kaltenbrunner and Himmler would get the Count's diaries. At the same time she was aiding Edda to save Galeazzo's life.

51. Susmel, *Vita sbagliata*, p. 332. This would have to be the night January 5–6 (Wednesday to Thursday).
52. Ibid. (The account here reverts to Harster's postwar testimony as its source.)
53. Ibid., pp. 332–33, where the narrative is again based on Harster's postwar testimony.

At this point the whole plan collapsed. Kaltenbrunner and Himmler had so far kept the plan secret, even from Hitler. Possibly they had hoped to confront him with an accomplished fact, and had reckoned on gaining his approval when they would submit the Ciano documents and diaries to him. Or it may have been that at the last moment they had misgivings and asked for the Führer's approval for the scheme which would have saved Ciano's life. In any case Hitler learned of the plan and immediately forbade its execution. General Harster recalled after the war that on the afternoon of January 6 he received a telephone call directly from Hitler himself who stated peremptorily that Harster would forfeit his own head if Ciano were enabled to save his. Harster immediately countermanded the whole operation. Frau Beetz was bitterly indignant at the role which she had been induced to play, but there was no other course open to her but to inform Ciano and then Edda and Lieutenant Pucci that her superiors had quashed the operation.[54]

Edda Ciano Escapes into Switzerland with the Diary

It was late in the night of January 6 as Lieutenant Pucci recalled (more probably the night of January 5), that he made his way back from Verona to Countess Edda at Ramiola. She was much upset by Pucci's

54. Ibid., p. 333, where the quoted paragraph is taken directly from Harster's postwar account. It is Harster who gives the date of January 6 for Hitler's veto. If this be correct, then there is an error of one day, as we have seen, in Pucci's report of May 24, 1945, and the foursome got back from Rome to Verona on the evening of January 5 rather than on the sixth.

Harster was, of course, in Verona at the time, and did not witness what happened in Berlin. He records that he heard later the version which circulated among the German high military: that Ribbentrop was tipped off by some one and immediately appealed to Hitler, who all along had opposed any compromise with Ciano. Hitler promptly summoned Himmler and Kaltenbrunner and gave them a tongue-lashing.

Hoettl, *Secret Front*, pp. 276–77, gives a somewhat different version. He states that Himmler and Kaltenbrunner got cold feet at the last moment, and asked Hitler's permission for the operation which was refused. He confirms that Hitler threatened to punish anyone who aided Ciano, but he does not mention a phone call, he gives no precise date, and he suggests that Hitler rather believed that Mussolini would not permit the father of his own grandchildren to be put to death.

Deakin, *Brutal Friendship*, p. 637, fn. f, states that Rudolph Rahn, the German ambassador to the Republic of Salò, told him after the war that at this time, just before Ciano's execution, he flew to Hitler's headquarters and urged that Ciano be allowed to escape into Switzerland. Hitler refused, it is recorded, and reiterated that the Germans must regard the Verona trials as exclusively the affair of Mussolini.

Giovanni Dolfin's diary, entry for January 7, confirms that Rahn was at Berlin at this time. *Con Mussolini nella tragedia: Diario del Capo della Segreteria Particolare del Duce 1943–1944* (Milan: Garzanti, 1949), p. 188.

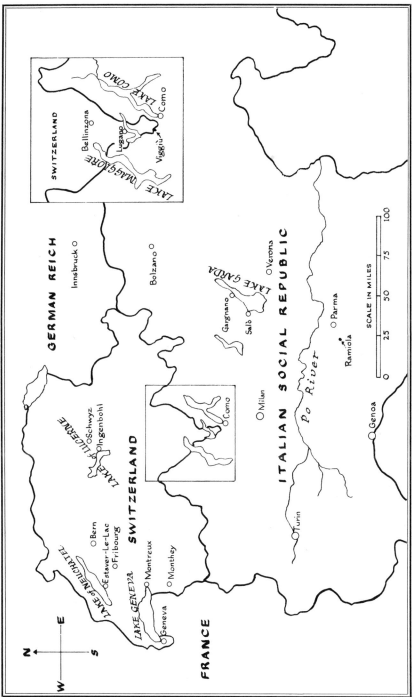

MIGRATION OF THE CIANO DIARIES

delay which she at first attributed to some new German trick. About noon of January 7 the two started off for the rendezvous with Galeazzo. They made a first stop in Milan where they picked up the seven booklets of the diary which they had hidden the day after Christmas. They put these seven booklets into one suitcase, packed the large parcel "Germania" in a second suitcase, and some letters and other papers of Edda in a third. They did not get off for Verona until about six o'clock in the evening.

An hour or so later they were on the Milan-Brescia highway. About halfway toward Brescia the two rear tires went flat. They decided that Pucci would stay with the car, and that Edda would go on alone as best she could, taking the diaries with her. Edda managed to thumb a ride as far as Brescia, and from there she walked and ran and even rode a stretch with a man on a bicycle, straining every nerve to reach the rendezvous point by 9:00 P.M. But she did not get to the ten kilometer mark until ten o'clock, an hour late. There she waited and waited in the bitter cold night. But her husband did not appear.

At about five the next morning, January 8, Edda hailed a ride with a truck and made it into Verona, dragging the suitcase with the booklets of the diary with her. She found Frau Beetz and together they went to General Harster, who merely remarked that the Germans had changed their minds. Frau Beetz apparently recognized what was in the suitcase but said not a word, and Harster did not have Edda searched. Frau Beetz managed to urge Edda to flee to Switzerland, and to explain that General Harster had been made personally responsible for Count Ciano. She also managed to slip secretly into Edda's hands a letter in which Galeazzo recorded his last wishes.[55]

Ciano's trial began this same day, January 8. The night before (January 7–8) there had been a rather strange intervention on the part of the Germans. Ambassador Rahn had gone to Berlin. He telephoned from there to the German Chargé d'Affaires Von Reichert urging that Ciano's trial be postponed for a few days. Von Reichert in turn got in touch with Pavolini, secretary of the Fascist party, who brought the proposal to Mussolini. The Duce declared bluntly: "That the Republican Government, given the publicity already made regarding the matter, could not consider it opportune to postpone the opening of the trial by even one day." But this curious intervention of the Germans at the last moment left Mussolini rather perplexed. He felt certain, at least, that the German action did not come from Hitler. He then turned to his personal secretary, Dolfin, and declared:

55. *Pucci Report,* pp. 5–6; "Relazione Pucci," *Libera Stampa,* September 9 1945. Cf. Susmel, *Vita sbagliata,* pp. 334–35.

No intervention now can halt the course of events! For me, Ciano is already dead. He will not be able now to maneuver around in Italy, to let himself be seen, to have a name. Whoever voted for Grandi's order of the day will be condemned for it.[56]

Lieutenant Pucci, who had stayed with the car while Edda went on, hoping to meet her husband, managed to get the tires fixed and reached Verona about noon. When he got to Edda she looked so distressed and worn out that he scarcely recognized her. They were not able to say very much for they were under constant surveillance by Gestapo agents. They started back for Ramiola, escorted this time by fourteen German police in three automobiles. When they got to the clinic the place was under guard both by the Germans and by neofascist police.

Not till she got to her own room did Edda read the letter from her husband which Pucci recalled ran something as follows:

Darling—meanwhile you are still living in the wonderful illusion that in a few hours we are going to be together again and free; for me agony has already started. . . . Bless the children and bring them up to respect and worship what is right and honorable in life."

Edda now broke down in the feeling of utter helplessness and frustration, knowing that her husband soon would be shot. The doctors worked over her for some time and only after midnight did Edda manage to pull herself together so that Pucci and she could plan the next step. Above all Pucci wished to help her escape into Switzerland, to take the diary with her, and threaten its publication if Count Ciano were not released. There were the problems of carrying the documents, of eluding the guards, of getting across the Swiss frontier.

It was quite out of the question for Edda to try to carry the whole diary and the remaining documents as well. Pucci selected the five booklets of the diary which covered the war years, wrapped them in a cloth which Edda then wound round her middle as a belt. Pucci had a flair with women's costumes! The first two booklets of the diary, the parcel of documents on "Germania," some personal papers of Edda, and some of her jewels were carefully wrapped up and the package was sealed with wax. Lieutenant Pucci then turned the whole thing over to one of the brothers Melocchi. The doctor assured Pucci that he would hide it where no one could find it, near the electric plant where there was danger of electrocution. The doctor was already initiated in the matter, and furthermore had connections with the Partisans. Dr. Melocchi swore that if

56. Dolfin, *Con Mussolini nella tragedia*, pp. 188–89. Cf. note 54 above.

Edda and Pucci should be caught and executed, he would turn the documents over to the Allies when they reached Ramiola.[57]

Pucci, in his air force uniform, approached the guards and showed them an appointment which he had at the air force medical institute in Ferrara where he was due for a physical examination following his illness. He was granted permission by the German police to go. At about noon, when there were fewer guards about the clinic, Edda went out through the basement and across the fields. It is said that she had pinned a Do Not Disturb card to the door of her room. Pucci and Edda made a clean getaway; they followed the back roads and made for Como where they stopped with friends.[58]

Late in the night of January 8, Pucci and Edda Ciano reached Viggiù (or Cantello-Ligurno) on the frontier of Switzerland. They stayed overnight at the Hotel Madonnina and there Pucci helped her to write out three letters. To General Harster she wrote:

[January 10, 1944]
General: For the second time I have entrusted myself to the word of the Germans with the outcome which you know. Now it is enough. If that is not done which was promised me I shall release against the Axis the most fearful campaign and thereby I shall make use of all the materials which I have and of all that I know. My conditions are: that within three days from the moment at which these

57. This is Pucci's own, firsthand testimony, *Report*, pp. 7–8; "Relazione Pucci," *Libera Stampa*, September 9, 1945.

On May 16–17, 1945 Allen Dulles visited the clinic at Ramiola and recorded: "At the time of her flight on or about January 5, 1944 (Dr. Elvezio Melocchi thought it was Friday or Saturday) Edda Ciano entrusted to Dr. Elvezio Melocchi her husband's diary for 1937–1938, one package containing a file which bore the mention in Italian, 'Ministry of Foreign Affairs—German-Italian relations'; two packages of phonograph records of Bruno Mussolini's voice; one case of jewels and many personal belongings including a quantity of furs. Edda took with her several other of her husband's diaries, concealing them on her own person, which made her look very bulky and gave rise to the rumors in Switzerland that she was to have a child. The documents and the diary left in Dr. Elvezio Melocchi's care represented the surplus which she was unable to carry with her." Memorandum for files, May 18, 1945, "Ciano Diaries for 1937 and 1938, as well as other important documents left by his wife in Italy at the time of her flight to Switzerland in 1944," item 12R, file "Edda Ciano Diaries," personal files of Allen Dulles.

Susmel, *Vita sbagliata*, pp. 335–36, mentions the sealed package given to Dr. Melocchi with the volume on "Germania," Edda's personal papers and jewels. He states further that the package contained twelve volumes of the conversations. If sixteen volumes of the conversations were recovered at Rome (p. 331), and if six were delivered to Harster (p. 332) the remainder should have been ten, not twelve.

58. *Pucci Report*, p. 8: "Relazione Pucci," *Libera Stampa*, September 9, 1945.

Susmel's account, *Vita sbagliata*, p. 336, is again quite at variance with Pucci's testimony, for he speaks of three booklets of the diary for the years 1936, 1937, and 1938 which were left at Como in the house of the Pessina family.

letters will be transferred to Frau B[eetz] my husband must be at the Bern railway station, accompanied only by Frau B. between 10:00 and 15:00 hours. If this should be carried out in a completely loyal way, we will retire into private life and let nothing more be heard from us. The diaries will be turned over to Frau B. by my husband on that same day. I enclose two letters on this same subject, the one to the Führer, the other to the Duce. Turn these over immediately together with a copy of this letter itself.

[signed] Edda Ciano

To Hitler she dictated:

January 10, 1944

Führer: For the second time I believed your word and for the second time I have been betrayed. It is only the fact of the soldiers who fell together on the battle-fields that restrains me from going over to the foe. In case my husband is not freed in accordance with conditions which I have specified to your general, no considerations will restrain me any longer. For some time the documents have been in the hands of persons who are authorized to use them in case anything should happen to my husband, to my children or to my family. If, however, as I hope and believe, my conditions are accepted and we are left in peace now and in the future, one will hear nothing from us. I am distressed to be forced to act in this fashion, but you will understand.

[signed] Edda

To her father Edda wrote:

January 10, 1944

Duce: I have waited until today for you to show me the slightest feelings of humanity and justice. Now it is enough. If Galeazzo is not in Switzerland within three days in accordance with the conditions which I have made known to the Germans, then everything which I have at hand in the way of proofs will be used without pity. If, on the other hand, we are left in peace and security against everything from pulmonary consumption to auto-accident, then you will hear nothing further from us.

[signed] Edda Ciano.[59]

59. Deakin, *Brutal Friendship*, pp. 642–43, gives the texts of these letters in English translation in his summary of Kaltenbrunner's telegraphic report of January 12, 1944. I have translated the letter to Harster from the German of Kaltenbrunner's report, the original of which is in the file, "Handakten Brobrick," in the *Politische Archiv* of the *Auswärtiges Amt* at Bonn. The microfilm is in the collection, microcopy T-120, serial 738, frames 267681–86, in the National Archives.

In a written report of January 13, 1944 addressed to Ribbentrop, Kaltenbrunner forwarded photostats of the original letters in Italian which were sent to Hitler and to Mussolini (738/267674-680). These originals each bore the date, January 10, 1944. The facsimile of Edda's letter to Mussolini, and the typed text were first published by the Milanese edition of *L'Unità*, June 23, 1945, p. 1. Cf. chap. 5 (Publications by *L'Unità* and Others).

The next day, Sunday, January 9, Pucci took Edda up to the frontier They stopped a few hundred yards from the line. He gave her a revolver to use—on either German or Italian guards if necessary, or on herself if they caught her. Pucci waited for an hour or so to make sure that she was across the frontier and then turned back.[60]

Pucci records that he got back to Verona late during the night at about 1:00 A.M. This must have been the night January 9–10. After some difficulty he was let into the hotel where the German agents lived, and he found Frau Beetz. The hotel is identified as the "Gabbia d'Oro" by Susmel. He assured her that Countess Ciano had got into Switzerland and with the diary. He added that she could let Ciano know of this, and he gave her the letters, urging her to hand them over as quickly as possible. Frau Beetz mentioned that the trial had not yet finished; and said she would wait until 8:00 A.M. or so to turn over the letters. This delay would give Lieutenant Pucci a bit of a head start in getting into Switzerland himself.[61]

The letters which Edda Ciano wrote, and deliberately misdated January 10, were delivered and before Ciano's execution which was at about 9:00 A.M. of Tuesday, January 11. According to Susmel, Frau Beetz on the evening of January 10, before making her usual visit to the Scalzi to see Ciano, went first to General Harster's office and delivered the envelope with the three letters, stating that they had been brought to her at the Hotel "Gabbia d'Oro" by Lieutenant Pucci. She added that she had also learned from Pucci that Ciano's wife had fled into Switzerland. General

60. *Pucci Report*, pp. 7–8, indicates that they left Ramiola on the afternoon of January 9, stayed overnight at the Hotel Madonnina, and that he escorted Edda to the frontier on the following day. In his later "Relazione," installment 5, *Libera Stampa*, September 11, 1945, this error is corrected and the time of crossing the frontier is given as 5:00 P.M. January 9.

The German police report of the frontier crossing, which was made a short time after the event, states: "On Saturday January 8, 1944 at 22:30 hours there arrived at the Hotel Madonnina in Cantello-Ligurno (the proprietor Rustini), 3 or 4 kilometers eastwards of Varese, a woman with two men. The woman was recognized from a snap shot without doubt as Frau R. The three stayed there overnight. On Sunday, January 9, 1944 at about 1:30 one of the men and the woman went toward the border. At about 17:30 hours the man returned alone. A short time later both men drove away. The woman gave her name as Emilie Santos of Rome." Kaltenbrunner to Ribbentrop; n.d., German Foreign Office Archives, Inland II geheim: "Geheime Reichssachen" 1944, vol. 15 (box 3). I have used the film, microcopy T-120, National Archives, serial 712/262452–53.

Susmel, *Vita sbagliata*, p. 336 correctly dates the frontier crossing as the evening of January 9.

61. Pucci must have reached Verona on the night January 9–10 as he stated in the "Relazione," *Libera Stampa*, September 11, 1945, rather than at 1:00 A.M. of January 11 as is indicated in his *Report*, p. 8.

The trial lasted for three days, January 8, 9, and 10. The remark by Frau Beetz could not have been made during the early hours of January 11.

Harster forwarded the letter addressed to Mussolini by a special courier. He transmitted the text of the letter to Hitler by a telephone call to the *Reichssicherheitshauptamt* in Berlin, and from there the text is said to have been retransmitted by telephone to Hitler's headquarters.[62]

Over at Gargnano, Mussolini had been following the course of the trial and the actions of the accused with great interest. At about 1:00 A.M. of January 11 he telephoned to his personal secretary, Dolfin, who did not at first recognize his voice. Mussolini asked if Dolfin had had any news of Edda. He had had none, he said, and he had no particular news from Verona.

Mussolini summoned Dolfin the next morning (January 11) at eight o'clock, a good half hour earlier than usual. The Duce was very upset and extremely tired. "Last night," he said, "a letter was delivered to me from Edda who has fled. In case Ciano is not set free within three days, she threatens to publish a complete documentary account of our relations with the Germans. I had known for some time that Ciano kept a diary on the events of these last few years, and a *dossier* which documented it, point for point. Ciano was clearly anti-German. His personal relations with Ribbentrop were never good, and toward the end they hated each other. The publication of this diary which aims to show the continuous German treachery toward us, even during the period of full alliance, could at this time provoke irreparable consequences!" With great bitterness Mussolini went on: "It is peculiarly my destiny to be betrayed by everyone, even by my own daughter. She has probably escaped into Switzerland." [63]

Back in Verona within the walls of the Scalzi prison at the close of Monday, January 10, the news soon spread that all of the Grand Councillors were condemned to death, all except Cianetti who was sentenced to thirty years imprisonment. Zenone Benini, Ciano's lifetime friend, was able to have a few words with him during the early part of that long night.[64] The Germans had at first refused even to permit him to confess and to take communion. The brunette lady, as Benini called Frau Beetz, was trying to get such permission. The permission was later granted and

62. "Relazione Pucci," *Libera Stampa*, September 11, 1945. See also Susmel, *Vita sbagliata*, p. 346, where the account is apparently based on Harster's postwar testimony to Susmel.

63. Dolfin, *Con Mussolini nella tragedia*, pp. 200–201.

64. Benini was not a member of the Grand Council of Fascism, but in the period before July 25, while minister of Public Works, he was active in the movement to oust Mussolini. After the formation of the Republic of Salò, Benini gave himself up to avoid reprisals against his family, and he was promptly thrown into the Scalzi prison where he had the opportunity to talk to Ciano. He was released on January 29, 1944 (*Vigilia a Verona*, pp. xlvii, 82, 168–69).

Don Chiot, the prison chaplain, was able to offer Count Ciano the last comforts of his faith.[65]

About midnight the chief of the province appeared to make an inspection. He said that since the beginning of the trial he had had to report continuously to Mussolini. Ciano, Benini records, was now free for a time from his German guardian angel, and the two friends walked the corridor of the prison, arm in arm. Ciano told Benini: " 'Forget about the plea for mercy: Let us speak of serious things. When you return among men, and this cursed war will have finished (and it will finish soon) do not abandon my children and my wife: they are the only things that I still have. Edda has conducted herself admirably toward me.'— Then he was silent; he wiped a tear with the back of his hand; murmured some words which I was unable to understand. Then he resumed. 'Now she is in flight and is trying to reach Switzerland, where the children have preceded her. She has with her my diary and other important documents, some of which I have written here. The transfer of these papers, the preparation and execution of all of this is mainly due to that noble creature whom the Germans set to spy on me. To her I have entrusted my political testament and other correspondence of great importance. I have also written to my friends letters of no political import, and she has left these with the Director so that they would be delivered through the appropriate authorities and that thus there would be no suspicion of a clandestine correspondence.

" 'Now if Edda succeeds in crossing the frontier with all the documentary material which she has, she will be in position at the appropriate moment, to demonstrate to the world how things really were, and to reveal the principal secrets and the behind-the-scenes moves which led to the alliance with Germany and to the war. It will be something of the greatest interest.' " [66]

Sometime later during that long night, the prison director, Dr. Olas, passed on to Benini the latest news from the prefecture. The countess, it appeared, had eluded both the Italian and the German police, who had been searching for her for days. The last word of her was that she was at the Swiss frontier. Toward dawn Benini went back to Ciano's cell. The German lady again was there. Ciano's face radiated satisfaction when he got that news.[67]

65. Benini, *Vigilia a Verona*, pp. 115–25.
66. Ibid., pp. 128–29.
67. Ibid., pp. 137–40.

Mussolini Attempts to Reach Edda
and Get the Diary

Although Countess Edda had got over the border and into Switzerland, her troubles were by no means over. On January 15 she was able to reach her children and tell them the horrible truth: Pappa had been shot because Grandpa insisted on it. Mussolini himself was embittered by his daughter's attitude and thoroughly alarmed by her threat to publish the diaries. Both he and the Nazi leaders during the year 1944 tried by one means or another to learn of Edda's whereabouts, to make contact with her, and to gain possession of the diaries.

On January 11 Vittorio Mussolini, at his father's instigation, tried to follow his sister's trail in order to get the diary, or at least to try to persuade her not to have it published. He got to Como and there at the house of the Pessinas learned that Edda had crossed into Switzerland.[68] He could follow the trail no further.

Later that same month Mussolini arranged to have Don Giusto Pancino visit him at Gargnano. This priest had been a childhood friend of Edda's; later he had been a chaplain in Albania when Edda served there as a Red Cross nurse. Don Giusto had not seen Mussolini since March of 1942 and he was shocked when he was ushered into the private study of the Duce on January 27.

Mussolini appeared emaciated, dispirited, worn out. Their interview lasted for more than half an hour. Mussolini explained how Edda had been pursued by the SS who were intent at any cost on getting possession of the diaries. Mussolini tended somewhat to play down the importance of the diaries in speaking to the priest. He mentioned that he himself had from time to time advised Ciano to record the events of the day. The main thing, he suggested, was to prevent the Germans from getting them. He urged the priest to go to the Vatican for help in getting into Switzerland to Edda Ciano.

Don Pancino reached Rome on February 2, spoke to Monsignor Tardini, deputy cardinal secretary of state, and received from him a letter of introduction to Monsignor Bernardini, apostolic nuncio in Bern. On February 5 Don Pancino was again with the Duce who directed him to say to Edda that her father's house would be open to her if she wished to return to it. After a second trip to Rome to secure a Swiss visa, Don Pancino was able to reach Bern on March 4.[69]

68. Susmel, *Vita sbagliata*, p. 359.

69. Don Giusto Pancino, "Tentai di riconciliare Edda Ciano e Mussolini," *Oggi*, September 22, 1954. Cf. Susmel, *Vita sbagliata*, pp. 365–66.

According to Don Pancino's testimony at the trial of Graziani, the Germans in Italy got wind of the discussions with Mussolini and of the intended mission into Switzerland in search of the diaries. Mussolini, the priest stated, was at the time nothing more than a prisoner of the Germans, who completely dominated the situation and knew his every move. Rahn and Wolff took pains to assure Don Pancino that this was the situation. When he got into Switzerland, German agents approached him with the offer of one hundred million lire if he would deliver the diaries to them.[70]

Edda Ciano was now practically a prisoner of the Swiss government which maintained a most careful watch over her. Only with difficulty was Monsignor Bernardini able to learn of her whereabouts from Pillet Golaz, head of the Political Department in Bern. When Don Pancino arrived at Ingenbohl, Edda was astonished to see him; she wondered how he had been able to find her. But she refused to hear anything from her father. She told the priest that Mussolini would be redeemed in her eyes only if he fled or if he killed himself. On returning to Italy with such negative results, Don Pancino first sought the advice of Cardinal Schuster before reporting to Mussolini.

It was not easy for Don Pancino to tell Mussolini, on March 29, what Edda had said. During the course of this discussion Mussolini learned that Hitler had got a copy of the Duce's own "diary" of the summer of 1943, "written by him during his detention on Maddalena and at the Gran Sasso and in which Mussolini remembered perfectly having expressed judgments scarcely flattering regarding Hitler and his policies." [71] It is said that this only increased Mussolini's concern lest the Germans gain possession of Ciano's notations.

In April, Mussolini for the second time summoned Don Pancino and persuaded him to go to Switzerland again to see Edda. On this second trip the priest carried a letter from father to daughter. Furthermore, he had some success, for he was able to make new arrangements for the manuscript of the Ciano diaries. Edda had but little money because most of Ciano's wealth had been confiscated by the Badoglio regime. She was in miserable health and feared for the fate of her three children in case of her death. The booklets of the diaries were now delivered over to Don

70. Testimony of Don Pancino at the session of January 21, 1949, Rodolfo Graziani, *Processo*, 3 vols. (Rome: Ruffolo editore, 1948–50), 3:1106. Cf. Deakin, *Brutal Friendship*, p. 777, n. c.

71. Pancino, "Edda Ciano e Mussolini." This is the priest's assessment. Actually the 'diary' of Mussolini of the summer of 1943 which the Germans got, the "Pensieri pontini e sardi," was politically innocuous. Although the Germans retained photostatic copies, the original was returned to Mussolini in January 1945. See chap. 6 (Mussolini's Writings of the Summer of 1943 Preserved in the German Foreign Office Archives).

Pancino who placed them in a strong box at the *Credit Suisse* Bank of Bern under joint names: that of Emilia Conte Marchi, a pseudonym chosen by Edda, and his own. In case of Edda's death, Don Pancino agreed to arrange for publication of the diaries with the proceeds to go for support of the children.[72]

In March 1945, Don Pancino undertook a final mission to Switzerland at the behest of Mussolini who now was hoping to make some contact with the Allies. The priest again saw Edda, quite secretly, for the Swiss authorities had refused him permission to visit her. She had left Ingenbohl and now was living in a clinic near Montreux.[73]

The next month came the triumph of the Allied armies in Italy, the rising of the Partisans in the North, and the end of the Republic of Salò. Edda had just turned her radio to the wavelength of the Milan station on April 28, when she heard the announcement that a great crowd had gathered at the Piazzale Loreto to see her father's corpse.[74]

The German Pursuit of Edda Ciano: Translation of the Supporting Papers

The Countess Ciano and the Marchese Pucci had neatly given the German guards the slip when they left Ramiola for the Swiss border on January 8. But when the guards discovered the empty room behind the Do Not Disturb sign, there was a quick call for reinforcements. The SD arrived in force and interrogated the Melocchi brothers. But they learned very little and they did not, at this time, carefully search the clinic. The diaries for 1937–38, the portion of the supporting documents, and the other possessions of Edda Ciano which had been entrusted to Dr. Melocchi remained safe.[75]

Meanwhile other German agents had picked up Pucci. After deliver-

72. Ibid. Cf. Susmel, *Vita Sbagliata*, p. 370.

73. Pancino, "Edda Ciano e Mussolini." Edda later mentioned something of this visit to Allen Dulles whose file has this undated notation:

"Justo Pancino—old friend of Musso—brought letters from Musso to Edda & Nuncio— Told Edda that Himmler wished Nuncio to advise Vatican that Germans wished peace & would let Am. & B's in; didn't want Russians—

"Told Musso re Himmler's plan & said the fools—should have done this 2 yrs ago—" (item 23R, file "Edda Ciano Diaries").

74. *Il Giornale del Mattino* (Rome) September 21, 1945, Jader Jacobelli, "Sono stato a Lipari e ho parlato con Edda." Cf. Anita Pensotti, "Edda Ciano parla per la prima volta," *Oggi*, September 25, 1959.

75. "Memorandum for Files. Subject: Ciano Diaries for 1937 and 1938, as well as other important Documents left by his wife in Italy, at the time of her flight to Switzerland in 1944," May 18, 1945, item 12R, file "Edda Ciano Diaries," personal files of Allen W. Dulles.

ing Edda's letters to Frau Beetz by whom they were passed on to General Harster, Lieutenant Pucci had hoped to make his own escape to Switzerland over the route through Sondrio. But he was ill to begin with; and then he had overtaxed himself and got very little sleep for several nights running. He pulled off by the side of the road and slept for several hours. When he tried to move on, the starter of his car failed to operate, and he went to a peasant's house for help. On his return, another car drew up on the road, full of Germans. They asked for his papers, and on learning his identity shouted with gleeful rage. Their first question was, "Where is the Countess?" [76]

Pucci was first taken back to Verona for interrogation and then on to Ramiola where there was further questioning in the presence of Dr. Melocchi. The doctor, it appeared, had told the Germans that Pucci was violently anti-Fascist and anti-German, but he explained to Pucci that he had said this to make the Germans believe he was on their side. After a few hours a German officer ordered Pucci to change from his uniform into civilian clothes and to be taken to Gestapo headquarters in the Hotel Regina. Here the Germans produced the hotelkeeper of Viggiù, who identified Pucci as the man who had helped Edda Ciano over the frontier. The Germans questioned Pucci from all angles regarding Edda, the diaries, the documents, and the children and beat him unmercifully when he refused to talk.

After some hours of torture Pucci was thrown into a cell in San Vittore prison with another prisoner who appears to have been an *agent provocateur*. Next day Pucci was brought back to the torture chamber and beaten so severely that his skull was fractured in several places. Fearing that he might betray his trust, Pucci tried to commit suicide with a razor blade which he had managed to conceal on his person at Ramiola. But he was handcuffed; the attempt failed; and the net result was that he was further weakened by loss of blood. [77]

The next day the beatings and questionings began again, but suddenly ceased. The Germans moved Pucci back to his cell, and treated him with decency. Frau Beetz appeared. What had happened? It seems that on January 14 Hoettl arrived back in Italy with a new mission for "La Burkhardt." She was to go to Switzerland, make contact with Countess Edda, and learn from her the hiding place of the remaining diaries and papers. She herself made the suggestion that the SD also make use of the services of the Marchese Pucci, who, because of his relationship with

76. *Pucci Report*, p. 9; "Relazione Pucci," *Libera Stampa*, September 11, 1945. Cf. Niccoletti, *Colliers*, April 27, 1946, p. 24.

77. *Pucci Report*, p. 9; "Relazione Pucci," installments 5 and 6, *Libera Stampa*, September 11 and 12, 1945. Cf. Niccoletti, *Colliers*, April 27, 1946, p. 74.

Countess Edda, might be able to persuade her not to use the diaries against the Germans. La Burkhardt burst into tears at the sight of Pucci covered with blood after his torturing. Furthermore, her conscience bothered her. She felt that her own haste in turning over Edda's letters to General Harster had been responsible for Pucci's quick capture. With tears and pleadings Pucci was persuaded to agree that he would give the message to Edda that both she and the children would be killed if she did anything against the Germans.[78]

The SD had little difficulty in getting Frau Beetz into Switzerland. Her cover was that of a temporary replacement of a clerical secretary in the German consulate in Lugano, and as such she was promptly issued a Swiss visa. With Pucci it was different. He had no proper papers. The SD, however, smuggled him across the border by boat during the night and once across he met Frau Beetz at a prearranged rendezvous.

As soon as he was in Switzerland, Lieutenant Pucci made very strenuous efforts to interest the British authorities, through the vice-consul in Lugano, Mr. Lancelot de Garston, in the Ciano documents. Perhaps he also asked about the possibility of asylum for Edda and her children in England. The British attitude was completely negative. The one thing that Pucci accomplished here was to give Mr. De Garston a note which he hoped would be delivered to Edda Ciano.

All this time Pucci had been simply going on his nerves. Now he suddenly collapsed. He got to a doctor who felt sure that his skull had been fractured, and thus it was that Lieutenant Pucci felt obliged to report to the Swiss police. He then entered a hospital in Bellinzona under the care of a Dr. Bettellini. Not until the end of March was the Italian air force lieutenant released from the hospital and sent to Estavayer-Le-Lac. For the rest of his stay in Switzerland he was under close supervision by the Swiss police.[79]

Pucci under internment was of no use to Frau Beetz and the Germans in their efforts to reach Countess Edda and to head off any attempt at publication of the diaries. Frau Beetz then tried, but quite unsuccessfully, to raise the money required as bail by the Swiss authorities in such cases as Pucci's. Possibly Pucci was able to learn Edda's address, and to write to her, urging her not to undertake any action against the Germans.

Frau Beetz also learned where Edda was staying, and made a trip to Ingenbohl, but without being able to see the countess. About this time she got some alarming news from her superiors. It appeared that a priest

78. *Pucci Report*, p. 12; cf. Niccoletti, *Colliers*, April 27, 1946, p. 74.

79. *Pucci Report*, pp. 12–14; "Relazione Pucci," installment 7, *Libera Stampa*, September 13, 1945. Cf. Niccoletti, *Colliers*, April 27, 1946, p. 74.

named Pancino had been able to visit Edda in her internment at Ingenbohl, and Frau Beetz suspected that Father Pancino was working for the
Germans as well as for Mussolini. It should be remembered that it was
through Frau Beetz that General Harster and the SD had got hold of
Ciano's supporting papers which had been sent to Berlin in January. She
had been a most useful and skillful agent. Now Frau Beetz was greatly
afraid that Edda would tell the priest of the part which she had played in
helping Edda to escape and to get the diaries into Switzerland. If the
R.S.H.A. were to learn of her true role, she feared they would arrest her
and torture her. She resolved to cover up her tracks by taking the initiative for the recovery of the remaining Ciano materials which she knew
were at Ramiola.

After her second Swiss visa expired, Frau Beetz returned to Italy.
There she enjoyed a couple of weeks vacation with her husband, whose
military leave was arranged by Kaltenbrunner. She was now directed to
make contact with Father Pancino and with his aid to reach Edda and
urge her to keep quiet. This second mission into Switzerland did not ma-
terialize because the Swiss government refused to issue a new visa.

In the summer of 1944, either through the direct participation of
Frau Beetz, or at her instigation, the *Sicherheitsdienst* was able to get its
hands on all of the materials which Edda and Lieutenant Pucci had left at
Ramiola in January. There are two or three different versions of this episode, varying in credibility and differing as to the precise time and
regarding exactly who took part. But there is agreement that it was the
summer of 1944 and that a fabricated letter played a big role.

The most convincing version comes from the Melocchi brothers. At
war's end, as we will note, Allen Dulles hastened over the border of
Switzerland into Italy, provided with precise directions for getting to
Ramiola, and with a genuine letter addressed to Dr. Walter Melocchi by
Edda Ciano, asking that he turn over to the American her husband's
diaries, certain other documents, and the case of her jewels. Here are the
exact words of Allen Dulles's report:

"1. On May 16th and 17th I called on the brothers Elvezio and
Walter Melocchi, doctors of medicine, who have a sanitorium (casa di
cura—'Ramiola') at Ramiola, Prov. of Parma. Countess Edda gave me a
letter addressed to Dr. Walter Melocchi in which she requested him to
turn over to me certain documents, parts of her husband's diary and a
case of her jewels which she left with him for safekeeping at the time of
her flight to Switzerland in January 1944.

"2. The doctors stated that all the documents and the box with Edda
Ciano's jewels were taken away by the Germans after Edda's departure.
Dr. Walter Melocchi, to whom Edda's letter which I brought was ad-
dressed, answered this letter in writing."

[Here follows an account of the searches in January 1944]:

"7. During this first interrogation, no questions were asked about any documents and the brothers did not volunteer any information about them. As a side remark Dr. Elvezio Melocchi mentioned that he had concealed the two diaries behind the books on the shelves of his office. The interrogation by the Germans took place in that room and they looked over some of the books without discovering the diaries. The remaining documents, phonograph records and the jewel case, Dr. Elvezio kept in his own room. None of these were taken away by the Germans at that time.

"8. Shortly afterwards the Italian police appeared at the Sanitorium, wanted to arrest the two brothers and to close the establishment because of its being connected with the Countess's escape. The brothers were convinced that there was an Italian spy among the establishment's personnel, who was reporting to the Italian police, often exaggerating the happenings in order to give himself more importance.

"9. It was not until some time in August that the next development took place. At that time there came to the Sanitorium a man who claimed to be a nephew of Professor Fossati, a well known gynecologist from Milan. This man stated that he came from Switzerland as emissary for Edda Ciano to obtain the documents left behind by her. Elvezio Melocchi was caught off his guard and asked for the written instructions from the Countess, as it had been arranged between her and the Doctors that the things left behind would only be delivered upon written orders from her. The man left but returned two days later bringing a letter purported to have come from the Countess. It was an obvious falsification and the doctors decided not to hand over the things, pretending that they were no longer at Ramiola which was not a safe place for them but that they had been taken away and hidden somewhere in Florence. The pseudomessenger left again. Dr. Walter Melocchi noticed that the car in which he had come had a German license identified as coming from Trieste.

"10. A few days later two agents of the S.D. from Parma appeared at the Sanitarium accompanied by an S.S. officer whom they recognized as one of those who conducted the original interrogation in January. Elvezio and Walter Melocchi were both taken to Parma, to via Carlo Alberto XIII (Stradone). A number of the German military were lined up on their entering the building and generally a show of importance was put on presumably to intimidate the brothers. By that time both of them were quite nervous and unwilling to take any chances on behalf of the Countess. Therefore when they were told that they would be taken to Florence to produce the documents left behind by Edda, they admitted without further difficulties that there was no point of going there as the documents were kept in the Sanitorium at Ramiola. They were taken

back and turned over to the German S.D. officials everything they had
for the Countess, including a handbag mentioned by them now, for the
first time during this narrative. Elvezio Melocchi stated that the Countess
had shown him the contents of this handbag which contained a number
of letters from Mussolini to her. The Countess qualified these letters as
being 'Important for future developments.' When asked whether they
had read those letters after Edda's departure the brothers answered in
the negative, saying that they never were interested in politics. I then
asked them whether they had read the contents of the Italian Foreign Office dossier left with them. Elvezio Melocchi said that they had not, inasmuch as, to avoid any complications, he wrapped and sealed with his
own seal, those documents, in the presence of Edda. They admitted,
however, having read some parts of the diary which dealt with the Spanish war events. One of the brothers said that they found the reading
nauseating and after a few pages did not read any more. I then remarked
that the diary concerning the Munich events was in these volumes, to
which one of the brother promptly reacted by saying that the relative
sheets, perhaps 10 or 15 in number were cut out. The brothers then admitted that they had looked for that particular topic as one they thought
would be interesting!! Both brothers stated that they made no copies of
anything at all nor did they make any photostats." [80]

The *Sicherheitsdienst*, chiefly through the operations of Frau Beetz,
now had the five or six volumes of records of conversations which Gen-

---

80. "Memorandum for Files, Subject: 'Ciano Diaries for 1937 and 1938, as well as other
important Documents left by his wife in Italy, at the time of her flight to Switzerland in
1944,' " May 18, 1945, item 12R, file "Edda Ciano Diaries."

A letter of Walter Melocchi to Countess Edda Ciano, dated May 16, 1945, relates substantially the same facts regarding the two booklets of the diary and other materials and it
repeats the statement of the arrest of the brothers by the SD in October of 1944, Walter for
five days and Elvezio for 53, item 20R, file "Edda Ciano Diaries." Cf. Niccoletti, *Colliers*,
April 27, 1946, p. 76.

Frau Beetz, at the end of the war in Europe and after she fell into Allied hands, seems
to have explained that she twice visited Ramiola in June 1944 and then with the aid of Dr.
Segna regained all of the materials. She herself then took the documents to Zossen where
she prepared a summary of them for Hoettl, chief of Amt VI B. It is not excluded that Dr.
Segna is the same person as was described by Dr. Melocchi to Allen Dulles.

Susmel, *Vita sbagliata*, pp. 369–70, gives an account which is apparently based on
postwar testimony to him by Harster, as follows. Segna remained convinced, despite the
failure to discover anything in January, that Edda Ciano must have left important materials
at Ramiola. He therefore fabricated a letter purporting to be from Countess Ciano in Switzerland to Dr. Melocchi asking that the materials be turned over for delivery to her. Thereupon Dr. Melocchi surrendered: the twelve volumes of the "colloqui"; the file "Germania";
the documents regarding Ciano's last mission to Hitler's headquarters in December 1942;
Edda's diary as a Red Cross nurse; and her correspondence with her father. The Ciano materials were sent on to Berlin; the others were held at Verona. Susmel's account is not so

eral Harster had got in January 1944 and had sent on to Berlin; the two diary volumes for the years 1937 and 1938, and the bound volume labeled "Germania" which had been taken from Ramiola in August. The two volumes of the diaries were quite like the other five calendar notebooks.[81] The volumes of the *colloqui* or memoranda of conversation must have been the copies which Ciano personally made or set aside while other official copies went into the *Archivio di Gabinetto* and have survived in microfilm form in the Lisbon Papers. The volume, Germania, must have been a kind of personal copy retained by Ciano of materials like those in files so labeled in the Lisbon Papers.[82]

Frau Beetz made a summary of the new materials seized at Ramiola in the summer of 1944, and then was directed to return to her home in Weimar to make a full translation of the whole collection. This work was done under careful security precautions. Each night after the day's work the original documents were placed in the safe of the Gestapo in Weimar. In the last month of the Nazi regime, that is in April 1945, Hitler ordered these Italian documents and the translations to be destroyed. Without the knowledge of her superiors, however, Frau Beetz had made an extra carbon copy of her translations. It has been suggested that she thought of using these in a book in case Countess Ciano would grant permission. Just before the end came, she buried this carbon set of translations in her garden, which some said was a rose garden.

The Americans Pick Up the Trail of the Ciano Diary

On June 4, 1944, the Allied armies entered Rome. In the next month *L'Unità*, organ of the Communist party in Italy, published a little note which was immediately echoed in the New York *Times* of the following day (July 30, 1944):

Interested parties are deliberately holding back the publication of the late Count Ciano's diary, the Communist newspaper *Unità*, charged today.

credible as that of the Melocchis. What Harster learned was secondhand, not what he himself saw or did.

Susmel makes no mention in this connection (pp. 369–70) of the diaries before 1939. He states, however, that after the recovery of the materials at Ramiola, Frau Beetz and Segna went on to Como and there picked up the three booklets of the diary, that is for 1936, 1937 and 1938.

I find no mention anywhere in Edda Ciano's correspondence with Allen Dulles of a diary for 1936. Edda Ciano in that correspondence frequently referred to the two notebooks for 1937 and 1938 respectively, and stated consistently that she had left them at Ramiola.

81. See above (Count Galeazzo Ciano).

82. See chap. 1 (Analysis of the Collection).

The diary, which Ciano kept from the beginning of the war until his arrest last summer, is said to be one of the most important historic documents of the Second World War. It was believed that his wife had taken the only copy with her when she fled to Switzerland, pursued by the orders from her father, Benito Mussolini, to get her, dead or alive. However, the Unità said that the diary was in Italy and had been hidden or suppressed by some who feared its revelations.

This note in L'Unità was apparently the first real alert to American intelligence agencies about the Ciano diaries.[83]

A bit later, that is about mid-August of 1944, American counterintelligence agents picked up Zenone Benini. Ciano had poured out his heart to Benini on that last long night before his execution, and almost his last words were of his hope that his widow would be able to publish his diary and notes and thus vindicate his memory.[84] Benini was able to give considerable information about the diary, information which was embodied in a fifteen-page memorandum by Lt. Col. Henry H. Cuming, assistant chief of staff, G-2, Peninsular Base Section and dated August 16.[85]

Benini mentioned that the diary was known to quite a number of people, and that Ciano on several occasions had mentioned his intention to have the document published abroad, perhaps in England or America. Benini also stated that the diary included:

a. Records of personal conversations between Hitler and Mussolini;
b. Terms of the so-called Pact of Steel;
c. Accounts of the Munich Conference;
d. Copies of all personal secret documents of Mussolini concerning the most important problems of foreign policy, particularly those bearing on Italo-German relations. (Ciano is understood to have copied these documents personally, in long-hand, trusting no one.) [86]

83. Interview with Mr. Allen W. Dulles, January 7, 1966. Mr. Dulles had learned of Edda Ciano's arrival in Switzerland in the winter of 1943–44; he had made inquiries with Magistrati, Italian minister in Bern and who had married Ciano's sister, by this time deceased, but had got no clue that she had the diaries with her (message Dulles to OSS, Washington, January 19, 1945 [paragraph 5], item 44R, file "Edda Ciano Diaries").

Sumner Welles knew of the existence of the diaries, but he did not publicly mention this fact until he wrote the introduction for the American edition of the diary which was issued in January 1946.

German intelligence agents, as noted, had been on the trail of the diary for some time. It is not excluded that there was a Communist penetration of the SD which enabled L'Unità to publish its note.

84. See above (Edda Ciano Escapes into Switzerland with the Diary).

85. Enclosure no. 2, despatch 703, August 25, 1944, Robert D. Murphy, United States Political Adviser, AFHQ, copy in file "Edda Ciano Diaries, item 65R.

86. Note that Benini, in speaking to Colonel Cuming, drew no distinction between the diary and the supporting papers.

Benini declared categorically that Ciano had told him: "They (The Germans and Republican Fascists) have stripped me of my possessions. I am poor now. But there is one treasure they have not taken which is of more value to me than all the rest: my Diary, now in the hands of my wife."

"Benini is convinced that, as life-long friend of Ciano and as financial manager of both Galeazzo and Edda, he can persuade the latter to make the document available to Allied authorities. He is equally convinced that Edda Ciano, now reported in Switzerland, has not turned the Diary over to the Germans, since she regards it as an instrument of eventual security for herself and children after the collapse of Germany and the Italian Republican Fascist government."

To assist the American authorities (and incidentally thereby to help his own cause as a former Fascist) and at the same time to fulfill the promise to Galeazzo, Benini on August 15 addressed a letter to Edda, entrusting its delivery to the Americans.

"I was in the Verona prison," Benini wrote, "from the 30th of November to the 30th of January and I was able to get in touch with Galeazzo in spite of the strict guard kept. I spent the last tragic night of January second [sic] with him, and I am burning with the desire to bring you his last wishes, his last words, and his advices." Somewhat cryptically Benini mentioned: "He praised all that you had done for him, upon you he placed the certainty that some day he will be truly understood as to his thoughts and actions in Italy and abroad. He has counted on you so that the world might have an irrefutable revelation of so many capital truths." [87]

Ambassador Kirk was consulted and suggested that the matter of securing the diary was of sufficient importance to warrant its being taken up through the War Department with a view to possible diplomatic action in Switzerland.

Between the arrival in Washington of Mr. Murphy's despatch 703 to the State Department, the arrival of whatever messages regarding Ciano's diary went to the War Department by its channels, and the next step, there was quite a lapse of time. But on the twenty-second of October the minister in Bern [88] received an instruction stating that the Department of State had reliable information that Count Ciano's diary was in the possession of his widow in Switzerland. The minister was directed to try to get the diary or a microfilm copy, and it was suggested that he might wish to make use of OSS help. [89]

87. The letter in English is enclosure no. 1 in despatch no. 703, August 25, 1944.

88. Leland Harrison (1883–1951), Envoy Extraordinary and Minister Plenipotentiary to Switzerland since July 13, 1937.

89. Copy of telegram as received, item 60R, file "Edda Ciano Diaries."

The head of the Office of Strategic Services network in Switzerland was Allen W. Dulles.[90] He operated in direct contact with the legation and was able to use its communications facilities for reporting to home base in Washington. He had managed to get into the bastion of neutral Switzerland just as the portcullis was being lowered following the Allied landings in North Africa and the German overrunning of unoccupied (Vichy) France.[91]

After discussing the problem with Minister Harrison, Mr. Dulles began, or rather renewed his search for Edda Ciano and the diary. Bellia, the Italian consul in Lausanne,[92] had served in Ciano's personal office; he knew Edda well; and from him Dulles gained the impression that Edda probably had the diaries with her. Mr. Dulles enlisted the services of a few people, a team, so to speak, in the quest for Edda and the diary. These were Cordelia Dodson, Mme. Louis de Chollet, an American woman married to a Swiss, and Paul Ghali, correspondent of the Chicago *Daily News*.[93]

Meanwhile Lieutenant Pucci, who had been released from the hospital at the end of March with the fractures of his skull healed, had been sent to Estavayer-le-Lac, and then to Fribourg. There he met Mme. de

90. Allen Welsh Dulles (1893–1969) was born in Watertown, New York, the son of the Reverend Allen Macy Dulles, a Presbyterian minister, nephew of John Welsh, ambassador to Great Britain during the Hayes administration, and brother of John Foster Dulles, secretary of state under President Eisenhower. After graduation from Princeton he spent a year traveling in Europe, India and the Far East, then took an M.A. degree in International Law and entered the diplomatic service in 1916. In Washington a few years later he gained an L.L.B. degree by attending night classes at George Washington University. Dulles served in Vienna, in Bern, at the Paris Peace Conference, at Berlin and Constantinople and returned to the department in 1922 as chief of the Division of Near Eastern Affairs. In 1926 he resigned with a public protest against the low salaries in the government service and joined the Wall Street law firm of Sullivan & Cromwell. Nevertheless his great interest in international affairs continued together with some participation.

After his wartime service in Switzerland Mr. Dulles in 1950 became deputy director of the Central Intelligence Agency and then director for the period 1953–61. Sometime after the Bay of Pigs affair he resigned but he continued to write. The extraordinary numbers who tried to crowd into the little Presbyterian Church in Georgetown for his funeral were testimony to the high regard and devotion felt toward him by those who served under him in the C.I.A.

91. See Dulles's own delightful account of his adventurous arrival in Switzerland: *The Secret Surrender* (New York, Evanston, and London: Harper and Row, 1966), pp. 12ff.

92. Franco Bellia, entered the Italian foreign service in 1933; in 1941 headed the "Ufficio della Segreteria" in the Ministry of Foreign Affairs.

93. Interview with Allen Dulles, January 17, 1966. Cordelia Dodson had known Pucci at Reed College. In the "Relazione Pucci," *Libera Stampa*, September 14, 1945, there is a vague reference to her as a former college friend ("una mia ex compagna di Università a Reed College—in America").

Chollet in the early autumn. Pucci abruptly turned down Mme. de Chollet's suggestion that he capitalize on his friendship with the Countess Ciano by writing some newspaper articles about her; but he gained the clear impression that the Americans were much interested in Ciano's widow.

At the end of October, Pucci, who had moved back to Estavayer, managed to see Edda in Lausanne. They talked at length about the diary and documents. Pucci asked her if he should contact the Americans and she agreed. Finally on December 6, Pucci managed to get permission to go to Fribourg along with a school group which made the excursion to see the procession of St. Nicholas. Although Pucci was not able to see Mme. de Chollet, he talked to her on the phone indicating that he wished to see her and had something of importance to say. But he did not wish to run the risk of directly mentioning the diary on the telephone.

A couple of days after this phone call, Mme. de Chollet arrived in Estavayer accompanied by Paul Ghali, and the two met with Pucci. At just about this time there had been newspaper stories of a marriage of Countess Ciano and Marchese Pucci. Ghali wanted to know about this. Pucci denied the rumor, but he brought up the subject of the diaries and indicated that Edda might be willing to let them out.[94]

The next step was the delivery to Edda Ciano of a copy of the letter which Zenone Benini had entrusted to the American authorities in Rome in August. To Mme. de Chollet, who served as messenger, Mr. Dulles wrote on December 15:

I do not know whether the original letter was sent to Washington or directly to the Countess by other channels. If she has not already received it, I feel sure she would desire to read it, and, of course, she may keep this copy, if she so desires.

From Rome I learn that Signor Benini is with the American military forces in the neighborhood of Rome and has given these authorities all information in his possession with regard to the importance of the Diaries, and of his willingness, in the interest of his friend and of the cause, to do what he can to help toward making them available, so that photographic copies can be made under conditions that would preserve to the rightful owners all rights of eventual publication.

I am sure that you will express to your friend my sincere conviction that it is important that the material we discussed be made immediately available under safeguards which will be scrupulously observed, and which will reserve to your friend and her children all rights of publication.

94. *Pucci Report*, pp. 14–15. This same period is covered in the "Relazione Pucci," *Libera Stampa*, September 14, 1945, but the participants on the American side are merely suggested by initials.

In conclusion Mr. Dulles mentioned that he had to leave for Paris next day but hoped to see Mme. de Chollet on his return which would be on December 20.[95]

We can well imagine Edda Ciano's feelings from the reply to Benini which she drafted on December 16:

Dear Zenone: Only today I have received a copy (in English) of the letter you wrote me on August 15th. It is useless, and I cannot tell you all I went through—a real hell—always with the thought that I was not able to do (for reasons beyond my control) what Galeazzo had written me to do.

Your letter, although late, arrives to the point. For that reason, before arranging anything, I would like to see you as soon as possible. It is very important. I beg you to be careful because if the Swiss (for reasons of quiet living) or above all the Germans knew of the dirty trick I am about to pull on them, my life (but that would not have any importance—I am so tired of everything) and that of my children would be seriously endangered.

But it is certain that even if I would have to die, I want first to avenge Galeazzo and to succeed in making him known such as he was.

I will be waiting for you. I embrace you affectionately.

[signed]   Edda [96]

After this reply by Edda, which was read and analyzed all the way from Bern to Caserta to Rome, the initial thought of the American intelligence authorities was to try to elicit another letter from Benini, in which he would specifically direct Edda Ciano to the next step. This time, however, Benini refused. Edda Ciano wanted Benini to come to Switzerland so that she could consult him directly. But Benini was under a blanket indictment for his Fascist activities, and the American intelligence officers did not wish to go so far as to move him into neutral Switzerland.[97]

Mr. Dulles in Switzerland had believed, after receiving the reports from Mme. de Chollet and Paul Ghali, that the situation was now ripe for filming the diaries. He made out a certificate that Daniel Schachter was officially authorized "to make photographic reproductions of documents, records and reports desired to complete the official documentation of United States Government Offices. Any documents so photographed by him are for official uses only." [98] Armed with this certificate, Schachter

95. Copy of the letter, Bern, December 15, 1944, item 57R, file, "Edda Ciano Diaries."
96. The holograph is in the file, "Edda Ciano Diaries," item 8R. A copy in English translation, item 53R; another such copy, item 44R, exhibit A.
97. Telegram, Caserta to Bern (for Dulles) December 29, 1944, item 61L; telegram, Bern to Caserta (for American political adviser) December 31, 1944, item 60L; telegram 837, Caserta to Bern (for Dulles) January 11, 1945, item 57L, file "Edda Ciano Diaries."
98. Copy of the certificate, item 58R, file "Edda Ciano Diaries," personal files of Allen Dulles.

was sent to Countess Ciano to make photographs of the diaries, but she refused. She stated that she was willing to go through with the matter of making the diary available to the United States government, but she insisted first on talking directly with Mr. Dulles.[99]

Countess Ciano got the same message to Mr. Dulles through another channel. In a letter sent December 20 to Mme. de Chollet she wrote, "when your 'important friend' comes back—please ask him to come and see me as soon as possible. I should like to talk with him because, though I am willing with all my heart to carry through the deal the whole thing is too important for me (and I am not thinking of money) to take wild chances blindfolded. . . . Your important friend could come with his car and take me for a ride (not in the American sense of it I mean to say)." [100]

In these circumstances, and despite the risk which was involved of a refusal by Countess Ciano to cooperate, or to spin the negotiations out and exploit a connection with Mr. Dulles, he determined to speak to her directly. He brought Magistrati into the picture at the time, and that influence probably was helpful. Magistrati was no longer minister in Bern. His prominent Fascist past might require investigation in anti-Fascist Italy. Dulles believed that Magistrati had worked conscientiously for the Allies since the Armistice, and he did promise to put in a good word for him at Rome if he would help to get the diaries.[101]

Allen Dulles Gets the Diary for the United States Government

On January 7, 1945, Allen Dulles motored to Monthey in the Valais, accompanied by Mme. de Chollet who had arranged for a meeting there with Edda Ciano. It was almost a year since Countess Ciano, with the help of Lieutenant Pucci, had been able to escape into Switzerland with the five booklets of Count Ciano's diary. This meeting in Monthey was secret. The war was still going on, and Countess Ciano was under rather close surveillance by the Swiss. The three spent a good part of the afternoon discussing the delivery of the diaries to the United States government.

99. Dulles's report to OSS, Washington, Bern, January 19, 1945, item 44R, file, "Edda Ciano Diaries." (This report is of basic importance and summarizes a great deal of Dulles's moves with respect to the diary.)

100. Holograph letter, undated but with envelope postmarked Monthey, 20 XII 44, item 7R, file "Edda Ciano Diaries."

101. Interview with Mr. Dulles, January 17, 1966; message of Dulles, December 30, 1944, item 52R, file "Edda Ciano Diaries."

On the one hand Edda wished to make the diaries available in accordance with what she now believed to have been her husband's last wishes. On the other she hated to give up her last assets. She wished to bargain, yet she wished at the same time to give the impression of a generous act toward America. She was anxious to get out of Switzerland and beyond the reach of the *Sicherheitsdienst*. She wanted to talk directly with Benini before coming to a decision. She needed clear assurances regarding her rights for commercial publication, and she was very anxious that her husband's political reputation be vindicated.

Mr. Dulles was chiefly anxious to move quickly. He took the position that the diaries were losing value every day; that this was Edda's last real chance to make a generous act; that the United States government was not interested in a bargain or in paying out money. He gave full assurances that her rights for commercial publication would not be impaired, but he could not state when, with the war still on, the diaries could be published. He was careful to explain that the U.S. government might conceivably wish to publish parts of the diary if it would help in the war.

In the end Edda agreed and arrangements were made for a team of photographers to make the reproductions. Dulles was impressed by Edda's great resentment at her father for failing to heed her intercession for Ciano's life, and by her fear and hatred of the Germans, above all of Ribbentrop. In his report of the discussion, Dulles suggested that if the American government were to publish any part of the diary, there should be consideration of her protection. But no such assurance was requested or given in the discussion of January 7.[102]

Next day Mr. Dulles sent his team. Capt. Tracy Barnes, a trained lawyer, supervised; Schachter did the actual photographing. These reproductions were regular photos, not microfilms. The men worked secretly in Countess Edda's room in the sanitarium in Valais where she was confined. They worked in great haste lest they be discovered by the Swiss authorities. The whole job was completed that day: Some twelve hundred pages were photographed of the five notebooks.[103]

Countess Ciano was not completely satisfied with Mr. Dulles's oral assurances although she recognized him, at their meeting, to be a gentleman whose word would be honored. Early next day (5:00 A.M. according to her account), she wrote to Mr. Dulles asking for certain specific guarantees:

102. Dulles's report to OSS, Washington, Bern, January 19, 1945 (paragraph 7), item 44R, file "Edda Ciano Diaries"; interview with Allen Dulles, January 17, 1966. Cf. Niccoletti, *Colliers*, April 27, 1946, p. 74.
103. Telegram, Dulles to Washington, January 11, 1945, item 58L, File, "Edda Ciano Diaries"; interview with Allen Dulles, January 17, 1966.

1. A formal acknowledgement from the government of the United States that she donated the diaries;

2. A written engagement from the American government that the materials be used only for political and military purposes, secretly; and that nothing be published without her consent;

3. For assistance in commercial publication of the diaries in the United States as soon as the government had gone over the material.[104]

At the secret meeting with Allen Dulles, Edda Ciano had mentioned that there were additional documentary materials of Count Ciano which were still in Italy, the "chocolates" as she liked to call them. She referred to these additional documents in her letter of January 8: "Another thing, the rest. The complement to the diaries are still in Italy—if you take me out of here, I am willing to go and fetch them, only Pucci and I know where they are. Pucci does not know that I know." [105]

There was no problem in understanding Countess Edda's motives. In his telegraphic report of January 11, Dulles recorded that "Today Hitler, Ribbentrop and her father are the chief objects of her hatred." But the guarantees which she asked were a different matter. Dulles stated:

In prior conversation I never accepted such conditions but told her I would give her personal letter of acknowledgement after diaries photographed and that in giving us copy, such rights as she might have regarding publication would be undisturbed. I specifically stated our Govt might wish to publish certain extracts.

On January 13, through Mme. de Chollet, Dulles sent the acknowledgement over his signature with the concluding sentence:

This will further acknowledge that the photographic copies of the diaries will be forwarded to Washington for the information of the government, together with a copy of the Countess Ciano's letter of January 8th, that the material in the photographic copies will be used for official purposes only, and that the giving of these photographic copies will not affect any rights which Countess Ciano may have with regard to the eventual commercial publication of the diaries.[106]

Edda Ciano had not stressed financial considerations, and Count Ciano had insisted that she not accept payment from the American government. But in Switzerland she was living on a very limited budget. The Swiss authorities saw to it that she did not get sufficient funds to move around easily in their neutral country. Mr. Dulles gave her an ad-

104. Letter, Edda Ciano to Allen Dulles, January 8, 1945, the holograph, item 5R; a typed copy, item 44R, exhibit B, file "Edda Ciano Diaries."
105. Ibid.
106. Item 48R, file "Edda Ciano Diaries."

vance of thirty-five hundred Swiss francs against future possible royalties.[107]

In reporting his success in gaining the Ciano diaries, Dulles acknowledged that he had no independent basis of judgment of their contents, but he felt completely sure of the authenticity of the materials. The twelve hundred pages covered the period January 1, 1939 through February 8, 1943, and Edda included Galeazzo's note of December 23, 1943 from his cell in Verona. Mr. Dulles noted, however, that there were some pages which were missing or had been cut, particularly those between January 25 and April 24, 1941, regarding the Greek war.[108]

The work of photographing the diaries had been done in secrecy and in great haste. It was feared that some of the filmed pages would prove to be illegible, that there would be double exposures, and that quite a few of the pages of the original notebooks would have to be retaken. At AFHQ they still had Benini on the hook. At Allen Dulles's suggestion they kept him there in case his intervention should be considered necessary to gain Edda Ciano's consent for the making of retakes. She was, throughout this time, extremely worried lest the Swiss authorities learn of her activities and expel her as an undesirable alien, or that the *Sicherheitsdienst* might learn of her disposition of the diaries and kill her.[109]

On January 16, however, Dulles was able to report that the rephotographing had been carried out successfully and that he had good, clear films of all elements of Count Ciano's diaries which Edda had admitted to having with her in Switzerland. There was now no need for any call on the services of Benini, and Dulles arranged for a copy of his report to

107. Telegram, Dulles to Washington, January 11, 1945, as cited.

108. At a subsequent stage the late Professor Gaetano Salvemini was able to examine the photographs of the diary, page by page. He noted that the sheet with the entries for October 27 and 28, 1940 had been removed and substituted. Susmel suggests that when Ciano was ambassador to the Holy See, he was able to make interpolations and mutilations in the day-to-day entries which he had made earlier (Susmel, *Vita sbagliata,* p. 78, fn. 1).

Allen Dulles suspected that Edda Ciano herself might have excised certain passages which she considered might have been offensive to the Anglo-Americans (interview with Allen Dulles, January 17, 1966).

Toscano, *The History of Treaties and International Politics,* 1:455, mentions that the American edition omitted certain topics which were considered to be of little interest to American readers, and states that the French edition, published directly from the original diary, is the most accurate.

Compare the entry for October 31, 1941 in the American edition (p. 400) with the entry for that date in the French edition, *Journal politique 1939–1943,* 2:74. Here is a whole paragraph regarding the arrest of an American, Fanny Patrizi, which does not appear in the American text. See the photographic reproductions of the original items from the diaries in the Illustrations.

109. Telegram, Bern to Washington, January 13, 1945, item 56L, file "Edda Ciano Diaries."

be sent to Caserta lest any complications arise from Ciano's friend who was anxious to clear up his Fascist past.[110]

On January 15, Captain Barnes had sent his chief a full report regarding the work of rephotographing. It listed all of the days where retakes were necessary. It listed the missing dates as follows:

1939	February 17–18
1940	April 13–18
1941	January 26–31
	February–entire
	March–entire
	April 1–23
	July 23–31
	August–entire
	September 1–21
1942	July 10–19
	August 17–24
	September 12–21

The only explanation given for the significant omissions in 1941 was that during the period January 26 through April 23 Ciano was a flight officer with the Italian Air Service. The Countess stated that she knew of no reason why the second big period was left out in 1941 nor for the shorter omissions occurring in other years.

There was another rather puzzling matter about the original diaries. There was a series of initials in red pencil and in capital letters at the right-hand top corner of many pages. "The Countess examined these rather carefully but said, and I believe truthfully, that she knew no explanation for them." [111] When Allen Dulles and his team were able to study these initials at leisure, it appeared that they corresponded with the initials of some of Galeazzo's lady friends—and apparently had been recorded for the appropriate days.[112] These markings argue rather strongly that the diary was genuine, and that there was but little retouching of the original entries by Count Ciano.

In his comprehensive report of January 19, Allen Dulles informed the OSS central office in Washington that the reproduction of the diaries would go forward the next day, hand-carried in the form of two sets of microfilm.[113] Apparently there was a reduction to microfilm after the ini-

110. Telegram, Bern to the American Political Adviser (AMPOLAD), Caserta, January 16, 1945, item 54L; telegram Bern to Washington, January 16, 1945, item 53L, file "Edda Ciano Diaries."
111. Report of Capt. Tracy Barnes to Mr. Dulles, 15 January 1945, item 45R, file "Edda Ciano Diaries."
112. Interview with Allen Dulles, January 17, 1966.
113. Item 44R, file "Edda Ciano Diaries."

tial photographing sessions by Capt. Tracy Barnes and Daniel Schachter. The two aluminum containers of the sets of film were designated respectively "A" and "B." Container "A" held the negatives of the initial filming done on January 8; container "B" the negatives for the subsequent refilming.[114] Mr. Dulles further reported that he was keeping one complete set of prints of each of the two films and was arranging to have them translated under the editorial guidance of Royall Tyler.[115]

These translations went forward rather rapidly with covering notes of February 19, March 1, and March 3, 1945.[116] The Washington central office of OSS, in accordance with Mr. Dulles's suggestion, promptly forwarded a print of the microfilm of the diaries to the Department of State.[117] As the translations reached Washington from Bern, OSS promptly forwarded copies to the Department of State. The series was completed on April 12, 1945, only a short time before the end of the war in Europe.[118]

Shortly after V-E Day, and as quickly as the border of Switzerland and Italy was opened up, Mr. Dulles hastened to Ramiola, in search of the supplementary materials which Edda had told him about. At Edda Ciano's request, Mr. Dulles supplied her with a film of the photographs of the diary, and promised that she would receive film copies of whatever additional materials he would be able to retrieve in Italy.[119] When he reached the clinic of the Melocchi brothers, he learned that the Germans had got there first. The "chocolates" had been gobbled up.[120]

Publication of the Diary

Paul Ghali, correspondent of the Chicago *Daily News,* had been of real service to Allen Dulles in making contact with Edda Ciano and in inducing her to make the diary available to the United States government.

114. Item 44R, exhibit E, file "Edda Ciano Diaries."

115. Report of January 19, 1945, as cited.

116. Respectively items 37R, 34R, and 33R, file "Edda Ciano Diaries."

117. Covering letter, Charles S. Cheston, acting director, OSS, to James. C. Dunn, assistant secretary of state, February 6, 1945, 103.918/2–645, Central Files, Department of State. When retired to the National Archives these files constitute Record Group 59.

The author, at this period, was serving in the Division of Southern European Affairs, and thus learned for the first time about the diary but had little time to study it. The film, so far as I recall, was carefully guarded and kept in the safe in Mr. Dunn's office.

118. Under cover of hand-carried letters, March 16, April 5, and April 12, 865.01/3-1645; 865.01/4-545; and 865.01/4-1245, Central Files, Department of State.

119. Edda Ciano to Mr. Dulles, May 3, 1945, item 25R; receipt by Edda Ciano, May 9, 1945, item 24R, file "Edda Ciano Diaries."

120. See above, (The German Pursuit of Edda Ciano).

Dulles felt under obligation for these services and, within the limits permitted by his official position, he assisted Ghali in getting first rights of publication. There were some difficulties for Ghali in making a bid. Use of commercial cable from Switzerland in describing the materials would promptly alert the authorities and jeopardize the status of Countess Ciano as a political refugee. If Ghali were to cross the border and telegraph from Paris his message might not get through the Allied censorship. Yet if he did not act there was the risk that Edda would become impatient and approach some other publisher. Toward the end of January Dulles reported to the OSS in Washington that he felt obliged to let Ghali go ahead in contacting his publisher. At the same time Dulles pointed out that any aid with communications would enable the OSS to keep control over the whole matter. Edda agreed orally to give the Chicago *Daily News* preference. She asked for twenty-five thousand dollars for the newspaper rights and for an additional offer for publication of the diaries in book form, but leaving Mme. de Chollet free to negotiate for a French edition to be published in Switzerland and France.[121]

The Chicago *Daily News* readily agreed to accept censorship of such materials in the diaries as might be judged necessary by the Department of State—the war was still on in Europe—but without seeing the material the newspaper felt able to offer only thirty-five hundred dollars for exclusive first publishing rights, leaving the publication in book form to await inspection of the manuscript.[122]

By the middle of March some of the staff in Chicago had been able to read a portion of the diary in translation. (At this time only the OSS and the State Department had the text of the whole manuscript.) After a second trip to Paris, Ghali returned to Switzerland at the end of March with full authorization to offer twenty-five thousand dollars for the exclusive first publication rights for newspapers and periodicals throughout the world, excepting only Switzerland and France.[123]

On April 7 Edda Ciano, acting for herself and for her three children, and Paul Ghali representing John Knight (Chicago *Daily News*) signed at Monthey, Switzerland, the formal contract for publication. The Chicago *Daily News* agreed to pay twenty-five thousand dollars for the rights of serial publication of the five booklets of the diary of Count Galeazzo

121. Telegram Bern (Dulles) to Washington, January 17, 1945, item 52L; telegram Bern to Washington, January 25, 1945, item 42R; undated message, by Ghali for John Knight, item 31R, file "Edda Ciano Diaries."
122. Telegram, OSS to Bern (via Department of State) February 14, 1945, item 36L; copy of letter, Paul Ghali to Edda Ciano, March 5, 1945, item 28R, file "Edda Ciano Diaries."
123. Telegram, OSS to Bern, March 20, 1945, item 26L; telegram, Bern to OSS, March 31, 1945, item 23L, file "Edda Ciano Diaries."

Ciano. Edda agreed to deliver to the firm a photocopy of the manuscript, and she formally guaranteed its authenticity. The Chicago *Daily News* further agreed to act as Edda Ciano's representative in arranging for publication of the manuscript in book form. She retained the right to accept, to reject, or to discuss such offers as would ensue. Switzerland and France were excepted.

Article 3 of the contract stated:

> There are references in the manuscript to certain documents which are not at the present time in the possession of Countess Ciano.
>
> If they should be retrieved, it is understood that she will send to the Chicago *Daily News* photocopies of such of those documents as clearly have the character of supplements or appendices to the manuscript.[124]

After V-E Day, Lieutenant Pucci decided to return to Italy, and he applied for permission of the Swiss police to travel to Bern in order to put himself at the disposal of the Italian authorities. The Swiss police promptly granted the request and at the same time notified him politely but very clearly that he was expected to leave Switzerland by the end of that month of May. On May 15 Pucci called on Ghilia, the Italian air attaché in Bern. Whatever may have been the chivalry of Pucci's aid to Countess Ciano in her escaping into Switzerland, or however admirable his courage under German torture, there was the basic fact that he was an officer of the Royal Italian Air Force, and he had been absent without leave.

Pucci identified himself to Ghilia, for he had a distinguished war record, but the attaché indicated that Pucci's actions had made him a political figure. He suggested that Pucci write out a complete account of his actions since September 1943. Pucci did not feel free to do this although he declared that he was willing to submit to an investigation or judgment by the Italian authorities. The suggestion was then brought forward that Pucci indicate that he had been aiding the Allies, and that he submit his case to the Allied authorities in Bern. Lieutenant Pucci explained the matter to Miss Dodson who was able to assure him that some favorable solution would be found.

A few days later Pucci again spoke to the attaché who indicated that the members of the Italian legation were quite pessimistic regarding his chances of returning to Italy. Ghilia thought there were only two possibilities: a statement by some Allied authority that Pucci was working for them; or an Allied declaration that he was a supporter of the Allies and that his return to Italy would be useful to them.[125]

---

124. Copy of the contract (in French), item 29R, file "Edda Ciano Diaries."
125. Memorandum by Pucci, undated, but written sometime between May 15 and May 24, 1945, item 16R, file "Edda Ciano Diaries."

It was Allen Dulles who represented the Allied authorities as far as Pucci was concerned and it was Cordelia Dodson who on May 24 got from him his most interesting account regarding his help to Edda Ciano and in preserving Galeazzo Ciano's diaries.[126] Apparently the intervention of Allen Dulles was promptly forthcoming and effective. Not long afterward Pucci returned to Italy, and he himself published the first accounts of his key role in saving the Ciano diaries.

Edda Ciano also returned to Italy not long after Pucci. In June, there was some press agitation in Switzerland against her presence, and her name was linked with others whose Fascist political activities had been notorious: Alfieri, Volpi, Bastianini. But the Swiss, despite the wars of their neighbors, have preserved a humane tradition. They did not wish to force Edda Ciano across the border into Italy if such action would result in her maltreatment or death. They asked if the Americans would accept delivery and assure her safety. Some sort of assurances seem to have been offered, and at the end of August Countess Edda was consigned to Allied authorities by the Swiss guards at the frontier. The *Risorgimento Liberale* (Rome) of August 31 told something of her life in Switzerland "including her alleged marriage to an Italian diplomat named Pucci and her confinement in Swiss sanitarium. Story concludes with report of Italian semi-official communiqué which has announced she might return to Italy safely and had nothing to fear from Italian or Allied authorities.[127]

For almost a year Edda was confined on Lipari Island, but without serious suffering or even real hardship. It was a very different kind of imprisonment from that which her father had inflicted on the anti-Fascists whom he confined on that island. On September 20 and 21, 1945, she gave some interviews to two Italian and three American journalists. She mentioned that she was reading the "Memoriale Pucci" which was being published in the *Giornale di Sicilia,* and on being questioned she declared that Pucci's published account was completely accurate and truthful. She declined, however, to reveal the name of "Signor X," explaining that if Pucci had not wished to mention it, she herself would not do so.[128]

We can infer that Edda Ciano managed to keep some contact with

126. Covering memo by Cordelia Dodson to Mr. Dulles, May 24, 1945, item 15R; covering letter, Pucci to Mr. Dulles, Bern, May 24, 1945, item 17R, file "Edda Ciano Diaries."

127. Bern telegram no. 3203, June 16, 1945 (740.0011EW/6-1645); departmental telegram to Bern, no. 2127, June 23, 1945 (740.0011EW/6-1645); Caserta telegram no. 3369, August 24, 1945 (740.0011EW/8-2445); Rome press telegram no. 2527, August 31, 1945 (865.00/8-3145), Central Files, Department of State.

128. Jader Jacobelli, "Sono stato a Lipari e ho parlato con Edda," *Il Giornale del Mattino,* Rome, September 21, 1945.

Frau Beetz. She told the newspaperman: "Signor X is a German who is now in an Allied concentration camp and the Allies know his name. He is perhaps the one German who is human." [129]

Countess Edda "reverted frequently" during her talk with the newspapermen to the memory of her husband, and eulogized him. "We all asked ourselves why this woman, who for so many years openly showed an extraordinary indifference to the conjugal bonds, should now instead be so bound up by his memory. Was this a true sentiment or only pretense?" [130]

On July 2, 1946, the newspapers of Rome announced that Countess Ciano had been granted her full freedom; she was released by the Ministry of the Interior from confinement on Lipari and free to move about and act on her own free will.[131] During her stay on Lipari Island, Countess Edda had kept up some correspondence with Marchese Pucci as she mentioned to the newspapermen in September 1945.[132] The rumors that she would marry Pucci persisted into 1947.[133]

Frau Beetz, as we have noted earlier, had been able to regain, directly or indirectly, the two booklets of the diaries of Count Ciano covering the years 1937 and 1938, the booklets which in January 1944 had been left at the clinic in Ramiola. Whether Frau Beetz was able to hold the originals, or merely to hide photostats or microfilms of these two notebooks after the final collapse of Nazi Germany is not clear. But the texts of Ciano's notations for 1937 and 1938 were restored to Edda Ciano prior to their publication in 1948. We read in the introduction:

Of the seven note books. . . . Edda Ciano . . . was able to bring with her only five, and precisely those of 1939, 1940, 1941, 1942 and 1943, which were edited two years ago by Rizzoli of Milan. Having learned that only those note books had been taken into Switzerland, to a secure place, and that the other two, which were of exceptional importance, had been left at the clinic where Edda had rested, the S.S. were charged to find them. The doctor of the clinic, to whom these notebooks had been entrusted, consigned them under threat of death, to the Reich police who demanded them. From that time on, until a year ago, there was no word of these diaries of the years 1937 and 1938, and it was thought that they had disappeared for good. Instead, they were in the hands of a third party, and their fortunate recovery permits us today to make them known to the public in their entirety.[134]

129. Ibid.

130. Ibid., September 22, 1945.

131. New York *Times,* item 14, Rome, July 2, 1946, file "Lanfranchi-Mussolini IV," personal files of Allen W. Dulles.

132. Jader Jacobelli, "Sono stato a Lipari" (September 21, 1945).

133. Newscutting, "Edda Ciano to wed friend of late husband," Paris, September 11, 1947, item 11, file "Lanfranchi-Mussolini IV," personal files of Allen W. Dulles.

134. Ciano, *1937–38 Diario,* p. xvii.

The "Rose Garden" Papers in Washington

Allen Dulles's trip to Ramiola at war's end was a complete disappointment as far as concerned "the chocolates." The *Sicherheitsdienst* had got there first. They had picked up the diaries for 1937–38, the bound volume marked "Germania," and the jewels and personal belongings of Countess Edda. But this was not the last round.

In May 1945, came the *Wehrmacht's* total defeat and unconditional surrender. Germany as a state ceased for a time to exist. Teams of Allied experts swarmed over the country searching for government archives; intelligence agents ferreted out the Nazi leaders and got accounts of their activities which could be used in the war criminal trials at Nuremberg; Special Counter-intelligence (S.C.I.) groups sought out the members of the *Sicherheitsdienst* and of the R.S.H.A. On June 30, Mr. Dulles received word via London that the S.C.I. detachment in Germany [135] had picked up Frau Beetz, who had mentioned something about having Ciano's diaries for his tenure of office. The message did not seem clear. In reply it was explained that the diaries for 1939 to 1943 had been obtained some months earlier, but that the diary for 1937–38 and the memoranda which Ciano prepared for Mussolini had been seized by the SD; if Frau Beetz could give any clue regarding these missing documents it would be of great interest. Four days later, on July 6, the report reached Allen Dulles that his detachment in Germany had obtained from Frau Beetz in German translation the memoranda of Ciano as foreign minister. The detachment had sent them on to the Documents Center of Twelfth Army Group Headquarters. [136]

It was almost a year later that the Department of State received official information about Ciano's supporting papers. In May 1946, Ambassador Murphy [137] informed the secretary of state:

135. The S.C.I. detachments were OSS elements. In Germany they were under command of the then Lt. Col. Andrew H. Berding, who was immediately under Allen Dulles. Lawrence E. de Neufville, who picked up Frau Beetz, was a civilian on Berding's Berlin detachment.

I interviewed Mr. Berding on November 28, 1967, but he was able to tell me nothing about Frau Beetz. He had refrained from keeping any personal records; he did not remember her; there was such a press of work that only with difficulty could they keep up with the day's tasks. He commented that as the flood of reports and intelligence swept in, they hoped and imagined that some fine day someone in Washington would carefully sort the material out. I said that I was trying to do just that for a small fraction of the materials with which I was familiar, but was encountering difficulties.

136. Telegram London to Bern, June 29, 1945, Item 7L; telegram to London, July 2, 1945, item 6L; telegram London to Bern, item 4L; file "Edda Ciano Diaries."

137. The various teams of experts which gathered up the German Foreign Office archives and began their microfilming operated as members of the staff of Robert Murphy.

I have the honor to report the information that complete copies of Ciano's records of conferences of Hitler, Mussolini and Ribbentrop, and all telegraphic and letter correspondence between Hitler and Mussolini were discovered by SCI detachment in May 1945. They were obtained from Hildegarde Beetz, a German S.D. agent assigned to Ciano while he was in jail in Verona. The documents in question were sent to the document center, 12th Army Group and then transmitted to War Department. I understand that in one of the file indexes is the name of Beetz.

Further information concerning these documents can be obtained from Lawrence E. De Neufville who originally obtained the documents from Frau Beetz.[138]

The author first heard of this collection on January 13, 1947, being at the time head of the Mediterranean Section, Historical Office of the War Department (since redesignated Office of the Chief of Military History or OCMH, Department of the Army). At luncheon that day, Professor Raymond J. Sontag, then on leave from Berkeley and serving as editor in chief of the *Documents on German Foreign Policy 1918–1945,* mentioned that he had learned of this most interesting find, possibly from the report, possibly from Ambassador Murphy directly.[139]

The next day I first telephoned and then sent a memorandum to Major Seeley, War Department General Staff, describing the papers on the basis of what I had been told by Professor Sontag, and asking that they be transferred to the Historical Office. My memorandum mentioned that

Ciano also kept certain materials, reports and memoranda in addition to the diary—materials which constitute a kind of appendix for the diary as published. The materials were seized by the Germans during their occupation of Rome and were translated from Italian into German by a woman employed by the German Foreign Office. While making this translation this woman made an extra copy of the translation for herself which she buried in a rose garden.[140]

Major Seeley promptly sent the material but I was not able, at that time, to learn much more about its acquisition than I had been told by Professor Sontag.

The papers consisted of a couple of bundles of loose sheets of carbon copies in German, without an index or table of contents. Because of the

138. Despatch no. 3614, Berlin, May 21, 1946 (840.414/5-2146), Central Files, Department of State.

139. I wrote to Professor Sontag on August 10, 1964, asking if he could tell me how he first learned of this collection. In his reply of August 21, 1964, he stated that he could no longer remember the circumstances of his learning of these papers (personal files).

140. Memorandum for Maj. Rudolph G. Seeley, WDGS, January 14, 1947, copy in personal files.

method of their acquisition there was a presumption of authenticity of the documents. After examining the materials the author became convinced that they were genuine, chiefly for two reasons: many of the accounts of conversations comprised in the collection tallied precisely with references in the published Ciano diaries to full records kept elsewhere; and scattered among the sheets of German carbon copies were a few stray items of Italian originals.[141]

I arranged the papers in chronological order, and numbered the pages with a stamping machine. I then prepared an index or table of contents of the papers initially sent to me which comprised:

> 4 items for 1939 (pp. 1–31)
> 56 items for 1940 (pp. 32–254)
> 32 items for 1941 (pp. 261–393)
> 19 items for 1942 (pp. 394–469)
> 6 items for 1943 (pp. 470–90)
> 117

In the Historical Office, War Department, we wondered what to call this collection. I had understood from Professor Sontag that it was dug up out of a rose garden and we dubbed it the "Ciano Papers: Rose Garden." The name stuck. This is the designation usually used in the citations to this material in the Historical Office, now Office of the Chief of Military History.[142]

Having put the materials in shape for our use we then received a bunch of additional sheets: some material for 1938; and a great deal for 1939. The integration of this additional material required a renumbering of the pages and the preparation of a revised index which now showed:

> 4 items for 1938 (pp. 1–13)
> 108 items for 1939 (pp. 14–290)
> 56 items for 1940 (pp. 297–519)
> 32 items for 1941 (pp. 520–652)
> 19 items for 1942 (pp. 653–728)
> 6 items for 1943 (pp. 729–49)
> 225

141. "Verbale del colloquio a Palazzo Venezia tra il Duce, von Ribbentrop e il ministro Ciano," Roma 28 ottobre 1938–XVII, item 2, 1938, revised paging 007–010; "Appunto, Salisburgo, 12 agosto [1939] XVII, item 11, 1939, revised paging 044–046; "Verbale del colloquio del Duce con von Ribbentrop presenti Eccellenze Ciano, Alfieri e Mackensen," 19 settembre 1940–XVIII, not listed as a separate item, initial paging pp. 196–99; "Colloquio Ribbentrop-Ciano, Schönhof," 4 novembre '40, not listed as a separate item, initial paging 223–24.

142. George F. Howe, *Northwest Africa: Seizing the Initiative in the West* (Washington, D.C.: Office of the Chief of Military History, Department of the Army, 1957); p. 4, fn. 5; Albert N. Garland and Howard McGaw Smyth, *Sicily and the Surrender of Italy* (Washington, D.C.: Office of the Chief of Military History, Department of the Army, 1965) p. 34, fn. 21.

The index for the revised paging lists two of the Italian original texts as separate items. Hence the total number of documents is 223.[143]

Professor Sontag in the spring of 1947 arranged for the State Department to borrow the material from the War Department and to have it microfilmed.[144] Thus the Ciano Papers: Rose Garden was assimilated into the collection of microfilms of the German War Documents Branch of the Historical Office, Department of State. A copy of the microfilm was sent to J. W. Wheeler-Bennett who at the time was British editor in chief of the *Documents on German Foreign Policy*, and thus a copy of the Ciano Papers: Rose Garden became available at the Public Record Office.

The carbon copies of the German translations made by Frau Beetz with the few, stray, Italian originals were held in the Office of the Chief of Military History, Department of the Army, for twenty-two years. In January 1969, they were turned over to the National Archives which had assumed the succession to the German Military Documents Section.[145]

These carbon sheets bear the revised page numbers, 1 to 749. The crossed-out page numbers reflect the revision which I made when the additional items were received at OCMH. The microfilm is held in the National Archives, listed as reel no. 4597 in the great series of films made by the German War Documents Project, the series designated microcopy T-120. The film is complete and gives the 223 documents. But I have no way of proving whether or not the collection comprises all of the supporting papers which Count Ciano originally set aside in his office in Rome.

One or two more descriptive comments. Throughout most of the materials there is merely the notation at the end of each document: "übersetzt" (translated). For the last two items of the collection, items 5 and 6 for the year 1943, on pages 742 and 749 respectively, is to be found the typewritten note "übersetzt" followed by the signature "Beetz."

The handwritten, arabic numbers enclosed in circles are in my writing, added when I listed the documents by year. The other series of numbers and letters, such as "7-y" (p. 007) or "7-x" (p. 044) were on the papers when they reached OCMH and apparently were notations made by Frau Beetz. It appears that she made some retouches on the materials

143. Cf. note 141 above.

144. Assistant Secretary of State J. H. Hilldring to Howard C. Peterson, assistant secretary of war, April 8, 1947, copy in files of the Historical Office, Department of State.

145. By letter of transmittal dated January 16, 1969, Col. H. A. Schmidt, chief, Historical Services Division, OCMH, to the Archivist of the United States (memorandum for the Record, National Archives, February 25, 1969).

GMDS was initially succeeded by the Captured Records Section of the Departmental Records Branch, TAGO, which in turn became the World War II Records Division of the National Archives and later evolved into the Modern Military Records Division, NA.

on turning them over to the Americans. We find such notations as the following and in English: p. 196, "This is separated from the sheet that should go with it. Translator"; p. 223, "Italian version"; p. 245, "List of necessary raw materials"; p. 484, "Separated from the sheets that belong with it. Translator."

Most of the letters and memoranda of conversations which are recorded in German translation soon appeared in printed form in *L'Europa verso la catastrofe*. In the editing of the *Documents on German Foreign Policy 1918–1945*, in accordance with standard practice, the usual reference, for purposes of comparison of German and Italian texts of the letters of Hitler and Mussolini, or for filling in gaps in incomplete records of the German Foreign Office, is to the published Italian text.

There are at least a couple of cases, however, of texts which are to be found in the Ciano Papers: Rose Garden which do not appear in the Lisbon Papers or in the published version of *Ciano's Diplomatic Papers*. Thus we have given the draft of the secret protocol dated Hendaye, October 23, 1940, but which clearly is Ciano's modified version which he had on November 3–4, 1940, at Schönhof.[146] What we printed in Washington is an English translation from an enlargement ("blowup") of a microfilm made from a carbon copy of a German translation of an Italian document, the original of which has disappeared.[147] We also printed Ciano's minute of December 8, 1940, which is not found elsewhere.[148]

We can now summarize the relationship of the "Lisbon Papers," the printed selections from them published under the title, *L'Europa verso la catastrofe*, and the Ciano Papers: Rose Garden. We can entertain no serious doubt of the authenticity of the Lisbon Papers because of our precise knowledge of their origin, travels, filming and restitution. They are only a fraction of the papers in the Cabinet Archives, yet they are by far the largest of the three collections here compared. The printed book in turn represents only a selection from the Lisbon Papers and in a few

---

146. *Documents on German Foreign Policy, 1918–1945*, ser. D, vol. 11 (Washington, 1960), Editors' Note pp. 466–467.

The German text was initially published by Donald S. Detwiler, *Hitler, Franco und Gibraltar: Die Frage des spanischen Eintritts in den zweiten Weltkriege* (Wiesbaden: Franz Steiner Verlag, 1962), pp. 118–19, and is now available in *Akten zur Deutschen Auswärtigen Politik 1918–1945*, serie D, band 11, 1 (Bonn: Gebr. Hermes, 1964), pp. 394–95.

147. But surely this is as close to the vanished original as is the reconstructed text, for example, of the "Defensor Pacis" to that missing original manuscript, as edited by Richard Scholz, *Marsilius von Padua: Defensor Pacis* (Hanover: Hansche Buchhandlung, 1932–33). See particularly the Introduction, pp. v–lxx.

148. *Documents on German Foreign Policy 1918–1945*, document no. 477, p. 823, fn. 7 (German text, *Akten zur Deutschen*, p. 686). See also ser. D, vol 12, document no. 17, p. 30, fn. 7.

cases the complete texts have not been reproduced. The duplication of many of the same documents in the Ciano Papers: Rose Garden only clinches the argument for the authenticity of the Rose Garden texts. They survive in translation only. The original Italian copies were destroyed in Germany. Possibly the collection is not complete. They are, however, the real "Ciano's Diplomatic Papers." They are what he himself set aside as the accompaniment of his diary.

3 / Documents from the Ministry of Popular Culture: The Work of the Italian Documents Section of P.W.B.

Development of the Ministry of Popular Culture

One of the hallmarks of fascism was its effort to achieve thought control; negatively through censorship of the press and other news media; positively through propaganda. As the personal dictatorship of Mussolini came to full bloom on the eve of World War II, this work of guiding the thinking of the Italian people and of creating influential groups of sympathizers abroad came largely to be concentrated in the Ministry of Popular Culture (*Ministero della Cultura Popolare*). Not the least among the foreign countries to be subjected to a very successful Fascist propaganda campaign was the United States of America where there were concentrations of recent immigrants from Italy together with first generation, so-called Italian-Americans, that is American citizens of Italian descent.

Mussolini's public career had been launched as that of a journalist, editor of the socialist daily *Avanti* before the outbreak of war in 1914, and then as editor of *Il Popolo d'Italia* after his conversion to the cause of intervention. Following the "March on Rome" Mussolini was appointed prime minister and head of the government (*Capo del Governo*). Although the *Statuto Albertino* was not formally abolished, the dictatorship began to emerge with the Fascist laws of 1925 and 1926 which made the head of the government independent of parliamentary control and granted him the authority to issue decree-laws with the force of law. A Press Office (*Ufficio Stampa*) was established, attached to Mussolini's office as *Capo del Governo.* Gaetano Polverelli served as chief of Mussolini's Press Office for the period 1932–33.[1]

On August 1, 1933, after the marriage of Galeazzo Ciano to Mussolini's daughter, Edda, Count Ciano was named chief of that office (*Capo dell' Ufficio Stampa del Capo del Governo*). The office for a period functioned in the Palazzo Chigi, attached to the Ministry of Foreign Affairs. After little more than a year following Ciano's appointment, the office was raised to an "Undersecretaryship for Press and Propaganda." On June 26, 1935, this undersecretaryship was made into a full-fledged ministry and Mussolini's son-in-law was thus invested with ministerial rank.[2] It is said that the Nazi Ministry of Enlightenment and Propaganda served as the model for this transformation and expansion of the Fascist institution.[3]

Count Ciano himself, as we have noted earlier, went on to greater and higher things. He served in command of a bomber squadron in the war against Ethiopia and then in June 1936 Mussolini named him his minister of Foreign Affairs.[4] Dino Alfieri succeeded Ciano as undersecretary for Press and Propaganda and was elevated to the rank of minister in 1936.[5] He filled this post until October 1939 when he was made ambassador to the Holy See.[6]

Meanwhile, on June 1, 1937, this department or office was redesignated the Ministry of Popular Culture. Alessandro Pavolini was made minister, a post which he held until Mussolini's last cabinet reshuffle in February 1943.[7] From February until Mussolini's overthrow on July 25, 1943, Polverelli, who had been undersecretary in the period immediately previous, was made minister.

1. Polverelli had followed Mussolini in 1914; collaborated in the very first issues of *Il Popolo d'Italia*; took part in the march on Rome, 1922; served as press attaché at the Lausanne Conference in 1923.

2. *Enciclopedia italiana,* Appendice 1, p. 412; Duilio Susmel, *Vita sbagliata di Galeazzo Ciano* (Milan: Aldo Palazzi editore, 1962), pp. 44–45.

3. William Ebenstein, *Fascist Italy* (New York: American Book Company, 1939), p. 105.

4. See chap. 2 (Count Galeazzo Ciano).

5. Alfieri kept Ciano informed about the affairs of the ministry during Ciano's leave in the Ethiopian War. P.W.B.'s special report no. 6 of the summer of 1945 comprises thirteen letters of Alfieri to Ciano, September 11, 1935, to January 12, 1936. See note 45 below.

6. Alfieri left some interesting memoirs, *Due dittatori di fronte* (Milan: Rizzoli, 1948), but he merely alludes (p. 3) to having been at his desk at the Ministry of Popular Culture on October 29, 1939, when he was summoned by Mussolini to be nominated ambassador to the Holy See.

7. Pavolini (1903–45) was a journalist by profession and had been one of the early supporters of Mussolini. After September 1943 he served as secretary of the Fascist Republican party. He stayed with Mussolini to the end; was captured and shot at Dongo on April 28, 1945. See chap. 5.

When the budding Press Office or Undersecretaryship of Press and Propaganda blossomed into cabinet rank, it took on the general features of an Italian ministry and the structure reflected the concentration of control over the domestic press, theater, motion pictures, radio, television, and propaganda, and the extension of influence abroad. The minister, Pavolini, was served by a *Capo di Gabinetto*, Celso Luciano, who held two offices, and by a personal secretary (*segretario particulare*), Ferdinando Gatteschi. The ministry comprised six bureaux or departments (*Direzione generale*) in addition to the bureau for administration and personnel, and one inspectorate, as follows:

Bureau of Administration and Personnel	Celso Luciano
Bureau for the Italian Press	Gherardo Casini
Bureau for the Foreign Press	Guido Rocco
Bureau of Propaganda	Ottavio Armando Koch
Bureau for Motion Pictures	Vezio Orazi
Bureau for Tourism	Giuseppe Toffano
Bureau for the Theater	Nicola de Pirro
Inspectorate for Radio Transmission and Television	Giuseppe Pession [8]

The main office was located at 56 via Vittorio Veneto but some of the bureaux had separate addresses.

When Mussolini was set up by Hitler as head of the Italian Social Republic and Duce of the Republican Fascist Party, he created a new Ministry of Popular Culture headed by Mezzasomma [9] which operated in the North. Some sections of the reorganized ministry operated at Milan but Mezzasomma's residence and the new Cabinet Archives were in the Villa Amadei on Lake Garda at the northern border of Salò.[10]

It proved very difficult to find office space and storage room for archives in the Republic of Salò. Its executive departments and their subordinate bureaux were scattered in dozens of locations in the North. The great bulk of the archives of the Royal Fascist Ministry of Popular Culture

8. See *Chi È? Dizionario degli italiani d'oggi 1940*, 4th ed. (Rome, 1940), p. xxxviii. Ottaviano Koch and Guido Rocco were professional diplomats. Also Luciano, Vezio Orazi, and Giuseppe Toffano were professional civil servants with the rank of prefect (*prefetto del Regno*). Gherardo Casini and Nicola De Pirro were journalists who had good records as Fascists. Casini had been chief of the Press Office in 1927. Pession was professor of physics (electromagnetic waves) and of radio at the University of Rome.

9. Fernando Mezzasomma (1907–45) had been in charge of the press in the last period of the Fascist regime. It is said that he asked Badoglio to keep him at his post. Pavolini brought about Mezzasomma's appointment in the Italian Social Republic. He adhered to Mussolini to the end and was shot at Dongo on April 28, 1945.

10. See Special Report of the Italian Documents Section, P.W.B., Activity April 27–May 31, enclosure in Rome despatch no. 1866, July 6, 1945 (865.414/7-645), Record Group 59, National Archives.

were simply left in Rome at 56 Via Vittorio Veneto and there they were when the Allied armies captured Rome on June 4, 1944. Only a few of the files were transferred to the North for the use of the Republican Fascist Ministry.

The Psychological Warfare Branch (P.W.B.)
and Its Italian Documents Section.

As the effort of the Allies gathered momentum during the course of World War II, they also developed a vigorous propaganda which aimed to undermine enemy morale and to shield the peoples on their side against too sharp reactions toward unfavorable political and military developments. This work of psychological warfare as it came to be called during the Second World War was conducted by a variety of agencies in Great Britain and the United States. Beginning in September 1939, British propaganda was carried out by the Ministry of Information, by the Political Intelligence Department of the Foreign Office, and by the British Broadcasting Corporation. A general control over Britain's propaganda came to be exercised by P.W.E., the Political Warfare Executive, a committee made up of representatives of the War Office, the Admiralty, the Foreign Office, and the Ministry of Information.[11]

After America's entrance into the war, President Roosevelt set up a special agency, the Office of War Information (O.W.I.), which took its functions and personnel from the former Office of Facts and Figures, the Office of Government Reports, the Division of Information of the Office for Emergency Management, and the Foreign Information Service of the Coordinator of Information. Elmer Davis was named director of O.W.I. and Robert E. Sherwood headed the overseas branch. With delightful disregard of the subtleties of the American language and the niceties of our constitutional structure and practice, the *Almanach de Gotha* listed Davis simply as minister of propaganda. By 1944 the O.W.I. operated chiefly in the foreign field. After the end of the war in 1945, the agency was abolished and its foreign functions were transferred to the Department of State.[12]

In North Africa and then later in Sicily and on the Italian mainland,

11. Great Britain, Public Record Office, *A Guide to the Documents in the Public Record Office* (London: H.M. Stationery Office, 1972), pp. 112–15; 'Forrest C. Pogue, *The Supreme Command* (Washington, D.C.: Office of the Chief of Military History, Department of the Army, 1954), pp. 84–85.

12. See the National Archives, *Federal Records of World War II*, vol. 1, *Civilian Agencies* (Washington: Government Printing Office, 1950), pp. 222, 284, 547–48; *Almanach de Gotha* (1943), p. 669; Dean Acheson, *Present at the Creation: My Years in the State Department* (New York: W. W. Norton and Co., 1969), p. 127.

British and American forces were combined. They operated under a combined and integrated headquarters, Allied Force Headquarters or AFHQ. In general AFHQ was organized on the American staff pattern with sections G-1 (personnel and administration), G-2 (military intelligence), G-3 (operations and training), and G-4 (supply and evacuation). To these was added G-5, control over civil affairs in occupied territory.

AFHQ also developed its own propaganda organ, which came to be called P.W.B., the Psychological Warfare Branch. This organization began to take form in conferences held in London in July 1942 by some officers of General Eisenhower's staff, a representative of O.W.I., and representatives of the Political Warfare Executive. On November 2 the headquarters team of psychological warriors set out for Gibraltar, springboard for the invasion of North Africa.[13]

At Gibraltar, immediately prior to the North African landings, the Psychological Warfare Service as it was initially called, was given an organizational pattern: an Administrative Section, a Planning Board, a Political Intelligence Section, and an Operations Section. Yet the service had no regular, military table of organization; in fact, throughout its history, P.W.B. as such had no table of organization. On December 3, 1942, however, it was given, by command of General Eisenhower, a "charter" which outlined its organization and functions. The chain of command for operations of the service was from General Eisenhower through the chief of staff to the head of the organization.[14] O.W.I. in Washington and P.W.E. in London inspired and guided the service and supplied a goodly portion of the personnel. In this field of propaganda, as in that of "intelligence," the British initially were far ahead and only gradually did the Americans close the gap between pupils and teachers.

But American and British policies, particularly regarding the House of Savoy, were definitely diverse. After Mussolini's overthrow, an American broadcast referred to Victor Emmanuel III as "the moronic little king," much to the annoyance of Churchill who is said to have rebuked Eisenhower for an unauthorized message to the Italian people. General

13. Wallace Carroll, *Persuade or Perish* (Boston: Houghton Mifflin Co., 1948) pp. 30–32; see also George F. Howe, *Northwest Africa: Seizing the Initiative in the West* (Washington, D.C.: Office of the Chief of Military History, Department of the Army, 1957), pp. 54–55.

14. "Psychological Warfare in the Mediterranean Theater" (a report to the War Department on the part played by the United States Army in the development of psychological warfare organization, policy, and operational technique in the North African, Sicilian, Italian, and Southern France campaigns), by Col. Donald F. Hall. Mimeographed, dated Naples, August 31, 1945. Colonel Hall was commander of the 2679 Hq. Co., P.W.B., and military director of P.W.B. The report is to be found in Microfilms of Allied Force Headquarters Records, reel 554-A, Record Group 331, NARS. See pp. 2–4. Hereafter cited as "Psychological Warfare in the M.T."

Eisenhower thereupon appealed to the Combined Chiefs of Staff for setting up machinery to enable P.W.B. to operate quickly and effectively in a crisis. In consequence a committee with three or four British and three Americans was set up in London in September 1943 with full power to issue directives to the theater commander and to coordinate the propaganda of the American and British governments.[15]

On January 5, 1943, well before the end of the campaign in North Africa, AFHQ was reorganized. An independent section for Information and Censorship was set up as part of that headquarters. This section had the three-fold responsibility for Allied censorship, for public relations, and for psychological warfare, with a special branch for each function. The Censorship Branch was transferred from G-2 (intelligence). The Public Relations Branch was the former, separate Public Relations Section. The Psychological Warfare Service thus became a "Branch." [16]

The staff memorandum which established I.N.C. in January 1943 gave it the official designation, "Information and Censorship Section," but it got to be generally known as the "Information, *News*, and Censorship Section," and this name came into general use in 1945.[17]

In August of 1943, when success of the Sicilian campaign was assured, a general optimism prevailed regarding a rapid advance up the Italian peninsula. All the while AFHQ had remained in Algiers in North Africa. In October a reconnaissance party was sent out to survey possible accommodations on the mainland. The group favored the old royal palace of the Neapolitan Bourbons at Caserta, about eighteen miles north of Naples. The palace was already housing the headquarters of the U.S. Fifth Army. Headquarters of the Fifteenth Army Group subsequently moved in. Initial plans called for an advance echelon of AFHQ to move to Caserta by December 15, 1943. But the Allied attack up the Italian boot bogged down in December and the big move to Caserta was postponed.

Not even an advance echelon of AFHQ was transferred to Caserta but only a small command post. In February 1944, the Supreme Allied Commander, Mediterranean Theater (SACMED), General Sir Henry Maitland Wilson, decided to move all of AFHQ as soon as the operational situation permitted. In May, when success of the Allied offensive seemed sure, the decision was made for the big move to Caserta with July 20 as the target date for the official opening at the new location.[18] All

15. Carroll, *Persuade or Perish*, pp. 178–81.

16. *History of AFHQ* (*History of Allied Force Headquarters and Headquarters NATOUSA*): *A History of Command, Administration and Organization at the Headquarters Level* (Caserta, Italy: Allied Force Headquarters, 1945), pt. 2, sec. 2, pp. 304, 306; "Psychological Warfare in the M.T.," p. 4.

17. *Draft History of AFHQ*, pt. 4, July 1944 to December 1945 (November 1946) p. 198.

18. *History of AFHQ*, pt. 3, sec. 2, Period of the Italian Campaign from the Winter Line to Rome (1 December 1943–30 June 1944), pp. 797–98.

questions of civil censorship policy remained with the I.N.C. section of AFHQ in Algiers, but in April 1944 the operational control of civil censorship in Italy was transferred to the Allied Control Commission.[19]

In this period of about one year between the attack on Sicily (July 1943) and the occupation of Rome (June 1944), there were several significant changes affecting P.W.B. On July 1, 1943, immediately before the launching of the Sicilian campaign, General Eisenhower issued a staff memorandum which specified and clarified the organization and functions of Psychological Warfare as a branch under the Information and Censorship Section of AFHQ. Under I.N.C., it stated, the Psychological Branch "amalgamated the activities performed by Office of War Information, Psychological Warfare Executive, Ministry of Information, and part of Office Strategic Services." Its headquarters continued to be located in Algiers at Maison d'Agriculture, 12 Boulevard Baudoin.[20]

All the while P.W.B., which had only a "charter" and a staff memorandum but no table of organization, had scrounged what military personnel and equipment it could. Rather naturally it had drawn heavily on Headquarters Company, Allied Force. On August 17, 1943, the very day the Sicilian campaign ended, the 2679th Headquarters Company, P.W.B. (Provisional) was activated with an allotment of 10 officers and 60 enlisted men which was later increased to 50 officers and 300 men. General order no. 61 which activated this company stipulated that the details of its internal organization and of its operations were authorized as requested by the chief of I.N.C.[21]

A huge expansion of P.W.B. followed the successful Allied landing at Salerno and the capture of the great port of Naples. Most of the Italian mainland remained under Axis control; Mussolini had been liberated by the Germans and set up as head of the Republic of Salò; each side possessed a figurehead with some appeal to the loyalties of the Italian people. The winning over of men's minds became a matter of crucial importance. Although the headquarters of P.W.B. remained in Algiers, field teams were sent out both with the United States Fifth Army, and with the British Eighth Army which operated along the Adriatic coast. In Naples the Fifth Army seized some splendid facilities for printing and for radio broadcasting. Large numbers of specialists, mostly civilians, were rushed to Naples. Many Italian and French nationals were recruited by the forward teams. At Naples it was estimated that the team had some three thousand Italian and French employees, most of whom were paid for by O.W.I.[22]

19. Ibid., p. 835.
20. "Psychological Warfare in the M.T.," p. 6 and Annex no. 3.
21. Ibid., p. 6.
22. Ibid., p. 7.

General Wilson, who had succeeded General Eisenhower as supreme commander in the Mediterranean, issued letter orders in February 1944 which redefined and clarified the operations of P.W.B. These orders established the position of Psychological Warfare Officer (P.W.O.): to serve as adviser to SACMED in matters of psychological and political warfare; to coordinate psychological warfare policy; to serve as director of P.W.B. When the Englishman, whom General Wilson had desired to appoint, was prevented by illness from becoming the new chief, Mr. Russell Barnes (U.S.) was named director and Psychological Warfare Officer. Mr. T. G. M. Harman (British) became Deputy Psychological Warfare Officer (D.P.W.O.).[23]

Under this new organizational plan four zones were set for P.W.B.'s activities, each with a Deputy Psychological Warfare Officer: North Africa; Central Mediterranean (Italy); Western Mediterranean (Southern France); and Eastern Mediterranean. The Eastern Mediterranean zone, including the Balkans was left a British responsibility at Bari. For Italy, however, P.W.B. continued to be combined and integrated.[24]

On June 4, 1944, the Allied armies captured Rome. This made available great facilities for radio broadcasts and for the printing of leaflets. Within a few days after the occupation the larger part of the P.W.B. staff at Naples moved into new quarters in the Italian capital. AFHQ made its move from Algiers to Caserta on July 27 and P.W.B. headquarters moved into Naples.[25]

When the Allied armies occupied Rome they found the files of the former Fascist Ministry of Popular Culture apparently intact. What a find! In competitive sports and other contests, in warfare and in psychological warfare as well, there is a fascination in the opponent's operations and setup, in what transpires on "the other side of the hill." In the very month that Rome was captured, P.W.B. set up an Italian Documents Section, headed by Mr. Dante Gnudi, a civilian. Its purpose was defined:

to examine and utilize for intelligence purposes the files of the former Ministry of Popular Culture. These reports are directed to three objectives: *Historical,* of offering documented information about personalities, organizations and movements of national and international significance; *operational,* of providing documentation for immediate intelligence operations; *anticipatory,* of making documented information available for control measures to be taken in respect to the activities of individuals and organizations and thereby providing a means for anticipating and preventing the growth of undesirable activities in the future.[26]

23. Ibid, pp. 9–10.
24. Ibid, pp. 11–12.
25. Ibid.
26. Special report, "Italian Documents Section, P.W.B. Northern Italy Assignment (Activity April 27–May 31)" a report in twenty-eight pages signed by Blanchard W. Bates, p. 1,

The Work of the Italian Documents Section
of P.W.B. in Rome

Although the archives of the former Ministry of Popular Culture had been left substantially intact in Rome when the Italian Social Republic was established in the North, they did not long remain in order after the Allied occupation of the Italian capital. Immediately upon their discovery various Allied "S" forces [27] went through the building like a storm. Each force, in its haste to find the materials relevant to its mission and function, gave no heed to possible requirements and needs of other agencies. Some files and index cards were destroyed or disrupted making subsequent research much more difficult. These various competing Allied agencies showed about as much regard for each other's needs and for the overall Allied purposes as carpenters, plumbers, electricians, plasterers, and painters show for each other's work and for the whole job when someone tries to get a house built. Dante Gnudi arrived in Rome on June 28. When the Italian Documents Section was set up to sift through the files of the Ministry of Popular Culture, the section's first task was to put the files back in order. These archives, however, suffered less than those of other ministries. Gnudi records, by way of comparison, that when the Allied Commission took over the building of the former Ministry of Corporations,[28] many of its files were simply thrown out into the street.

The task of putting the files in order was rendered somewhat easier because the newly established Italian Documents Section was set up in a couple of rooms of the main building of the former Ministry of Popular Culture at 56 via Vittorio Veneto. The section worked closely with the

enclosure in Rome despatch no. 1866, July 6, 1945, (865.414/7-645), Central Files, Department of State. When retired to the National Archives, these files constitute Record Group 59.

27. "S" force, a single intelligence force whose operations included the investigation and examination of industrial plants, scientific establishments, counterintelligence elements, war crimes matters, and others which had not been included in the normal functions of intelligence. Such planned forces which moved in to secure known targets as well as targets of opportunity are said to have demonstrated their value when the Allies occupied Rome.

28. Report by Dante Gnudi, December 8, 1944, pp. 385–82, file 20905/A/2, "Archives Policy—Modern Archives—Liaison with G-2, February 1944–October 1945" (stamped pages 259–429), Subcommission for Monuments, Fine Arts, and Archives (10,000/145/320), Allied Commission Records, Record Group 331, National Archives and Records Service. Hereafter in citations the Monuments, Fine Arts, and Archives Subcommission will be indicated by the initials MFAA; National Archives and Records Service will be NARS. Several of the files of the MFAA Subcommission were built up in the field in reverse chronological order, and the page numbers were stamped in later. Many papers several pages in length were included in such files and with these the stamped page numbers run backward.

Allied military authorities. It cooperated also with the Italian government, which was still a monarchy under the house of Savoy but one
whose survival after the war had been placed under heavy mortgage.
Victor Emmanuel III had made his own retention of the throne impossible by his twenty-one years of close association with Mussolini followed
by his complete mismanagement of the surrender to the Allies in 1943.
The Royal Italian government was a "cobelligerent" alongside the Allies,
but after the occupation of Rome, the effective constitution was Decree-
Law 144 of June 25, 1944 which provided for determination of the permanent form of government by the Italian people following the end of
hostilities.[29]

The anti-Fascist government of Italy, particularly after the reoccupa-
tion of the capital, proceeded rather vigorously at first to purge its personnel of Fascist elements. Defascistization and epuration commissions
were set up and they frequently got documentary evidence in the files
made available by the Italian Documents Section.[30]

Initially Mr. Gnudi had intended that his section would limit its
work to checking the records of former staff members of the Ministry of
Popular Culture who were employed or who might seek employment
with various Allied agencies including P.W.B. itself, and to investigating
the past records of Italian newspaper men. But on digging into the files it
became apparent that they would be important not only for immediate
use but also for future study and analysis of the Fascist propaganda
machine. The mission of the section was broadened: It was decided to
make a thorough screening of the files in Rome and to make copies of
great numbers of documents showing the activities of numerous persons
in the service of the Fascist government or working for it. By early December of 1944 the Italian Documents Section had compiled well over
one hundred reports.[31]

29. See my article, "Italy: From Fascism to the Republic," *Western Political Quarterly* 1,
no. 3 (September 1948):205–22.

30. Memorandum by the assistant deputy director P.W.B., AFHQ to the Civil Affairs
Section Allied Commission, July 21, 1945, "Records of Italian Ministries," pp. 1786–84, file
"Archives Rome Central Ministries June 45–Feb. 46," MFAA Subcommission
(10,000/145/329), Allied Commission Records, Record Group 331, NARS.

31. Report by Dante Gnudi, December 8, 1944, as cited in note 28 above.

On December 22, 1944 a meeting was held to discuss future work in Italian official
archives. P.W.B., the embassies of the United States and of Great Britain, the Allied Commission, G-2 of AFHQ, and the India office in London were represented at the meeting.
The record of the meeting is to be found on pp. 1723–1722, file "Rome Central Ministries,
pt. 1 (20905/C/4/C)," MFAA Subcommission, 10,000/145/328, Record Group 331, NARS.

At this meeting Mr. Gnudi circulated a memorandum entitled "Reports Published up
to the 18th December 1944," pp. 391–386, file "Archives Policy—Modern Archives—Liaison
with G-2, February 1944–October 1945" (20905/A/2), MFAA Subcommission, 10,000,145/320,

Copies of most of these reports were forwarded to the Department of State by Ambassador Kirk under cover of a series of six despatches, October 19–December 9, 1944, as follows:

October 19, despatch no. 449 (reports 1–36)
October 27, despatch no. 468 (reports 37, 38)
November 11, despatch no. 522 (reports 39–44)
November 20, despatch no. 556 (reports 61–70)
December 6, despatch no. 614 (reports 33A and 71–80)
December 9, despatch no. 633 (reports 79A and 81–95).

These reports are typewritten transcripts. They were batted out in a great number of copies. The distribution list varied somewhat during the course of the section's operations, but seven to nine copies were sent out, and extra copies were left over in the rooms at 56 Via Vittorio Veneto after the section folded up in the summer of 1945. Report no. 1 and the immediately following ones of the autumn of 1944 were distributed as follows:

Foreign Office, London—2 copies;
State Department, Washington—2 copies;
Mr. J. Rayner, D.P.W.O.—1 copy;
Mr. G. Edman, A.D.P.W.O.—1 copy;
File—1 copy.

One consequence of the wide distribution of these reports is that they are to be found, in the typewritten transcript form and also on film, in several different locations in Washington and London.[32]

Why the laborious and time-consuming method of reproduction by typewritten transcription was chosen, I have not been able to determine.[33] There is also the probability of error in typed copying which does not arise with microfilm or photostat. Cameras and film apparently were available. I can offer only the conjecture that labor, including that of typists, was dirt cheap at this time in Rome; and it may have been sound social policy to provide jobs for human beings even by employing the obsolete method of transcription.

Record Group 331, NARS. This report lists 100 numbered reports by the Italian Documents Section. However, report 15 comprises 12 items, 15A through 15L. Report 28 is followed by 28A. Report 31 is followed by 31A through 31D. Report 33 is followed by 33A. There are reports 60 and 60A, 71 and 71A, 97 and 97A, a total of 21 listed additional items.

32. See below (Declassification of the P.W.B. Reports).

33. A letter to the author by Professor Bates, February 22, 1970, states that the practice had already been established when he joined the Italian Documents Section in the autumn of 1944. He himself had a camera. Blanchard W. Bates (b. 1908), A.B. Bowdoin, 1931; A.M. Harvard, 1933, Ph.D. Princeton, 1941; is now professor in the Special Program in European Civilization, Princeton University. As a member of OSS he had been assigned to the Italian Documents Section of P.W.B. in the autumn of 1944.

Between December 1944 and the end of hostilities in Europe the Italian Documents Section prepared 37 more numbered reports, thus bringing the total to 137.[34]

These typewritten reports made by the Italian Documents Section comprise such topics as:

Mussolini's letters: and Miscellaneous (report no. 1);

Reports from Grandi on Italian Propaganda in England, from October 1935 to June 1936 (report no. 2);

A letter from Grandi to Mussolini concerning Mosley, and a letter from Mosley to Mussolini and De Miege (report no. 11);

Ambassador Grandi's letters to Mussolini and Ciano on his propaganda work with Mosley (report no. 13);

Secret report on the effect of the Allied bombing of Berlin and Munich, dated March 13, 1943 (report no. 14);

Italian Press Service in the U.S.A., Edgar Sisson, Mr. Lamont of Morgan & Co. 1927 (report no. 33);

Report on Muriel Curry, OBE (report no. 34);

A complete list of all subsidies given to Italian newspapermen, artists, and writers during the period 1933–43, from the secret funds of the Ministry of Popular Culture (report no. 42);

Report on William Randolph Hearst (report no. 46);

Miscellaneous documents from files on the United States, 1920–27 (report no. 71);

Continuation of documents taken from files on the United States (report no. 71A);

---

34. The reports sent in to the Department of State between January 10 and April 24, 1945 were in a series of twelve covering despatches by Ambassador Kirk in Rome as follows:

January 10, despatch no. 783 (reports 96, 97, 97A, 98, 99, 100, 101, 102, 102A, 102B, 103);
January 13, despatch no. 803 (special report on Labh Singh, member of Indian Nationalist Movement);
January 27, despatch no. 872 (reports 104–11);
February 9, despatch no. 957 (reports 112, 112A, 113–16);
February 19, despatch no. 997 (reports 109A, 117–19);
March 12, despatch no. 1137 (reports 120, 121, 122);
March 17, despatch no. 1155 (reports 122A and 123);
March 29, despatch no. 1242 (reports 124 and 125);
April 17, despatch no. 1368 (reports 126–34);
April 24, despatch no. 1419 (reports 135, 135A, 135B, 136);
April 24, despatch no. 1420 (report 137).

Despatch no. 1157 of March 17 forwarded an index of personalities mentioned in reports 1–31D, and despatch no. 1243 of March 29 forwarded an index to personalities mentioned in Reports 32–71A.

Luigi Villari (report no. 82);

List of OVRA spies on the payroll of the Ministry of the Interior (report no. 93);

Ezra Pound, broadcasts January to June 1942 (report no. 137).[35]

In the course of its screening of the files of the defunct Ministry of Popular Culture, the Italian Documents Section discovered a set of the reports made by the Italian Armistice Commission in France. A selection was made of these documents and these too were transcribed and copies were sent to AFHQ, and to various offices in Washington and London. There were 26 such special reports distributed in March and April of 1945, with copies to the Department of State as follows:

> March 12, despatch no. 1138 (special report 1–9)
> March 17, despatch no. 1156 (special reports 10 and 11)
> March 29, despatch no. 1244 (special reports 12 and 13)
> April 17, despatch no. 1369 (special reports 14–22)
> April 24, despatch no. 1421 (special reports 23–26)

A final word about P.W.B. itself. In October 1944, while the Italian Documents Section was busy sifting and copying documents from the Ministry of Popular Culture, the Psychological Warfare Branch was removed from its position in I.N.C. It became a special staff section (as distinguished from a general staff section) under the civilian director, Mr. Barnes. But it still was called a "Branch," P.W.B., and this continued to be its title in the Mediterranean theater until the end. In mid-July 1945, after the surrender of the German forces in North Italy, the operations of P.W.B. for Italy, as an integrated program, were closed down.[36] When a program and an organization for the conduct of psychological warfare were set up for the European theater, there was a different nomenclature. Here the organization was designated the Psychological Warfare Division.[37]

The Italian Documents Section and North Italy

In the early spring of 1945 everyone knew that the final defeat of the German armies and the collapse of the Republic of Salò were but a matter of time. Each Allied agency and office was making plans for the liberation of the North. The Italian Documents Section of P.W.B. was busy gathering and exchanging information with other intelligence agencies

35. A complete list of these reports, which I obtained in the Central Files, Department of State, is available at the National Archives.

36. *Draft History of AFHQ*, pt. 4, July 1944 to December 1945 (1946), pp. 100, 198–99, 214–15.

37. Carroll, *Persuade or Perish*, p. 189.

about the archives and operating files of the executive departments of the
Italian Social Republic. A special Documents team for the North, also
designated P.W.B. Unit 12, was appointed by the assistant deputy director of P.W.B., Mr. Radford. This team consisted of two men, Dr. Bates
and Dr. Costas. Its mission was "that of taking, in conjunction with the
competent sections of A.C., AMG, the proper steps for locating and
safeguarding of the various archives and hence for the ensuring of the
subsequent investigation of the documents by Allied organizations."
The U.S. Fifth Army granted permission for the Documents team to
operate with the Fifth Army's "S" forces.[38]

Because of lack of transportation it was not possible for the Bates-
Costas team to move promptly forward, after reporting on April 28 with
Fifth Army's "S" forces. Thereupon Colonel Culver of the Allied Commission authorized the pair to go ahead with another P.W.B. unit which
was attached to the "S" forces for Milan. This apparently was P.W.B.
unit 16, whose office was set up at via Cesare Cantù 3. Thus Bates and
Costas began their operations in Milan, feeling confident that they would
be able from there to get transportation to their further targets. This first
phase of the team's survey of the archives of the North took up the
period May 2–7.

In Milan, Bates and Costas had considered their particular target to
be the Milanese section of the neofascist Ministry of Popular Culture.
They quickly discovered, however, that during the last days of the Italian
Social Republic many offices and files from outlying locations had been
moved to the Lombard capital and that plans and programs had been initiated for additional movements.

In the Palazzo Clerici at via Clerici, 5, they discovered the central
seat of the ministry. The building, however, had been requisitioned by
the Republic of Salò only in December 1944 and occupation of the edifice
had begun only on March 1, 1945. It had been planned to set up the following offices: (1) *Ufficio di Collegamento* (Liaison Office) Dr. Fuscà; (2)
Ufficio del Sottosegretariato di Stato per il Ministero (Office of the Undersecretary for the Ministry [Cucco]); (3) *Ufficio della Stampa Estera* (Office
of the Foreign Press); (4) Office for the representative of the *Scambi Cul-
turale* (Cultural Exchange). In fact, however, only the first office, that of
Dr. Fuscà, had moved into the new location. The rest were only in the
planning stage. There was evidence that fires had been started in the

38. "Italian Documents Section, P.W.B., Northern Italy Assignment (Activity April
27–May 31)," a twenty-eight-page report signed by Blanchard W. Bates plus twelve pages of
appendices. The report is not dated but Appendix G comprises material of June 14. Forwarded in despatch no. 1866, July 6, 1945 (865.414/7-645), Central Files of the Department of
State. National Archives.

courtyard and in the building, but it was not certain if there had been an organized attempt to destroy documents. The only materials of significance which were recovered were some index cards from the *Direzione Generale Stampa Italiana* (Bureau for the Italian Press) which had been removed from Rome to Venice and then transferred from Venice to Milan by truck on April 19, 1945 along with the files of the Bureau for General Affairs and of the Bureau for the Foreign Press and Radio. It was reported that prior to the arrival of Bates and Costas an Allied officer had carried away some cases of documents which had been in the courtyard.

On May 5 the team visited an apartment building at Piazza Castello, 24, which had been the location of the office dealing with Foreign Radio (*Radio Estera*). This branch had continued in operation, preparing broadcasts and recording interceptions until the close of work on April 25. It was quite apparent to Dr. Bates that considerable documentary material had been burned, but the physical equipment of the office appeared to be complete. The few, scattered papers that remained were of no significance.

In the winter of 1944–45 the propaganda offices of the Ministry of Popular Culture had been moved to a palace on the via Francesco Sforza. Here too the files appeared to have been burned; the operational documents which remained at the time of Bates's visit on May 3 were of little significance. There was, however, a considerable body of propaganda material left behind. The team planned to make a selection for appropriate American and British archives, but while Bates and Costas were looking for transportation, the custodian of the building allowed the printed matter to be carted away for pulping. Throughout the tour by the Bates and Costas team in the North they repeatedly saw things, made recommendations, and left orders but were powerless to enforce them. It was the usual plight of civilians in a military theater.

On May 7, Bates and Costas visited the prefecture of Milan province which was located at via Monforte, 31. It quickly appeared that a considerable variety of documentary records from various offices had been concentrated there in the last days of the Republic of Salò. Among these were materials from Mussolini's private archives (*Segreteria particolare del Duce*) and from his unclassified correspondence (*carteggio ordinario*). We will deal with these documents later when we take up the problem of Mussolini's Private papers.[39]

There were other documents in the prefecture which the P.W.B. team learned about secondhand. The Prefect Lombardi stated that there were some twenty-eight to thirty-five wooden cases of documents in the

---

39. See chap. 5 (The Flight to Como and Beyond, April 25–26).

basement. In the early days of May they had been consigned to an OSS commission on the understanding that they would be opened only in the presence of a member of the CLN (Committee of National Liberation). This was not done; and what was to be the final disposition of the documents was not known. It was thought that these cases were a portion of the files of the Ministry of the Interior.[40]

The period May 8–May 28 constituted the second phase of the survey of archives in North Italy undertaken by Bates and Costas, P.W.B. unit 12. Their activity during this period was largely confined to the province of Brescia, a zone of concentration for the neofascist offices which had been transferred from Rome after Mussolini's reinstatement by Hitler. "The center of the area," reads the report, "was the Salò-Gargnano region on Lake Garda. Since there was no full movement of "S" forces through the entire r. ~ion, and since the neofascists had time to prepare for the cessation of work, the files in this region presented a different appearance. In general, they were left in order by the functionaries of the ministries, but the lack of Allied protection for a considerable space of time permitted some amount of tampering with documents. P.W.B. Documents team, upon arrival in the area, established contact with the Documents Section, G-2, Fifth Army (Captain Ciforelli), with Captain Goodman, AMG officer of Salò, and with the intelligence organizations working in the region. Every effort was made to cooperate with the Fifth Army Documents Section for the protection of archives; action had to be taken rapidly, inasmuch as the villas used by the former ministries were soon requisitioned by [Allied] military authorities as billets for various army units." [41]

Altogether during this second phase of their work, Dr. Bates and Dr. Costas examined the records of a dozen Fascist ministries or agencies and of two German offices, the German embassy in the Villa Maria at Maderno, and the SS in the Villa Besana at Gardone. Many of the subordinate elements of the neofascist ministries were widely dispersed. Office rooms of the Ministry of Popular Culture were found in the Villa Amadei (at the northern outskirts of Salò); the residence of the Minister Mezzasoma and seat of the Cabinet Archives, at the Villa Speranza; and at the Villa Angelini. The Republican Fascist Ministry of Foreign Affairs was distributed in six separate buildings; the Ministry of the Interior was quartered in two school houses, one palace, three villas, and one town hall, that of Vobarno which was nine kilometers outside Salò.

In some cases the offices had not been targets listed in advance but

40. Bates's Report, as cited in note 38 above. Hereafter this will be cited simply as Bates's Report.

41. Ibid., p. 7.

were discovered through local intelligence. In the case of the school building at Mompiano (four kilometers north of Brescia) which housed parts of the Ministry of the Interior, Bates and Costas were the first Allied intelligence officers on the spot. More often, the P.W.B. team made its survey only after other Allied intelligence elements had already reached the target. Mussolini's archives had been housed in the Villa Feltrinelli at Gargnano. When Bates and Costas got there they learned that the Documents Section of G-2, Fifth Army, had taken custody of the documents.[42] After making whatever arrangements they were able to achieve for the protection and exploitation of the archives in the province of Brescia, the team released all of the targets in that area by May 28.

Bates and Costas next surveyed a couple of establishments located respectively in the provinces of Como and Bergamo, and then during the four days June 11 to 14 they inspected a group of offices in Venice. In the Volpi Palace they discovered offices of the Ministry of Popular Culture which had been active until the last days of the Republic of Salò. In April these offices were in the process of being shifted to Milan. The documents discovered represented the remainder which had not been transferred before the end of hostilities. Dr. Bates made arrangements for these materials to be moved into the Palazzo Foscari at Ponte Widmann, just outside Venice. The Volpi Palace itself was needed by the Allied military authorities. After checking over a couple of other targets in the area of Venice the team finished its work there by the middle of June.

In its search for—and survey of the records of the neofascist regime, the Bates and Costas team constantly kept in mind the intelligence needs of the Allies. These were not a matter of operational military intelligence, but of identifying Fascists who might attempt to flee, to disguise their records, or to go underground. The team kept in close touch with G-2 of Allied Military Government and with the "S" force command. They also cooperated with the Italian authorities who were concerned with such state documents. In many cases the custory of neofascist records was turned over directly to newly constituted Italian authorities. Where important finds were made, the team tried to provide for security of the records.

Since the autumn of 1944 the neofascist regime had begun making plans for concealing or destroying documents and it proved difficult to estimate the amount of destruction which had taken place. "The responsibility for the destruction seems, in most cases," Dr. Bates reported, "to be nearly equally divided between the planned operations of the neofascist leaders and the often uncontrolled actions of the patriot forces." Fi-

42. Ibid., p. 21.

nally there was the lack of coordination of the various groups on the Allied side who were interested in documentary intelligence. "Not only was there an unnecessary amount of repetitious moves, which made for inefficiency, but there was also a failure to adhere regularly to the general security understanding in respect to the targets, as established by military intelligence practices. Files and parts of archives were hastily removed before others had examined them; such an arbitrary step not only prevented examination of the target but more important, by going counter to the most elementary rule of handling documents, it endangered the security and final value of archives." [43]

The general impression which Dr. Bates gained from his examination of the papers of the Italian Social Republic was their mediocre interest, a reflection of official work carried out in a perfunctory, uninspired manner. "Their chief significance is the internal evidence of the wasting away of the Fascist organism in the last months; otherwise," Dr. Bates recorded, "the papers are of limited interest to the Allies (the older files are more fertile)." [44]

Whereas in Rome the main value of P.W.B.'s documentary work was in the great series of reports from the files of the Ministry of Popular Culture, the search and survey conducted by Bates and Costas constituted the principal accomplishment in the North. Only a few, miscellaneous documents from the files of the Republic of Salò were selected for duplication and transmission to Washington and London. These documents, like those from the files of the Ministry of Popular Culture in Rome, were typewritten transcripts. The copies were forwarded to the Department of State under three covering despatches signed by Ambassador Kirk in the summer of 1945 and dated July 18, July 26, and September 20.[45]

43. Ibid., pp. 26–27.
44. Ibid., p. 28.
45. Despatch no. 1936 of July 18, 1945 (National Archives, 865.414/7-1845) forwarded three reports:
Report no. 1, an outline history of the Ministry of Foreign Affairs (General Affairs, November 1943–January 1945);
Report no. 2, a series of monthly reports by the prefecture of Milan to the German *Kommandatur* on the general conditions of the province of Milan, July–November 1944;
Report no. 3, comprises eleven reports, October 1941–November 1944, regarding the activities and attitudes of Italy's German ally.
Despatch no. 1984 of July 26, 1945 (National Archives, 865.414/7-2645) forwarded three reports:
Report no. 4, various reports on conditions in parts of North Italy including a list of persons to whom Mussolini granted audiences during the final days (mostly from the prefecture of Milan);
Report no. 5, reports by the Republican National Guard to the prefecture of Milan on Partisan activity and public attitudes in April 1945;

What became of the originals of the documents which were copied by P.W.B.? They never left Italy. They were held for a time by the Italian Documents Section and then returned directly or indirectly to the custody of the Italian government. Actually there was little chance for any other course. In January 1944, well before the Allied occupation of Rome, what had been the Monuments and Fine Arts Subcommission of the Allied Commission was expanded to include archives. The records of the Monuments, Fine Arts, and Archives Subcommission suggest that its members had little concern for the "intelligence" requirements of the Allies and even less for possible Allied use of documents of the Fascist era for historical purposes. Their attention was focused almost exclusively on preserving intact not only the historic archives of the towns, monasteries and principalities of medieval and renaissance Italy but those of the modern era as well. They were intent on getting back all of the Fascist documents into the control of the cobelligerent Italian government as fast as possible.

On June 28, 1945, the Civil Affairs Section of the Allied Commission sent this rather peremptory message to P.W.B.:

1. It is understood that P.W.B. is at present holding the complete records of the former Italian Ministry of Popular Culture. These are in part in Rome, in part at Venice.

2. It would be appreciated if you would notify the Allied Commission what arrangements have been made for the return of these records to the Italian Government, and when this is likely to take place.

3. Could this please be treated as a matter of urgency.

For the Chief Commissioner
[signed] G. R. Upjohn, Brig.,
Vice President Civil Affairs Section [46]

Mr. C. A. Raleigh Radford, assistant deputy director of P.W.B., was able to reply only in the third week of July. He stated in regard to the records of the Ministry of Popular Culture, both those seized in Rome and those which had been shipped back from the North, that they were being held by P.W.B. by agreement with G-2 of AFHQ and could be released to the Italian authorities only with the consent of G-2.

The Psychological Warfare Branch itself faced dissolution. Hence Mr. Radford regarded arrangements for the transfer of the documents in its

Report no. 6, a series of letters of Alfieri to Count Ciano during the Ethiopian War.

Despatch no. 2309 of September 20, 1945 (National Archives, 865.414/9-2045) forwarded a single report:

Report no. 7, letter of Mussolini to Hitler, July 20, 1944.

46. File "Archives—Rome Central Ministries (June 3, 1945–February 1946)" stamped p. 1757 (10,000/145/329), Record Group 331, NARS.

custody as a matter of urgency. He had addressed a letter to G-2, AFHQ, to the British and American embassies in Rome, and to the chief commissioner of the Allied Commission asking for a decision. There appeared to be three possible courses: (a) return of all archives to the Italian ministries concerned, subject to a guarantee of free access by Allied organizations; (b) the transfer of custody from P.W.B. to the Allied Commission with permission for Italian access as at present; (c) the transfer to G-2, AFHQ with similar permission. Radford's own preference was for return to the Italian ministries.

Mr. Radford mentioned that the Rome files of the Ministry of Popular Culture had been in some confusion when taken over by P.W.B. but the Documents Section had put them in order and made them available for consultation by the Allied military organization and by the Italian government, the Epuration Commission particularly. The files of the Ministry which had been recovered in the North had been brought to Rome and had been—or were in the process of being—incorporated in their proper places.

Some files of the Ministry of Foreign Affairs of the Republic of Salò had also been brought to Rome and stored at 56 via Vittorio Veneto. The crates could be opened if their examination were a matter of urgency. By arrangement with G-2 of AFHQ, P.W.B. had taken charge of a railway car of other documents of the neofascist Ministry of Foreign Affairs and of the Ministry of the Interior. The Branch also had nine sacks of files of Farinacci. But P.W.B. was serving only as a temporary custodian. The whole intelligence organization of P.W.B. had closed down and there was only one responsible officer dealing with the documents.

At this time plans were being made for a rather large scale research operation desired by the Department of State and the Foreign Office. P.W.B. was not regarded as suitable for the new undertaking, but it would serve as custodian of the Italian archives to be examined until the new project got under way.[47]

Declassification of the P.W.B. Reports

I myself first saw the P.W.B. reports when they arrived at the Department of State in the latter part of the year 1944 and the first of 1945.

47. Letter July 21, 1945 to the Allied Commission, Civil Affairs Section, file "Archives—Rome Central Ministries (June 3, 1945–February 1946) stamped pages 1786–1784 (10,000/145/329), Record Group 331, NARS.

The new project alluded to was the La Vista-Thompson Organization which microfilmed the Mussolini Private Papers. This is described in chap. 5.

Dr. Bates was asked to stay on in Rome to work on the new project but was unable to work out satisfactory arrangements with La Vista who had been sent over from Washing-

During that period I was attached to the Italian desk in the Division of Southern European Affairs with the title of "Country Specialist." Because of my historical training, documents and background materials were shunted to me as a matter of course. I got a glimpse of the enclosed Italian documents; I endorsed many of the covering despatches by which Ambassador Kirk forwarded the copies to the department; but I had no time to study the contents. The titles and summaries made one's intellectual mouth water. Here would be the proof, if anywhere, that a number of prominent Americans, who should have known better, had been playing footsie with the Fascists. But there was such a press of work for each calendar day at the desk that there was no time for careful scrutiny of the P.W.B. reports. Like so many others in positions high or low in the department I looked forward to the congress which, avoiding the mistakes of Versailles, would establish the peace; let the world return to normalcy and me to academic life. Then I might be able to study these records of the Fascist era with the appropriate leisure.

The documents themselves and Ambassador Kirk's covering despatches went to the Central Files of the department with their usual security classification of "Secret." Years passed. In due course the despatches of 1944 were transferred to the National Archives as part of an allotment while those of 1945 remained in the Central Files. All retained the security markings originally given them during the wartime emergency. Thus they were not available for scholarly research.

The security classifications on Kirk's despatches and on the P.W.B. reports, that is on the transcripts originally made in Rome, did not, however, provide for complete secrecy. The reports had been made in numerous copies, as we have noted earlier, and they had been distributed to several agencies other than the State Department and the British Foreign Office. At least one series of the P.W.B. reports was sent to Allied Force Headquarters. In accordance with an Anglo-American agreement, the original documents of AFHQ, after screening and microfilming in Rome, were deposited in London. The United States received the microfilm copy of these records. (The reverse distribution was made of the SHAEF papers with the originals deposited in Washington and the film copy in London.) The microfilm records of AFHQ are deposited at the National Archives. Under certain restrictions [48] they have been available for years. Reels 87E to 99E reproduce the P.W.B. reports from the

ton. After closing down the operations in the documents office Dr. Bates prepared to return to Washington in September (letter of Bates to the author, February 22, 1970).

48. Access to the AFHQ film collection is through the Department of the Army. In recent years the army has followed a practice of granting access to scholars as follows according to origin of the materials: (a) open for strictly American; (b) open for combined British-American; (c) closed for strictly British. Information supplied by telephone by Mr.

Ministry of Popular Culture in numerical sequence. Reel 100E comprises the Index of Personalities mentioned in these reports. Reels 100E and 101E reproduce P.W.B.'s reports on the Italian Armistice Commission in France.[49]

We have already noted that in the summer of 1945 when P.W.B. was being phased out, a new Anglo-American agency was set up to film some of the Italian documents discovered in the North, Mussolini's Private Papers particularly.[50] This agency, headed by the American, La Vista, and by the Britisher, Colonel Thomson, called itself the Joint Allied Intelligence Agency. It made microfilm copies of 135 of the 137 special reports made by P.W.B.'s Italian Documents Section in Rome.[51]

Hohman, NARS, October 16, 1968, recorded in a memorandum by the author, submitted that same date to Dr. William M. Franklin, director of the Historical Office, Department of State. Copy in personal files.

49. The exact title of the AFHQ documents is: "Combined British-American Records of the Mediterranean Theater of Operations in World War II." The film collection is comprised in Record Group 331 of NARS.

See the guide prepared by Kenneth W. Munden, *Analytical Guide to the Combined British-American Records of the Mediterranean Theater of Operations in World War II* (Headquarters Military Liquidating Agency, Allied Force Records Administration, Rome: 26 March 1948; xxvi and 290 pages, mimeographed), pp. 112–13.

Not all items in the AFHQ films are listed in detail in the Munden *Guide*. For the use of the archives's staff only, there is the *Catalogue of the Combined British-American Records of the Mediterranean Theater of Operations in World War II* (exclusive of the records of the Allied Commission for Italy), compiled by Archives Division, Allied Force Records Administration, 3 vols. (Rome: 1948, typewritten on legal size paper, 10 by 13 inches).

50. See note 47 above.

51. All except reports nos. 16 and 137. Mussolini's Private Papers are designated microcopy T-586 at the National Archives. The collection is organized by "jobs." The following job numbers have copies of the P.W.B. reports as listed:

Job Number	P.W.B. Report	Job Number	P.W.B. Report
15	1–14	32	77–80
17–18–19	15	33	81–88
20	17–25	34	89–95
21	26–29	35	97–102
22	28; 28A–D	36	102A–7
23	22 (cont'd)	37	108–9A
24	30–35	38	110–17
26	36–44	39	118–21
27	45–48	40	122–23
28	49–56	41	124–26
29	57–61	42	128–34; 136
30	62–70	43	135
31	71–76		

Jobs 44–51 provide microfilm copies of the reports of the Italian Armistice Commission in France.

In England also there are at least three sets of copies of the P.W.B. reports. Two copies of each were sent to the Foreign Office, one set is with the original papers of AFHQ. The "file copies" probably went to England and P.W.E. received a set.[52] What arrangements or regulations have been made for access to these records in England I do not know. Some of them at least were made available several years ago to F. W. Deakin, then Warden of St. Antony's College, Oxford, when he wrote his exhaustive study of the relationship of Mussolini and Hitler during World War II.[53]

For November 1968 the National Archives planned a conference on Captured German and Related Records. I was invited to speak about "Italian Civil and Military Records on Microfilm." Inasmuch as I was quite familiar with the Italian documentary collections in Washington and had been working on this monograph in my spare time for several years, I was most happy to accept. My paper was delivered as part of the morning session, Wednesday, November 13.[54] In my lecture I hoped to be able briefly to describe the P.W.B. reports and in October I urged Dr. Franklin, director of the Historical Office, Department of State, that steps be taken for the declassification of these documents. In a memorandum which I addressed to him on October 16, 1968, I described the reports and pointed out that although Ambassador Kirk's covering despatches and the typewritten transcripts were classified, they were available in other collections in microfilm form.[55] There was not, however, sufficient time prior to the conference for all the steps necessary for declassification to be taken, and in my oral presentation I made no mention of the P.W.B. reports.

The problem of removing the security classifications from these reports was rather complicated because the jurisdiction over the reports was not clear. Although the Department of State had received two copies

52. See above, regarding distribution.

53. *The Brutal Friendship: Mussolini, Hitler and the Fall of Italian Fascism* (New York: Harper & Row, 1962).

See pp. 716–17, Appendix A to Deakin's chap. 11, where he prints in English translation "A Note Handed by the Duce to the Fuehrer (July 20, 1944)." This is P.W.B., Special Report 7, forwarded to the Department of State in Ambassador Kirk's despatch no. 2309, September 20, 1945. This is identified as from the "Italian Collection." On p. 820 Deakin mentions, as part of the "Italian Collection," that "a considerable amount of documentary material of uneven interest was found by the Allies in the vaults of the Ministry of Popular Culture in Rome in 1944."

54. Plans and preparations are under way for publication by the National Archives of the various papers presented at the conference together with a record of the discussions at each session.

55. Memorandum entitled: "Declassification of P.W.B. Reports; Present accessibility to scholars of the files of the three groups of reports." Copy in personal files.

of each of the reports, the Psychological Warfare Branch apparently had been subordinate to AFHQ and it was necessary to gain the concurrence of the Department of the Army which in any case controlled the AFHQ microfilms. On December 17, 1968, Dr. Franklin wrote to Mr. Ollon D. McCool,[56] proposing declassification of all of the P.W.B. reports: the 137 numbered reports; the 26 reports of March and April 1945; and the special reports, 1 to 7, of the summer of 1945 regarding North Italy.[57]

There was some difficulty regarding the seven special reports, copies of which were not found in the National Archives, but the State Department's copies were made available to the army for examination. In February of 1969, after its scrutiny of the special reports, the army expressed full concurrence in removing all restrictions on the use by scholars of all the P.W.B. reports. Within the Department of State it was arranged that the despatches and reports of the year 1945 which were still in the Central Files would be transferred to the National Archives so that the collection would constitute a unity available in one place. Dr. Franklin also recommended to the National Archives that the declassification be extended to Ambassador Kirk's covering despatches in addition to the reports, a proposal which found prompt acceptance.[58] With Dr. Franklin's letter of March 17, 1969, to Mr. Mark Eckhoff [59] and Eckhoff's reply of March 21, the arrangements were completed. Notice of the declassification was sent out to several of the leading professional journals so that appropriate announcement would be made to the scholarly public.[60]

In the National Archives there is no particular designation of the P.W.B. documents. They merely form a part of the records of the Department of State, Record Group 59.

56. Chief, Office Management Division, Office of the Adjutant General, Department of the Army.

57. Copy in files of the Historical Office, Department of State.

58. Letter, McCool to Franklin, January 15, 1969; Franklin to McCool, January 17, 1969; McCool to Franklin, February 27, 1969; Memorandum of Dr. Franklin to Mr. Donald J. Simon, chief, Records Services Division, Department of State, March 17, 1969; copies in files of the Historical Office.

59. Director, Diplomatic, Legal and Fiscal Records Division, NARS.

60. See the *Newletters* of the American Historical Association, vol. 7, no. 5 (June 1969), p. 33.

4 / The Italian Military Documents The *Aktensammelstelle Süd*

Dissolution of the Royal Italian Army

On September 8, 1943, the Royal Italian Army numbered some sixty divisions. They were miserably armed; their record in World War II was unrelieved by any successes without German help or direction; they, the product of the Fascist era, were comparatively a much poorer force than the Italian army of World War I. Nevertheless they were a large body of trained men and comprised many officers and soldiers who, given effective weapons and skillful direction, would have given a good account of themselves. From the point of view of the chain of command and of the orders which were issued prior to Marshal Badoglio's announcement of the Armistice, we may consider that the Royal Italian Army was made up of three groups of forces.

1. The army around Rome consisted of three corps under the immediate command of General Mario Roatta, the chief of the Army General Staff (*Stato Maggiore Regio Esercito* [S.M.R.E.] and also called *Superesercito*). It was a force of about eight divisions if one included the 220th and 221st Coastal Divisions.

2. There were a number of armies or headquarters in the Italian homeland or in occupied France and Yugoslavia which were under command of *Superesercito:* [1]

1. There was a curious bifurcation in the high command of the Italian ground forces between the Army General Staff and the Armed Forces General Staff which was rather analogous to the separation in Germany between OKW and OKH theaters. For the development of this split see my article, "The Command of Italian Armed Forces in World War II," *Military Affairs* 15 no. 1 (Spring 1951):38–52.

(1) Fourth Army, in Southern France and Liguria

(2) Sixth Army Headquarters, responsible for the territorial defense of Milan and Bologna

(3) Fifth Army, in Tuscany and on the coast of the Gulf of Genoa

(4) Eighth Army, whose divisions had fought in Russia, were being brought back to strength, and were distributed along the northeastern frontier

(5) Headquarters, Armed Forces Sardinia

(6) Seventh Corps on the island of Corsica

(7) Seventh Army in Southern Italy

(8) Second Army in the Yugoslav areas annexed by Italy during the war, Slovenia, Croatia, and Dalmatia.

3. In the Balkans, Greece, and the Dodecanese, the Italians had the following forces:

(1) Army Group East, in Albania and Montenegro

(2) Eleventh Army, on the Greek mainland and on Crete

(3) Headquarters, Armed Forces of the Aegean, which were on the Dodecanese.

Army Group East, the Eleventh Army and the forces of the Aegean were under command of the Armed Forces General Staff (*Comando Supremo*) whose chief was *Generale d'Armata* Vittorio Ambrosio.[2]

From the end of July until the very moment of General Eisenhower's announcement of the Armistice on September 8, the Badoglio regime had

2. I studied the original documents which at the time were in the custody of the United States government, the collection which is here being described and which can be verified in: the National Archives, microcopy T-821, "The Italian Military Records Collection," file IT 10d, roll 8, "Quadro di battaglia alla data del 1 agosto 1943," and file IT 10, map "Situazione complessa 1. IX 1943."

See also Francesco Rossi, *Come arrivammo all'armistizio* (Milan: Garzanti, 1946) pp. 173–176 and 404–7; and Ruggero Zangrandi, *1943: 25 luglio–8 settembre* 2d ed. (Milan: Feltrinelli, 1964), pp. 975–89.

No exact statistics are available. The round numbers are given for this time of 1,700,000 men mobilized of whom 800,000 were within the frontiers of metropolitan Italy. Of these about half made up the regular divisions and the other 400,000 were in coastal divisions, antiaircraft units, and nondivisional forces. For Italian troops in France and Corsica we have the round number of 230,000 for which see *Il Processo Carboni-Roatta: L'Armistizio e la difesa di Roma nella sentenza del tribunale militare* (Societa Editrice "Temi," n.d.; Estratto dalla "Rivista Penale" maggio-giugno 1949, Fasc. 5–6), p. 42, and Rossi, *Come arrivammo* pp. 181, 188.

These round numbers are probably underestimates. Official statistics record that on September 30, 1942, Italy had a total of 2,944,619 men mobilized (microcopy T-821, file IT 1178, roll 136). There is nothing to suggest that between September 1942 and September 1943 Italy lost or demobilized more than a million men. The actual count must have been more than Rossi and the Military Tribunal were willing to admit. We do have real statistics for Sardinia for which Rossi (p. 181), gives the estimate of 70,000. Data provided by the Ministry of War at the trial of General Basso indicate that there were 5,011 officers and 111,552 men on the island. See Antonio Basso, *L'Armistizio del settembre 1943 in Sardegna* (Naples, 1947), pp. 60, 104.

been searching for a way out of the war, hoping at first that the Germans would permit Italy to withdraw, and then, after the pattern of the German occupation became clear, that the Allied invasion would save them from the Germans. Badoglio's was a very zigzag course; he was impelled one way and then another by his subordinates; if he had any convictions they are hard to discover. Badoglio at all times during his forty-five-day period was extremely cautious. He was intent on going no further than the king's express instructions. The king himself finally got irked by Badoglio's refusal to formulate any program or course of action. Eisenhower's peremptory demand on September 8 that Badoglio keep his pledge to surrender forestalled by one day the ultimatum which Hitler had prepared.

While Badoglio was seeking terms from the Allies, and even more important, trying to make sure that their attack would come near Rome, the Germans successfully withdrew their Fourteenth Armored Corps from Sicily, a force of more than three divisions. Rested, refitted, and brought up to strength, these units were combined with the Seventy-sixth Armored Corps to form the German Tenth Army, pointed after August 22 to meet the Allies at Salerno. During the month of August, Hitler also moved some eight divisions (including two overstrength armored divisions) into Northern Italy, that is above the line of the Northern Apennines. These constituted Army Group B under command of Field Marshal Rommel.[3]

What were the plans, what were the orders actually issued to the Italian army prior to Badoglio's announcement of the Armistice on September 8? For the forces around Rome which were immediately under General Roatta's command, there was some planning that the capital would be defended. But these plans, as September 8 neared, were based on the hope and expectation that the Allies would land within striking distance of Rome and on the belief that the main Allied invasion would not come before September 12. The regrouping and reinforcement of this army were only in process when the Armistice was proclaimed. When the Italian high command discovered that the Allied amphibious attack was headed for Salerno, Badoglio was persuaded to cancel Giant II, the aerial drop into Rome by the Eighty-second Airborne Division and to attempt to renege on his pledged word. Reluctantly and tardily, Badoglio announced the Armistice. Next day, September 9, Roatta, with a most ambiguous order, turned over command of the forces around Rome to General Carboni, one of the corps commanders.

3. Albert N. Garland and Howard McGaw Smyth, *Sicily and the Surrender of Italy* (Washington, D.C.: Office of the Chief of Military History, Department of the Army, 1965), pp. 288–93, 382, 469–72.

Although Badoglio had authorized General Castellano to sign the terms of armistice at Cassibile on September 3, he limited himself to summoning the chiefs of staff (armed forces, army, navy, air force) and stating that "His Majesty has decided to negotiate for an armistice" and orally telling each to make appropriate dispositions. But he declined to put the order in writing for fear that too many people would learn of the decision.[4]

For the armies and headquarters under command of the Army General Staff, General Roatta drew up Memoria 44. It made no reference to any possible armistice or to any eventual cooperation with the Allies. It was based purely on the premise of a possible German aggression to seize control of the country and restore fascism.

Memoria 44 listed a number of preparations to be made against possible German aggression: protection of railways, command posts, and other centers against possible German attacks; interruption of German traffic; grouping of troops to pass over to the offensive when the situation clarified. For the Seventh Army in Southern Italy, for the forces on Sardinia and Corsica, in fact for each of the armies or headquarters under command of S.M.R.E. specific measures in respect of the Germans were outlined. Memoria 44 was to be executed on order from S.M.R.E. or on the initiative of the local commander in case the Germans took the offensive. The order also gave the exact location of each of the German units in Italy.

Between September 2 and 5 this order was hand carried to all of the headquarters under command of the Army General Staff. Each recipient, after receiving his copy of the order, was directed to burn it in the presence of the courier, except for the last page which was to be signed as a receipt.[5]

Following the meeting with Badoglio, Ambrosio, chief of the Armed Forces General Staff, composed a memorandum for the deputy chief, Francesco Rossi, outlining the instructions for the air force, the navy, and for Army Group East. On September 6 the *Comando Supremo* issued Promemoria 1. This was a general directive and was essentially defensive. For the army it was complementary to Memoria 44. It was like Memoria 44 in that there was no reference to an armistice or to cooperation with the Allies. It was in reference to a collective and general German aggression as distinguished from local, irresponsible German actions. The Army General Staff, on receipt of Promemoria 1, issued on September 6 a new directive to the headquarters under its command.

4. Ibid., p. 483.
5. Ibid., p. 481.

This was Memoria 45, and it included those points in Promemoria 1 which had not been listed in Memoria 44.

Because of the close intermixture of German and Italian divisions in the Balkans, Ambrosio determined to issue instructions to Army Group East as late as possible, and he apparently reckoned that he would have the time up to September 12 to do this. On September 6 a directive for Army Group East and for the troops in Greece was drafted. This was Promemoria 2. But its transmission was held up. It contemplated diverse actions for the three different areas. In Herzegovina, Montenegro, and Albania (the Sixth Corps, Nineteenth Corps, and the Ninth Army) the troops were to withdraw toward the coast and maintain possession of the ports of Cattaro and Durazzo. The Eleventh Army in Greece and Crete was to tell the Germans frankly that the Italians would not fight against them unless the Germans themselves resorted to force. The troops were to be concentrated in proximity to the ports as quickly as possible. In the island of the Aegean the contemplated order was substantially offensive: the Italians were to disarm the German troops whenever it was foreseeable that the Germans would resort to acts of force.[6]

Comando Supremo, before issuing Promemoria 2, wished to discuss the situation in the various areas with staff representatives. General Cesare Gandini, chief of staff of the Eleventh Army was summoned to Rome and received a copy of Promemoria 2 in the evening of September 6. He got back to his headquarters at Athens in the morning of September 7. General Emilio Giglioli, chief of staff of Army Group East, was summoned to Rome on September 7, received a copy of Promemoria 2 the next day, but because of bad flying weather was unable to return to his headquarters at Tirana prior to Badoglio's public announcement of the Armistice.[7]

The crisis came on September 8 when General Eisenhower threatened the dissolution of the Royal Italian government if Badoglio did not announce the Armistice as agreed. Ambrosio realized that Promemoria 2 had not reached the headquarters in Tirana, Athens, and Rhodes. He repeated and reaffirmed the points of the earlier directive, but he added the final clause: "Do not in any case take the initiative in hostile acts against the Germans." Roatta refused to transmit this directive to the forces under command of S.M.R.E. because it was too much in conflict with his Memoria 44. But during that fateful night Roatta declined to issue any order to put Memoria 44 into effect; he put the decision up to Ambrosio. Ambrosio in turn felt it was Badoglio's decision, but Badoglio

6. Rossi, *Come arrivammo*, pp. 215–16.
7. *Processo Carboni-Roatta*, p. 48.

could not be found. The army was left without orders, and meanwhile the Germans everywhere were systematically attacking.[8]

In the very early hours of September 9, in the face of the concentric German attack which left only the Via Tiburtina open—this is the road leading to the Adriatic Coast—Badoglio and the King decided to escape while there was still a chance. They took with them not the civilian ministers but the high command. Around 5:00 A.M. the party in five automobiles left the city. Just on leaving, Roatta turned over command of the forces around Rome to General Carboni. Throughout the night the wires to the *Comando Supremo* and to S.M.R.E. hummed with inquiries as to what to do in the face of the German attacks. There was no response, no direction.[9]

At Pescara the royal party on the evening of September 9 boarded the corvettes *Scimitarre* and *Baionetta* and sailed south under escort of the cruiser *Scipione*. At about 2:30 P.M. of September 10, the royal family, Badoglio, and the Italian high command debarked at Brindisi, finding safety behind the Allied lines. Throughout the voyage from Rome the royal army was left without direction. These critical two days sealed its fate. When Roatta on September 11 issued by radio a general order to all army commanders to consider the Germans as enemies, it was too late. The army was the victim of the Armistice.[10]

In sharpest contrast to Badoglio's lack of decision, Hitler had been intuitively certain since the overthrow of Mussolini that the king and Badoglio were planning "treason" to the Axis. He began formulating plan *Achse* on July 26, the day after Mussolini's overthrow. Final revision of the orders for Operation *Achse* were issued on August 30. The main attention of the German forces in Italy was directed against the Italians who were to be disarmed except for those who might wish to fight on the German side. Kesselring's two divisions near Rome were to seize the city. The German Tenth Army was to fight a delaying action in the South against the Allies and retire northward. Rommel's Army Group B was to devote its entire attention to disarming the Italian forces in its area. Rommel was forbidden to send any of the units under his command south of the line of the Northern Apennines.[11]

8. Garland and Smyth, *Sicily*, pp. 514–15.

9. Ibid., pp. 516–18.

10. Ibid., p. 535; Zangrandi, *1943*, pp. 388–89. See also Col. Gaetano Giannuzzi, *L'eser-cito vittima dell' armistizio* (Turin: P. Castello, 1946), passim.

11. Garland and Smyth, *Sicily*, pp. 283–84, 287–88, 473–74. The diary kept at Hitler's headquarters which I used in the original form in the research for the OCMH has since been published and the reader may now consult it: Percy Ernst Schramm, general editor, *Kriegstagebuch des Oberkommandos der Wehrmacht (Wehrmachtführungsstab), 1940–1945*, 4 vols. in 7 parts (Frankfurt am Main: Bernard & Graefe Verlag für Wehrwesen, 1961–65),

Poised as they were, and with most precise orders, the German forces in Italy made short work of the Italian units. In the area of Army Group B the disarming of the erstwhile allies was more in the nature of a police action than warfare. It was all over in a couple of days. In the Balkans and in Greece the German roundup of the Italian troops took a couple of weeks but the result was the same.

Eight days after the announcement of the Armistice all that remained of the Italian army were some nine divisions: the *Mantova,* the *Piceno,* and the *Legnano* behind the Allied lines in Southern Italy; four divisions in Sardina; and one each on Cephalonia and in the Dodecanese. The rest of the Italian army could be written off; it was surrounded by the Germans and finished, declared General Ambrosio to Eisenhower's emissary.[12]

For the most part the documents of the Italian army were abandoned where they were and the Germans proceeded promptly to sweep them up too.[13]

The Germans Set Up the Document Collection Center-South

Rather early in the course of World War II the Germans had made elaborate plans and had set up a considerable organization for the writing of their history of that conflict. In 1940 the department, Armed Forces War History (*Abteilung Wehrmacht Kriegsgeschichte*) was established under Keitel, chief of the Armed Forces General Staff (OKW). In 1942 this office was placed directly under Hitler and its head, Col. Walter Scherff, was promoted to brigadier general (*Generalmajor*) and named "Commissioner of the Führer for writing the War History" (*Beauftragter des Führers für Kriegsgeschichtsschreibung*).[14]

As the basic step for the history which was to be written the Germans systematically began collecting documents. They prepared their

with a supplement, *Der Krieg in Finnland, Norwegen und Dänemark vom 1. Januar–31 März 1944,* ed. Andreas Hillgruber (1969). See vol. 3 for the year 1943, Walther Hubatsch, ed. (1963), pt. 2, 837–38, 868–70, 977–78, 1038–39, 1061–62, 1065–70.

12. Garland and Smyth, *Sicily,* pp. 542–43.

13. A transcribed memorandum dated September 17, 1943, evidently composed at Headquarters of Army Group B, gives a general list of the Italian documents seized by the Eighty-seventh Army Corps, by the Fifty-first Mountain Corps, by the Second SS Armored Corps and by the Seventy-first Infantry Division. (The National Archives, microcopy T-78, "Records of Headquarters of the German Army High Command," roll 8, "Oberkommando des Heeres, Der Chef der Heeresarchive," file H/40/75, "Italienische Akten, Heeresarchivrat Böhm, 1943," frame 679605.)

14. Schramm, *Kriegstagebuch des Oberkommandos der Wehrmacht,* vol. 4, pt. 2, p. 1782.

own diaries at various levels of command, beginning with the one which
was maintained at Hitler's headquarters. They seized and began cataloguing the military documents of every country which they overran:
Poland, Yugoslavia, Greece, Denmark, Norway, Belgium, the Netherlands, France, and, in part, Soviet Russia. Under the overall direction of
the Army Archives at Potsdam, various branch collecting centers were
set up to organize the captured enemy records. Thus the *Aktensammelstelle West* began indexing the seized French military documents.[15] Some
of the documentary records captured by the Germans were put to propaganda use during the first phase of the war.[16]

It was immediately after the dissolution of the Royal Italian Army
that the Germans determined to set up the Document Collection Center-
South (*Aktensammelstelle Süd*). On September 14, General Scherff directed
Ruppert, chief of the Army Archives, to send Archivist Gerhard Böhm to

15. See in general the National Archives, National Archives Records Service, NARS,
General Services Administration, Guides to German Records Microfilmed at Alexandria,
Va., no. 12, *Records of Headquarters of the German Army High Command*, pt. 1 (Washington,
D.C., 1959), pp. 9, 11, with descriptions of files H/40/120, H/40/126, H/40/183. These consti-
tute parts of microcopy T-78.

A table of organization and personnel of March 1944 shows the following archives and
collecting centers:

    I. *Chef der Heeresarchive* (Potsdam)
        Ministerialdirigent—Karl Ruppert
        Heeresoberarchivrat—Dr. Bernard Poll
   II. *Aktensammelstelle West* (Wannsee)
  III. *Aktensammelstelle Südost*(Vienna)
        Major z. V. Kurt von Regenauer
  IV. *Heeresarchiv* Potsdam
   V. *Heeresarchiv* Wien
        Heeresarchivdirektor Rudolf Kiszling
  VI. *Heeresarchiv* München
        Heeresarchivdirektor Dr. Maximilian Leyh
        Heeresarchivrat Herbert Knorr
        Heeresarchivrat Otto Freiherr von Waldenfels
 VII. *Heeresarchiv* Dresden
VIII. *Heeresarchiv* Stüttgart
  IX. *Heeresarchivzweigstelle* Danzig
   X. *Heeresarchivzweigstelle* Prag.

File H/40/126, "Beauftragte des Führers für die militärische Geschichtsschreibung, Diverser Schriftwechsel, January–July 1944," National Archives, microcopy T-78, serial 14, roll
14, frames 687744–45. Hereafter rolls and frames will be indicated within brackets and separated by an oblique stroke thus (14/687744).

16. See for example: Germany, Auswärtiges Amt, 1939/41 Nr. 6, *Die Geheimakten des
französischen Generalstabes* (Berlin: Zentralverlag der NSDAP. Franz Eher Nachf. GMBH.,
1941), a selection of 70 documents from a carload of materials which were found at the
railway station of La Charité after the French collapse of 1940.

the Headquarters of Army Group B, that is Field Marshal Rommel's headquarters, which were at Garda in Northern Italy. Böhm's mission was to survey the captured material and to suggest how the records of the former Italian armed forces could be secured for the writing of the German war history. On the basis of *Archivrat* Böhm's report, Scherff would decide whether a special collection center would be set up.[17]

Archivrat Böhm sent in his initial report on September 20. He stated that large amounts of documentary materials had been seized by units of Army Group B who were maintaining them in their custody. He urged that the troops be relieved of such duties as soon as possible; recommended that in view of the general situation the documents be sent to Germany; and noted that the *Abwehr* and the *Auswärtiges Amt* and possibly the navy and the Luftwaffe would be interested in the captured Italian documents. He proposed that a separate collecting center be set up at a suitable location in South Germany, and that he, Böhm, be assigned to headquarters of Army Group B with responsibility for despatching the documents to Germany. He asked for an assistant, for some workers, a couple of translators, and an auto and a truck together with drivers. He suggested that documentary materials which could be determined on the spot to be of no significance for military history or of no interest otherwise from the German point of view be not forwarded but left in place. Finally he asked for a decision whether such materials should be held or turned over to officials of the restored Fascist regime.[18]

Böhm made a quick trip to Danzig in the latter part of September, and on the return to Army Group B it was arranged that he stop in Munich to confer with *Heeresarchivdirektor* Ruppert and Dr. Leyh regarding the establishment of the *Aktensammelstelle Süd*.[19] General Scherff left the decision regarding the establishment of a separate Document Collection Center-South to the heads of the Munich Army Archive.[20]

It apparently was easier to reach the decision to establish the *Aktensammelstelle Süd* than to find a suitable location. Initially there seemed to be no problem about the delivery of Italian records, for it appeared that quantities of these began to arrive in the Berlin area while the search was going on in South Germany for proper quarters for the new collection

---

17. File H/40/75, "Italienische Akten, Heeresarchivrat Böhm, 1943," (8/679611). The letter bears the typewritten date October 14 but the stamp of the *Chef der Heeresarchive* shows receipt on September 17. A correctly dated transcript, September 14, is on (8/679612).

18. Ibid. (8/679608–9).

19. Letter, *Chef der Heeresarchive* to Commissioner of the Führer for writing the war history, September 27, 1943 (8/679628–29).

20. Telegram (draft), *Chef der Heeresarchive* to *Heeresarchiv, München*, September 27, 1943 (8/679630).

center. A minute dated September 30, 1943 and evidently recorded at Potsdam reads:

This morning an officer telephoned from "Zeppelin" [code name for Zossen]—I did not catch his name—and said that a carload of Italian documents had arrived in Berlin. A decision was necessary regarding the freight car. I said that the Document Collection Center-South was in the process of being established, and the documents could not be taken over in Berlin. Probably the Document Center would be set up in Traunstein. Thereupon the freight car was directed to Traunstein. I asked the officer immediately to notify the *Heeresarchiv* at Munich because that office was assisting in setting up the Document Collection Center-South.

B. Poll[21]

Maj. Josef Karl Brennfleck, a professional archivist from Vienna, had been designated to head up the new center. The very day that the carload of Italian military records arrived in Berlin, he sent in a report that Traunstein was not suitable, a report based on a personal inspection conducted on September 29. The coffeehouse "Weinliste" which had been suggested had already been requisitioned for the Reich defense commissar and in any case it could accommodate only one carload or so of documents. Although the police barracks of the town were at the time empty, there were plans for their prompt conversion into a police hospital and auto repair shop. The army supply depot at Rosenheim was then also empty but was soon to be stocked with valuable communications equipment. The military barracks were already overloaded. No appropriate civilian space was available. The requirements which Army Group B would have for its rear area staging zone quite took priority over the needs of the Document Center. For these reasons Major Brennfleck planned to look for some suitable location between Munich and the Danube.[22]

After rather extensive search by the *Heeresarchiv* of Munich, it was possible to fix on Ingolstadt as the location for Major Brennfleck's new

21. The working copy of this minute (*Aktennotiz*), a transcript with the typed signature of Dr. Poll, is in the collection being described, microcopy T-821, The Italian Military Records, file IT 5739, "Aktensammelstelle Süd, München-Kraftfahrbetrieb, Transportwesen." Correspondence and other records concerning the shipment of Italian records to the *Aktensammelstelle Süd* and the occasional disappearance of shipments" (roll 467/000069). This copy bears a typed notation signed by Ruppert, dated November 29, 1943, stating that it was forwarded to *Heeresarchiv* of Munich for the *Aktensammelstelle Süd* with the request for further investigation.

A similar copy is in the file H/40/77, "Italienische Akten, Archivrat Dr. Nemetz 1943" (microcopy T-78, 8/679904) and the signed original as well (8/679816).

22. Report to the *Chef der Heeresarchive*, Potsdam, dated Munich, September 30, 1943 (8/679817).

center. Appropriate space was made available by the deputy corps commander.[23] Accordingly the archivists who had already been despatched to areas formerly occupied by the Italian armies were notified of the definitive location of the Document Collection Center-South.[24]

Unfortunately these messages were much delayed in transmission and the archivists in the field simply used their best judgment in forwarding the documents which they collected. Some of the initial gatherings were despatched to Vienna; some were directed to Munich; and some were lost.

The reported arrival of a carload of Italian documents at Zossen at the end of September proved to be a case of mistaken identity. Initial inquiries about the car were made by the chief of the army archives with the Armed Forces Screening Center (*Wehrmacht-Sichtungsstelle*) in Berlin which ascertained the number of the shipment and the point of origin which proved to be Meran (Merano) and the time of departure, September 24. The commissioner for War Economy with Army Group B was able to supply the information that the records were not captured Italian documents but were the papers of the former German War Economy Officer in Italy whose office had been dissolved. Major Brennfleck could write this one off by the first week of December.[25]

No significant shipments of documents reached Ingolstadt in the autumn of 1943. Major Brennfleck reported about the middle of November that he had received a few individual documents from the Evaluation Center at Bozen (Bolzano) and nothing more. He wrote that he planned to stay a few more days at Ingolstadt with his secretary, Weinbeck, and then to move back to Munich where he could be of use at the *Heeresarchiv*. He asked that the transfer of Major Wietersheim be held up until there was some real work for him to do.[26]

In December 1943, the Document Collection Center-South was dissolved and its few, miscellaneous holdings were moved to Army Archives-Munich at 57 Leonradstrasse. Major Brennfleck directed the archi-

23. Telegram, *Heeresarchiv*, Munich to *Chef der Heeresarchive*, Potsdam, October 11, 1943 (8/679829).

24. Telegram (draft) *Chef der Heeresarchive*, Potsdam to the Commissioner with the Document Collection Center-West, October 13, 1943 (8/679831); telegram (draft) to Major Regenauer (Belgrade), October 10, 1943 (8/679832); telegram (draft) to *Heeresarchivrat* Dr. Nemetz, Rome, October 22, 1943 (8/679833).

25. *Wehrmacht-Sichtungsstelle*, Berlin to *Chef der Heeresarchive*, October 28, 1943 microcopy T-821 (467/000084); *Sonderbeauftragter OKH WaA Italien*, Como, to *Aktensammelstelle Süd*, November 13, 1943 (467/000072); Longhand draft of letter of Major Brennfleck to *Chef der Heeresarchive*, December 4, 1943 microcopy T-821 (467/000070); the signed original microcopy T-78 (8/679903).

26. Brennfleck to *Chef der Heeresarchive*, November 18, 1943 (8/679905).

vists serving in the field to despatch the Italian records to that office with freight shipments addressed to the main railway station of Munich.[27]

Meanwhile a very important shipment had gone forward from Rome. Dr. Nemetz in October had notified his former office, the Army Archives of Vienna, that he had despatched to them almost a full carload of Italian military records. After some time had passed and the freight car failed to show up, *Heeresarchiv* of Vienna began making inquiries. The railway station of Ingolstadt reported finding no trace of the car. Archive director Kiszling on December 13 reported to Potsdam all of the circumstances which he could learn about the missing shipment: Nemetz's notice of the shipment was dated October 5; the car was not quite filled and at the Tiburtino station some electrical parts had been loaded on, and also some chests for the signal training school at Neissen; the car's number was E 1027340; the train number 694225.[28]

After Major Brennfleck received notice of the missing shipment, he personally undertook a search at the Ingolstadt station with the aid of two railway officials. There was no record that the car ever reached there. A stray Italian document found at the station had at first seemed to be a clue; on inspection it proved to be a membership list of Italian veterans of Ciampino dating from 1934. Brennfleck made inquiries at the signal training school at Neisse, at the branch office of that school at Glatz, and also at Halle and at Ansbach. There was no trace of the missing carload of Italian documents.[29]

During the spring of 1944 materials began to arrive in quantity for the *Aktensammelstelle Süd* in Munich. On June 2, Major Brennfleck reported to Potsdam:

> The Document Collection Center-South has taken on such a range of documents and breadth of exploitation that one cannot carry on without regular help.
>
> Some 550 bundles of files were already received and organized, and then on May 21 a freight car arrived with documents sent in by both of the commissioners in Italy which in part were completely unsorted, and notice has been received of additional shipments due from Army Archivist Nemetz.
>
> Almost every day small shipments arrive from *Fremde Heere West* and from

27. Telegram (draft) December 20, 1943, Brennfleck to Regenauer, Böhm, Nemetz and Preyer, microcopy T-821, file IT 5746, "*Aktensammelstelle Süd*, Organization" (467/000147).

28. Ingolstadt railway station to *Heeresarchiv*, Vienna, December 8, 1943 (467/000034); Kiszling to *Chef der Heeresarchiv*, December 13, 1943 (467/000033).

29. Brennfleck to *chef der Heeresarchive*, with information copy to *Heeresarchive*, Vienna, January 13, 1944 (467/000032); *Heeresarchiv München* to *Wehrmachtkommandantur Neisse*, February 8, 1944 (467/000065); *Heeresnachrichtenschule II*, at Glatz, to *Heeresarchiv München*, February 17, 1944 (467/000063); *Heeresnachrichtenschule I*, at Halle, to *Heeresarchiv München*, February 24, 1944 (467/000061); *Heeres—Nebenzeugamt, Ansbach*, to *Aktensammelstelle Süd* (Munich) March 10, 1944 (467/000031).

Amt Ausland. From time to time documents come in from these offices which request them back for re-examination so that their immediate processing is required.

Major Brennfleck ended his report with a plea that he be allowed to retain the services of Dr. Ohnsorge, the man who had accompanied a shipment of materials which had arrived from Italy on May 20.[30] Major Brennfleck failed to be granted the services of Ohnsorge as we shall note when we examine Böhm's work in Italy [31] but he soon had even more pressing problems.

In August the collection was moved to Dillingen on the Danube and to nearby Donaualtheim. By now the Allied aerial bombing of Munich had grown so devastating that it was feared that the whole collection would be destroyed if it were left in the building on Leonrodstrasse. Major Brennfleck reported that the move had been carried out on August 3. Up to this time about seven hundred bundles of files had been sorted out and arranged and about half of these were moved to Donaualtheim by August 3. The rest of the organized files were expected to follow as soon as a truck became available.

The uncatalogued and unorganized files and Major Brennfleck's office were set up in some space in the *Ludwigskaserne* which was made available by the deputy corps commander of the Seventh Army Corps. Incidentally the major reported to Potsdam that as a result of the air raid of July 16, he himself had lost practically everything. His house and all his belongings had gone up in flames. He had been able to save only some clothes, cooking utensils, and odds and ends.[32]

The Collecting Work of Archivist Böhm in Northern Italy

Military Archivist Böhm's recommendations for setting up a special collection center for the Italian military records having been accepted, he himself returned to Northern Italy at the end of September 1943. His mission was defined in a letter sent September 27 from the Commissioner of the Führer for the Writing of the War History to the Headquarters of Army Group B. Böhm was formally attached to that headquarters and was assigned a translator as assistant. He was made responsible not only for gathering up the documents of the former Italian army but those of

30. Brennfleck to *Chef der Heeresarchive,* June 2, 1944; longhand draft (467/000007–8); typed copy (467/000005–6).

31. See note 49 below.

32. Brennfleck report no. 391, August 6, 1944, file H/40/75 "Italienische Akten, *Heeresarchivrat* Böhm, 1943," microcopy T-78 (8/679694–95).

the navy and air force as well. Materials of political significance were to be despatched to the Foreign Office. He was directed to cooperate with the *Abwehr* offices, to turn over to them such documents as were of counterintelligence interest, yet at the same time Headquarters Army Group B was asked to see to it that the *Abwehr* officers left the files in proper order after their screening so that Böhm's work would not be rendered more difficult.

Böhm was directed to select and to send to Germany all documents important for the history of the war, especially war diaries, operational orders, and supporting documents (*Unterlagen*) regarding Italo-German cooperation in the current war. Austro-Hungarian documents of the period of World War I which might be found were to be confiscated and sent to the *Heeresarchiv* in Vienna. Böhm's area for collecting documents was defined as exactly the same as the zone of operations of Field Marshal Rommel's Army Group B. However, for expediting the movement northward of materials gathered in the Balkans, he was directed to cooperate in the strip of territory Pola-Trieste-Laibach (Ljubljana) with Major von Regenauer, commissioner in Belgrade of the chief of Army Archives. Likewise he was ordered to cooperate in the forwarding of materials from Southern France, the zone assigned to Major Knor as commissioner of the chief of Army Archives. *Heeresarchivrat* Nemetz had been selected for the area defined by the boundaries of *Oberbefehlshaber Süd* (Field Marshal Kesselring's forces) which essentially was Italy south of the Northern Apennines and included the capital, Rome.[33]

Such Italian documents as were neither of historical interest nor of direct political interest, so far as could be verified on the spot, that is to say documents regarding administration, regarding reserve forces, those concerning the administration of military justice, and the correspondence of subordinate units were not to be despatched to Germany but were to be left in place. It was indicated that Traunstein would probably be the location of the *Aktensammelstelle Süd* but this was not definite. The hope was expressed that the new collection center would promptly be activated.[34]

33. See "Befehlsgliederung in Italien vom 9.9.1943," Schramm, *Kriegstagebuch des Oberkommandos der Wehrmacht 1940–1945*, vol. 3, pt. 2, pp. 1460–61. Cf. above (Dissolution of the Royal Italian Army).

34. Transcript of draft of message sent September 27, 1943, Az 13n, Nr. 2689/43, Chef. H. Arch., signed by order by Dr. Poll, file H/40/75, "Italienische Akten, Heeresarchivrat Böhm, 1943," microcopy T-78, roll 8, frames 679631–32, National Archives. Hereafter such a film citation will be indicated as (8/679631–32).

A typewritten transcript of this message is to be found in the film collection being described, "Records of the Italian Armed Forces," microcopy T-821, file IT-5746, roll 467, frames 000123–24, National Archives.

Heeresarchivrat Böhm's period of service in Northern Italy lasted from the beginning of October 1943 until the second half of May 1944 when he submitted his final report and despatched his last quota of confiscated Italian documents. During this time he was able to gather about two freight-car loads of materials which he forwarded to the *Aktensammelstelle Süd*. These were first brought together at a Collection Depot which he set up in Verona, part of which subsequently was moved to Garda.

At one time or another between October and May Böhm's staff comprised: *Gefreiter* (Corporal) Beck, an interpreter made available by the *Dolmetscher-Kompanie* of Munich; *Obergefreiter* Niederkorn who served as chauffeur until mid-March 1944 when he was called back into frontline service and supplanted by an Italian civilian; and a second translator, *Sonderführer* Z. Küttner, who served the whole time.[35] Petty Officer (*Unteroffizier*) Dr. Werner Ohnsorge also served on Böhm's staff from October 22, 1943, until May 19, 1944, when he conducted the second carload of documents from North Italy to the *Aktensammelstelle Süd* in Munich.[36]

On October 4, Böhm reported to Potsdam that he had begun his work. He had given *Archivrat* Nemetz the guidelines to search especially for war diaries, operational orders, and documentary evidence regarding Italo-German cooperation. He felt that his cooperation with Major Prager of the *Abwehr* was good, but he was particularly conscious of the need to carry out his mission quickly. Mussolini, now reestablished as Duce of the revived Republican Fascist party, and set up by Hitler as head of the Italian Social Republic, would naturally wish some military forces of his own and might make claim to the documentary records of the former royal army. Böhm had received the orders to cooperate also with *Amt Ausland Abwehr* (Office of Foreign Counterintelligence), but as late as October 9 he still had not been informed of the location of the *Aktensammelstelle Süd*. In his reports to Potsdam he announced that he planned to forward the documents which he selected to Garmisch.[37]

During the first half of October, Böhm looked through the Italian materials in Verona and Genoa but found very little of significance—possibly one chest full. Such documents as he discovered were in

35. Summary report on the activity of the commissioner of the chief of the Army Archives in the zone of Upper Italy, 1944–45, June 21, 1944, signed by Werner Ohnsorge, file H/40/75 (8/679684–91).

36. dr. Ohnsorge on returning to Germany was first assigned to the staff of the *Aktensammelstelle Süd* in Munich on June 5, but the next day his orders were changed and he was assigned to Liegnetz (microcopy T-821, file 5738, roll 467, frames 000012–15.)

37. Letter, Böhm to *Chef der Heeresarchive*, October 4, 1943 (8/679644);telegram (draft) Böhm to Nemetz, October 2, 1943 (8/679645); letter, *OKW/Amt Ausland*, to *Chef der Heeresarchive*, October 9, 1943 (8/679641).

a very bad condition. In two cases they were simply shoved aside in waste piles in the barracks. On the other hand he was lucky enough to be issued an automobile by Headquarters of Army Group B, but the intelligence officer (Ic) of that headquarters made it very clear that *Heeresarchivrat* Böhm would have to keep his staff small.[38]

By the middle of November, however, Böhm was able to report that he had gathered up some Italian documents of real interest. In Florence he found the operational records of the Italian Fifth Army and the personal papers of its commander, General Caracciolo. He screened many documents regarding the technical preparations for sabotage of installations and interruption of communications—railways, bridges, port installations—documents which he forwarded respectively to Headquarters of Army Group B, or to *O. B. Süd*. In Padua, Böhm's search revealed nothing. The records there had apparently all been destroyed. In this his first search at Venice he found only a portion of one document. In Treviso, Böhm picked up six cartons of records of the *Comando Difesa Territoriale*, and an hour by hour record of the developments between September 8 and 12.[39]

Archivrat Böhm requested and received leave to visit his sick father in Munich from the sixteenth to the twenty-seventh of November, during which time his staff continued the work in Verona and Modena. On his return to Italy he found that the chain of command in Italy had been redrawn. Hitler at last had made up his mind that it would be possible to defend Italy south of Rome. The Führer decided that the Italian peninsula would constitute a single theater instead of comprising as before

38. Böhm's report to *Chef der Heeresarchive*, Potsdam, October 17, 1943 (8/679647–48). These reports by Böhm to Potsdam which are gathered in file H/40/75, "Italienische Akten, Heeresarchivrat Böhm, 1943" and filmed on roll 8 of microcopy T-78, are all in longhand, a sure indication that his staff was kept to a minimum. Typewritten transcriptions of a few of his reports are to be found among the records kept by Major Brennfleck at the *Aktensammelstelle Süd*. The same difficulties of inadequate personnel, the same complaints regarding the ignorant indifference of combat troops toward documents, and regarding the priority granted intelligence agencies are to be met on the Allied side as soon as these documents again changed hands.

39. Böhm's report to *Chef der Heeresarchive, Potsdam*, November 15, 1943 (8/679649–50). Cf. NARS, *Guide to Records of the Italian Armed Forces*, pt. 1 (Washington, 1967), pp. 43ff. See particularly pp. 59–60 regarding the personal papers of General Mario Caracciolo. General Caracciolo in 1946 published his diary under the title: *"E poi?" La tragedia dell' escercito italiano* (Rome: Casa editrice libraria Corso) with an interesting explanation (pp. 9ff) of its origin. The Germans made a translation which, except for the first 48 pages, was available in Washington in the GMDS as no. EAP-21-a-14/32.

Caracciolo's diary is one of the best pieces of evidence that it was lack of decision by, and lack of orders from Badoglio and the Italian high command which doomed the Royal Italian Army, July 26–September 8, 1943.

two separate headquarters in echelon with Kesselring's as *O. B. Süd* in the south and Rommel's Army Group B in the north. Field Marshal Kesselring with the title, commander in chief, southwest, was given overall command. The zone of operations in North Italy which had been assigned to Field Marshal Rommel in the summer of 1943 now became the zone of the Fourteenth Army.[40] Böhm continued his gathering of Italian military documents within the same geographical area as before, but was attached, first to the headquarters of the Fourteenth Army and then to the staff of the Plenipotentiary General of the German Armed Forces in Italy (*Bevollmächtigter General der deutschen Wehrmacht in Italien*), General Rudolf Toussaint, who was placed in command of German occupied Italy.[41]

In the first week of December Böhm was able to report that he and his staff had made quite a haul in Verona, seventy bundles of documents of the Italian Second Engineer Regiment, documents showing the emplacement of mines between the Julian Alps and the Brenner. These documents, however, were demanded by Headquarters of the Fourteenth Army, and Böhm felt obliged to turn them over, so that he feared they would be lost for the purposes of military history.[42] As it turned out, however, the engineer commander at Fourteenth Army Headquarters already had the materials which he needed, and the documentary evidence regarding the border fortifications could be included in a shipment which Böhm despatched from Verona to Ingolstadt on December 11. In Brescia, Böhm gathered up the documents of the *Lupi di Toscana Division* for the years 1939–42, some of which were included in the shipment which was conducted to the *Aktensammelstelle Süd* by Dr. Ohnsorge. Fourteenth Army Headquarters relieved Böhm of one great anxiety by issuing an order that no documents of the former Royal Italian Army (except for personnel files) were to be turned over to the new Italian armed forces which were being organized by the Republic of Salò.[43]

By mid-January 1944, Böhm was able to report that in the last month he had worked through the Italian records which had been confiscated at Mantua, Milan, and Turin. He found very little material in Milan-a few records of the Swiss defense measures against Italy. In Mantua he picked up the war diary of the Fourth Italian Antiaircraft Regiment, and in

40. Schramm, *Kriegstagebuch des Oberkommandos der Wehrmacht*, vol. 3, pt. 2, pp. 1256–58, and pp. 1465–66, "Befehlsgliederung in Italien von 6.11.1943."

41. Böhm's report of December 2, 1943, was dated at Headquarters, Fourteenth Army; that of January 26, 1944 at the Office of the Plenipotentiary General.

42. Böhm to *Chef der Heeresarchive*, December 2, 1943 (8/679651–52).

43. Telegram, Böhm to *Chef der Heeresarchive*, Potsdam, December 11, 1943 (8/679653); report, Böhm to *Chef der Heeresarchive*, December 20, 1943 (8/679656–57).

Turin he got a big quantity of materials—possibly half a freight-car load which were sent on to the Collecting Depot at Verona. Most of these documents were of the Italian First Corps and comprised extensive records of the preparations along the frontier. Many top copies of the documents were sent directly to Headquarters of the Fourteenth Army so that the secondary copies could be retained for the *Aktensammelstelle Süd*. By this time the Collection Center had been moved into Munich, which action and change of address was acknowledged in Böhm's report.[44]

During the first part of February, Böhm made several new finds in Vicenza of documents of great importance for the Military Geographical Group, South (*Militärische geographische Gruppe Süd*) and in Udine he acquired a number of records of the Italian Twenty-fourth Corps. But by this time the Allied bombing of Verona had grown so severe that he transferred the more important documents to a new, auxiliary collecting depot at Garda. He forecast that with one more month's work he would be able to complete his assignment and wind up affairs: He and Dr. Ohnsorge would then report to the staff of *Heeresarchiv*, Munich. He had nothing to report regarding *Archivrat* Nemetz with whom he had been unable to establish contact.[45]

By March 1, Böhm had picked up considerably more material regarding the Italian fortifications along the French border, mostly documents of the Italian Second Corps. The automobile which had been issued him by Headquarters of Army Group B had been involved in a collision on February 23 and was out of commission for the rest of the month. Quite by accident Böhm learned that his colleague Nemetz had for some time been confined in a hospital in Verona.[46] During the month of March Böhm scoured the country and made visits to Cremona, Piacenza, Reggio, Parma, Rovigo, and Ferrara but did not find many records. Because of the accident to his auto, he now forecast the closing down of his operations for the end of April. Corporal Niederkorn, who hitherto had served as Böhm's driver, was called up to frontline duty and his place was taken over by an Italian civilian.[47] Whatever the feverish activity of the German archivists in Italy, the auxiliary evidence in their records of the strain on German manpower and of the intensified Allied bombing offers testimony to the tightening ring around *Festung Europa*. But nowhere does one find any expressions of doubt as to how long the Germans themselves would be able to hold on to the documents which they had seized from their erstwhile ally.

44. Böhm to *Chef der Heeresarchive*, January 15, 1944 (8/679665–666); typewritten transcription, file H/40/126, serial 14, roll 14/687682–83.

45. Böhm to *Chef der Heeresarchive*, February 11, 1944 (8/679668–69).

46. Böhm to *Chef der Heeresarchive*, March 1, 1944 (8/679672–73).

47. Böhm's report to *Chef der Heeresarchive*, April 1, 1944 (8/679670).

In April, Böhm again visited Venice and luck was with him. Half by accident he found in the naval commissariat (*Marine Intendantur*) sixty-six cases of records of the Italian Second Army, the army which had occupied Croatia and Dalmatia during the course of the war. Most of these materials were of the years 1942 and 1943. Some documents appeared to be of first rate historical importance, but there was also much which *Archivrat* Böhm considered to be worthless. He at first thought to send the selected materials directly to Munich, but decided later to forward them first to Verona. Accordingly he forwarded by rail from Venice to Verona some fifteen chests of materials including three cases of maps, but left many records in place: personnel records, judicial matters, documents regarding civil affairs. He notified the *Aktensammelstelle Süd* in Munich that he would forward approximately a carload of documents as soon as that center would be ready to receive them. For his diligent work in Italy Böhm was promoted to senior military archivist (*Oberheeresarchivrat*).[48]

On returning to Verona, Böhm received a tip about materials that had initially been passed over in Florence. He spent four days in early May sifting through some eight to ten hundredweights of records of the Italian Second Corps dealing with its service in Russia as part of the Italian Eighth Army. On May 19 the materials which had been collected since December at the document depot in Verona were carefully loaded into a freight car and despatched to the *Aktensammelstelle Süd*. At the same time Böhm sent on ten cases of documents which had been forwarded to Verona by *Archivrat* Nemetz. Dr. Ohnsorge accompanied the shipment just as he had done for the earlier one of December 1943. Böhm's office at the headquarters of General Toussaint was deactivated and he himself returned to the staff of *Heeresarchiv*, Munich.[49]

Petty Officer Dr. Ohnsorge did not revert to the Munich War Archives as Böhm had intended, but succeeded in getting himself transferred back to the *Staatsarchiv* of Dresden. In June he sent in a summary report which he had drafted at Liegnitz on behalf of Böhm registering some complaints and underlining some of the difficulties in the work of military archivists in the field. First was the need to act quickly before the documents disappeared. Troops were not suitable guardians or custodians of documents. The prior claims of the intelligence services and the carelessness of intelligence officers in handling documents were serious hindrances. (How often were these same complaints raised later on the Allied side in the search for the German records of the Nazi era!)

48. Böhm to *Chef der Heeresarchive*, report dated Venice, April 15, 1944 (8/679674); report of May 2, 1944 (8/679671).

49. Böhm to *Chef der Heeresarchive*, May 23, 1944 (8/679679).

Ohnsorge noted that: "With the passing of time the conditions for work became constantly less favorable. The officials of the newly forming Italian military gathered the documents which in part they undoubtedly needed (such as personnel records), and they were not disposed to turn over their own materials. The reactivation of the Italian armed forces and the transfer of garrisons, war colleges, and the like to the Italian units continuously cut the ground from under the commissioner. The attitude of the Italians was mostly passive, as is understandable, if not, as for example, in Alessandria where it was consciously negative.

As the overall result it can be affirmed that through the assignment of the Commissioner of the Chief of the Army Archives to the area of North Italy, the unique opportunity which arose from the war was exploited and a great quantity of important materials of the Italian armed forces were secured for Germany.[50]

The Work of Archivist Nemetz in Central Italy

For the work of collecting the Italian military documents in the zone of the German commander in chief, south (*Oberbefehlshaber Süd* or *O. B. Süd*), the chief of the Army Archives selected a member of the staff of the Vienna War Archives, Dr. Walter Nemetz. His work extended over the period from late September 1943 until June 1944 and can be traced through a series of eight or nine reports which he submitted to *Ministerialdirigent* Ruppert at Potsdam. These begin with an eight-page account of October 10 and conclude with a formal report of May 30 plus a supplementary statement of June 22 of which only one page is preserved.

Archivrat Nemetz worked under serious difficulties. There were interruptions in the communications with the main office (*Chef der Heeresarchive*) in Potsdam. There were even greater difficulties in forwarding the assembled documentary materials to Germany. For a time Nemetz was pulled off his assigned archival work to serve as keeper of the war diary at Field Marshal Kesselring's headquarters. He had a bad bout with influenza which put him in the hospital in Verona in February and a much more serious time with an infected leg injury in May which necessitated an amputation. Part of his time of service he had the use of a typewriter and part of the time he had an automobile at his disposition. After the middle of January he had the assistance of M. Sgt. (*Oberfeldwebel*) Friedrich Müller who served as translator.[51]

50. Ohnsorge report, Liegnitz, June 21, 1944 (8/679680–91).

51. The records of Dr. Nemetz's collecting work in Central Italy are practically all in the file H/40/77, "Italienische Akten, Archivrat Dr. Nemetz 1943" which is microfilmed in microcopy T-78, roll 8 beginning with frame 679812. (Hereafter roll and frame will be indicated thus: 8/679812.) Microcopy T-78, "Records of Headquarters of the German Army High

Dr. Nemetz on September 25 was named commissioner of the chief of the Army Archives (*Beauftragter des Chefs der Heeresarchive*) with the mission to seize the documents of the Italian army as war booty. He was directed to report to the Headquarters of *O. B. Süd* (Kesselring). That same day he departed for Italy. His instructions were in general the same as those issued to *Archivrat* Böhm in North Italy: To screen the materials on the spot; to cooperate with the Foreign Office, with the intelligence offices of the Reich, and with the operating headquarters; to be on the lookout for Austro-Hungarian documents considered to have been unjustly seized by the Italians following the Armistice of Villa Giusti in November 1918. On October 19 he received a telegram instructing him to cooperate with Böhm, and three days later a telegram was sent out directing that the materials which he gathered be sent to the Document Collection Center-South at Ingolstadt.[52]

On September 27 Nemetz reported at the Headquarters of the Commander in Chief, South, which shortly before his arrival had been moved from Frascati to a new location northwest of Rome, about twelve kilometers away from the railway line. Next day he reported to the commandant of Rome whose staff proved to be very cooperative. As a consequence of the developments in September, Rome was regarded by the Germans as a captured city, with the same rules applying as in occupied enemy territory. In general Dr. Nemetz considered the situation in respect of military documents in the Italian capital as quite unfavorable, partly because of plundering by the Roman mob before the consolidation of German control.

One of Dr. Nemetz's first steps was to visit the Italian War Ministry. It appeared that immediately after the withdrawal of the last Badoglio troops, the German forces had seized all of the documentary materials which they found in the building and had sent them on to Berlin to the Department of Foreign Armies West (*Abteilung Fremde Heeren West*). The Italians themselves, Nemetz was told, had burned their operational documents at Monterotondo when the Army General Staff (S.M.R.E.) had pulled out of that location. Italian officers again staffed the Ministry of War in Rome where the Germans had only a liaison officer whose op-

Command (pt. 1)" is indexed in Guide no. 12, *Guides to German Records Microfilmed at Alexandria, Va.*, issued by the National Archives (Washington, 1959).

52. The minute of September 25, 1943, records Nemetz's assignment (8/679813); telegram, *Heeresarchivdirektor* Kiszling, Vienna to *Chef der Heeresarchive*, Potsdam, September 25, 1943, reports Nemetz's departure that day (8/679814); the instruction to cooperate with *HAR* Böhm was acknowledged in telegram of *Heeresarchiv* Munich, October 19 (8/679835); draft telegram of October 22 directed Nemetz to forward materials to Ingolstadt. Additional material on Nemetz's assignment is to be found in 8/679965–73.

posite number was an Italian captain at the Headquarters of *O. B. Süd.* Accompanied by this Italian officer, Dr. Nemetz on September 29 visited the War Ministry where renewed assurances were given by the Italian staff that the documentary materials had all been removed. The Italians appeared to know nothing regarding the location of documents from the First World War which, it was indicated, had been removed to Orvieto because of the danger of aerial attack.

Dr. Nemetz, however, insisted that at least he be allowed to visit in person the building and the rooms where the files of the Italian War Ministry had formerly been stored. Accordingly he first was shown some bare rooms with empty shelves, but he noticed the inscription, *"Ufficio istorico"* (Historical Office) on certain doors which appeared to lead into quarters occupied by the Italian auxiliary police. Nemetz refused to accept the explanation that only empty shelves lay behind these doors and boarded up windows, and he made a great find. Once the cat was out of the bag the Italians made no further difficulties. The documents were confiscated, loaded into a freight car, and despatched to Vienna.[53]

During the course of his operations in Rome, Nemetz learned that he was expected to report regularly at the headquarters of Kesselring. He promptly presented himself to *Generalmajor* Westphal and the rest of the staff. He gave a full explanation of his assignment and mission to Lieutenant Colonel Langenscheidt, the first general staff officer (*Ia*), and asked that he at least be assigned an interpreter. Nemetz's initial discoveries in Rome put him on the trail of the documents of the Italian Eighth Army Corps and of those of the Twenty-first (*Granatieri di Sardegna*) Infantry Division. With the aid of a list of the barracks Nemetz during the next few days visited the command posts of most of the Italian units in Rome during the last of the forty-five days of Badoglio.

In general the situation was deplorable. Nemetz reported:

> The condition of the documents left behind by the Italians was everywhere the same. Ripped out shelves, broken book-shelves, left over food, underclothes shoved in between, parts of uniforms and filth. If some detachment of the Wehrmacht had subsequently been quartered in the same barracks, then they found no other course in the brief time available but to sweep all the mess into a room or two, or, what was often unfortunately the case, to heave the verminous stuff into the court yard and burn it.

Nemetz separated out all of the printed, technical descriptions of Italian matériel. Then on October 7, he got a tip about important political materials west of Lake Bracciano, which led to the seizure of the private

---

53. It was this carload of documents which was lost, the search for which is described above and in footnotes 28 and 29.

papers of the Italian Foreign Minister Tittoni (1855–1928) in the neighborhood of Manziana.

As a result of this early activity in and about Rome, Nemetz had seized about five hundred bundles of files, and some four hundred cartons of maps and such material. He felt that he would need two middle-sized rooms for temporary storage of the materials, and another room for the twelve hundred volumes or so of printed matter. In his report to Potsdam he asked for a translator-interpreter (*Dolmetscher*) plus the service of one or two helpers for four months. Unless he should get help for screening on the spot he proposed to forward the materials to the Military Archives of Vienna.[54]

Potsdam's message regarding the location of the *Aktensammelstelle Süd* at Ingolstadt had still not reached *Archivrat* Nemetz by mid-November when he sent in a second report to the chief of the Army Archives describing his activities, October 10 to November 14. Lacking any positive directive, he reported, he had sent the first carload of materials to the office whence he had set out, the Vienna War Archives. He governed his activity in this period in accordance with the priorities of urgency: first collecting the documents most threatened with destruction or disappearance, the operational materials (*Truppenakten*), next the papers of the Army General Staff at Monterotondo, and finally the records of the *Comando Supremo*.

For the first two weeks of this new period *Archivrat* Nemetz searched the barracks of Rome and the forts around the city. The operational papers at such places were most in jeopardy for they had been left in a chaotic state by the Italian troops and were threatened with being swept out and burned in case the buildings were newly occupied by German units or by Italian security police. By his prompt action Nemetz was able to gather up considerable material of the Second Grenadier Regiment and of the Thirteenth Field Artillery Regiment in Rome and of the Eighth Engineer Regiment in Petralia. Of the records of the Eighth Armored Regiment, however, but little remained.

Dr. Nemetz's next step was to search the castle at Monterotondo where the Army General Staff had been located in September. There, in back of some framework, he found a dozen or so steel safes with records showing the buildup of Italy's defenses after 1936, maps of operations in Slovenia and Dalmatia, and memoranda of the S.M.R.E. which showed precisely the locations of its branches in Tivoli, Monterotondo, Fara Sabina, and Orvieto. This wide dispersal was to require much time on the

54. Nemetz's own report to Ruppert, *Chef der Heeresarchive,* in Potsdam, was in longhand. A typewritten transcription in 8 pages plus 2 pages of annex of the report, dated October 10, 1943, is found in Nemetz's file (8/679860–69).

part of the German archivist. A test probe in Orvieto, where the Italian historical office had been located, confirmed the accuracy of the memoranda. But before rounding up the materials of the Army General Staff, Nemetz wished to finish his work in Rome, that is, to secure the papers of the Armed Forces General Staff (*Comando Supremo*).

This staff had been located in the Palazzo Vidoni, a five story edifice. Although some of its documents had been burned by the Badoglio troops, much had been saved because the German commandant had sealed off the building in order to keep its furniture and office equipment in reserve for German use. In several rooms the documents were piled knee-high on the floor. It soon appeared that the Italians themselves had lost control of their documents by their hasty emptying of drawers and shelves. Most of the records of the Operations Division seemed to have been destroyed but there were some valuable papers of the last days of the *Comando Supremo* and a great number of military-diplomatic papers which, for the most part, lay next to the floor underneath piles of other documents.

Luck was with Nemetz in finding a plan of the building and list of its offices so that he could at least in part restore the order of the documents. He found the stationery supply-room of the *Comando Supremo*, another stroke of luck which he exploited in filing his own reports. But in other respects he was less than fortunate. He had to contend with a chronic shortage of help and a dearth of transportation in setting up his primary collecting depot. This was first located in a building next to a German barracks but then was moved to an old, stone structure sadly in need of repair. It was without light, or water, or window glass but it was fireproof.

For a time Nemetz had a volunteer helper. This was an Italian who had excellent command of French through which the *Archivrat* could give instructions to the auto driver. Unfortunately the helper got involved with the police for stealing Italian uniforms. He simply checked out. Nemetz again had to work alone, packing the documents into heavy sacks and loading them into whatever auto was available. Every ten days or so Nemetz made the fifty-kilometer trip to Headquarters of *O. B. Süd* where he delivered such documents as he judged to be of contemporary intelligence interest to the intelligence officer (*Ic*, as such is termed in German) Lieutenant Colonel Zolling. Here he was promised the use of a typewriter. He expressed the hope that his current report would be the last in longhand, and that he could begin with the job of indexing.[55]

---

55. Nemetz to the chief of the Army Archives at Potsdam, Rome, November 14, 1943, a typewritten transcript in 4 pages (8/679889–92).

True to his forecast, Dr. Nemetz was able to send in his next report to Potsdam in typewritten form. But it was an Italian typewriter which was supplied him, its keyboard was different from what he was accustomed to, and his operation of the machine was rather clumsy. This report of November 24 is essentially a supplement to that of November 14. In the new ten-day period Nemetz had been able to discover the Map Office of the Italian Ministry of War, largely because of the clue offered in a military telephone book of Rome. He had got no confirmation of the initial shipment to Vienna: The freight car appeared to have been lost. The German military authorities in Rome regarded the Palazzo Vidoni chiefly as a reserve supply of office furniture; they placed the building under sequestration; and though Nemetz had got out much of the material of the *Comando Supremo*, he felt sure that there were significant files that he had not been able to claim. The Wehrmacht itself stood in his way.

Because of the heavy winter rainfall the Allied attack in the south had been brought to a standstill. But most of the departments and offices in Rome, so Nemetz learned, were preparing to move to the North where Mussolini had set up the central offices of the Italian Social Republic. Nemetz was worried about his own primary collecting point because it was located in an insecure neighborhood of Rome. He had meanwhile received notice that the *Aktensammelstelle Süd* at Ingolstadt had been dissolved and that its staff had been moved back to Munich. He requested permission to accompany the shipment of the *Comando Supremo* materials to Munich.

The principal development which Nemetz was able to report was that he had put many of the groups of documents of the Armed Forces General Staff back into order. Furthermore he had made real progress with an index of these papers. He had started typing this out in duplicate, using the Italian typewriter and the reverse side of the stationery of the *Comando Supremo*. He sent the top copy of the first six pages of his index to Potsdam with the request for approval.[56]

In a brief report of December 2, 1943, *Archivrat* Nemetz forwarded the continuation of his index, pages 7–16. The initial report had comprised bundles one through eleven of *Comando Supremo* documents. These additional pages indexed bundles 12–77. Meanwhile Kesselring's command had been redesignated commander in chief, southwest (*Oberbefehlshaber Südwest*). A telegram from Vienna arrived there for Nemetz

56. Nemetz to the chief of the Army Archives at Potsdam, Rome, November 24, 1943 (8/679915–20). The six pages of index (*Aktenverzeichnisse*) were attached as an annex to the report, (8/679921–27). One film frame (679922) is interpolated showing the obverse side of a sheet of *Comando Supremo* stationery.

stating that his initial carload of Italian military files had not arrived either in Vienna or in Ingolstadt. The archivist reported that he desperately needed chests for packing the documents. He had organized about half of the *Comando Supremo* files into 114 bundles. The other half of that material was still unsorted.[57]

Under cover of a report dated January 24, 1944, *HAR* Nemetz sent to Potsdam a general survey of the files which he had so far examined, plus pages 17–25 of the index.[58]

This diligent work by Dr. Nemetz in sorting, classifying, and indexing the Italian military documents has endured. Of these twenty-five pages of index matter, the top copy was sent to the main office at Potsdam. Later, at the end of May, a carbon copy was forwarded from Verona to the *Aktensammelstelle Süd*. This carbon copy, with a couple of additional sheets, and with the insertion of file numbers in red crayon, became volume two of the entry book which Major Brennfleck set up at the Document Collection Center-South.[59] In turn the entry book was the basis for the American catalogue of the *Aktensammelstell Süd*. When, after many years, the Italian military documents were microfilmed, the catalogue in turn served as the basis and scheme of organization for the three *Guides* to these films which were issued by the National Archives.

For weeks and weeks, however, *Ministerialdirigent* Ruppert at the main office remained quite ignorant of Nemetz's operations. The carefully prepared reports sent from Rome on November 24 and December 2, 1943, and from Headquarters, *O. B. Südwest* on January 24, 1944, did not reach Potsdam until February. Meanwhile Dr. Nemetz's archival work had been seriously interrupted by illness, and plans for his future employment had radically changed. Dr. Ruppert was happy to accept the index of materials prepared by Nemetz, but he notified him that as soon as he had recuperated he was to report back to Headquarters of *O. B. Südwest* to keep the war diary (*Kriegstagebuch* or KTB) of that command. Ruppert added that he had visited the Army Archives in Vienna and had spoken to the director, Dr. Kiszling: There was still no trace of the carload of documents which Nemetz had despatched to Vienna. He expressed the

57. Nemetz to the chief of the Army Archives at Potsdam, Rome, December 2, 1943 (8/679928). The annex with index pages 7–16 listing bundles 12–77, is filmed on frames 679929–32.

58. The report is 8/679940; the general survey (*Inhaltsübersicht*) is on frames 679941–44; the additional index pages are on frames 679945–54. These are not filmed strictly in order. The last frame, 679954, is for page 23; page 25 is filmed on frame 679952; and page 26 which appears later at the *Aktensammelstelle Süd*, is missing.

59. Cf. below (Major Brennbleck's Entry Book). Cf. frame 8/679921 with vol. 2, p. 1 of the *Bestandbuch* which is at the National Archives.

hope that the confiscated materials would arrive at the Army Archives of Munich whither the *Aktensammelstelle Süd* had been transferred.[60]

Only in April was Dr. Nemetz able to send a comprehensive report concerning his activities and misadventures since the beginning of December 1943. Lieutenant Colonel Zolling, first general staff officer (*Ia*) at Headquarters of *O. B. Südwest*, approved the plan to move the collected Italian war documents out of Rome, and Nemetz chose as his new depot Ostiglia, a small industrial city on the main line to the North. There were many difficulties in the loading. Nemetz faced a shortage of labor. He had hoped that the maps would already have been sent on: but the officer who had so freely offered his help had been transferred before he could make good on his promises, and the job fell back on Nemetz himself. After that officer's transfer, unauthorized persons had entered the storage rooms, had helped themselves to what they wished, and left everything behind in disorder. Nemetz originally had hoped to gather together in the new depot all of the materials which he had ferreted out, but at the last minute the freight car promised him was not made available and he could carry out his plans only partially.

The local commander of Ostiglia proved to be very obliging. He assigned the archivist, as working space, a couple of classrooms of a school building which had been commandeered by a German unit. But the unit was promptly moved on; the heat was cut off; and Nemetz was unable to get a guard. He therefore sought and was granted permission to move his documents a further stage northward, that is to Verona. Meanwhile his documents remained in the unheated, unguarded school rooms in Ostiglia.

Working conditions were miserable. Nevertheless, just before Christmas all of the *Comando Supremo* documents were securely packed in chests ready for the next move. Then on the night before Christmas Eve (December 23–24) the lock on the door was broken off, the rooms were forcibly entered, and all of the chests on the floor were ripped open. Nemetz promptly reported the burglary and thefts to the local commander and to the *Carabinieri*. Apparently it was a group of schoolboys, thoroughly familiar with the building, who had broken in and taken maps, books, and a few documents just for the lark. After dire threats of punishment most of the stolen material seems to have been restored. Fortunately for Nemetz, the things the boys had taken were chiefly printed materials.

In Verona, Archivist Nemetz managed to get a couple of rooms on the ground floor of a private house as a storage depot, and while waiting

60. Ruppert to Nemetz, Potsdam, February 23, 1944 (8/679955–56).

there for the collection of documents to be forwarded from Ostiglia, he received notice from Lieutenant Colonel Beelitz to report back to Headquarters of *O. B. Südwest*. Nemetz got the documents moved into the new depot only after considerable difficulty. The railway station at Verona had been practically obliterated. He left Verona in the morning hours of New Year's Day 1944, but by this time the Allied aerial bombardment of the Italian railway lines was so severe that it took him four days to get to the Headquarters of the Commander in Chief, Southwest. There he learned that his new assignment was to keep the war diary (KTB) of that headquarters. He was to report back within two weeks. He could retain his mission as an archivist only as an auxiliary function.

On returning north to Verona Dr. Nemetz set to work to get his documents in proper order for the final move to the *Aktensammelstelle Süd*, but at this point his health broke down. For the next five weeks he was confined to the hospital in Verona. While there in bed and much to Nemetz's surprise his interpreter-helper, whose services had been promised back in October, arrived and reported for duty. This was M. Sgt. Friedrich Müller.[61]

Not until February 24 was Nemetz released from the hospital and the next day he started back to Field Marshal Kesselring's headquarters. During Nemetz's illness, *HAR* Böhm had apparently moved the documentary materials northward to the *Aktensammelstelle Süd*. On the return trip southward there was a long halt at Florence and Nemetz used this stopover to make further inquiries for Italian war documents. Thus it was that he was able to pick up a collection of regulations for artillery of the Seventh Army Corps. Sergeant Müller saw to it that these new materials were shipped on to Verona.

At Headquarters of *O. B. Südwest*, Dr. Nemetz was able to enlist the help of the German liaison officer with the commandant of Rome and thus to acquire another considerable group of Italian military publications.

The work of Dr. Nemetz as keeper of the war diary at Kesselring's headquarters did not last very long. The Luftwaffe colonel who had formerly kept the KTB was restored, and the archivist was thus freed to follow up certain leads to materials which he had first uncovered at Monterotondo in the early autumn. He was able to pick up three steel filing cabinets in Palombara Sabina, twelve in Fara Sabina, and three more in Tivoli, altogether about sixty bundles of files. The archive commissioner was particularly proud of one find—a document dated September 1, 1943, delineating the occupation of Rome by the "Red Party," that is, Badoglio

---

61. Telegram, Nemetz to *Chef der Heeresarchive*, Potsdam, January 15, 1944 (8/679978).

troops, one armored division and one motorized division which together formed a corps.

After collecting this new material Nemetz again traveled northward to Verona. He arrived April 7. He announced his plan to await the arrival there of the other materials which he had gathered in his assigned zone, and then to accompany the shipment into Munich. The difficulties of transportation had become so great that he felt it unsafe and unwise to assemble any considerable quantities of documents at any point south of the Apennines. For all its difficulties, Verona was the best assembly point.[62]

In a separate report of the same date (April 11, 1944) *HAR* Nemetz gave some additional details about his assignment as KTB keeper. The previous keeper of the war diary was an older air force colonel. He had been very much hurt at being relieved. By the time Dr. Nemetz got to Kesselring's headquarters after his stay in the hospital in Verona, conditions at Headquarters, *O. B. Südwest* had greatly changed and the Luftwaffe colonel had managed to get restored to his former task. There was not enough work for two men; Nemetz asked to be discharged; and thus he was granted permission to resume his archival work.[63]

For his careful and conscientious work Nemetz was awarded the War Service Cross (*Kriegsverdienstkreuz*) which he acknowledged in his reports of early May, but he confessed that he felt he had really done no more than his obvious duty. Since being relieved of the job of KTB keeper at *O. B. Südwest*, he had pushed on with the gathering up and shipping northward of the materials from the Villa Braschi and the Villa Greci at Tivoli, that is of Army General Staff materials some of which had gone forward in December. To his regret the materials from Fara Sabina and Palombara-Sabina and some of those of Tivoli had to be sent on in complete disarray. He felt sure, however, that the documents from the *Ufficio Ordinamento* would provide a good insight into the working methods of the Italian high command, and that the tables of organization and the strength reports of the *Ufficio Mobilitazione* would be most useful for the future war histories. The documents taken out of safes and from locked filing cabinets could be sorted on the spot, but Dr. Nemetz could not sift through the rest of the materials.

Working conditions were not easy. Archivist Nemetz could get away from headquarters only around noon, and then there might be an au-

---

62. Nemetz to *Chef der Heeresarchive*, Verona, April 11, 1944, report on activities December 1, 1943–April 10, 1944, an eight-page typewritten report (8/679986–93).

63. Nemetz to *Heeresoberarchivrat* Dr. Poll at Potsdam, Verona, April 11, 1944 (8/679994–96).

tomobile trip of some hours. There were guerrilla bands in the hills so that as much as possible Nemetz and his driver traveled by daylight.

In order to make sure of the safe arrival in Verona of all of the materials which he had assembled, those screened as well as those not sorted, Nemetz managed in four days and nights personally to escort them. For the stretch from Florence to Verona he had got a freight car; he stayed with it day and night. *HAR* Böhm had meanwhile been in Verona. The two had not been able to meet but Nemetz was glad to receive the written offer from Böhm of some shipping space for moving his materials on the last stage, over the Alps to Munich.

The freight train which had picked up Nemetz's car of documents was due in Verona by midnight. Near Bologna, however, there had been a couple of air raid alarms which caused considerable delay but no damage. Then at Isola della Scala, just outside Verona, there was another alarm shortly after 2:00 A.M. May 3. Nemetz's car was shunted onto a siding. Here in the night he was standing against the footboard on the side away from the station. He failed to see the starting signal; and, because of the rapid acceleration of the electric train, when he tried to swing onto the car he missed his footing and fell. Fortunately his car was the last. His leg was not severed but he incurred a double fracture of the shinbone. After receiving first aid treatment by some German railway men at about 5:00 A.M. of May 3, Nemetz found himself back in the same military hospital where he had been confined during the winter.

It was a compound fracture but aside from considerable bleeding at the start, it did not seem to threaten loss of the leg. The staff doctor indicated that Archivist Nemetz would be able to walk again after about four weeks. There seemed to be but little fever, not too much pain. The military hospital was not far from the depot for the documents and Nemetz hoped that his helper, Master Sergeant Müller, would be able to supervise the moving of the materials to the *Aktensammelstelle Süd*. The day after his accident Nemetz made out his report and was busy with plans for indexing the S.M.R.E. materials in the same fashion as he had done those of the *Comando Supremo*.[64]

For three weeks with his leg in a cast and with his head full of plans for further work—there is something admirable about this man's zeal—Dr. Nemetz appeared to make good progress. Then one day, quite suddenly, he felt sharp pains in his whole right leg. The cast was removed at the end of the fourth week and Nemetz was transferred to the orthopedic hospital in Cortina d'Ampezzo. Blood poisoning had set in. The leg had

64. Nemetz to the *Chef der Heeresarchive* in Potsdam, May 4, 1944, a five-page, single-spaced, typewritten report with Nemetz's signature (8/679997–680001).

to be amputated above the knee and Nemetz had to remain in Cortina d'Ampezzo. Master Sergeant Müller took care of the work of forwarding the documents collected by *HAR* Nemetz in Central Italy to the *Aktensammelstelle Süd*.[65]

By the end of May, Dr. Nemetz was back at work in Verona. He forwarded to the *Aktensammelstelle Süd* the carbon copy of the index of materials of the *Comando Supremo* which he had prepared earlier, and sent to Potsdam a detailed listing of the documents, maps, and printed materials which had been sent from Verona to Munich on May 19 along with the materials gathered by *Archivrat* Böhm. He asked for instructions as to what to do with the unsorted materials which he still had at Verona.[66]

Sometime in June *Heeresarchivrat* Nemetz seems to have finished his work, but only a fragment of his longhand report of June 22, 1944, survived.[67] And that freight-car load of documents, despatched from Rome to Vienna in October of 1943, what became of it? The surviving German records do not say. Nevertheless a great deal of materials of the *Comando Supremo* did reach the *Aktensammelstelle Süd* and were later shipped to the United States and microfilmed. These materials may have been shunted to Ljubljana or some other depot; they may have been intercepted by a rival or competing intelligence office and forwarded later; in any case many reels of such records are at hand in the National Archives and the original documents are now back in Rome.[68]

France and the Balkans

Compared to the rich harvest of Italian military records gathered by Senior Archivist Böhm in Northern Italy or by Dr. Nemetz in Central Italy, the zones of France and the Balkans yielded but little. We need only brief mention of each area.

The Germans already had a branch office in Paris of their Document Collection Center-West (*Aktensammelstelle West*) which was located at Wannsee. Herbert Knorr, army archivist on the staff of the Munich War

65. Unsigned report, enclosure in Ohnsorge's report of June 21, 1944, Böhm file, H/40/75 (8/679682). Cf. note 50 above.

66. Nemetz to *Chef der Heeresarchive*, May 30, 1944 (8/680004). Annexes to this report: listing contents of 10 crates (8/680005–10); special index-artillery regulations, Seventh Corps (680001); guides to maps, scale 1:100,000 (680012–28); guides to maps, scale 1:500,000 (680029–35); of various scales (680036–37).

67. Ibid. (8/680038).

68. See "Comando Supremo" in the index by provenance in the *Guide to Records of the Italian Armed Forces*, pt. 1, pp. 140–41; pt. 2, p. 126; pt. 3, p. 159.

Archives since April 1937, and who had been called back in the reserves
with the rank of major, was in charge of this office which was attached to
Headquarters of the German Military Commander in France. Thus it was
that when Italy collapsed, Major Knorr was directed to go to the area of
Southern France which had been occupied by the Italian Fourth Army
and to seize its records.[69]

Major Knorr had scarcely begun his searches in Southern France
when he fell ill. Senior Archivist Freiherr von Waldenfels of the Munich
Army Archives happened to be in Paris at this time and volunteered to
undertake the mission.[70] In the six days granted him, November 12–17,
Waldenfels visited a score or more of places which had served as headquarters of various units of the Italian Fourth Army. He listed the places
where he had located Italian records, but these were not very numerous
because that army had already begun its movement back into Italy in
August. Quite properly the Italians had turned over certain of their administrative records to the German Nineteenth Army which relieved
them. For lack of transport it was not possible to forward to Paris the materials which had been located. Waldenfels recommended that the next
step should be to examine the documents on the spot.[71]

Chief of Army Archives Ruppert apparently hoped that Waldenfels
would be permitted to remain another three or four weeks in France to
follow up with the screening of the Italian records which he had discovered. The Army Archives of Munich, however, needed his services for
their transfer into new quarters and insisted on his return. At the

69. Knorr, born August 7, 1888, is listed as *Heeresarchivrat* in the file H/40/126, "Beauftragte des Führers für die militärische Geschichtsschreibung, Diverser Schriftwechsel, January–July," microcopy T-78, serial 14, roll 14, frame 687745. A notation in the final column
reads: "als Major d. R. Beauftr. d. Ch. d. H. A. in Paris, 1.8.38(?)." The question mark is
appropriate. It does not seem probable that the Paris branch office was set up a year before
the outbreak of war.

Most of the records regarding the collecting work in southern France are in the file
H/40/251, "Beauftragte Frankreich: Archivdienst, Fundmeldungen über Beuteakten und
Bücher, 1940–44," microcopy T-78, serial 30, roll 30, frames 702894–703415. This file is in re-
verse order. A few scattered references are in the Böhm file (H/40/75) or in the Nemetz file
(H/40/77) which have already been cited.

70. Otto, Freiherr von Waldenfels, born August 10, 1889, was appointed *Heeresarchivrat* on the staff of the *Heeresarchiv* of Munich on April 1, 1937 (file H/40/126–14/687745).
Some time before the autumn of 1943 he had been promoted to senior archivist (*Heeresoberarchivrat*) for he was referred to as such in the memorandum of November 25, 1943
(8/679821). Waldenfels reported Knorr's illness by letter of November 4, 1943 to the military
commander in France and asked permission to visit Lyon, Marseilles, Toulon and Nice during the period November 12 to 17, 1943 (30/702941).

71. Waldenfels to the *Chef der Heeresarchive* in Potsdam, Paris, November 19, 1943
(30/702935–37). Another copy in Nemetz's file (8/679823–26).

beginning of December, Major Knorr resumed the work of collecting the papers of the Italian Fourth Army.[72]

During the first fortnight of December, *HAR* Knorr visited Cannes, Grasse, Antibes, Nice, Villafranche, and Beaulieu. At Cannes in the Hotel Mont Fleury he found a pile of records from the Italian 166th Coastal Regiment and from the staff of the 223d Coastal Division. There were about three cubic meters of papers, all in a mess. The building was being used as a branch office of the Security Service (*Sicherheitsdienst* or SD) whose headquarters were at Nice. One pile, about one and one-half meters high, appeared to have documents of historical interest. Knorr requested the SD to forward them to the Document Collection Center-South at Ingolstadt.

There were no records at all in the Hotel Victoria at Grasse, but at Antibes in the Hotel Royale, *Archivrat* Knorr found a couple of chests with records of the 156th Artillery Group. He sifted through these and forwarded a selection by service mail to Major Brennfleck in Munich.

In general, *HAR* Knorr considered his trip as scarcely satisfactory. He had been directed especially to get the maps and plans of the Italian border fortifications, but he was not able to find such materials. He reported that his work had been severely handicapped: by the severe reduction in railway service, by the incessant delays of the passenger trains, by the overcrowding of the auto buses, and the shortness of the daylight working hours. Furthermore Knorr's predecessor (Waldenfels) had listed the locations of Italian documents as given him by the German units which had moved in immediately after the Italians. Meanwhile other German units had supplanted the initial ones and they knew nothing of the Italian documents or reports about them. The various garrison headquarters along the Côte d'Azur had only recently been set up and consequently had not been brought into the picture regarding the collecting of Italian records. Knorr planned another trip to Southern France after the holiday-season restrictions on service travel would be lifted and he asked for appropriate authorization.[73] From Paris Knorr by letter renewed the request that the SD forward to the *Aktensammelstelle Süd* in Munich the service regulations and other Italian documentary materials held in the branch post at Cannes.[74]

By letter of March 7, 1944, Major Knorr notified the Munich Army

---

72. Ruppert to Paris, November 25, 1943 (8/679821); *Heeresarchivdirektor* Leyh (Munich) to Ruppert, December 1, 1943 (8/679827).

73. Copy, Knorr to the *Chef der Heeresarchive* at Potsdam, Paris, December 15, 1943 (30/702928–30).

74. Major Knorr to Garrison Commander, Cannes, December 27, 1943 (30/702924). These materials were finally sent forward by freight on March 30, 1944 (Garrison Com-

Archives that he had that day forwarded two packages of documents and maps of the Italian Third Aerial Torpedo Training Squadron (*nucleo addestramento aereosiluranti*).[75]

In Waldenfels's report of his trip to Southern France in November he had explained that a goodly portion of the records of the Italian Fourth Army had been turned over to the relieving German Nineteenth Army. He mentioned this orally to Major Brennfleck after his return to the Army Archives in Munich. Brennfleck referred to these materials and in April urged Major Knorr to obtain them from the *Ic* at German Nineteenth Army Headquarters at Avignon. Accordingly on May 10, Knorr wrote to the intelligence officer of the Nineteenth Army staff asking that he send these materials to the *Aktensammelstelle Süd* in Munich.[76]

The surviving records do not indicate whether or not these Italian documents were ever sent on from France. In any case Operation Overlord, the main blow of the Western Allies against Nazi Germany, was less than a month away. Although the German forces in France knew neither the time nor the place of that assault, they certainly knew that something was coming.[77] The intelligence staff of the German Nineteenth Army had more important things to worry about than captured Italian documents.

The Paris branch of the German Army Ordnance Office did turn over to Major Knorr some confidential materials regarding the Italian Alpine fortifications along the French border. Knorr forwarded these by courier, apparently to Potsdam.[78]

Major Kurt von Regenauer, the officer in charge of the Document Collection Center-Southeast (*Aktensammelstelle Südost*), was charged with the duty of collecting the documents of the Italian military forces in the Balkans.[79] It was this office, located in Vienna, which had seized the records of the Yugoslav General Staff following the Balkan campaign of 1941, records which were restored to the Yugoslav Republic shortly after

mander, Cannes to the Commissioner of the Chief of the Army Archives attached to Military Commander in France, April 7, 1944—30/702918).

A note by Major Brennfleck dated April 14, 1944 acknowledged the arrival of these two chests of Italian documents on April 12 (30/702916).

75. Ibid. (30/702921).

76. Major Brennfleck to Major Knorr, April 27, 1944 (30/702912). Carbon copy, Major Knorr to Headquarters Nineteenth Army, *Ic*, May 10, 1944 (30/702914).

77. See United States Army in World War II, the European Theater of Operations, Gordon A. Harrison, *Cross-Channel Attack* (Washington, D.C.: Office of the Chief of Military History, Department of the Army, 1951), pp. 258ff.

78. Knorr to the *Chef der Heeresarchive*, May 19, 1944 (30/702911).

79. Von Regenauer was born August 3, 1888; and had been head of the Document Collection Center-Southeast on December 18, 1939, microcopy T-78, serial 14, roll 14/678774. He was named "Commissioner of the Chief of the Army Archives" as is indicated on his correspondence.

When the Axis dominated Europe. *Front row, left to right:* Göring, Mussolini, Hitler, and Ciano. Courtesy of the U.S. Information Agency, National Archives.

Allen W. Dulles (1893–1969), head of the OSS in Switzerland during World War II. Photograph taken in 1947. Courtesy of Mrs. Allen W. Dulles.

Emilio Pucci skiing in the Cascade Mountains while a student at Reed College (1936–37). Courtesy of the Alumni Director, Reed College.

Emilio Pucci, taken on the occasion of his return to Reed College in 1962 to deliver a lecture. Courtesy of the Alumni Director, Reed College.

Col. Henry Hartford Cuming, Jr. (1905–45), photographed in 1941 when he held the rank of major. Courtesy of Mrs. Lawrence Lee, former widow of Colonel Cuming.

Frau Dr. Karl Heinz Purwin, née Hildegard Burkhardt. During World War II she was married to Capt. (and subsequently Major) Gerhard Beetz. Photograph taken in 1960. Courtesy of Heinz Engels, Pressehaus, Heussalle, Bonn, Germany.

Count Galeazzo Ciano (1903–44), Mussolini's son-in-law and Italian Minister of Foreign Affairs, 1936–43. Reprinted by permission of Wide World Photos.

Countess Edda Ciano, photographed while she was interned on the island of Lipari. Reprinted by permission of Wide World Photos.

Countess Edda Ciano in 1942. Reprinted by permission of Rizzoli Press, Milan, Italy.

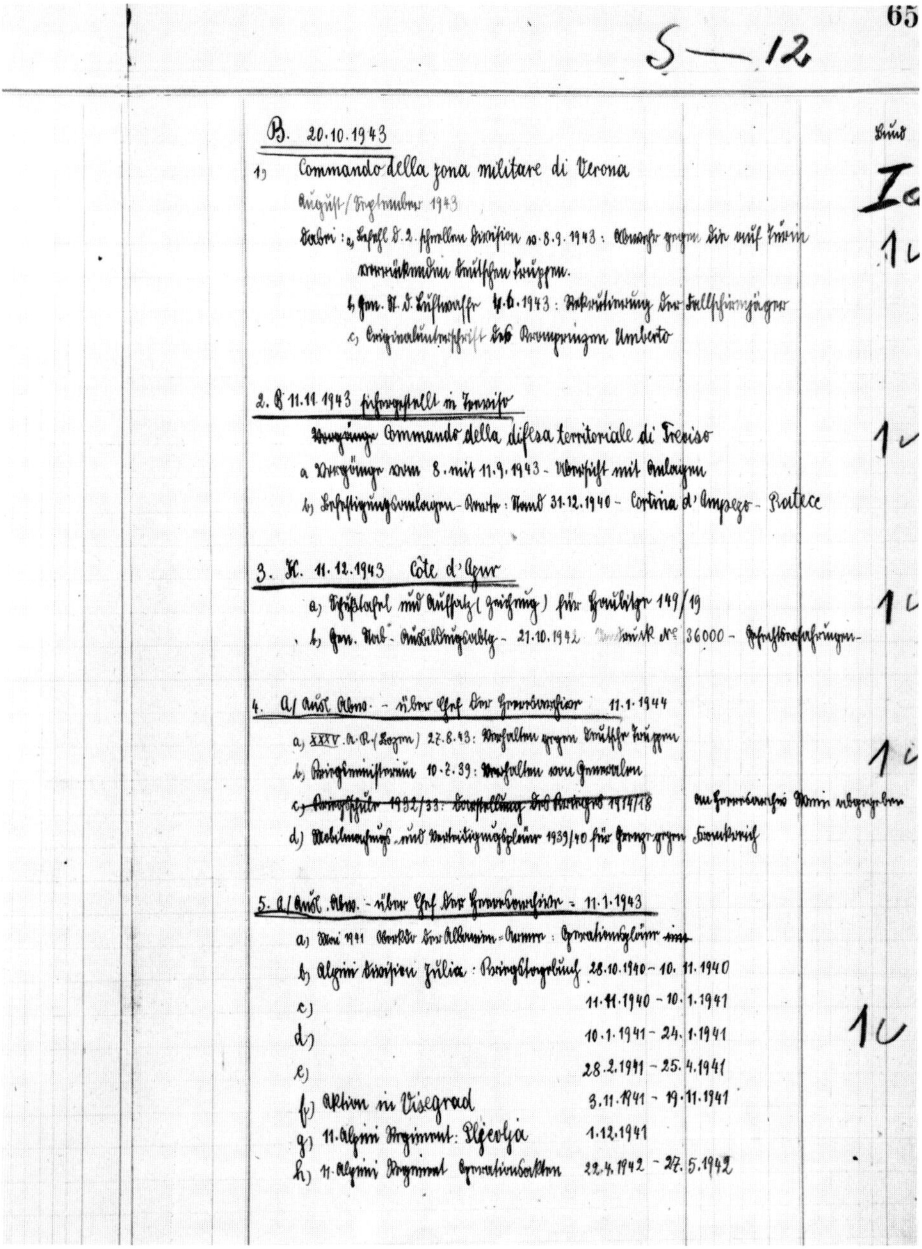

B. 20.10.1943

1) Commando della zona militare di Verona

    August / September 1943

    [handwritten text, largely illegible] 8.2. *[...]* Division 10.8.3.1943: *[...]*

    b) *[...]* 4.6.1943: *[...]*

    c) *[...]* Kronprinzen Umberto

2. *[...]* 11.11.1943 *[...]*

    [...] Commando della difesa territoriale di Treviso

    a) *[...]* vom 8. mit 11.9.1943 - *[...]* mit Anlagen

    b) *[...]* Karte: Band 31.12.1940 - Cortina d'Ampezo - Piatiece

3. K. 11.12.1943 Côte d'Azur

    a) *[...]* für *[...]* 149/19

    b) *[...]* 27.10.1942 *[...]* No 36000 - *[...]*

4. a) *[...]* Abw. - über Chef der *[...]* 11.1.1944

    a) XXXV. A.R. (Bozen) 27.8.43: *[...]* gegen Deutsche Truppen

    b) *[...]* 10.2.39: *[...]* von General *[...]*

    c) *[...]* 1932/33: *[...]* 1917/18   *[...]*

    d) *[...]* 1939/40 für *[...]* gegen Frankreich

5. a) *[...]* Abw. - über Chef der *[...]* - 11.1.1943

    a) Mai 1941 *[...]* Albanien - Armee - *[...]*

    b) Alpini Division Julia: *[...]* 28.10.1940 - 10.11.1940

    c)   11.11.1940 - 10.1.1941

    d)   10.1.1941 - 24.1.1941

    e)   28.2.1941 - 25.4.1941

    f) Aktion in Visegrad   3.11.1941 - 19.11.1941

    g) 11. Alpini Regiment: Pljevlja   1.12.1941

    h) 11. Alpini Regiment *[...]* 22.4.1942 - 27.5.1942

Bestandbuch I, first page. Courtesy of the National Archives.

Comando Supremo

I. ABTEILUNG

a) Sachgebiet oestlicher und westlicher
   Kriegsschauplatz .   Va

20 Tagesberichte des Oberkommandos des Heeres   30.5.1940
1235   (Superesercito) an das Comando Supremo Va 271   bis
                                                        30.4.1941

                                                        222
   1136 Handstreiche bei der Eroeffnung der Feind=
        selickiten   Juni 1940

   1137 Offensive an der franzoesischen Grenze   Juni/Juli 1940

21 Truppenversammlung im Padana-Tal 1138   Juli/Aug. 1940

   Vorfallenheitsberichte 1139   Juli/Okt. 1940

   Studie ueber Flottenunternehmungen gegen
   Jugoslavien (Projekt) 1140   Aug. 1940

   Lagemeldungen aus Albanien 1141   Mai/Dez. 1940

                                                        273
   Exp.20 Stand der Operationen in Albanien 1142   Nov. 1940
   Exp.19 Massnahmen fuer die Winterperiode 1143   Nov. 1940
   Exp.14 Neue Bereitstellungen   1144   Jan. 1941
22 Exp.15 Neue Richtlinien fuer die (ital.)Ostfront 1145 März 1941
   Exp.15A Kriegsvorbereitungen gegen Jugoslavien 1146 März/Mai 1941
   ─── Wortlaut von militaerpol.Zusammenkuenften 1147 März 1941
   Exp.15B Zusammenarbeit mit Deutschland 1148   März/Mai 1941
   Exp.15D Denkschriften u.ä. 1149   März/Mai 1941

                                                        224
23 Gruppierung der Landstreitkräfte 1150   März/Apr. 1941

   Jugoslaviens Kapitulation 1151   Apr. 1941

   Neue Grenzziehungen   1152   Mai 1941

   Korfu   1153   Feb. 1941

Bestandbuch II. Courtesy of the National Archives.

2. Armee

V. Armeekorps

5447	Notiziario	1.1. – 31.5.	1943	880 ✓
5448	"	1.6. – 6.9.	1943	881 ✓

VI. Armeekorps

5449	Notiziario	27.12.1942 – 22.4.	1943	882 ✓
5450	"	23.4.1943 – 1.9.	1943	883 ✓

XVIII. Armeekorps

5451	Notiziario	1.1.1943 – 31.8.	1943	884 ✓

Fernsprechvermittlung

5452	Notiziario	V. Armeekorps	2.8.1943 – 5.9.	1943	
5453		VI. "	6.8.1943 – 12.8.	1943	885 ✓
5454		XI. "	4.8.1943 – 7.9.	1943	
5455		XVIII. "	5.8.1943 – 31.8.	1943	

Reste

5456	Französ./ital. Grenzkommission : ankommende Fernsprüche	8.8.1941 – 20.1.	1942	II d
5457		28.4.1942 – 7.5.	1942	
5458		abgehende Fernsprüche	29.4.1942 – 15.5.	1942	
5459	2. Armee : Denkschrift über die Insel Pago		1942	886 ✓
5460	" : führer durch Kroatien und Aufmarschräumen		1940	
5461	Division Emilia (155.) : Abwehr-Grenzsicherung im Raume Cattaro		1943	
5462	Division Perugia (151.) : Standort Almissa		1942	
5463	II A.K. (Art.Rgt.) : Operationen Tätigkeit des Artillerie-Rgts.	9.9.1941 – 9.6.	1942	

Bestandbuch III, final page. Courtesy of the National Archives.

AKTENSAMMELSTELLE SÜD.
Page 1.

I a :bundle 1:

B.3o.1o.1943.
1) Commando della zona militare di Verona
August/September 1943
Dabei:a)Befehl d.2.schnellen Division v.8.9.1943:Abwehr
    gegen die auf Turin vorrückenden deutschen Truppen.
    b)Gen.St.d.Luftwaffe 4.6.1943:Rekrutierung der
    Fallschirmjäger
    c)Orginalunterschrift des Kronprinzen Umberto.

2.B.11.11.1943 sichergestellt in Treviso
    Commando della difesa territoriale di Treviso
    A)Vorgänge vom 8.bis 11.9.1943—Übersicht mit Anlagen
    b)Befestigungsanlagen-Karte:Stand 31.12.194o-Cortina d
    d'Ampezo-Ratece

3.K.11.12.1943 Cote d'Azur
    a)Schußtafel und Aufsatz(Zeichnung)für Haubitze 149/19
    b)Gen.Stab-Ausbildungsabt.21.1o.1942.Umdruck Nr 36 ooo-
    Gefechtserfahrungen

4.A/Ausl.Abw.-Über Chef der Heeresarchive,11.1.1944
    a)XXXV.A.K.(Bozen)27.8.1943:Verhalten gegen deutsche
                        Truppen.
    b)Kriegsministerium 1o.7.1939:Verhalten von Generalen
    c)Mobilmachungs- und Verteidigungspläne 1939/4o
    für Grenze gegen Frankreich.

5.A./Aus.Abw.-Über Chef der Heeresarchive.11.1.1943
    a)Mai 1941 Oberkdo der Albanien Armee:Operationspläne
    b)Alpini Div.Julia:Kriegstagebuch 28.1o.194o-1o-11.194o
    c) "   "   "   "   11.11.194o-1o. 1.1941
    d) "   "   "   "   1o. 1.1941-24. 1.1941
    e) "   "   "   "   28. 2.1941-25. 4.1941
    f)Aktion in Visegrad   3.11.1941-19.11.1941
    g)11.Alpini Regiment:Pljeolja   1.12.1941
    h)11.Alpini Regiment Operationsakten
                    22.4.1942-27.5.1942

bundle 2:

6.Gen.St.d.H.-Fremde Heere West-Über Chef der Heeres-
archive-11.1.1944.
    a)Verteidigungspläne einiger englischer Inseln
    b)7 Hefte Commando supremo-Kräfteverteilung 1.1.1943-
                                   1.7.1943
    c)(in Bund 14)
    d)7 Hefte Gen.St.d.H.-Kräfteverteilung Jan-Juli 1943
    e)6 Umdr.-Cdo supremo,Kräfteverteilung der Miliz
                              1.1.1943-1.6.1943
    f)7.Umdr.Cdo.supremo-Kräfteverteilung 1.1.1943-1.7.1943
    g)k:Cdo supremo:Istatürken Januar-August 1943
    h)Ge.St.d. H.2o.2.1943-Austellung des leicht mot.Reiter-
                            regiments Lucca.

Catalogue of *Aktensammelstelle Süd,* first page. Courtesy of the National Archives.

In the days of his glory: Mussolini speaking to a crowd in Rome. Courtesy of the U.S. Information Agency, National Archives.

Walter Audisio, "Colonel Valerio" (1909–73), the man who shot Mussolini, speaking to a mass meeting in Rome in 1947. Reprinted by permission of Wide World Photos.

The horrible picture: The bodies of Mussolini, of Claretta Petacci, and of Achille Starace, suspended upside down at the garage on the Piazzala Loreto on April 29, 1945. Courtesy of the U.S. Office of War Information, National Archives.

Mussolini's last great audience: The crowd milling about the Piazzala Loreto on April 29, 1945. Courtesy of the U.S. Army Air Force' National Archives.

a) Passate con fischio o spauracchio al volo (esclusi i valichi montani) abrogato dal 1 gennaio 1928, per R. D. L. 27 dicembre 1927, n. 2518) . . L. 400,—

d) Paretai, copertoni e prodine con contrappesi . . . . . L. 400,—

e) Boschetti e tordere, con panie e con richiami (esclusi i valichi montani e la spiaggia al mare) . . L. 400,—

f) Appostamenti stabili, con preparazioni di sito, per caccia con armi da fuoco (anche per i gruppi di capanni formanti unico sistema) oltre la tassa di cui al n. 16 (abrogato con R. D. L. 3 agosto 1928, n. 1997). . L. 250,—

Licenza annuale permanente per la caccia e l'uccellagione nelle riserve di che l'art. 8 e 9 della legge 24 giugno 1923, n. 1420, rilasciata dal proprietario delle medesime a terzi L. 30,—

Fabbricazione e vendita armi

a) Licenza dell'Autorità Circondariale di P. S. per la fabbricazione, per la raccolta, a fine di commercio ed industria, per lo smercio od esposizione in vendita delle armi in genere, escluse quelle da guerra, ai sensi dell'art. 30, primo comma, del testo unico delle leggi sulla P. S. 6 novembre 1926, n. 1848 . . . . . . L. 500,—

Vidimazione annuale della detta licenza . . . . L. 100,—

b) Licenza per l'importazione delle dette armi: per ogni arma : L. 5,—
(Col massimo di L. 500)

c) Licenza per la vendita ambulante di strumenti da punta o da taglio, ai sensi dell'art. 36, 2° comma, della citata legge . . . . . L. 100,—

Vidimaz. annuale della licenza L. 20,—

La licenza annuale per la caccia e l'uccellagione è soggetta al pagamento delle seguenti tasse:

a) licenza di caccia anche con porto di fucile, lire 100:

b) archibugio o altra arma da getto a cavallotto o spingarda su barche senza motore, lire 300; ogni arma in più, lire 185;

c) archibugio o altra arma da getto a cavalletto con appostio fisso, lire 96; ogni arma in più lire 60;

d) panie e panioni, con o senza richiami (uccellagione mobile), lire 100;

e) paretai, copertoni o prodine senza contrappesi, lire 250;

f) roccoli, con o senza passate, lire 400;

g) bressanelle, lire 400;

h) paretai, copertoni e prodine, con contrappesi, lire 400:

i) boschetti e tordere con richiami, lire 400:

l) licenza annuale, permanente per la caccia o l'uccellagione nelle riserve, rilasciata dal proprietario a terzi, lire 30.

All'atto del rilascio della licenza di caccia o di uccellagione del versamento all'Ufficio del registro della tassa di bollo per le tabelle indicanti il divieto di caccia nelle bandite e nelle riserve o l'appostamento, dovrà versarsi all'Ufficio del registro anche l'importo della seguente soprattassa:

1° per ogni licenza di caccia anche con porto di fucile. . . . L. 10

2° per ogni licenza di spingarda o di altra arma impostata . . . L. 25

3° per ogni licenza di panie e panioni (uccellagione mobile) . . L. 10

4° per ogni licenza di uccellagione con appostamento fisso . . L. 25

5° per ogni licenza di panie e panioni (uccellagione fissa) . . L. 25

6° per ogni tabella indicante il divieto di caccia nelle bandite e nelle riserve o l'appostamento, lire 0.10.

Similmente per ogni lire 100 o frazione di lire 100 di imposta erariale per le riserve, verrà imputato al riserva maggiore onere di lire 10, da riscuotersi nei modi che verranno indicati dal regolamento per l'esecuzione della presente legge.

Licenza per la pesca lacuale e fluviale rilasciata dalle Prefetture, ai sensi dell'articolo 20 della legge 24 marzo 1921, n. 312:

a) a pescatori di mestiere . L. 12,—

b) a pescatori dilettanti . » 25,—

c) per gli stranieri che risiedono provvisoriamente nel Regno . . L. 6.—

Ciano Diary, January 1, 1939. Initial entry in the American edition (1946), showing reference to supporting papers. Courtesy of the National Archives.

OTTOBRE
26
SABATO

s. Evaristo papa

300-66

Sorge il sole ore 6,55, tramonta ore 17,19
Luna nuova il 26

OTTOBRE
29
MARTEDI

s. Quintino vescovo

303-63

Sorge il sole ore 6,59, tramonta ore 17,14
Luna nuova il 30

Ciano Diary, October 28,
1940, showing reference
to supporting papers.
Courtesy of the National
Archives.

Ciano Diary, October 31, 1941. Only the first paragraph is given in the American edition (1946). The whole of the second paragraph regarding Fanny Patrizi is simply left out of the American edition. Courtesy of the National Archives.

the entrance of American troops into Vienna toward the end of World War II.

On October 30, 1944, Von Regenauer sent in a general report to Potsdam regarding the Italian military records, chiefly those of the Italian Second Army, which he had surveyed after being charged with the new task on October 3. In general, he reported, the operational documents of the Italian Second Army had been found and had been forwarded to Ingolstadt. At the same time important documents had been sent to Rommel's headquarters and to the headquarters of the German units which had moved in to the zone of Trieste-Fiume. Furthermore they had supplied the *Abwehr* office in Trieste with the key to an Italian code.

Von Regenauer initially had hoped that the German Navy would send a Lieutenant Commander (*Korvettenkapitän*) to assist with the naval records, but at the last moment the Navy decided to operate alone, to do its own screening of the Italian and former Austro-Hungarian naval documents. Von Regenauer visited Trieste for the period October 15–18 and again on the twenty-second and twenty-third. It was established beyond doubt that the headquarters of the Italian Twenty-third Corps and of the Eleventh Corps had burned their classified papers two days before the capitulation. However, he did retrieve a steel cabinet with terrain descriptions and plans of fortifications which were useful for the immediate conduct of operations. The unclassified archival material of the period 1920–29 was in complete disorder. Examination of it revealed nothing of significance. The Italian intelligence staff had burned its files. The records of other former Italian command posts which Von Regenauer visited appeared to have completely disappeared when German troops moved into the buildings, although the *Ic* (intelligence officer) of Army Group B had seized a few documents.

In the state archives of Trieste, *HAR* Von Regenauer located 567 bundles of Austro-Hungarian naval legal records. The naval archive of Vienna was immediately notified. But there was no trace of regimental records of the old imperial and royal army. It appeared that some very important records had been transferred by the Italians from Trieste to Moderzo in the province of Treviso. Von Regenauer alerted the staff of Army Group B.

On October 19 and 20, Von Regenauer visited Fiume and Sušak. He learned that the building which had served as command post of the Italian Second Army had been damaged by aerial attack, but that headquarters, without doubt, had left all of its records behind at the time of the surrender. In the meantime partisans had occupied Sušak for a brief interval and had removed two steel cabinets or safes. Von Regenauer broke open the third. It held some code keys, operational reports 1941 into 1943, and other important documents. These he packed in five crates and made arrangements for them to be forwarded to the *Aktensammelstelle Süd* at Ingolstadt.

Von Regenauer visited Udine on October 24. Here it appeared that only recently had the records of the Italian Twenty-fourth Corps been destroyed by German troops passing through. *HAR* Von Regenauer found one steel case which he was able to break open. It held nothing of significance. There were also two safes which the archivist himself could not crack. He left this task to the German security division which occupied Udine and whose commander promised a full account of the disposition of the materials.

In conclusion Von Regenauer reported that he had fully informed the *Heeresarchiv* of Vienna, the Naval Archive, and *HAR* Böhm of his work. He had tried to make contact with Böhm but had got no response to his messages. It appeared that the intelligence officer of Army Group B had issued an order to the German forces occupying the area Trieste-Fiume-Laibach (Ljubljana) that all Italian and Communist (Partisan) records which were seized were to be sent to a depot at Ljubljana. Von Regenauer promised to ascertain if such records could be released for despatch to Ingolstadt.[80]

During the first week of November, Von Regenauer arranged with the intelligence officer of Army Group F that the records of the Italian Army Group whose headquarters had been at Tirana would be forwarded, after their exploitation for intelligence purposes, to the *Aktensammelstelle Süd* at Ingolstadt.[81]

Senior Archivist Böhm's reports of April 15 and of May 2, 1944, wind up the surviving sources regarding the German retrieval of Italian military records from the Balkans.[82] I have discovered no German records regarding their confiscation of the documents of the Italian military forces which, under the alliance with Germany, occupied the lower parts of the Balkan Peninsula and Greece. Very few of these records ever reached the German Document Center-South to be later captured by the United States Seventh Army and to be listed in the *Guides* issued by the National Archives.

80. Regenauer to *Chef der Heeresarchive* at Potsdam, October 30, 1943, a four-page typewritten report, original, file H/40/75 (8/679634–37); note of Regenauer to *Aktensammelstelle Süd*, Ingolstadt, October 30, 1943 (IT 5739, 000079); note of Regenauer to *Heeresarchive*, Munich, November 1, 1943 (IT 5739, 000077).

81. Letter, Von Regenauer to *Heeresarchive*, Munich, November 2, 1943, file H/40/77 (8/679882). Another copy is in IT 5739/000076.

82. See above (The Collecting Work of Archivist Böhm in Northern Italy).

Major Brennfleck's Entry Book

Some of the Italian military documents which were gathered up by the Germans went first to the intelligence staffs of the armies in the field and only at a later stage reached the Document Collection Center-South. Others were immediately circulated and read by other agencies and offices. As was the case with the German handling of the *Palazzo Chigi* archives,[83] so it was with the military records. The Germans were looking for evidence of "treason" toward the Axis.[84] Professor Schramm, who maintained the diary kept at Hitler's headquarters during this period, records that it was a particular satisfaction for him in the second semester of 1943 to be able to use General Roatta's records of conferences with General Rintelen in his entries concerning the work of the German military attaché in Italy.[85] But, for the most part, Major Brennfleck and his staff organized and indexed the captured Italian records for the use of later historians.

The inventory or entry book (*Bestandbuch*) which was compiled by Major Brennfleck for the materials which he received at the Document Collection Center-South constitutes the basis for all of the subsequent cataloguing and numbering of the files of the Italian military documents seized by the Germans. It consists of three parts or volumes. Each has a hand-lettered label, "*Aktensammelstelle Süd—Bestandbuch*" and the appropriate Roman numeral.[86]

Volume one is a bound, hardback covered, mottled brown ledger book, 8¼ inches by 13 inches, with printed page numbers. The numbered pages 1 to 62 have been torn out. The initial sheet, pages 63–64, is blank. The written entries run from page 65 to 192.

83. See chap. 1, note 49.

84. In vol. 3 of the *Bestandbuch*, pp. 95–98, we find some typewritten, inserted sheets with some detailed descriptions of documents in files 4549 to 4559 indicating the "treasonable" relations of General Gambara, commander of the Eleventh Italian Army Corps, with the Slovenes, and of peace feelers being conducted through the British ambassador at the Vatican, the Duke [sic] of Osborne. These notations, without doubt, were for immediate submission to Major Brennfleck's superior.

85. Schramm, *Kriegstagebuch des Oberkommandos der Wehrmacht*, vol. 4, pt. 2, pp. 1783–84, and vol. 3, pt. 2, p. 979, fn. 1. General Enno von Rintelen was German military attaché in Rome and after December 1941 had the additional title of German General at the headquarters of the Italian Armed Forces. He recorded his experiences in his book: *Mussolini als Bundesgenosse: Erinnerungen des deutschen Militärattachés in Rom, 1936–1943* (Tübingen: R. Wunderlich, 1955).

86. The original *Bestandbuch*, not being an integral element of the Italian military documents, has been retained in Washington in the National Archives. It is also available on film along with the guide to the files of the *Aktensammelstelle Süd* which was based on it, in microcopy T-821, roll 493. See *Guide to Records of the Italian Armed Forces*, pt. 3 p. 155.

In the left-hand ledger column there is a continuous enumeration of folders or files. The mid-portion of the sheet has a description or designation of the file, usually in German but sometimes in Italian. These entries in volume one are in ink in the neat and legible hand of Major Brennfleck. It has a listing of files from 1 to 3845.

On the right side of the page are the *Bund* (bundle) numbers. A group of thin files, in some cases a single thick file, made up a bundle. In some cases, as we have noted particularly with the work of Archivist Nemetz, the files arrived at the *Aktensammelstelle Süd* already arranged. In other cases the related material was sorted out and organized at the center, and a fair sized group of files was formed into a bundle.

The bundle numbers are entered in red crayon in the ledger column on the right side of the sheet. Thus we have on the initial page (p. 65) the entries for files 1 to 5. These make up *Bund* 1 entered on the right.[87] Or again, on printed page 78 of the *Bestandbuch* we have at the left a listing of files 99 to 106. Opposite the file number, 99 a–c, we have in mid page the designation or description: "Comando Supremo: Kampf auf Sizilien 9.7.43–17.8.43." Files 99 through 106 make up bundle 55. The final entry of *Bestandbuch I* (p. 192) lists files 3842 to 3845 which make up *Bund* 616.

Bestandbuch II is on the same general pattern as volume one with the file numbers on the left and the bundle numbers on the right. Otherwise it is quite different. Its cover is a manila folder. Its pages are the reverse sides of form sheets of the *Comando Supremo* whose obverse sides bear that printed inscription. Thus there is only one page per sheet. There are twenty-five numbered pages (approximately 8½ inches by 12¾ inches) plus two supplementary pages (*Nachträge*). These individual sheets are stapled together. All of the entry descriptions are typewritten except for those of the two supplementary pages which are handwritten in ink. But both the file numbers on the left and the bundle numbers on the right are handwritten in red crayon. The typed file descriptions clearly were done first; then the file numbers and bundle numbers were entered later. The outside cover, besides the title *"Bestandbuch II"* bears the description *"Einlieferungen von H. A. R. Nemetz"* (Deliveries from Army Archivist Nemetz).

What we have, in fact, in volume two of the *Bestandbuch* are the carbon copies of the index material which *Archivrat* Nemetz had prepared in Italy. He had sent the top copy of these sheets to Potsdam in his reports of November 24 and December 2 of 1943 and of January 24, 1944.[88] Then at the end of May he had sent a complete carbon copy of

87. See the facsimile in the Illustrations.
88. See notes 56, 57, and 58 above.

this index, that is pages 1 to 25, to the *Aktensammelstelle Süd*.[89] The file numbers and bundle numbers were inserted after the arrival of the materials at the Document Collection Center-South, and there the two supplementary pages were added.

Numbered page 1 begins with files 1119 to 1135 which make up bundles 253 and 254. The volume lists files 1119 to 1600 with corresponding bundles 253 to 267.

Bestandbuch II has a very puzzling discontinuity. At page 8 the files run to number 1235 (the last file listed in bundle no. 271) and then jump back to file 1136 which is the first file listed for bundle 272. (Some bomb must have hit nearby at about this time; there is no explanation on rational grounds.) The German inventory keeps up with the error from file 1136 to file 1214, and then goes from there to the final entry, file 1600. Thus the *Bestandbücher* have an error of duplication; there are two sets of files numbered 1136 to 1214. The second set of files with these numbers recorded in volume two are grouped in the bundles 272 to 291.[90]

Volume three of the *Bestandbuch* in its material composition resembles volume one. It is a bound, black, printed ledger book, with printed pages 52 to 394, approximately $8\frac{1}{4}$ inches by 12 inches. Only a portion of these printed pages have been used, beginning with page 59 and ending with page 140. The initial file entered is file 3846 (in bundle 617) and the final file is 5463 which is part of the last bundle, no. 886. The entries designating or describing the files are again in the neat, clear handwriting of Major Brennfleck. File numbers at the left are entered in ink and the bundle numbers at the right are in red crayon.[91]

This was the index which was at hand when the American army seized the collection of Italian military records from the Germans. It may be that Major Brennfleck's work of indexing had not been completed when the center was captured. In 1951 an examination showed that there were numbered files IT-1 through IT-5490 and sixty-five boxes of uncatalogued Italian military records.[92] These may have come from the *Aktensammelstelle Süd* or they may have been seized by American forces in other places.

89. See note 66 above.

90. See the facsimile in the Illustrations. See also the note in the index by G.W.S.F. (George Washington Salisbury Friedrichsen) dated December 2, 1955, and the British document EDS/DOCS/20, "The *Aktensammelstelle Süd* Collection," June 1966, copy in the National Archives.

91. See the facsimile in the Illustrations.

92. Memo by M/Sgt. Michael Halyshyn to Chief, GMDS, "Report on the Italian Military Records Section," 13 December 1951, copy in the National Archives.

American Seizure of the Aktensammelstelle Süd:
The Catalogue

When the United States Seventh Army overran Southern Germany in the spring of 1945 the German Document Center-South fell into American hands. Since the autumn of 1944 there had been considerable combined planning by the United States and British governments for seizing the documentary records of Nazi Germany. For the civilian agencies there was set up a Combined Intelligence Committee which collected all of the information which it could get about archives and collections of documents, this through the CIOS, the Combined Intelligence Objectives Subcommittee. The targets which this subcommittee listed were strictly civilian.[93] The military documents of Nazi Germany were carefully left as targets for the military intelligence sections: G-2 in the American staff system, and their British opposite numbers. Their cooperation in the search for, and exploitation of military documents was regulated by the Bissell-Sinclair agreement.[94]

This agreement provided in Article 5 for continuation in the period of SHAEF and of AFHQ of arrangements already worked out in the field whereby the London Branch of the Military Intelligence Research Section (MIRS) would obtain from SHAEF and AFHQ the selected archives and documents required for War Office and War Department research.

At the end of the SHAEF period the Washington Branch of MIRS was to be deactivated (Article 8). At the beginning of the occupation period, the London Military Document Center was to be set up as a clearing house for German military documents, to receive them, to circulate them to authorized agencies in the United Kingdom, and then to transmit them to the United States. At the same time G-2 agreed to establish in or near Washington a central German military document collection where these materials would be received. It was to be known as the German Military Document Section (GMDS) of the Military In-

93. Something in regard to this preliminary work before Germany's surrender may be found in *Foreign Relations of the United States, 1945*, vol. 3, *European Advisory Commission; Austria; Germany* (Washington: U.S. Government Printing Office, 1968), pp. 1099ff. Considerably more information is in the Central Files of the Department of State, file 840.414. Dr. Ralph Perkins, who headed the group of American documents experts who worked first in London and then on the continent after Germany's surrender, kept a personal file for the period 1944–46 which he was kind enough to lend me.

94. Of May 1945. Copy in the files of the German Documents Branch, Historical Office, Department of State. The agreement was signed respectively by Maj. Gen. Clayton Bissell, assistant chief of staff, G-2, War Department, Washington, D.C., and Maj. Gen. John Alexander Sinclair, Director of Military Intelligence, London.

telligence Division or MID (Article 9). "The implementation of this agreement will make a German military document collection available for post-war historical research."

The seizure of the *Aktensammelstelle Süd* was, in a sense, an accident. It came as a by-product of the search for Nazi military records. Apparently the collection of Italian materials was seized in April 1945 and initially was stored in the Document Center at Frankfurt am Main. The collection was carefully arranged on labeled shelves. A group of American soldiers, mostly of German descent and with a good knowledge of the spoken language, did the work under the supervision of Lt. Col. J. L. Austin, British Intelligence Corps. He had formerly served on the SHAEF intelligence staff under Brig. Kenneth W. D. Strong, Eisenhower's top intelligence man. The typed catalogue was prepared at this time, the catalogue which accompanied the collection when the documents were shipped to the United States. What this work amounted to was a careful following of the scheme of organization in files and bundles which Major Brennfleck has worked out in his *Bestandbuch*. His handwritten entries (for volumes one and three) were now typed out. But the numbering by files and bundles remained the same. When these amateur archivists came to the duplicate file numbers, the duplication which we have noted in *Bestandbuch II*, they simply added the letter "A" for the second series.

The catalogue made at Frankfurt had some omissions, for it recorded only those files actually at hand on the shelves when it was composed.[95] During this early period many documents apparently were borrowed by other agencies or even by individuals and were not recorded, even though they had been transferred to the German Document Collection-South and had been logged in, in Major Brennfleck's *Bestandbuch*.[96]

One of the men who served for a time under Dr. Ralph Perkins in the Foreign Office-State Department team was a Britisher, Capt. T. H. Frame. Some time in late August or September 1945 when he was working out of Marburg in the search for civilian records, he visited the U.S. Seventh Army Document Center which by then had been transferred to Heidelberg. An officer at this center pointed out to Captain Frame a

95. I have tried carefully to restrict the use of the term "Catalogue" to the index prepared by Americans at Frankfurt for the *Aktensammelstelle Süd* with its rather curious mixture of German, English, and Italian, and with its direct substitution of "bundle" for *Bund*. I have used only the terms "entry book" and *"Bestandbuch"* for the index prepared by the Germans. I have reserved the term *"Guide"* or *"Guides"* for the later index of files and microfilms prepared in Washington, D.C. See the facsimile of page 1 of the Catalogue (in the Illustrations) with its listing of bundles, rooms, pages and shelves, with the letter "S" indicating shelf.

96. Memorandum on three typewritten pages by G. W. S. Friedrichsen, British liaison official attached to OCMH, dated Washington, December 5, 1956 (OCMH files).

group of about one thousand bundles, each containing five or six files of Italian army documents. These, the officer explained, had been brought from Italy to the *Aktensammelstelle Süd* after the Italian surrender in 1943.

It was further explained that the collection had been discovered in a restaurant outside Dillingen on the Danube. A German major had been in charge, working from an office in the Dillingen library. There were two dispersal points for the documents and when these were cleaned up they yielded not only the Italian military records but also the Bavarian army archives and the Bavarian police archives. The German major had not been taken into custody and had got away without being interrogated. A Captain Nussenbaum, Seventh Army G-2, had supervised the transfer of the Italian files to the Seventh Army Center at Heidelberg. Captain Frame sampled some of the documents, noted that they all appeared to be strictly military, and turned in a brief report.[97]

97. Report, undated, in one page, entitled "Italian Military Documents Brought By Germans From Italy to the German Document Center (South)," attachment to despatch no. 937, United States political adviser, Germany (Robert Murphy) to the secretary of state, September 10, 1945 (840.414/9-1045), Central Files, Department of State.

This undated report by Captain Frame, a British officer serving under the American, Dr. Ralph Perkins, in the combined British-American search for German civilian records, is the only documentary evidence which I have been able to discover regarding the seizure of the *Aktensammelstelle Süd* by the U.S. Seventh Army.

I have looked diligently (and, I hope, intelligently) for some military record of this capture. (1) There are, in the National Archives, some miscellaneous records which originated with Headquarters Seventh Army, "Miscellaneous Reports of Hq. U.S. Seventh Army." These documents apparently accompanied the shipment of the files of the former *Aktensammelstelle Süd* from Europe to the German Military Documents Section which was set up in accordance with the Bissell-Sinclair agreement. After a considerable lapse of time these documents were transferred to the National Archives, but they do not include any record of the seizure of the collection center at Dillingen.

(2) At the suggestion of Mr. Donald Spencer and of Mr. Robert Wolfe I called the NARS record center at Suitland, Maryland, and at my request a search was made in the "After Action" reports of the United States Seventh Army, and in the records of some of its units: the Third Infantry Division, the Twelfth Armored Division. Records of the assistant chief of staff, G-2, and records of the Office of Military Government for Germany were also scrutinized. The capture of Dillingen and of Donaualtheim by CCA of Twelfth Armored Division on April 22, 1945 is recorded, and the support rendered by the Seventh Infantry Regiment of the Third Infantry Division. But there is no mention in these unit records of the seizure of the *Aktensammelstelle Süd*.

(3) At my request a search was made in the retained records of the Seventh Army at the Federal Records Center, 2306 East Bannister Road, Kansas City, Missouri. There too the results of the search were negative. In an interview with Mr. Philip Brower, March 3, 1965, he mentioned his doubts that I would be able to find any documents regarding the seizure of the *Aktensammelstelle Süd* at that Records Center. He himself had been out there and had made a search but found no pertinent papers. He did learn that some of the army's records on the collecting of enemy documents had been destroyed.

Suggestions, anyone?

One group of files of top political and strategic interest was transferred to London in the autumn of 1945. Apparently at some time in October a representative of the Political Intelligence Division of the British Foreign Office visited the Seventh Army Document Center and was given a copy of a goodly portion of the catalogue. (Possibly the catalogue at this time was just being typed out.) In any case a memorandum dated October 18 records the transmittal of the balance of the detailed index of the *Aktensammelstelle Süd*, pages 149 to 183, which were forwarded to the Political Intelligence Division (PID), Foreign Office, London, in accordance with the verbal request made the day before by Dr. Raymond Klibansky.[98]

On October 24 the Processing Section of Seventh Army Document Center despatched twenty items of the *Aktensammelstelle Süd* collection to the Political Intelligence Division of the Foreign Office, London, as follows:

1) Index, *Aktensammelstelle Süd, Nachtrag*, 3 pages.

2) Index, *Aktensammelstelle Süd*, new pages 153–54.

3) From bundle 500, file 3029-C-3, "Condotta politicamilitare della guerra da parte dell' Asse," a summary of the major points of disagreement between Germany and Italy, 1940–43. Prepared by the Italian high command for the Conference of Tarvisio, 6 August 1943.

4) From bundle 56, file 107. Meeting of Hitler and Mussolini, 18–20 December 1942 [sic].[99]

5) From bundle 56, file 109. Meeting of Hitler and Mussolini, 7–10 April 1943.

6) From bundle 254, file 1127. Conversation Mussolini-Kesselring, 22 April 1943 (photo).

7) From bundle 254, file 1135 and bundle 500, file 3032. Conversation Abrosio-Kesselring, 27 June 1943.

8) From bundle 500, file 3029. Exchange of telegrams Mussolini-Hitler, 12–18 July 1943.

9) From bundle 500, file 3029. "Appunto per il Duce in data 14 luglio 1943." A summary of the Italian high command.

10) From bundle 254, file 1127 and from bundle 500, file 3027, Conversation Mussolini-Kesselring, 15 July 1943.

11) From bundle 500, file 3029. "Convegno di Feltre." Meeting of Mussolini-Hitler, 19–20 July 1943.

12) From bundle 500, file 3031. Same as 11, in summary.

13) From bundle 254, file 1135, and bundle 500, file 3037, Conversation Ambrosio-Kesselring, 24 July 1943.

14) From bundle 253, file 1121. Events of 25 July 1943.

98. The memorandum is signed by 1st Lt. Charles Winnick, Processing Section, Office of the AC of S, G-2, Seventh Army Document Center (Miscellaneous Reports, Hq. U.S. Seventh Army, National Archives).

99. This is an erroneous description. It was Ciano who met with Hitler on this occasion. See Garland and Smyth, *Sicily and the Surrender of Italy*, pp. 34–35 and fn. 22. Cf. Schramm, *Kriegstagebuch des Oberkommandos der Wehrmacht*, vol. 2, pt. 2, p. 1153.

15) From bundle 254, file 1135 and bundle 500, file 3037, Conversation Ambrosio-Kesselring, 26 July 1943.

16) From bundle 500, file 3029, Summary of the Italian military situation 1 August 1943, prepared by the Italian high command for the Conference of Tarvisio.

17) From bundle 500, file 3029. Conversation at Tarvisio, 6 August 1943.

18) From bundle 724, files 4555 & 4556. The British ambassador, Duke of Osborne. August 1943 (photo).

19) From bundle 262, file 1226. Diary Ambrosio, in part only. Balance to follow.

20) From bundle 254, files 1127–40. Microfilmed (3 small rolls).

The memorandum concludes with this statement: "The above are either original Italian documents (additional copies of the same documents were included in the collection and remain with it) or photographic reproductions of such documents, except for items (1) & (2) which are part of the index. Only items (5) and items (19) are copies prepared here, and the originals of these documents (Items 19 handwritten) remain with the collection." [100]

Then on November 13, a box numbered Parcel 170 was despatched with a dozen bundles of original files, addressed to the London Military Document Center, 40 Hyde Park Gate, London SW 7, bundles listed as follows:

253	263
254	264
256	265
260	266
261	267
262	268

Receipt of these bundles was acknowledged in London on November 19, 1945. [101]

At the time that these twelve bundles were loaned or transferred to London, the catalogue in its various copies as prepared by Seventh Army Document Center was marked at each appropriate spot with a rubber stamp, "LMD," indicating London Military Document Center (or Section).

This group of documents was "lost" for several years. Dr. Klibansky, a medievalist by trade, apparently went back to his academic pursuits as did many other British and American scholars who had filled up the intelligence offices in London and Washington (and not without competence) in the emergency of World War II. Klibansky resumed the editing of the *Corpus Platonicum Medii Aevi* for the British Academy and his lec-

100. Miscellaneous Reports Hq., U.S. Seventh Army, National Archives. The reader will note that first bundles and then files are listed.

101. Despatch note, Hq. Seventh Army, Office of the AC of S. G-2, Miscellaneous Reports, U.S. Seventh Army, National Archives.

turing at Oriel College, Oxford. No one was at hand to exploit the Italian documents which apparently remained unpacked in their box in a corner of the Foreign Office Library until 1955.

Klibansky in 1949 brought out a very nicely edited English translation of Mussolini's memoirs of the years 1942–43, but there is no indication that he used the borrowed military files for this work.[102]

Now that the Document Center of the U.S. Seventh Army had taken over the collection of Italian military documents originally seized by the Germans, and had made copies or even originals of parts of the collection available to whoever expressed a keen and legitimate interest, they wondered what to do with the collection. The buck was passed up the line, to the commanding officer, Document Control Section, Office of the Assistant Chief of Staff, G-2, Headquarters, United States Forces European Theater (USFET). The memorandum dated November 20, 1945, subject "Disposition of Documents," reads as follows in the second and third paragraphs:

"2. There seems to be some question regarding the documents disposition. It is believed that all but the last item could be of some use to the German Military Document Center at Camp Ritchie, Md.

"3. The Documents will be retained at this Center pending further instructions from USFET." [103]

USFET apparently acted on the suggestion that the documents might possibly be of use to the German Military Document Section which was being set up at Camp Ritchie. In any case the Italian military documents, about one thousand cubic feet as archivists then reckoned, were packed in 101 boxes and shipped to Camp Ritchie, Maryland (WDGS-7-GMDS VI) in January 1946. They came as part of a shipment, a special cargo which weighed about fifteen tons, occupied about three thousand cubic feet of space, and which was accompanied by two officers and three enlisted men headed by Capt. Leo Baer.[104]

Initial Exploitation of the Italian Military Documents at OCMH

From Camp Ritchie, Maryland, the collection of Italian military documents was transferred in 1946 to the basement of the Pentagon. Things

102. Benito Mussolini: *Memoirs 1942–1943, With Documents Relating to the Period*, trans. Frances Lobb, Introduction by Cecil Sprigge (London: George Weidenfeld & Nicolson, Ltd., 1949).

103. Memorandum, signed by 1st Lt. Charles Winnick, chief, Processing Section, Miscellaneous Reports, Hq., U.S. Seventh Army, National Archives.

104. Theater shipping document, WE-AGO, Form 450-40, Miscellaneous Seventh Army Records, National Archives.

were rather slack with the American military establishment at that time. The Historical Office of the War Department, redesignated in 1950 Office of the Chief of Military History (OCMH), Department of the Army, was very comfortably housed in the Pentagon where space then was easy to come by. The Italian records occupied a few shelves among the hundreds of feet of German military records in the Pentagon underground. It was there that with the aid of Mr. Detmar Finke I began my acquaintance with this group of Italian records.

At no time after my first examination of some of the files of the *Aktensammelstelle Süd* did I harbor any doubts as to their authenticity. We knew this much about the collection: that it consisted of Italian files which had been gathered up by the Germans after Italy's surrender to the Allies in 1943. The catalogue, marked *Aktensammelstelle Süd,* which accompanied the collection and which in large part was in the German language, was in itself a record of what had happened. What was uncertain was how much the Italian government or Italian historians and archivists knew about the collection.

Work at the OCMH was challenging. There was for several of us a real problem of gaining a background in military organization, tactics, strategy and terminology. But even for those such as Dr. Hugh M. Cole, an historian who had also had training at the Command and General Staff College, there was the "clean slate" represented by World War II. There were in 1946 no bibliographies; the memoirs and other printed works were just beginning to come out. There was scarcely any catalogue of the documents.[105] We historians at OCMH had first to do the spade work of locating the collections of source materials before we could start the work of synthesis and composition, each for his own topic. I cherished that German catalogue of the *Aktensammelstelle Süd* for these files were at least partially organized.

I spent several months working through this typewritten listing of the Italian military records, checking and examining the files in accordance with the entries. My primary object was to search out those files and documents which were relevant to my projected volume in the history of the United States Army in World War II, Mediterranean theater of operations, *The Sicilian Campaign and the Surrender of Italy.*[106] At the same time I noted any material which might be of use to my colleague in the Mediterranean section, Dr. George F. Howe, who wrote the initial

---

105. The excellent guide, *Federal Records of World War II,* vol. 2, *Military Records,* issued by GSA-NARS, National Archives, appeared only in 1951.

106. The volume was not published until 1965, with Lt. Col. Albert N. Garland as co-author and with the slightly modified title, *Sicily and the Surrender of Italy.* See particularly the reference in the Bibliographical Note, p. 568, to the captured Italian records.

volume in the Mediterranean series, *Northwest Africa: Seizing the Initiative in the West* (Washington, D.C., 1957). Here these materials are cited as "Italian Collection." [107]

Also in checking through the typed catalogue and in examining these files I was at pains to note those which appeared to me to be of enduring historical importance. Thus I was greatly interested in item 26, the records of the series of conferences of Field Marshal Kesselring with General Ambrosio in the Spring of 1943; in those items which gave contemporary reports of the movement of the German Army Group B into Northern Italy beginning on August 1; and in the Italian intelligence reports before the announcement of the Armistice by General Eisenhower on September 8, 1943. Here was the real documentary evidence on some of those much disputed and controversial points where so much imagination had been employed by Italian authors such as Monelli, whose *Roma 1943* appeared in 1945 and which was reissued in several editions. Here were the real sources regarding Italo-German relations during the forty-five days of Badoglio for which his own account offers so much obfuscation.[108]

These Italian military records initially collected by the Germans provided the full and authentic texts of many documents which first became known to the Italian reading public in mutilated or garbled form when they were printed by certain of the generals and other actors in the tragic drama of Italy's surrender and collapse.[109]

I was most happy to find the file designated 99*a*, 99*b*, 99*c*, which was the record of the daily reports to the Italian armed forces high command

107. See p. 502, fn. 5, with the reference to the Italian Collection, item 26. See also p. 512, fn. 23; p. 513 fnn. 24 and 25 and further.

108. *L'Italia nella seconda guerra mondiale: Memorie e documenti* (Milan: Mondadori, 1946).

See Garland and Smyth, *Sicily and the Surrender of Italy*, the section entitled "Friction Along the Alps," pp. 288–95.

109. Rossi, *Come arrivammo*, prints as Appendix 1, pp. 324–35, "Appunti sulle dichiarazioni di Hitler in occasione del suo incontro con Mussolini a Feltre il 19 luglio 1943." This garbled text omits some of Hitler's harshest criticisms of the Italian conduct of the war. The complete original may now be found in IT 3031, roll 251, frames 000957–75. On pages 335–39 Rossi prints a text labeled "Appunti sui colloqui Gen. Ambrosio-Mar. Keitel." This is a fusion of two documents, the first and second discussions of Ambrosio and Keitel. The originals of these are now also in IT 3031, on film at the National Archives, microcopy T-281, roll 251, the first discussion frames 001009–11, and the second discussion 001015–20.

The work *Hitler e Mussolini: Lettere e documenti* (Milan: Rizzoli, 1946), prints as document no. 67, pp. 190–209, three reports of discussions at the Tarvis, conference of August 6, 1946. The initial report, pp. 190–97, has a serious omission as compared to the text in IT 3029 (251/000777–000812). This discrepancy, however, may not indicate suppression of the missing part, but merely the existence of two different texts of the same document.

during the Sicilian campaign, a source of the highest importance for that phase of World War II. This item I translated word for word and my translation is now, in accordance with the regulations of OCMH, stored with my notes in the repository for federal records at Suitland, Maryland.

In checking through the Italian military documents which had been seized and catalogued by the Germans, I was somewhat puzzled at the large number of papers with descriptions of the Italian fortifications along the Alps. These appeared to me to be of very minor importance for the history of World War II. Then I remembered that these records had been gathered by the Germans in 1943, before the detonation of the first atomic bomb, before the German unconditional surrender in May 1945, when it was, perhaps, reasonable to regard World War II simply as the last but not concluding chapter in the book of Europe's balance of power wars, when it was natural to regard war as a permanent institution of mankind, and to look to the final phase of the last one for the guidelines for the next.

Mostly, however, I was haunted by the fear that we in OCMH would suddenly be confronted by a demand by the Italian republic for the return of its documents. I had no doubt whatsoever that these records were the property of the Italian state. I knew that since September 1943 the tide had turned and now was running swiftly in a pro-Western, pro-American direction. What I did not then know was the full story of the collection of these files by the Germans, and how little knowledge there was in Italy about them.

My hope when I was on active service at OCMH was that in case of a formal request or demand for the restoration of these files to the Italian state, we would be ready and prepared. Thus it was that I alerted the chief historian to this danger, and I prepared a selected list of what I considered to be the most important documents from an historical point of view.

No move toward reclaiming the documents was made by the Italian government, somewhat to my puzzlement. In any case my list of selections was at hand so that if necessary OCMH could initiate a rapid program of microfilming prior to the actual physical return of the originals to Italy. No such request ever came during my period of active service with the OCMH, August 1946 to August 1952. I retained a couple of copies of my list of priorities for microfilming and several years later I gave one copy to Professor Howard Ehrmann when he served as advisor for the filming program which was actually undertaken.[110]

In the work of checking through the catalogue of the *Aktensammel-*

110. See below (Microfilming of the Italian Military Documents).

stelle Süd I was persistently annoyed and frustrated by the entries for the twelve missing bundles and miscellaneous items. The descriptions indicated that these files were of the highest political importance. Each entry had the overprinted stamp mark, "LMD" indicating the London Military Document Section or Center. At my request Mr. G. W. S. Friedrichsen, British liaison officer attached to OCMH, repeatedly wrote to London asking for a search for these missing bundles. The replies which came from London during all the time of my service at OCMH were constantly negative.[111]

I myself left OCMH in August 1952 to work with the captured German Foreign Office records which were then housed in Whaddon Hall, near Bletchley, Bucks, England.

The first published notice of the Italiam military records appeared in 1957 when the collection had been transferred to the custody of the Adjutant General's Office (TAGO). It was given the designation: "Record Group 1058—Records of the Italian Armed Forces 1935–1943" and a brief description was printed for official use.[112] Mr. F. W. Deakin visited Washington in January of 1958 in the course of his researches for his book, *The Brutal Friendship*. He was granted clearance for research in the captured Italian military records and consulted some of them. Although it is doubtful that his brief stay in the Washington area during that visit would have allowed for much more than a cursory examination of some of the more interesting documents, his application for clearance resulted somewhat later in the declassification of these records.[113]

Retrieval in London of the Missing Bundles

My work with the German Documents Project at Whaddon Hall where the German Foreign Office records were housed for the decade 1948–58—they had been moved out of Berlin at the order of General Clay when the Russians imposed their blockade—was of a different nature from the history of military operations in the Mediterranean theater in World War II. But I continued my work on the volume for OCMH in my

111. See Friedrichsen's memorandum, December 5, 1956, "*Aktensammelstelle Süd,*" para. 12, OCMH files.

112. Departmental Records Branch, Administrative Services Division, the Adjutant General's Office, *Guide to Seized Records: Reference Aid Nr. 17*, ed., Philip P. Brower, Archivist, Departmental Records Group, Record Group Summary Nr. 1058.

113. Memo, "Request for Clearance for Dr. Deakin," dated 10 January 1958, authorization by the assistant chief of staff, Intelligence; Routing slip memo Goldbeck to Bauer, General Services Administration, May 5, 1960. Copies in the National Archives.

spare time. I was permitted by special arrangements to bring many of my notes with me and to borrow some records from Washington.

I explained the matter of the missing bundles of the Alexandria collection of Italian military documents to the Honorable Margaret Lambert, British editor in chief of the *Documents on German Foreign Policy 1918–1945*. Miss Lambert kindly began inquiries. For three years I heard nothing. Then one dull, dreary, English, autumn day I received the exciting news that these documents had been found. Miss Lambert phoned from her office in Cornwall House, Stamford Street. They had been in that building, lying undisturbed for years in a crate which had been shoved into a closet off one of the gloomy hallways of the Foreign Office Library.

Miss Lambert had alerted the Historical Section of the Cabinet Office which promptly took custody of the documents. She put me in touch with Mr. Brian Melland whose office in Queen Anne's Chambers, 41, Tothill Street, SW 1, I visited a few times late in 1955. There I had my first glimpse of the missing files of the *Aktensammelstelle Süd*. My spare time away from my duties at Whaddon Hall was quite restricted and a trip to London from that isolated country house usually cost a couple of hours each way. I was able in these weekend visits to Melland's office to make only a cursory examination of these important papers. I was never able really to exploit them for the volume prepared for OCMH, a matter of distinct regret on my part.

I insisted vigorously both with Miss Lambert and with Mr. Melland that these files were an integral part of the collection of Italian military documents and should be returned to the main collection in Alexandria, Virginia. I notified the Office of the Chief of Military History that the missing files had been located, and that I had been assured that they would be restored to American custody. In a letter dated December 20, 1955, Brian Melland wrote me: "Since your last visit here we have completed our detailed examination of the fourteen folders of Italian military archives of 1943 and I attach a copy of our Contents List. I am also sending a copy to Washington." [114]

The Historical Section of the Cabinet Office not only made the very detailed listing of the fourteen folders of the *Aktensammelstelle Süd*, they

114. Original in my personal files. The contents list (copy no. 3), dated Enemy Documents Section, November 1955, is very detailed, 23 typewritten, folio pages and describes each file 1119 through file 1232 (folders 253 through 267–68).

The miscellaneous, listed documents borrowed by Raymond Klibansky in 1945 were apparently grouped into two bundles or "folders." Hence the reference to 14 folders, rather than to the 12 bundles sent from the U.S. Seventh Army on November 13, 1945. Cf. notes 100 and 101 above.

also microfilmed them. These British microfilms were made available to F. W. Deakin for his work, *The Brutal Friendship*. The originals were returned to the main collection in Alexandria only after the British had a complete film copy.[115]

Microfilming of the Italian Military Documents: The *Guides*

In the introductory statement of my problem I have mentioned the extraordinary program of microfilming of German military and other records which was launched by a committee of scholars in 1955 which in the following year became a Committee of the American Historical Association.[116] It had initially been my hope that the captured Italian military documents would be included in the schedule of Record Groups to be screened, microfilmed, and catalogued by the committee. In August 1960, Dr. Willard Fletcher, on leave from the University of Colorado, took over the chairmanship of the microfilming team operating under the Committee. In December of that year Herman Goldbeck of the National Archives broached the matter of the Italian military documents to Fletcher; showed him the collection and its German language catalogue; emphasized that the Italian documents had been declassified. Dr. Fletcher replied that he already had a full program with German records and could not take on additional groups. But he assured Mr. Goldbeck that he would report the matter to Professor Howard Ehrmann, representative of the American Historical Association's Committee and himself a specialist in the field of modern Italian history.[117]

I was in touch with Howard Ehrmann at this time and knew of his zeal for getting materials of World War II on microfilm. But the committee's financial support from private foundations was drying up. After preparing some forty *Guides to German Records Microfilmed at Alexandria, Va.*, which were issued between 1958 and 1964, the funds from private sources ran out and the committee's work ended in July 1963.[118]

115. Friedrichsen's memo of December 5, 1956 records:
"It was subsequently discovered that they [the missing bundles] had been sent from Frankfurt in 1945 to the LMDC earmarked for the Political Section of the Foreign Office, then at Bush House, London. They remained at the F.O. for ten years in oblivion, until they came to light in 1955 and were passed to the Cabinet Office from whence they will be returned to the CRS [Captured Records Section] National Archives." See note 111 above.
116. See Introduction, note 1.
117. Memo, "The Italian Records and A.H.A.," December 6, 1960, initialed "H[erman] G[oldbeck]," National Archives.
118. The first guide issued by the committee, unnumbered, was prepared by Ernst

Fortunately, however, the program of microfilming the captured Nazi records before returning them to the German Federal Republic was continued by the National Archives and Records Service itself. I then urged on all in authority who were concerned with this program that the Italian military documents, Record Group 1058, be included in the new schedule. I like to believe that my urgings had some effect. But Professor Howard M. Ehrmann, now emeritus, but then as always very active, was certainly as much interested as I in seeing that the Italian military documents were filmed before their return, and his influence counted a great deal. Record Group 1058, I was assured, would be filmed.

Late in 1963 I learned that the plan for filming the Italian military documents had lapsed. At the meeting of the American Historical Association I had a brief conversation with Professor Gerhard Weinberg [119] of the University of Michigan to whom I bewailed the fact of cancellation, and urged the danger that if the Italian government were to learn the whereabouts of its records it might legitimately demand their return. Not long after getting back to Washington I had a phone call from Dr. Weinberg. He told me that the Italian collection had been reinstated. Filming would start in May 1964; it would be selective and systematic and would be done by government employees rather than by private contract. For further details I might consult Mr. Robert Wolfe at the National Archives. I promptly recorded this in a memorandum to Dr. William M. Franklin, director of the Historical Office, Department of State, and gave a copy of the memo to the late E. Taylor Parks, then chief of the Advisory and Review Branch of the Historical Office. [120]

Later in January I tried to call Mr. Wolfe [121] but he was out of town.

Schwandt, and was entitled, *Index of Microfilmed Records of the German Foreign Ministry and the Reich's Chancellery Covering the Weimar Period, Deposited at the National Archives* (Washington, 1958). This work has been superseded by *A Catalog of Files and Microfilms of the German Foreign Ministry Archives 1920–1945*, comp. and ed. George O. Kent (Stanford, 1962–72).

Guide no. 40, *Records of German Field Commands, Army Groups, Part 1* (Washington, 1964), was issued jointly by the committee and by the National Archives.

119. Professor Weinberg in 1956–57, then of the University of Kentucky, had directed the work of the first microfilming teams working in the German documents then housed in Alexandria, and the preparation of the initial guides of the series. He has kept in close touch with the work ever since. Among other things buried in the mountains of German records shipped to Alexandria, Dr. Weinberg discovered the suppressed typescript of *Hitler's Secret Book* which was published in English translation by Grove Press, Inc. (New York), in 1961.

120. Memorandum, Smyth to Franklin, January 3, 1964, "Filming of the Italian War Department Documents." Copy in personal files.

121. Then Specialist in German Records, National Archives.

I then turned to Mr. Philip Brower who was then deputy director, Archival Projects Branch, Military Records Division of the National Archives and Records Service. From him I learned that Dr. Robert Bahmer [122] had decided for inclusion of the Italian military documents; the hope was that the work could begin in July or August of that year, 1964. However, the papers of the martyred President Kennedy had been assigned the first priority for filming at the National Archives, a development which might delay the work with the Italian records. At Brower's suggestion I phoned Dr. Bahmer who mentioned that the work of screening the Italian papers had begun with two competent men working through the files and making purport cards which would serve as guides for filming and as a basis for the index or guide which would be published. He mentioned that they were in touch with Professor Ehrmann and were getting his advice; they would appreciate mine also if I had any suggestions to offer. [123] I had kept in touch with Howard Ehrmann and on learning that he would serve as advisor regarding the selection of files and documents for filming, I turned over to him a copy of the list of important files which I, many years earlier, had made as a member of the Office of the Chief of Military History. [124]

The first step in this project undertaken by Uncle Sam—members of the academic community take note that the federal government undertook it and saw it through—was to put all of the documents and files in order. There were at hand Major Brennfleck's entry book and the typed catalogue based upon it which had been compiled by American soldiers at Frankfurt. The twelve bundles plus miscellaneous documents (sometimes reckoned as two additional bundles) which had been sent back from London to the main collection were put in their proper places as indicated in the catalogue. But *Bunde* or bundles ceased to be used from this point on as a method of classification. The documents were grouped simply into folders or files. However, the file numbers as initially given by the Germans in the *Aktensammelstelle Süd* were retained.

The sixty-five boxes of uncatalogued Italian military records were assimilated to the existing numerical scheme. There also were Italian military documents which appeared as stray copies among the German military records and these were put into appropriate files. In North Africa and in Sicily the United States Army had directly captured other Italian military materials. All of these were assimilated. Individual documents

---

122. Robert H. Bahmer, deputy archivist of the United States, 1956–66; subsequently archivist of the United States, January 16, 1966–March 9, 1968.

123. Memoranda of telephone calls, January 22, 1964, Personal Files.

124. Cf. above (Initial Exploitation of the Italian Military Documents at OCMH) and note 110.

were grouped into files and the "new" files were given numbers which continued the sequence started by the Germans.[125]

What of the duplicate listing in the entry book, the two sets of files numbered 1136 to 1214? In compiling the American catalogue at Frankfurt, this problem was solved simply by the addition of the "A" series, the separate listing of files A-1136 to A-1214. These "A" numbers for the given, described files were retained in the *Guide,* that is in the final reorganization of the files in Washington. They were not retained, however, as a separate series but only individually. Each "A" numbered file in the *Guide* is listed immediately after the regular number. Thus we have file IT-1136 followed immediately by IT A-1136; file IT-1137 followed by IT-A-1137; and so through IT-1214 followed by file IT-A-1214.[126] When one reckons with 5463 files in the German Document Collection Center-South, this is by accepting the German figure given on the last page of their entry book. One should add the "A" list of 79 files which would bring that total to 5542.

I have not attempted to achieve complete numerical consistency in this description but only the approximate outlines. Some files for purposes of indexing were broken into two parts. Some extraneous items have been added such as items from the administration of the *Aktensammelstelle Süd* and from the Italian embassy in Berlin.[127] Such a task would not be worth the labor. The *Guide* lists a total of 6833 files or IT item numbers on 490 rolls of film.

After the ordering of the files and their listing in one continuous numerical series came the next step, their description. This was done on purport cards. The files were examined, one by one. The contents of each were recorded on an index card; sometimes individual documents were noted. This work was done by Mario Fenyo and Cleveland Collier with

---

125. Interview with Philip P. Brower, March 3, 1965; letter of Brower to the author, August 5, 1965, personal files. This letter gives the following figures:

Items in the original *Aktensammelstelle*	
Süd	5463
Items added later	1342
Items in the entire collection	6805

or by volume:	
In the original German collection	
(5463 items)	420 cubic feet
Added later	82 cubic feet
Total	502

126. See *Guide to Records of the Italian Armed Forces,* pt. I, pp. 94–121.
127. Ibid., pt. 3, p. 156.

the editorial assistance of Luis E. Baños. Something similar to this indexing had been started while the collection was in the custody of the German Military Documents Section. Sfc. Frank Drasovec had made a card file in English for files IT-1 through IT-1360.[128] How much this initial card index was used in making the purport cards is not clear. Philip P. Brower and Donald E. Spencer supervised the whole operation.

After the preparation of a complete card index covering all of the files of Italian Military Documents in American custody came the step of selection for filming. The microfilming was done selectively; that is to say, not all files or folders were filmed, not all of the documents within each file. Roll 492 of this collection of microfilms gives the purport card descriptions of those files which were not filmed. The rough estimate was that about 60 percent of the total of Italian military materials in the custody of the National Archives and Records Service were photographed. On the basis of the descriptions recorded on the purport cards, a committee with the assistance of Professor Ehrmann determined which files or documents merited filming, which were to be omitted.[129]

On May 23, 1966, Mr. Donald Spencer was kind enough to telephone me that the filming of the Italian military documents had been completed and that the preparation of the guides to the collection was under way. These guides were to be in the same format as those for the German military records and for the Nazi ministries and agencies other than the Foreign Office.

The guides themselves were issued in three parts the following year.[130] At the National Archives this collection is designated microcopy T-821 and is open to general use. The indexing and filming is an excellent job. Each volume or part of the *Guide* comprises in the preface a brief statement regarding the collection, how it was acquired and augmented, how the filming was done, together with an explanation of the organization of the Italian armed forces during World War II. For each item or file the *Guide* shows the provenance, usually the originating office or the place where filed, and the item number as originally assigned in the *Aktensammelstelle Süd* catalogue or in the continuations added after arrival and sorting of the documents in Washington.

Within each roll or reel of microfilm the frames are numbered in

128. Memo by M/Sgt. Michael Halyshyn to Chief, GMDS, 13 December 1951 (first cited in note 92 above).

129. Interview with Philip P. Brower, March 3, 1965; letter of Brower to the author, August 5, 1965; Preface, *Guide to Records of the Italian Armed Forces*, pt. 1.

130. *Guide to Records of the Italian Armed Forces.* Pt. 1, items 1–1331 (rolls 1–196); pt. 2, items 1332–4248 (rolls 197–335); pt. 3, items 4249–6833 (rolls 336–506 plus reels R507 and R508).

sequence, but the numbering of frames is not continuous for the entire collection. Each roll begins anew. Thus roll 1 (of microcopy T-821) comprises the files, folders, or items 1 through 5, and includes frames 000001 through 001106. Item 4 which is wholly comprised within roll 1 can quickly be located by the given initial frame number, 227 (000227). Or again, reel 59 comprises items IT 557 through IT 573 in frames 000001 through 000906. The file, folder or item IT 569, "Comando V Corpo d'Armata—Operazioni Zona Gospic," can quickly be spotted within roll 59 by the initial frame number, 000526. Thus the roll or reel number is essential in the use of this microfilm collection. This is in contrast to the collection of the German Foreign Ministry Records (microcopy T-120), or to the collection of Mussolini's Private Papers (microcopy T-586) where the frame numbering is continuous for large groups of reels or for the entire collection.

When the Germans assembled the collection of the Italian military records which they were able to retrieve, they did not organize the files by provenance, that is according to the originating office. Thus the files which stemmed from the Armed Forces General Staff (*Comando Supremo*) are scattered; they are found in various places and not in sequence. To assist the reader in the use of microcopy T-821 each part of the *Guide* has an index by provenance listing all of the items from a given originating office or staff. Finally there is a tariff for purchase by scholars (and others) for duplicate copies of the microfilm by complete roll or by frame.

Return of the Originals
to the Italian Government

The first suggestion for the return of the captured Italian military records was made after they had been in American custody for only about five years. The German Military Documents Section, of which the *Aktensammelstelle Süd* was considered to be a part, was at that time, as a section of the Departmental Records Branch, under The Adjutant General's Office (TAGO). On December 27, 1950, Maj. Gen. Edward F. Witsell, the adjutant general, wrote to G. Bernard Noble, chief of the Division of Historical Policy Research, in regard to the collection of Italian military records. He suggested that in view of the new status of Italy after the ratification of the Treaty of Peace in 1947 it would be appropriate to consider the matter of restitution of these records even though the Italian government itself had made no request for their return. General Witsell proposed that his letter serve as a basis for bringing the question to the appropriate officials of the Department of State and to the attention of the Interagency Conference on Captured Enemy Documentation.[131]

The adjutant general assured Dr. Noble that the Department of the Army had completed its historical and intelligence exploitation of the Italian documents. In any case, he stated, they had been used relatively little. His own office had made no attempt to determine whatever interest other federal agencies might have in the collection, or if the British government were interested.[132]

In January of 1951 copies of General Witsell's letter were sent out to various offices of the Department of State. None offered objection to the return of the Italian military documents to Italy, but the Division of Western European Affairs suggested that if British troops participated in their capture, the British government should first be consulted.[133]

On February 2, Dr. Noble discussed the problem with Mr. Jamieson of the British embassy who stated that the Foreign Office wished that some British military officers examine the materials for the benefit of their military historians. On February 7, Dr. Noble replied to General Witsell that the Department of State considered that the documents might appropriately be restored to the Italian government. He added, however, that the matter had been discussed with the British government which wished to examine the documents, and General Witsell was notified that British military authorities would get in touch with him in order to arrange for transfer of the documents to London for examination.[134]

131. Copy in file "Captured Italian Documents," Historical Office, Department of State.

132. On finding a copy of this letter I was astonished at the assertion that the Department of the Army had completed its historical exploitation of these Italian military records. On July 19, 1968, I telephoned Dr. Stetson Conn, chief historian, OCMH, and asked him if OCMH had been consulted when this letter was sent. He said he remembered the name of General Witsell; but he could not check the files of OCMH for that period because they had been retired. He rather doubted that OCMH had been consulted. He said that he well remembered that the policy of Maj. Gen. Harry J. Maloney, the first chief of Military History, and of his successor Maj. Gen. Orlando Ward, was to retain records first captured by the Germans, such as those of the Netherlands or of Italy.

I myself was in OCMH at the time and heard with dismay the scuttlebut regarding the move to return the *Aktensammelstelle Süd* collection to Italy. I was then the chief user of the collection and more thoroughly acquainted with it than any one else; and no one had asked for my views. As the rumor came to OCMH, so far as I can accurately recall, responsibility for initiating the move was ascribed to Dr. Noble. Such documentary evidence as I have been able to gather indicates this to be quite incorrect.

133. W E (M. H. Colladay) to G. B. Noble, January 11, 1951, File, "Captured Italian Documents," Historical Office, Department of State.

134. Letter, G. Bernard Noble to Maj. Gen. Edward F. Witsell, the Adjutant General, copy in file, "Captured Italian Documents," Historical Office, Department of State.

What further moves were made along this line I do not know. But neither the whole collection of the Italian military records nor any large part of it was sent to London during this period although subsequently there was considerable small-scale borrowing by the British.[135]

Some years passed. The collection remained in Alexandria where it was consulted by a few American and British scholars. The fourteen or so bundles which had been "lost" in London were returned to the main collection, as we have noted earlier, and then in the mid-sixties the program for microfilming was initiated and carried out by the National Archives. All of this time the Italian government and Italian scholars apparently remained completely in ignorance regarding the collection.

In 1965 at long last the Office of the Chief of Military History issued the volume which I had written in collaboration with Lt. Col. Albert N. Garland, *Sicily and the Surrender of Italy*. We had made very extensive use of the Italian collection whose items were cited by the file numbers initially given them by the Germans at the *Aktensammelstelle Süd,* and we offered a clear description of the collection in the bibliographical note (*Sicily*, p. 568). I sent a complimentary copy of the work to the late Mario Toscano. That extraordinarily productive scholar and busy man was then wearing three or four hats: professor of international relations at the University of Rome, editor in chief of the *Documenti Diplomatici Italiani*, head of the Italian delegation at the Assembly of the United Nations. As historical adviser to the Italian Ministry of Foreign Affairs, Toscano enjoyed the rank of ambassador. The book, mailed to him in Rome, followed him back across the Atlantic to New York. On Sunday, October 10, 1965, through the kindness of the Italian ambassador in Washington, Sergio Fenoaltea, there was a luncheon party for Dr. Franklin and me to talk over with Professor Toscano certain aspects of the book and problems of editing diplomatic documents.[136]

Prior to this luncheon meeting the counselor of the Italian embassy had called by appointment on Dr. Franklin, director of the Historical Office, Department of State. At the instigation of Ambassador Toscano, Sig-

135. Years later Mr. Philip Brower, who was in charge of the collection of Italian military documents when it was housed in the old torpedo factory at King and Union Streets, Alexandria, told me that he had very frequently sent documents from the *Aktensammelstelle Süd* to the British; he had done this whenever a request was received. This was at considerable expense to his office, yet the British had not paid one cent for such service. On the other hand he felt that the British with whom he dealt had not been very candid or open about their holdings of certain captured German records (interview with Mr. Brower, March 3, 1965).

136. Draft, memorandum of discussion with Ambassador Fenoaltea, Professor Toscano, and Counselor of Embassy Rinaldo Petrignani (Dr. Franklin and Smyth) October 11, 1965, personal files.

nor Petrignani asked about the availability of certain files of the Department of State which were cited in *Foreign Relations of the United States* (1943). He also asked directly about the Italian military documents cited in *Sicily and the Surrender of Italy*, and if they were open to scholars. Next day, Friday, October 8, Dr. Franklin telephoned Petrignani and gave him a full description of the Italian military documents which at that time were in the process of being microfilmed in Alexandria. The files were completely open to scholars, as was verified by a telephone conversation with Mr. Donald Spencer who estimated that the microfilming project would probably be completed by December of that year.[137] The cat was now out of the bag. But the fear which had haunted me for years, that a demand by the Italian government for the return of its documents might be made before we in Washington were ready, was completely exorcised by the knowledge that the microfilming program was nearing completion.

During the course of the Congress of Archivists, which was held in Washington in 1966, two visiting Italian archivists, Dr. Lombardo and Dr. Sandri, looked over the collection but made no particular comment about it.

The estimate of October 1965 that the microfilming of the Italian military documents might be completed by the end of that year proved to be somewhat optimistic. On April 7, 1966, however, Mr. Spencer telephoned that a close estimate indicated that there remained about three more weeks of work for the microfilming team.[138]

All along I had made it a point to keep Dr. Franklin thoroughly informed of the progress of the microfilming of these records as well as regarding matters relating to the other Italian collections in the capital area. After a telephone call from Franklin, the archivist of the United States formally wrote to Col. Paul Hinkley, chief, Histories Division, OCMH, explaining that the Department of State would initiate a proposal for the early return to Italy of the collection of military documents.[139]

It was about the middle of April 1966 that the formal offer of the return of the Italian military records was made by the Department of State to the Italian ambassador. The note of the acting secretary of state mentioned: "The collection which has now been microfilmed, will be catalogued in the near future and the films will be made available to scholars

137. Draft, memorandum of conversations, October 10, 1965, personal files.
138. Longhand memo, April 7, 1966, personal files.
139. Letter, Robert H. Bahmer to Colonel Hinkley, April 12, 1966, copy in files of the Historical Office, Department of State.

at the National Archives in Washington." In May Ambassador Fenoaltea on behalf of his government accepted the collection.[140]

On October 5, 1967, the Davidson Transfer and Storage Company, acting as agents of the Italian embassy, picked up the collection for shipment over Baltimore to the Ministry of Defense in Rome.[141] At the end of that same month the director general of the Italian State Archives, Giulio Russo, wrote to the archivist of the United States explaining that in accordance with Italy's archival legislation, documents of a restricted character became available for consultation only fifty years after their given dates, and personal papers were opened up only after seventy years had elapsed. These restrictive rules, he stated, were dictated by political considerations and by clearly evident need. He explained further what was even more clearly evident that the application of these rules would be imperfect if copies of the documents were made available in Washington. He proposed a joint program whereby access to the microfilm copies would be on the same restricted basis as Italian law provided for the originals.[142]

After consultation with the Department of State, Dr. Bahmer replied that while it might be useful to the National Archives staff to know what restrictions would be applied in the consultation of the documents which were being sent back, they could not at that late date place such restrictions on the microfilms in Washington. Nor was there, he added, any practical way to control the subsequent use of the microfilm after it had been sold.[143]

What is one to think of this request by the director of the Italian Archives? In England, thanks largely to the crusading efforts of Donald C. Watt, there has been a reduction of the closed period of the British archives from fifty to thirty years. Dr. Watt, after a period of work in the United States, was impressed by the comparatively freer access to government documents on this side of the Atlantic.[144] He touched a sensi-

140. Carbon copy of note dated April 18, 1966, and note of the Italian ambassador, May 17, 1966, files of the Historical Office, Department of State.

141. Letter, Robert W. Krauskopf, director, Modern Military Records Division, National Archives, to William M. Franklin, October 11, 1967, files of the historical Office, Department of State.

142. Dr. Russo to Dr. Bahmer, October 31, 1967, Copy in files of the Historical Office, Department of State.

143. Letter, Bahmer to Russo, December 5, 1967, copy in files of the Historical Office, Department of State.

144. "United States Documentary Resources for the Study of British Foreign Policy, 1919–1939," *International Affairs* 38, no. 1 (January 1962): 63–72; and "Restrictions on Research: The Fifty-Year Rule and British Foreign Policy," *International Affairs* 41, no. 1 (January 1965): 89–95.

tive spot with British students of contemporary and recent politics when he expressed his annoyance at having to rely heavily on American records regarding the words and actions of British statesmen since World War I. Britain has become an exception. But in general the non-Communist governments of Europe apply the fifty-year rule to their political archives.[145] Italy, in respect of its state archives, is no different from the rest of the countries of Western Europe.

But Italy is certainly in a very different situation from that of Western Germany, the successor regime to her erstwhile Axis partner. The Nazi archives of the Foreign Office, of the Wehrmacht, of the Nazi party itself and of numerous other agencies were seized and have been filmed wholesale. The United States and Great Britain with the aid of France systematically screened the records of the former *Auswärtiges Amt* and published selections so that the world would have a real insight into the nature and workings of the Nazi regime. Furthermore, when the German Foreign Office records were restored to Bonn, it was stipulated that the German Federal Republic "will keep the returned files in an orderly manner, and grant German and foreign scholars access to the files at all times." [146]

Possibly the Department of State made a mistake in not stipulating such free access to the Italian military and other records which came into custody of the United States in consequence of World War II. There are real and important distinctions between Italian and German fascism. But surely it is just as important that the nature and operations of Mussolini's dictatorship be explored and exposed as it is for Hitler's.

This task of breaking the fetters on free inquiry, of getting rid of traditional restrictions on the consultation of state papers for such time until the questions to which they might give answers cease to be matters of current policy or relevance, would now appear to devolve on the Italian historians and other scholars. Such restrictions are perhaps appropriate for a monarchy but certainly not for a republic. I personally can only regret that my powers are not strong enough to evoke the ghost of Gaetano Salvemini to give the appropriate snort of indignation at any attempt under the Italian republic to lock the door to the documentary evidence about the Fascist regime.

145. See the pamphlet issued by the Historical Office, Bureau of Public Affairs, Department of State, "Public Availability of Diplomatic Archives," (May 1968), 25 pages, mimeographed. For the new regulations in Great Britain see p. 10, for Italy see p. 13.

146. Transfer of Archives, Agreement between the United States of America and the Federal Republic of Germany, effected by exchange of letters signed at Bonn and Bonn/Bad Godesberg, March 14 and April 18, 1956, *Treaties and Other International Acts Series 3613*.

5 / Mussolini's Private Papers

Mussolini's Archives: The Three Parts

Benito Mussolini, prime minister of Italy, head of the government, and duce of the Fascist party from the early twenties until his overthrow on July 25, 1943, maintained an extensive archive. A great many reports and messages were sent to him directly and in addition he received copies of the important papers of the various executive departments of the Italian government: the Ministry of Foreign Affairs, the Ministry of Popular Culture, the Ministry of Italian Africa, documents of the secret police (O.V.R.A.), reports of the armed forces, intelligence and counterintelligence reports. In the Fascist era the police sent in numerous reports on the activities both of the enemies of the regime and of its supporters. A significant portion of Mussolini's archives was made up of dossiers on individuals. These were an essential part of his system of control. These archives were made up of three parts: the open or general files (*archivio ordinario*); the secret military documents (*archivio militare segreto*); and the private papers (*archivio riservato*).

Originally these archives were maintained on the second floor of the Viminale Palace with the open files stored in the left wing. In August 1941, the confidential files were transferred to the Palazzo Venezia where the secret military archives occupied one huge room and the reserved archives another. The windows of each were protected by iron gratings. The open files remained in the Palazzo Viminale and during the period

164

1941–42 they were screened; a great number of papers were judged to be of no importance and were thrown out.[1]

Seizure of Mussolini's Archives by Badoglio

After Mussolini's overthrow, the Badoglio government quickly seized his private archives. The high command of the armed forces (*Comando Supremo*) took over the main part of the *archivio militare segreto*. These papers were packed in ten cases and were moved from the Palazzo Venezia to the Palazzo Vidoni. The Duke of Acquarone, minister of the royal household, took charge of the *archivio riservato* and removed most of the dossiers which Mussolini had maintained on the members of the royal family.[2]

The suggestion was made to Marshal Badoglio that the rest of the private papers be assimilated into the central state archives, but nothing was done for the time being and both the secret military files and the private papers were put back into storage in the Viminale Palace.[3]

1. See Emilio Re, *Storia di un archivio: le carte di Mussolini* (Milan: Edizioni del Milione, 1946), pp. 10–18.

Commendatore Re in October 1944 was appointed head of the Italian archive service. After the capture of Rome by the Allies he worked closely with the Monuments, Fine Arts, and Archives Subcommission of the Allied Commission.

Re's book, which was issued in 1946 in a limited edition of six hundred copies, was premature. Mussolini's Private Papers, as we shall see, had not yet at that time been restored to the Italian government. The book leaves the incorrect impression that they never were restored.

See also the report in eleven pages by Dante Gnudi, chief of the Italian Documents Section of P.W.B., January 22, 1945, enclosure in Rome despatch no. 885, January 30, 1945 (865.002/Mussolini/1-3045), Central Files, Department of State. When retired to the National Archives, these files constitute Record Group 59.

It seems probable that Gnudi gained some of the information in his report from *Commendatore* Re.

2. Report by Dante Gnudi, January 22, 1945, as cited above; Re, *Storia di un archivio*, p. 18.

Acquarone apparently did not get them all. When Mussolini was captured on April 27, 1945, he had with him a file on Umberto di Savoia. See note 75 below.

3. Subcommission for Monuments, Fine Arts, and Archives, "Final Report on Archives," January 21, 1946, p. 26, file "Archives Policy-General, May 1942–April 1946," 20905/A/1, National Archives and Records Service (NARS), Record Group 331, 10,000/145/319 AC, National Archives.

Hereafter the Subcommission for Monuments, Fine Arts and Archives will be cited simply as MFAA Subcommission; the National Archives and Records Service will be NARS.

Cf. Re, *Storia di un archivio*, pp. 18–19. It seems quite likely that it was Re who suggested to Badoglio that Mussolini's Papers be restored to the state archives.

See also Hillary Jenkinson and H. E. Bell, *Italian Archives During the War and at its Close*

Mussolini's Retrieval of His Archives

After the ignominious flight of Badoglio, of the royal family, and of most of the members of the Italian high command on September 9, 1943, Mussolini, whether he wished it or not, was restored to power by Hitler. As a result of the German occupation of Rome, Mussolini regained control of all three parts of his archives, the personal papers, the secret military files, and the *archivio ordinario*. Not only that, but he was able to make several significant additions, because Badoglio, in his hasty flight, had left many important documents in Rome.[4]

Mussolini's Private Papers, that is the *archivio riservato*, were moved out of Rome to the North and were housed in the Villa Feltrinelli at Gargnano sul Garda where the Duce was established by the Germans as head of the Italian Social Republic. The transfer of these archives apparently took place in December 1943.[5]

Early in 1944, the secret military files which had been taken over by the *Comando Supremo* in July 1943 were found at the railway station in Milan. No one seems to have known how they got there except that they were consigned to the Swiss frontier. The crates appeared to have been practically untouched. These secret military documents promptly rejoined the classified private papers in Mussolini's villa.[6]

(London: H.M. Stationery Office, 1947), p. 20. Both Jenkinson and Bell were members of the MFAA Subcommission and drew heavily on the official report of January 21, 1946 in composing their published pamphlet which was "Issued by the British Committee on the Preservation and Restitution of Works of Art, Archives and Other Materials in Enemy Hands."

4. These were picked up by the Police Chief, Tulio Tamburini. On December 21, 1943, the prefect, Giovanni Dolfin, private secretary to Mussolini, wrote to Tamburini asking that the Badoglio files be sent to him because his superiors wished to see them. In February 1944 Dolfin wrote again, insisting that he "receive the files from Badoglio's office which were seized by you in Rome."

These letters are filmed in the microfilm collection which we are now describing, "Mussolini's Private Papers," microfilm publication T-586, file "Segreteria Particolare del Capo del Governo—Administration of Mussolini's Secretariat," job 154, frames 045 373, 045 328, National Archives.

Hereafter this file will be cited simply as job 154 with the appropriate frame numbers.

Two bundles of documents of the Badoglio period seem to have been forwarded in November. See note 14 below.

5. An unsigned memorandum of the *Segreteria Particolare* of Mussolini dated December 10, 1943, mentions the arrival of 16 cases of archival material at the Villa Feltrinelli and the expectation that two hundred additional cases would soon arrive from Rome (job 154/045 371–72).

I have found no evidence that the two hundred additional cases were ever sent from Rome.

6. Report by Dante Gnudi, January 22, 1945, as cited in note 1 above; Re, *Storia di un archivio*, p. 19.

How much did these two sets of documents amount to? We can get an approximate idea from some of these records themselves which have survived from the Italian Social Republic. In the autumn of 1944 the Germans and Italians began to consider a withdrawal into an Alpine redoubt where they would make a last stand. Mussolini rather favored the Valtellina, north and east of Lake Como.[7] A memorandum dated October 11, 1944, refers to some such contemplated move and states:

The military and restricted correspondence comprises 23 cases.

The first concerns the war in Africa and the present war up to July 25, 1943, and was recovered by the Ministry of the Armed Forces when it was on the way to the Swiss frontier.

The second comprises the files on military and civilian persons who had positions of command in the military or in the government during the Regime.

For transporting this correspondence a normal sized truck would be required.[8]

We have only a general notion as to what happened to Mussolini's military records. In any case no military files as such were filmed in the course of the program to be described. All of the filming was from the *Segreteria Particolare*. As will be explained, Mussolini's Private Papers were first assembled, screened, and parts were translated by G-2 of AFHQ. G-2 apparently pulled out all documents of a strictly military nature.[9]

After G-2 had examined the military files of Mussolini, it apparently sent them on to the Allied Commission for return to the Italian government.[10]

The private papers, the military files, and some additional dossiers on persons which were selected from the *archivio ordinario* at Rome and transferred to the North, were the documents which Mussolini had at

7. See Frederick W. Deakin, *The Brutal Friendship: Mussolini, Hitler and the Fall of Italian Fascism* (New York and Evanston: Harper & Row, 1962), pp. 727–29.

8. Job 154/045 300.

9. See below (Difficulties of the J.A.I.A.: Its Work of Microfilming) item 11 in the letter of October 14, 1945, which mentions "approximately 5 tons of documents which are the remainder after selecting and eliminating all documents of a strict military nature which have already or will be processed by G-2."

10. A letter of Brig. Gen. A. L. Hamblen, AC of S, G-5, November 20, 1945, states:

"2. Seven cases, containing military documents with minor administrative matters, constitute the remainder of Italian documents held by the Headquarters for intelligence exploitation.

"3. These cases are being dispatched to you under separate cover for return to the Italian Government."

MFAA Subcommission, file "Archives, Rome Central Ministries June 3, 1945–February 1946" (10,000/145/329), stamped page 1951.

hand when he composed his last published work *The Time of the Stick and the Carrot*.[11]

The *Archivio Ordinario* in Rome.

The great bulk of the files of the *archivio ordinario* remained in Rome. In preparation for the movement of the capital of the Italian Social Republic to the North, Vittorio Mussolini, who exercised a general supervision over his father's political secretariat and private secretariat,[12] appears to have ordered that a selection be made in the files of the *archivio ordinario* and that the remaining files be destroyed. Colonel Nani, the archivist in charge of the open files, objected to their destruction. With the support of the chief of police, he urged that the files which remained after selection of the important materials also be shipped north, even if they had to be housed in temporary quarters. His estimate indicated there would be 130,000 files left over after selection.[13] During the month of November, 949 files were removed from the *archivio ordinario* and together with two batches of materials from Badoglio were transferred to the minister of the interior.[14]

But the efforts which were made to find or to erect suitable quarters for the *archivio ordinario* in the North were unsuccessful. In January 1944, Colonel Nani recommended that the archive be left in place in Rome, at least for the time being. He urged that if the files, (some one hundred

11. Re, *Storia di un archivio*, pp. 19–20. The book, *Il tempo del bastone e della carota: Storia di un anno* (ottobre 1942–settembre 1943) originally appeared as a "Supplemento del Corriere della Sera, no. 190 del 8-9-1944 XXII." There is an American translation by Max Ascoli, *The Fall of Mussolini: His Own Story by Benito Mussolini* (New York: Farrar, Strauss and Co., 1948).

Mussolini borrowed his title from Churchill who at the Trident Conference in May 1943 had told reporters in reference to Italy that we would use a stick and a carrot on that donkey. See the English edition edited by Raymond Klibansky, *Benito Mussolini: Memoirs 1942–1943 With Documents Relating to the Period* (London: George Weidenfeld & Nicolson, Ltd., 1949), p. xvii. The reference is to the *Christian Science Monitor*, May 27, 1943. See also *The War Speeches by the Rt Hon Winston S. Churchill*, 3 vols., comp. Charles Eade (London: Cassell & Co., Ltd., 1952), 2:462.

12. By action of October 21, 1943, which placed Vito Mussolini in charge of the political secretariat, and the Prefect Giovanni Dolfin in charge of the private secretariat (job 154/045320).

13. Memorandum by the archivist, Col. Renato Nani, for the private secretariat of Mussolini, November 13, 1943 (job 154/045367); Giovanni Dolfin to Colonel Nani, November 14, 1943 (job 154/045365–66).

14. The list of these files, together with the receipt on behalf of the minister of the interior dated November 1943, is filmed in job 154/045329–58. For the most part these selected files appear to be dossiers on persons. The righthand column of the list gives the number which the file bore in the *archivio ordinario*.

thousand he now estimated) were packed and put in temporary quarters in the North, there would be no possibility of consulting them, whereas if they remained in Rome, any particular file could easily be pulled out for examination.[15] The temporary solution became the permanent one: the *archivio ordinario* remained in Rome and Colonel Nani with it.

After the Allies entered Rome in June 1944 the *archivio ordinario* was discovered, apparently intact (save for the files sent North), by a member of the Subcommission on Monuments, Fine Arts and Archives (MFAA) of the Allied Control Commission. This was reported to be "a valuable collection of 100,000 files, housed in the Viminale." About this time Emilio Re made contact with the members of the MFAA Subcommission: it is not excluded that he assisted in the discovery of the *archivio ordinario*. Colonel Nani had remained with that archive and was able to give information regarding the *archivio riservato* which had been transferred to Mussolini's villa of Feltrinelli on the shores of Lake Garda.[16]

I have found no evidence of systematic filming by the Allies of the files of the *archivio ordinario* of Mussolini. Possibly some of the dossiers on persons were consulted by the Allied authorities; some data from them may have gone into the biographic summaries which were made by the American filming team.[17] But we can feel sure that *Commendatore* Re would have made a strong protest in case those files had been held for long. The reasonable inference is that the files of the *archivio ordinario* passed promptly back to the custody of the Italian government.

Mussolini's Plans for His Private Papers

Meanwhile in the North, Mussolini continued to maintain the reserved archives under his immediate control. While these private papers were housed in the Villa Feltrinelli, Carlo Silvestri joined Mussolini's camp. Earlier he had been an anti-Fascist journalist; he had been imprisoned and had suffered other punishments because of his opposition to fascism. Now, however, he had a change of heart. After Mussolini's death, Silvestri came out with several books in defense and explanation of the Fascist dictator and in apology for the Republic of Salò. He claims to have enjoyed some fifty interviews with Mussolini in the period between December 1944 and April 1945. Silvestri assures us that it was Mussolini's custom to draw forth various files and thus to produce the

15. Memorandum dated January 4, 1944 (job 154/045368).

16. See the report by Dante Gnudi of January 22, 1945 (as cited in note 1 above; see also MFAA Subcommission, "Final Report on Archives, January 21, 1946" (as cited in note 3 above); Jenkinson and Bell, *Italian Archives*, pp. 20, 22.

17. See note 203 below.

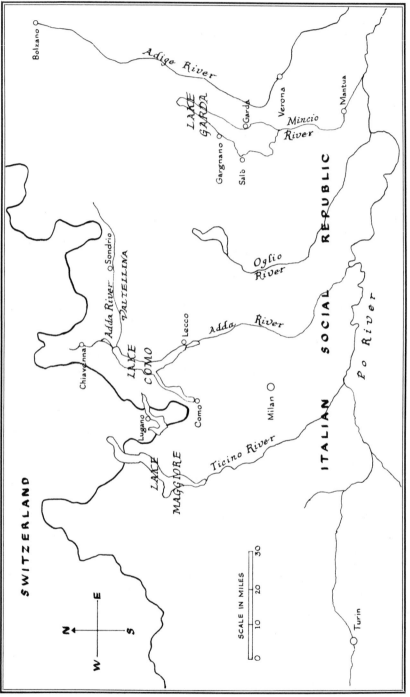

NORTH ITALY: THE PO VALLEY

documentary evidence for what he told him in regard to Matteotti, or as to what Turati had said, or on whatever other topic formed the subject of discussion.[18]

In this final period Mussolini was only the shadow of his former self; tired, depressed, indecisive. He was preoccupied with fears of his death and regarding his historical reputation. Apparently he toyed with the idea of turning over his private archives to Carlo Silvestri, that ingratiating and obliging journalist. The plan was that Silvestri would secrete them in some safe place. Then, after the political situation had quieted down, Silvestri would turn these precious archives over to a committee of illustrious Italians. Benedetto Croce, Vittorio Emanuele Orlando, and Alcide de Gasperi are mentioned among the names of those who were said to have been considered. The committee would guarantee the eventual return of the documents to the Italian government as part of its historical patrimony.

But the plan was never put into effect. For one thing Mussolini felt that a very detailed catalogue of the papers ought to be prepared prior to their turnover. Furthermore, he refused almost until the end, until April 25, 1945, in fact, to believe that the Germans were negotiating behind his back for a surrender of their armies in Italy.[19]

Various other plans, schemes, or notions passed through Mussolini's mind during these last days at Gargnano. Pavolini, secretary of the Fascist party, urged a fight to the last in Milan, that they make Milan "the Italian Stalingrad." Graziani, commander of the Armed Forces of the Italian Social Republic, vigorously opposed this idea: He argued with effect that the result would be to draw down on the capital city of Lombardy the weight of Allied air attack. Mussolini then dropped this idea and reverted to the notion of a last stand in that Alpine valley, the Valtellina, "because," he declared, "whatever the place, Fascism had to fall heroically." This theme was developed at the last Council of Ministers held at Gargnano on April 16, at which Mussolini announced that the next meeting would be held in Milan. The transfer of the capital of the Italian Social Republic was made to Milan on April 18, and Mussolini set up his headquarters in the prefecture on the via Monforte. At the opportune moment, it is said, he planned to retreat into the Valtellina. Pavolini promised that he would assemble several thousand men for this last ditch stand, men drawn from the Black Brigades and from the Republican National Guard.[20]

18. Carlo Silvestri, *Mussolini, Graziani e l'antifascismo (1943–45)* (Milan: Longanesi & C., 1949), pp. 9, 23–24.

19. Ibid., pp. 29–30.

20. Rodolfo Graziani, *Ho difeso la patria*, 4th ed. (Milan: Garganti, 1948), p. 490.

The plan for turning the archives over to Silvestri could not be carried out. Apparently Mussolini gave an order to his personal secretary, the Prefect Luigi Gatti, to have the bulk of his private papers burned.[21] The order was not carried out. The bulk of the files of Mussolini's private archives were left in the Villa Feltrinelli at Gargnano and were subsequently picked up by the United States Fifth Army.[22]

His Selection of Parts on Leaving Gargnano

Before his sudden departure from the shores of Lake Garda, Mussolini made a selection of what he considered to be the very most important of his papers. Possibly he was thinking of the chances of his capture and wished to have the documents as supporting evidence in his defense in case he were tried by an international tribunal.[23] If he did have with him on the final flight, as is suggested or asserted by several persons claiming to know it for fact, a file of correspondence with Churchill, such exchanges, if brought out in anything resembling a court, might have proved very embarrassing to the British prime minister. Possibly the Duce hoped to reach Switzerland and enjoy political asylum and there publish a defense of his regime. What is certain is that to the end Mussolini had the urge to write. He may possibly have hoped to hold out in the Valtellina for some time and to use the papers for a final work which would help to assure his place in history.

These especially selected documents, the very cream of the private papers as Mussolini himself judged them to be, were said to have been

21. Silvestri, *Mussolini, Graziani e l'antifascismo,* p. 24.

Quinto Navarra, *Memorie del cameriere di Mussolini* (Milan: Longanesi & C., 1946), p. 274, states that Gatti returned to Gargnano to oversee the transfer of the staff to Milan and to burn the larger part of the archives, but he does not mention any actual burning. He states, rather, that on April 23 Gatti departed, taking with him many packages of reserved documents.

See also Rachele Mussolini, *La mia vita con Benito* (Milan: Arnoldo Mondadori, 1948), p. 263.

22. Ivone Kirkpatrick, *Mussolini, A Study in Power* (New York: Hawthorne Books, Inc., 1964) p. 649, states that after Mussolini had carefully selected the files to be transported with him, the remainder were taken out in a boat and sunk in Lake Garda. No reference is provided for this statement which is in glaring contradiction to the bulk of the evidence.

23. As suggested by Charles F. Delzell, *Mussolini's Enemies: The Italian Anti-Fascist Resistance* (Princeton: Princeton University Press, 1961), p. 541.

Article 29 of the Long Terms of Armistice stipulated: "Benito Mussolini, his Chief Fascist associates and all persons suspected of having committed war crimes or analogous offenses whose names appear on lists to be communicated by the United Nations will forthwith be apprehended and surrendered into the hands of the United Nations. Any instructions given by the United Nations for this purpose will be complied with."

packed into two zinc boxes. The one, bound with iron bands, was taken from the Feltrinelli Villa to Milan by the Prefect Gatti at Mussolini's express order. It is asserted that this case contained the Duce's correspondence with Churchill, Roosevelt, Hitler, Laval, and Pétain, that it constituted a veritable synthesis of the diplomatic activity of fascism. The other zinc case, it is said, contained autographs of letters and speeches by Mussolini and had been sent on to Milan earlier.[24] There must, however, have been other boxes, bundles or packages of Mussolini's Papers which were removed from the Feltrinelli Villa at the time of the move to Milan. The two metal cases so frequently referred to are less than what can be established with certainty as having reached the prefecture of Milan.[25]

The Meeting with Resistance Leaders on April 25

On April 25, Mussolini met with spokesmen of the Resistance in the palace of Cardinal Schuster to discuss the possibilities of surrender. Before going to the meeting, Mussolini drew out some of the documents from one of the metal boxes and packed them into two large leather briefcases. Carlo Silvestri assisted Mussolini in making this selection. He assures us that these documents constituted proof of how much the republican government had done to avoid civil war, and to avoid complete submission to the Germans. They also offered proof, says Silvestri, of the English malevolence which led to the war, and information on the massacres which were being planned by the Communists.[26] It is said that before the meeting, Mussolini declared to his son Vittorio: "I'm going to prove, with Hitler's letters, that I saved Switzerland from invasion." [27]

In making the movements to Milan and thence to Como and beyond,

24. Bruno Spampanato, *Contromemoriale*, 3 vols., vol. 3, *Il segreto del nord* (Rome: Copyright by "Illustrato," 1952), p. 272.

See also Ezio Saini, *La notte di Dongo* (Rome: Casa Editrice Librario Corso, 1950), p. 143. Saini's work is a very thorough monograph on Mussolini's capture and execution and on the disappearance of the treasure of Dongo, and it also has considerable information on the fate of the final portion of Mussolini's private archives. Saini's book has the merit of making full use of the evidence which Gen. Leone Zingales was able to gather in his initial, judicial investigation of these matters.

25. Cf. note 21 above. Navarra states clearly that Gatti took with him "many packages of classified documents" (*molti pacchi di documenti riservati*).

26. Carlo Silvestri, *Mussolini, Graziani e l'antifascismo*, pp. 227–28.

27. Laszlo Bush-Fekete, "The Last Four Days of Mussolini," *Life*, January 12, 1948, p. 94. The author's source is not given. Vittorio himself merely records a discussion about the documents with his father who said that he had some of them with him in a brief case, and mentioned that it would be better if they were not all in one group. Vittorio Mussolini, *Vita con mio padre* (Milan: Arnoldo Mondadori, 1957), pp. 217–18.

Mussolini not only arranged to bring numerous documents, he also took along a great deal of currency. At some time before leaving Milan, Mussolini made some very heavy withdrawals from the banks which carried the accounts of the Italian Social Republic.[28] When Mussolini's secretary, Gatti, packed up selected documents from Mussolini's archives at Gargnano on April 23, he was seen to pack three suitcases with sixty-five kilograms of gold and banknotes.[29] This currency came to be known as the "Treasure of Dongo." The fate of the documents, of the treasure, and of Mussolini himself were destined to become inextricably intertwined.

Time was running short for Mussolini and for the German forces in Italy as well. Without informing their Italian allies the Germans had for some time been negotiating with Allied Force Headquarters for a military surrender.[30] In moving the capital to Milan, Mussolini had hoped to shake off the coils of German guardianship which had grown ever tighter. Early in April the Germans had sent a special SS detail to Gargnano under the command of *Hauptstürmfüher* Otto Kisnat of the SD. His orders were to prevent Mussolini from fleeing abroad; even to use force in case Mussolini attempted to escape into Switzerland. The Duce was practically the prisoner of SS Captain Kisnat who accompanied him to Milan and there obtained his promise not to remain but to return to Gargnano. Kisnat himself returned to Gargnano for a few days to attend to some personal matters, but he left a detail to guard Mussolini, a squad of twelve men under the immediate command of Lieutenant Birzer. He warned Mussolini not to attempt to flee into Switzerland.[31]

The news from the front spelled disaster. Allied forces reached the Po on April 23; Tito's Partisans occupied Fiume; Genoa revolted. Mussolini at this time was apparently keeping his options open. One course was for the leaders of the Italian Social Republic to seek asylum in Switzerland, a course which was strongly advocated by the former Minister

28. Testimony of Pellegrino Giampietro, minister of finance in the neofascist regime, as reported in Saini, *Notte di Dongo,* pp. 110, 204.

29. Navarra, *Memorie del cameriere,* pp. 274–75.

30. Allen W. Dulles, *The Secret Surrender* (New York, Evanston, and London: Harper & Row, 1966), pp. 119, 183.

31. Ricciotti Lazzero, "Un passo verso la verità sulla morte di Mussolini: Dongo," *Epoca,* August 11, 1968 [pp. 41–43].

This is a very important and detailed article on Mussolini's last days, based on the "collaboration" of numerous participants and witnesses who are listed at the end of the article, plus research extending to the Pentagon files and to the National Archives. Kisnat is apparently himself the source regarding his role.

The article is in three parts: 1, August 11; 2, August 18; and 3, August 25, 1968. No page numbers are given. Hence they are determined by interpolating between the printed page numbers of the respective issues of *Epoca.* Hereafter citations to the article will read: Lazzero, "Un passo," the part and its date, and the page number in square brackets.

of the Interior, Buffarini-Guidi. Another option appeared to be that last-ditch stand in the Valtellina which Mussolini discussed on April 21 with Graziani, who scoffed at the idea, and with Pavolini, who promised to assemble the necessary forces. The next day the Duce ordered that preparations for such a final Fascist defense be expedited.

A third course which seems to have crossed Mussolini's mind was to prepare to face a trial. On April 23, the same day on which he sent Gatti to Gargnano to gather up his papers, Mussolini drafted a letter to Churchill. This draft reminded the prime minister of some of his former words about Italy and asked, not for clemency, but merely for the opportunity for Mussolini to justify and defend himself. The Duce mentioned that he knew of the negoiations that were going on between Great Britain and the United States with Germany. The letter assured Churchill that Mussolini could offer most interesting documentation. The draft was apparently typed out by Mussolini himself who made arrangements for its forwarding over a British consulate in Switzerland, but he held back the order for delivery.[32]

Still another option for Mussolini was to see what terms might be arranged with his Italian enemies. Shortly after his move to Milan, Mussolini made certain approaches through Cardinal Schuster, Archbishop of Milan, to the political leadership of the Resistance, the Committee of National Liberation of Upper Italy (CLNAI).[33]

The CLNAI, although still underground, held a plenary session on April 25. In response to Mussolini's peace feelers it reiterated the demand for unconditional surrender. It issued a decree proclaiming the insurrection and the transfer of all political power to itself or to the various local Committees of National Liberation. An amendment of the next day added the Corps of Volunteers of Liberty (Corpo Volontari della Libertà or CVL) as a third element of revolutionary political power.

A second decree established popular courts of assize, tribunals of war, and commissions of justice to deal with those guilty of criminal acts during the civil war against the patriots. By implication this appeared to mean Mussolini's execution, for article 5 stipulated the death penalty for members of the neofascist government and hierarchs, for those guilty of suppressing constitutional guaranties, of creating the Fascist regime, and guilty of betraying the fate of the country. The original Fascists, the organizers of the "insurrection of 1922," were to be punished according

32. Lazzero, "Un passo," 1, August 11, 1968 [pp. 49–50] where the text is printed. The agent was SS Lt. Franz Spoegler, a man whom Mussolini felt he could trust. The text apparently was stranded in Germany when the war ended.

33. Delzell, Mussolini's Enemies, p. 523; Deakin, Brutal Friendship, pp. 776–77, 780, 795, 797–98.

to the Criminal Code of 1889; those guilty of crimes against the Italian state since September 8, 1943, were to be punished in accordance with the laws of war effective at the time.[34]

In midafternoon the insurrectional strike began. Both workers and businessmen gathered at the industrial plants to guard them against German sabotage, the threatened scorched earth policy. Others simply went home. A strange hush fell over the city.[35] It was the calm before the outbreak of the revolutionary storm.

Late in the afternoon the CLNAI met again and designated three of its members for the discussion with Mussolini. These were: Gen. Raffaele Cadorna, who held the position of military adviser to the CLNAI; Achille Marazza, representative of the Christian Democrats; and Riccardo Lombardi of the Party of Action. These spokesmen of the Resistance were given closely binding instructions: to demand unconditional surrender; to state that Fascist troops which surrendered would be treated in accordance with international law; to limit the discussion to one hour. If Mussolini agreed to surrender, he was to be held in the office of Cardinal Schuster.[36]

Mussolini arrived at the palace of the Cardinal Archbishop at about 5:00 P.M. He was accompanied by Marshal Rodolfo Graziani, commander of the armed forces of the Republic of Salò; by the minister of the interior (Zerbino); by the undersecretary of the presidential office (Barracù); the prefect of Milan (Bassi); and by Gian Riccardo Cella, an industrialist who had served as a go-between with Cardinal Schuster. The Resistance spokesmen made their appearance an hour or so later.

There were no salutes or handshakes. Mussolini asked what conditions would be offered. Marazza bluntly told him, in accordance with the instructions of the CLNAI, that they demanded unconditional surrender. Cadorna stated, however, that the terms would preclude a slaughter of the Fascist militia, would spare the families of the Fascist leaders, and assure the treatment of members of the diplomatic corps according to the norms of international law.

When Graziani declared that they would not agree to a capitulation behind the backs of their German allies, that they could not repeat the betrayal of September 8 (1943), Marazza and Cardinal Schuster broke the news that the Germans had already begun discussing terms of surrender. Mussolini appeared to be greatly incensed at this information. He

34. Delzell, *Mussolini's Enemies*, pp. 524–25, citing Catalano, *Storia del CLNAI*, pp. 413–19. Delzell provides a translation of a good part of the decree.

35. Massimo Salvadori, *The Labour and the Wounds: A Personal Chronicle of One Man's Fight for Freedom* (London: Pall Mall Press, 1958), pp. 224–25.

36. Delzell, *Mussolini's Enemies*, p. 525.

blurted out that the Germans had always treated the Italians like servants, that at the end they had betrayed him.

What outcome would the Fascist leaders expect? In explaining that the Allies had agreed on granting all members of the Fascist armed forces the treatment of prisoners of war, General Cadorna immediately added the qualification that this did not apply to specific war criminals. He records that the atmosphere again became very strained at this point.[37]

This was the stumbling block for Mussolini. He had mentioned that he accepted the discussion because various guaranties had been offered for himself, for the Fascists and for their families. He now faced the option of giving himself up to face a speedy trial by the revolutionary forces and probably execution, or possibly to be turned over to the Allies in accordance with the Long Terms of Armistice. Such a course would, however, have drastically cut down the further shedding of blood in Italy, and Cardinal Schuster urged him strongly to accept it. At the end of the discussion he asked for an hour in which to decide.

The Cardinal was so confident that Mussolini would return that he had a bed prepared for him in the palace. But after waiting for well over an hour, the Resistance leaders insisted on telephoning to the prefecture, demanding that Mussolini reply or return to the archiepiscopal palace to give himself up. Much to the surprise of everyone there, the word came back that Mussolini had departed and had left the order for a negative answer.[38]

The Flight to Como and Beyond, April 25–26

Back at the prefecture there was a great hustle and bustle in the crowded courtyard. Mussolini was offered all sorts of advice. Some urged

37. Raffaele Cadorna, *La riscossa: Dal 25 luglio alla liberazione* (Milan: Rizzoli, 1948), p. 250.

38. For this conference we have the testimony of three participants: Ildefonso Cardinal Schuster, *Gli ultimi tempi di un regime* (Milan: "La Via," 1946), pp. 158–70; Cadorna, *La riscossa*, pp. 250–53; Graziani, *Ho difeso la patria*, pp. 507–14.

There are useful secondary accounts in Delzell, *Mussolini's Enemies*, pp. 525–27 (from the point of view of the Resistance, and with careful attention to the background on the revolutionary side), and in Deakin, *Brutual Friendship*, pp. 807–10 (with focus of attention on Mussolini).

Franco Bandini's book, *Le ultime 95 ore di Mussolini*, 3d ed. (Milan: Sugar Editore, 1963), is a very detailed study of the last 95 hours and 10 minutes of the Duce which are reckoned from 5:00 P.M. April 25 at the cardinal's palace to 4:10 P.M. of April 28 when Mussolini was shot near the gate of the Villa Belmonte on the outskirts of Giulino di Mezzegra.

Bandini's interpretation of the meeting with the Resistance leaders (pp. 56–76) is quite at variance with most of the other accounts and it conflicts with some of the testimony of participants. Bandini asserts that Mussolini was master of the situation in that strange that they remain in Milan and make a last stand in the prefecture. Some, perhaps, even urged a return to Cardinal Schuster's palace. But Mussolini feared a trap. The memory of July 25 was still vivid and he favored almost any course over the risk of a new imprisonment. The snap decision was made to move on to Como and a column of some passenger automobiles and trucks was hastily organized. A unit of the *Muti* Brigade, which had two armored cars, provided some escort. But that was not all. In making the move to Milan, Mussolini had not been wholly successful in getting away from his German guardians. The SS unit, which had served as a personal guard at Gargnano and very effectively controlled his movements, had followed to Milan and now was at hand, under command of Lt. Fritz Birzer, to make up another part of the escort. Strict orders had been issued to Birzer to stay immediately attached to the Duce and to make sure that he arrived within the borders of the Reich.

Before leaving the prefecture, Mussolini relieved the Italian soldiers of their oath of loyalty and took farewell of some of his followers who chose to remain. It is recorded that when he first came down from his office he had a tommy gun slung over his shoulder and at this point he entrusted the two leather cases of documents to a certain Carradori. Pavolini, secretary of the Republican Fascist party, remained in Milan to organize his group of Blackshirts for the last stand in the Valtellina.[39]

The various Italian histories which deal with Mussolini's last days are in general agreement that the two metal cases of documents were loaded onto a light truck at the prefecture, a truck which was destined to

game of poker; that he was better informed than the others there; that Mussolini, the consummate actor and politician, was only putting on an act in his outburst of indignation against the Germans (pp. 59–60). He explains that on April 14 Mussolini had been informed of the German peace initiatives by Wolff, leader of the SS in Italy. Bandini dismisses the talk about a last, heroic stand in the Valtellina as mere talk; he insists that Mussolini's plan from the start had been to seek political asylum in Switzerland.

While there is much evidence to indicate that Mussolini had Switzerland in mind from the start, it may have been only as one alternative. But Bandini's assertion that Mussolini was master of the situation quite leaves out the testimony regarding his physical and psychic deterioration, and the evidence that he was surprised and overtaken by events.

39. See Giorgio Pini and Duilio Susmel, *Mussolini, l'uomo e l'opera*, vol. 4, *Dall'impero alla repubblica* (Florence: La Fenice, 1955), pp. 517–19. This four-volume work is inspired with great sympathy toward Mussolini and fascism, but it embodies a very great deal of painstaking research, it is thoroughly documented, and is rich in the detail which it presents.

See also Graziani, *Ho difeso la patria*, pp. 511–12. Massimo Salvadori, *The Labour and the Wounds*, pp. 225–26, gives a picture of the confused situation shortly after Mussolini's departure.

Bandini, *Ultime 95 ore*, pp. 81–83, describes the confused scene, but considers the move to Como, near the Swiss border, as carrying out a decision already made by Mussolini before the meeting with the Resistance leaders.

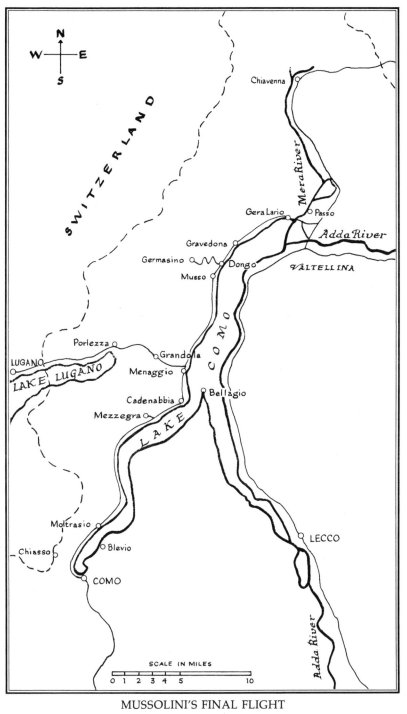

MUSSOLINI'S FINAL FLIGHT
179

disappear by being intercepted by Partisans between Milan and Como. Gatti prepared the metal cases and supervised the loading onto the truck which was known as the "Balilla." In addition to the cases of documents the vehicle carried the driver, a police agent, and Maria Righini, the personal chambermaid of Mussolini. Vittorio Mussolini was the last to leave the prefecture and followed some time after the light truck with the documents.[40]

The truck never got to Como, it is certain. But only one of the metal cases left the prefecture, and there must have been other packages of documents which went along in the convoy or reached Como in some fashion—these in addition to the two leather cases of documents which Mussolini kept close to his person.

The Duce and his column reached Como about 9:00 in the evening of April 25 where they were received by Celio, the local Fascist prefect, and by Buffarini-Guidi, the former minister of the interior who had gone on ahead. Mussolini promptly asked about the light truck and the documents. He was greatly disturbed to learn that they had not arrived.[41]

Apparently the truck broke down somewhere near Garbagnate. Maria, the chambermaid, managed to make her way to Como and report the breakdown. Mussolini then summoned Gatti who retraced the whole route back to Milan but found no trace of the missing truck.[42]

One of the metal cases remained in the prefecture in Milan and for this we have documentary evidence of greater weight than incidental mentionings by Italian journalists. When P.W.B. Unit 12, the Bates and Costas team for North Italy, visited the prefecture on May 7, they found a variety of documentary records which had been assembled from various departments in the last days of the Republic of Salò.[43] Bates reported:

In the storeroom on the right side of the courtyard there were two boxes of documents: the first consisted of communiqués and telegrams from various offices of the Fascist Republic; they proved to be of no interest; the second box was a light metal trunk, filled with documents belonging to the Mussolini archives. These documents, part of the Segreteria Particolare del Duce, consisted of the following items: discourses, letters, communiqués, prefaces to books, articles, interviews, varied items, composed in the years from 1922 through 1940 and presented in

40. Bandini, *Ultime 95 ore*, pp. 84–85; Spampanato, *Contromemoriale*, 3:272; Saini, *Notte di Dongo*, p. 143.

41. Graziani, *Ho difeso la patria*, p. 515 (the reference here is to one case only).

42. Spampanato, *Contromemoriale*, 3:274.

Cf. Bandini, *Ultime 95 ore*, p. 85; Pini and Susmel, *Mussolini*, 4:520.

According to Ermanno Amicucci, *I 600 giorni di Mussolini* (Rome: Editrice "Faro," 1948), pp. 267–68, the light truck had a breakdown; its contents were sacked; but some things were recovered and brought on to Como.

43. Cf. chap. 3, note 39.

manuscripts and in typewritten copies corrected by the Duce (all in blue folders); a second group is made up of the manuscripts of telegrams sent by Mussolini, 1922–39 inclusive; index lists of all these materials are included (the telegrams and index lists are contained in pink folders).[44]

When Bates and Costas made a return inspection of the prefecture on May 31, they noted that the cases had been transferred to a second storeroom at the rear of the courtyard, first floor. Here they found additional records and they reported:

There was a box of papers and a small amount of documents lying on the floor. These files were made up of various items: there were about forty files from the Mussolini archives, largely carteggio ordinario, which contained letters, requests, denunciations addressed to Mussolini or to Gatti; files of notes for Mussolini; notes of Mussolini's April audiences at Milan; military bulletins from the Ministry of War; documents representing the political, economic and military reports made by the Prefecture during recent months. Seven files were removed on May 7 from this storeroom and consulted by P.W.B.; this was done with the consent of the Prefect. They were returned on May 31.[45]

The further vicissitudes of the various boxes of documents from Mussolini's archives which remained in the prefecture of Milan after April 25 are not clear. Bates's report tells us only that they were left in the custody of the prefect, Lombardi, and that the only protection was what was afforded by the general guard at the entrance to the prefecture.[46] These files may have got into the hands of the Partisans who for a time were the ruling element in North Italy. They may have been taken over by the Joint Allied Intelligence Agency, the organization which we are soon to describe. Another possibility is that they were recovered by the Italian State Archives without ever having been microfilmed.[47]

What of Mussolini's actions at Como? Donna Rachele's published autobiography states that she did not see her husband in Como but that he sent her a letter mentioning that he and his party would have to move

44. "Italian Documents Section, P.W.B., Northern Italy Assignment (Activity April 27–May 31," p. 5. This is a twenty-eight-page report signed by Blanchard W. Bates, forwarded in despatch no. 1866, July 6, 1945 (865.414/7-645), Central Files of the Department of State, Record Group 59, National Archives.

45. Ibid., pp. 5–6.

46. Riccardo Lombardi, who had represented the Party of Action in the discussion with Mussolini on April 25, was made prefect of the province of Milan by the CLNAI the next day. When Colonel Poletti, representing Allied military government, arrived in Milan on April 29, he gave tentative approval to the appointments made by the CLNAI. See Delzell, *Mussolini' Enemies*, p. 529.

47. Bandini, *Ultime 95 ore*, p. 98, fn. 28 refers to twenty-two cases regained by the *Archivio di Stato*, citing an article by Roberto Mario in *Tempo* of October 7, 1950. That article has not been available to me.

on to the Valtellina, and he urged her to try to cross into Switzerland with the younger children. She adds that he repeated the same advice to her that night over the telephone. Sometime during that night of April 25–26, she records, she drove to the frontier but the Swiss police refused to let her cross, although Benito had told her that the Swiss authorities had promised him that they would admit her. The monumental biography of Mussolini by Pini and Susmel, the "official version" as Bandini calls it, follows closely Donna Rachele's account.[48]

Bandini presents a quite different view of the night of April 25–26 at Como. He insists that Mussolini saw his wife at the prefecture of Como and that this was their farewell rather than a week earlier at Gargnano. A year before writing her autobiography *Signora* Mussolini told a newspaper correspondent:

What displeases me greatly is to have lost the correspondence with Benito, the package of our private correspondence. There was also the file on Ciano—Buffarini-Guidi, the manuscript for the *Storia di un anno* and the record of imprisonment on Maddalena. Mussolini gave me these at our farewell two days before the tragedy. Later I left them in a house in Como and they disappeared from there. There was nothing that I could do but denounce the proprietress to the sequestrator. I was able to keep only the last letter which my husband sent me before taking the road toward the Valtellina.[49]

Bandini refers also to a file of correspondence between Mussolini and Churchill. This file, it is stated, was in a black leather folder which Mussolini gave to his wife on April 24 [sic] along with other documents and objects of great value while Donna Rachele had taken refuge at the Villa Mantero with the minor children, Romano and Anna Maria. In case of threats to her safety Mussolini advised his wife to make contact with the English; the file of correspondence would serve as a safe-conduct.[50]

48. Rachele Mussolini, *Vita con Benito*, pp. 267–71; *Mussolini*, 4:520–21.

49. Bandini, *Ultime 95 ore*, pp. 97–98, citing an interview of April 1947 by Federico Patellani with Donna Rachele published initially in *Tempo* of May 8, 1947. Lazzero, "Un passo," 2, August 18, 1968 [p. 45] also states that Rachele saw Benito then.

50. Bandini, *Ultime 95 ore*, pp. 85–86, fn. 26, citing an article by Pietro Giordanino in *Tempo* of April 22, 1950. The date, as is stated by Bandini, should, of course, be April 25–26.

It is not clear exactly what documents and items of personal property Donna Rachele had with her in Como or were seized there. In *Vita con Benito*, pp. 273–74, she mentions only that on learning of Mussolini's death she consulted the children who agreed that it would be well to notify the CLN of their presence in Como. Shortly thereafter three men made a search of the house and the next day, April 29, she and the children were taken to the Questura. She makes no mention here of documents.

There is a signed statement by the prefect of Como dated April 29, 1945 which lists thirty-one objects of value, the property of Mussolini, which were discovered on April 28 by the Patriots Arnaldo Visco, Mario Bianchi, and Vincenzo Cassarino. See Saini, *Notte di Dongo*, document no. 16, pp. 239–40. There is no mention here of documents.

At Como there was renewed argument among the Fascist bigwigs as to the next course. There now appeared to be two options open to Mussolini. One was to rally the Fascist forces available and make the final heroic stand in the Valtellina, or possibly to move still further on and join the Germans. The other course was to seek refuge in Switzerland, a course for which Mussolini believed he had made diplomatic preparations. If a firm decision for a military action had been made, there was, at this time, a substantial superiority of Fascist forces over the patriots in the immediate zone. Along the road northward to Moltrasio there were only 104 Partisans. Against these were some 5,000 Fascists in the area of Como, and in the city itself there was a Black Brigade of some 900 men. There was also the Black Brigade *Manganiello* which had but recently arrived from Tuscany with tanks and armored cars. Within a few kilometers of Como were the barracks of Italian and German SS units, about 500 men.[51]

Mussolini, however, did not favor the military action. He did not try to rally the Fascist forces in the area. He did not wait for Pavolini's troop which was expected at 5:00 A.M. but simply gave orders to his adjutant, Casalinuovo, to meet Pavolini.[52] Mussolini tried to start off in his car without any armed escort and accompanied only by Bombacci and the *Federale* (provincial party secretary) Porta. Lieutenant Birzer, however, suspected something. He blocked the departure of the Duce's auto which was thus diverted northward along the highway that skirts the western shoreline of Lake Como. After Mussolini's departure, Graziani heard from Buffarini-Guidi that it had been decided that the members of the Fascist government would try to get into Switzerland by way of the pass of Porlezza.[53]

This day, April 26, was a day wasted in futile moves and countermoves, a period of increasing doubt, panic and despair among the shrinking band of Mussolini's followers. For the Duce himself it was a day of complete frustration. The net outcome for him was to learn that all roads into Switzerland were closed.

Mussolini and his little party plus his German escort appear to have reached Menaggio about 5:30 A.M. where Birzer was able to add ten German soldiers to his platoon. General Graziani, General Bonomi, commander of the air force of the Republic of Salò, Mussolini's personal secretary Gatti, and the ministers who had followed from Milan to Como reached Menaggio an hour or so later. Only shortly after their arrival

---

51. Lazzero, "Un passo," 2, August 18, 1968 [p. 46]. Bandini, *Ultime 95 ore*, p. 139, estimates the number of Fascist troops in the area at four thousand.

52. Lazzero, "Un passo," 2, August 18, 1968 [p. 47].

53. Graziani, *Ho difeso la patria*, pp. 516–17; See also Pini and Susmel, *Mussolini*, 4:521; Bandini, *Ultime 95 ore*, p. 135.

Gatti gave the group the order to move back down the road to Cadenabbia. The large number of people gathered in Menaggio, he said, were attracting too much attention. This strange order, which most certainly emanated from the Duce himself, provoked strong murmurings among the hierarchs. Mussolini, apparently, wished to try to reach Switzerland by way of Grandola and Porlezza. The less conspicuous his party, the better, he believed, would be his chances of crossing the frontier.

By this time Graziani had had enough. He realized that his services would not be needed to command the last ditch stand which Mussolini talked about but did not really intend. He bethought himself of his troops, the Army of Liguria, and took the road back to Como, hoping to get back to his command post at Mandello in order to arrange a surrender. General Bonomi shared Graziani's views and went back with him.[54]

The civilian Fascist officials at Cadenabbia decided to return to Menaggio, to confront Mussolini, and to demand a clarification of the situation. They seem to have been willing to follow the orders of their Duce but they wished to know what those orders were. On this their second move northward toward Menaggio, Pavolini caught up with them. Surprised to learn that the Duce had departed from Como for Menaggio, Pavolini left his troop in Como and highballed up the road to find Mussolini. He too wanted a clarification of the situation, a statement of his orders.[55]

Mussolini himself managed to get a short and disturbed sleep at Menaggio, disturbed among other things by the arrival of his mistress, Claretta Petacci. She and her family apparently had tried to slip across the frontier into Switzerland but failed because their guides did not show up. They then attached themselves to Mussolini's party. At about 10:00 A.M. Mussolini indicated that they should move up the lateral road which leads to Grandola and thence to Porlezza and to the Swiss frontier. Meanwhile the Fascist hierarchs who had retraced their way from Cadenabbia also followed the lateral road and overtook Mussolini. The whole party stopped for a time at the Miravalle Inn and had a meal during the course of which Mussolini produced some documents showing Swiss

54. Graziani, *Ho difeso la patria,* pp. 517–19.

At Como Graziani consulted with his subordinate generals and then, on learning that Wolff was at the Villa Locatelli in Cernobbio, he sought out the SS general and turned over to him the power to surrender the Italian forces (Graziani, pp. 522–24). Dulles, *Secret Surrender,* p. 194, prints an English translation of this transfer of power.

Graziani was later saved from a lynching by the courageous intervention of General Cadorna. He was tried by the postwar government of Italy and acquitted, and thus was enabled to write his memoirs.

55. Bandini, *Ultime 95 ore,* pp. 145–47.

agreement to the exodus of Fascist leaders and their families into Switzerland.[56]

According to Bandini this meal at the Miravalle Inn was at about two o'clock in the afternoon. Mussolini, he explains, had already tried to shake off his German escort and, accompanied by only a few persons, had tried to sneak out of the rear of the hotel and to head for the frontier. Once again Lieutenant Birzer thwarted Mussolini's attempt to get to the border.[57] While the main party halted at Grandola, Buffarini-Guidi and Tarchi drove westward on the road to Porlezza. At this juncture, while Mussolini was awaiting word from these two, *Hauptsturmführer* Kisnat, who had the full responsibility for guarding the Duce, caught up with him. When he asked what those two were doing up the road, Mussolini candidly replied that they had gone to negotiate with the frontier authorities for passage into Switzerland for Mussolini and his followers.[58] Buffarini and Tarchi did not even reach the Swiss frontier but were arrested by the Italian Finance Guards who had come out openly on the side of the Partisans. One man of the party got back to Grandola to report this failure to reach Switzerland. After this misadventure it was clear to everyone that none of the Fascist chieftans would be able to make such an escape.

It was a gloomy afternoon for the Fascist hierarchs and Mussolini waiting in the hotel. Elena Curti Cucciati, an illegitimate daughter of the Duce, had also joined the group. Claretta Petacci mistook her for a rival mistress; she yelled so loud at Benito that he had to shut the window. He was now utterly tired out. For some thirty hours he had had almost no sleep. He stumbled and fell in the room and badly bruised his cheek. Late in the afternoon he gave the word to move back down the valley to Menaggio where, he said, they would meet with Pavolini and his troop of Blackshirts.[59]

What of Pavolini and his actions since Mussolini left him at the prefecture in Milan following the meeting at Cardinal Schuster's palace? He had done very well. In Milan he had assembled some two to three thousand men drawn from eight Black Brigades of the various areas of the Republic of Salò, and two hundred military trucks. They reached Como in good order. Here Pavolini got the disconcerting news that Mussolini had moved on to Menaggio. Pavolini left his troop in Como; he took an armored car to find the Duce; and on the road, as we have noted,

56. Pini and Susmel, *Mussolini*, 4:523–24.

57. Bandini, *Ultime 95 ore*, pp. 153–59.

58. Lazzero, "Un passo," 2, August 18, 1968 [p. 52]. Here again the source apparently is Kisnat.

59. Bandini, *Ultime 95 ore*, pp. 162–63.

he caught up with the Fascist officials whom Gatti had sent back to Cadenabbia.[60]

The bare facts of Pavolini's activities for the rest of the day and night of April 26 are clear, but their interpretation is a matter of basic disagreement. He overtook the Duce and talked with him; he went back to Como to speak to his Blackshirts; late during the night Pavolini rejoined Mussolini at Menaggio. Only a dozen or so of his troop volunteered for the last ditch stand. About 4:00 A.M. of April 27 Mussolini learned of this forlorn hope.

The "official version," the encyclopedic life of Mussolini by Pini and Susmel, throws the responsibility on Mussolini's followers for the failure to reach the Valtellina for a final, heroic stand where the Duce and his devoted ones would go down with the Fascist banner waving high and proudly. They failed him in his last hours of need and like rats deserted the sinking ship. It is implied that Pavolini's absence for several hours while searching for Mussolini was a great mistake: a whole day was lost by the absurd halt at Como. A general psychological collapse took place among the troops there during Pavolini's absence. With a determined leader, Pini and Susmel have stated, those forces might have reached the Duce; the whole outcome might have been different.[61]

Bandini views the actions of Mussolini during this day in an utterly different light. Pavolini, he shows, had to search out Mussolini, who failed to wait for the rendezvous or to leave instructions. Which way was Mussolini going when Pavolini got to him: northward along the highway on the shore of Lake Como and toward the Valtellina, or toward the Swiss frontier? There is no record of the discussion which took place between Pavolini and the Duce about midday of April 26. Both men were shot two days later and the content of their conversation is purely a matter of conjecture. The probability, argues Bandini, is that the discussion was a bitter and protracted one, with a clear indication that Mussolini's aim was to save his own skin. When Pavolini got back to his troops in Como he thought first of them and helped to save their lives by assisting in the negotiations for a surrender. But with a few determined followers he heeded the call of loyalty and returned to Mussolini's side. Once again, in the bitter words of Bandini, as has so often happened in the history of modern Italy, the failure of nerves was with the leader, the cowardice and betrayal of responsibility was at the top, and not on the part of the followers.[62] The "official version" will not stand up against the penetrating critique of Bandini.

60. Pini and Susmel, *Mussolini*, 4:522; Bandini, *Ultime 95 ore*, pp. 145–46.
61. *Mussolini*, 4:524.
62. Bandini, *Ultime 95 ore*, pp. 140–42, 146–50.
Interestingly enough Lazzero barely mentions Pavolini's meeting with Mussolini at

Sometime after midnight of April 26–27, Mussolini summoned Captain Kisnat and asked about the strength of Lieutenant Birzer's platoon. He reported that he had thirty SD men plus the ten police troops he had picked up in Menaggio. Mussolini then declared they would head for the Valtellina. He still had with him the currency and gold which he had packed in Milan. One metal case of documents and numerous boxes of papers had been left in the prefecture of Milan. Mussolini had lost at least one zinc case of documents between Milan and Como: he may have given a bundle of documents to his wife in Como. Others possibly may have been left there. But he still had with him the two leather cases of records which Carlo Silvestri had assisted in selecting at the prefecture in Milan.

The Capture of Mussolini, April 27

Early on April 27 the caravan of Mussolini and his followers moved off again, northward along the highway which hugs the western shore of Lake Como. While at Menaggio they attached themselves to a German antiaircraft unit under the command of a Lieutenant or Captain Fallmeyer. This group comprised about 175 men. They had forty motor vehicles (one armored car, some automobiles and some trucks) and were hoping to reach Merano in the Tyrol by way of the Stelvio Pass. What with the German escort under Lieutenant Birzer, the fleeing Fascists had a rather formidable guard. Mussolini took his seat in the armored car, and along with him rode Carradori with the two leather cases of documents.[63]

At about 7:30 A.M. the column with the armored car in the lead reached Musso. The Partisans apparently had strewn nails in the road; the lead car blew a tire and a bit further on a tree trunk across the road brought the column to a halt. Some shots were fired from the hills.[64] At this point a Partisan leader stepped forward, gave a military salute, and started pourparlers with Fallmeyer. This patriot was "Pedro," from

Grandola and attributes no particular significance to it ("Un passo," 3, August 25, 1968 [pp. 43, 45]). That author tends to follow the "official" version and to place the blame on Pavolini for the failure to join up with the Duce with his whole force at Menaggio. He states that Pavolini started off from Milan with some three thousand men, sixty trucks, machine guns, mortars, and small cannon, but failed to start off in time to meet Mussolini in Como at 5:00 A.M., a failure to which he attributes great importance. Mussolini, however, had already left Como before the hour set for the meeting with Pavolini's forces.

63. Pini and Susmel, *Mussolini*, 4:526–27; Bandini, *Ultime 95 ore*, pp. 172–73, quoting a report of Sergeant (*brigadiere*) Giorgio Buffelli of the Finance Guards, dated February 10, 1946.

64. Pini and Susmel, *Mussolini*, 4:527.

whom we have a firsthand account of the arrest of Mussolini.[65] He was commander of the Fifty-second (Garibaldi) Brigade.[66]

"Pedro" introduced himself as the Partisan commander and stated that he had orders to halt any enemy column and not let it pass farther. The Luftwaffe officer,[67] who spoke some Italian, declared that his orders were to press on to Merano to continue the fight against the Allies. But there does not seem to have been much fight left in him at this point. "Pietro" (Michele Moretti), had descended to Musso with Pedro, and also the Swiss, Alois Hofmann, who served as an interpreter on the Italian side, but there were, at this time, only about eight other Partisans at Musso, and perhaps twenty more could be called down from the mountains. "Bill" (Urbano Lazzaro), second in command under Pedro, joined up, and while Pedro was talking to the German, walked along the column to estimate its strength. There were twenty-nine trucks, ten autos, an armored car, and about two hundred men, considerably better armed than the Partisans. Pedro's only hope was to bluff and to stall for time so that the other Partisan units along the road could throw up barricades and mine the highway at bridges and other critical points.[68]

65. Pier Luigi Bellini delle Stelle (Pedro) and Urbano Lazzaro (Bill) *Dongo ultima azione* (Milan: Arnoldo Mondadori, 1962). Hereafter cited as Bellini, *Dongo ultima azione*. Although the book was not published until seventeen years after the events described, Bellini had at hand his contemporary notes and Lazzaro his contemporary manuscript, considerable portions of which are quoted directly. These quoted passages are in italics. On several occasions prior to the book's appearance, both men had granted interviews regarding their respective roles.

66. Each Partisan took a battle name and his true name was not known to the others lest it be revealed under torture on capture. A regular Partisan division consisted of three brigades of three battalions each. A battalion was made up of three detachments (*distaccamenti*).

The Fifty-second (Garibaldi) Brigade was rather irregular in its organization for it was made up of four detachments: "Puecher," "Mogni," "Gramsci," and "Cravero." According to the CVL regulations of April 1945 it was more the equivalent of a battalion.

The "Puecher" detachment, most directly involved in the capture of Mussolini, was composed of three squads of ten or eleven men each. It took its name from Giancarlo Puecher Passavalle who had been shot by the Fascists in January 1944. There was a strong Communist influence in the Fifty-second Brigade. The "Puecher" detachment had been reorganized under the leadership of "Pietro" (Michele Moretti), a Communist political commissar, and of Captain "Neri" (Luigi Canali), also a Communist.

The Fifty-second (Garibaldi) Brigade formed part of the First Lombard Division under Commandant "Nicola" (Dionisio Gambaruto). Bellini, *Dongo ultima azione*, pp. 13, 21–22; Bandini, *Ultime 95 ore*, p. 209; Cadorna, *La riscossa*, pp. 300–306.

67. The exact rank of the officer is not clear. Bellini refers to him consistently as a captain. Pini and Susmel, *Mussolini*, 4:527–28, write of him as a lieutenant. Bandini, *Ultime 95 ore*, p. 173, gives the rank of lieutenant colonel.

68. Bellini, *Dongo ultima azione*, pp. 113, 132–37.

Pedro insisted that he had to know the composition of the German column, whereupon Fallmeyer replied that there were some Italians in the armored car, but he added that he had no responsibility for them; he would negotiate for his own men only. After consultation with his staff and without too much hesitation Fallmeyer accepted Pedro's insistence that he needed the consent of his divisional commander before letting the column move on. Fallmeyer also accepted the proposal that they go together to seek Commandant "Nicola" who, Pedro said, was only a few kilometers away.

At about eight o'clock Pedro took off in a car with Fallmeyer, accompanied also by Pietro and Hofmann. It was a great bluff and a wild goose chase. The Partisan groups up the road had been alerted and were working furiously and Pedro made sure that Fallmeyer would see them. At each bridge he warned the driver to move slowly and with caution lest they detonate the mines. Pedro finally was able to speak to Nicola at Chiavenna while Hofmann in another vehicle remained with Fallmeyer. What was to have been a trip of an hour and a half was stretched out to almost six. Many more Partisans were in evidence on the return trip than earlier in the day. The protracted delay had worked enormously to the advantage of the patriots: by early afternoon there were eleven road blocks between Dongo and Ponte del Passo. Meanwhile the German troops marked time; the one thing they did was to remove the tree trunk from the road in order to be able to move forward if permission were granted.

At Dongo, Pedro stated his terms: (1) Further passage up the road was granted to the German troops and vehicles, but all of the Italians and their automobiles would surrender to the Partisans; (2) All of the vehicles were to halt at Dongo and submit to search, and the Germans would be required to show their documents proving identity; (3) At Ponte del Passo the German column would again halt and await further authorization from Partisan headquarters to proceed. In any case the Germans would be required to follow the route of the Valtellina. Fallmeyer asked for half an hour to discuss the terms with his officers.[69]

While Pedro at Dongo was waiting for the German reply, some Partisan came up and reported that there was a group of Italians at the tail end of the column, possibly including some of the ministers of the neofascist republic. Pedro then sent ten men down to Musso to prevent the escape of any Italians by turning back to Como.

Fallmeyer got back to his column at Musso at about two in the afternoon, and confirmed that the Germans might move on, the Italians

69. Ibid., 138–44.

might not. He was willing, however, to take Mussolini along if he would disguise himself as a German. Lieutenant Birzer, who since April 18 had kept such a close, protective guard about Mussolini, also recommended that course, as did several of the Italians who urged that it was the Duce's duty to save himself. Mussolini apparently was at first reluctant to make the switch; possibly it was Claretta's tears that pushed him to the decision. He donned a Luftwaffe coat and helmet and moved into the third German truck. At this same time he took back the two leather cases of documents from Carradori, and the five large suitcases of currency which Gatti, his personal secretary, had packed at Gargnano.[70]

Once the column started northward from Musso, it took only a few minutes to reach Dongo, the first check point. Some of the hierarchs now tried to escape by turning back toward Como. Pavolini yelled out that they should plunge into the waters of Lake Como; he dove in and Barracù, Utimperghe, Casalinuovo, Carradori, and Gasperini followed. The Partisans reacted quickly. The driver of the Petacci's car was shot. Carradori and Pavolini tried to hide in the water but were promptly discovered. Pavolini was shot and forced to come out although the wound was not serious.[71]

Shortly after 5:00 P.M. the inspection began, and Mussolini was soon spotted. Several individuals later claimed to have been first to recognize the Duce. Lazzaro states that while he was checking the documents of the German soldiers, some one yelled: "Bill! Bill!" It was Giuseppe Negri, the shoemaker of Dongo, who said he saw Mussolini. Bill went to the German truck where there was one person not accounted for. The Germans tried to pass him off as a drunken comrade, but Bill called out, "Cavaliere Benito Mussolini," whereupon the Duce climbed out. Bill took Mussolini's weapons, a tommy gun (*Mitra*) and a pistol, and proclaimed that he made the arrest in the name of the Italian people. At the same time he assured the Duce that if he made no resistance he would be safe. A crowd quickly gathered, shouting, "We have taken Mussolini." He was then conducted into the town hall.[72]

At the time of his capture Mussolini still had the two leather cases of documents. He carried the one into the town hall. The other was said to have been carried by his aide, Casalinuovo.[73]

Lazzaro records that the one was a large case of chestnut brown leather, and he states:

70. Pini and Susmel, *Mussolini*, 4:528; Bandini, *Ultime 95 ore*, pp. 200–203.
71. Pini and Susmel, *Mussolini*, 4:529.
72. Narrative of Urbano Lazzaro ("Bill") as printed in italics in Bellini, *Dongo ultima azione*, pp. 160–66; Buffelli's report, printed in Bandini, *Ultime 95 ore*, pp. 176–77.
Cf. Pini and Susmel, *Mussolini*, 4:530.
73. Spampanato, *Contromemoriale*, 3:274.

I took it and put it on the table. I was about to open it when Mussolini took my arm and said in a low voice: "Take note that the documents which are in there are secret. I warn you that they have a very great historical importance." [74]

Lazzaro did not reply; he remained undecided for a moment and then opened the case which had four partitions with a file in each. The first file was blue and was marked "Assigned to Benito Mussolini." Lazzaro cut the blue ribbon and a great number of documents unfolded: some regarding Trieste, some referring to passage into Switzerland, and letters about the Partisans. The second file consisted of letters between Hitler and Mussolini, all typewritten, German texts with attached translations into Italian. The third file pertained to the Verona trials. It had all of the interrogations and many letters written to Mussolini by the prisoners. The last file was a dossier on Humbert of Savoy. At the bottom of the brief case was some currency: 177 gold pound notes; three checks for 500,000 lire each, one for 50,000 and four for 25,000, all issued by Italian banks.[75] There is no question that there were two leather cases of documents seized at Dongo, but we have no precise record of the contents of the second case.

The other parts of the Treasure of Dongo—the five suitcases of paper money and gold which Mussolini still had with him on departing from Menaggio, were apparently left in German hands after the seizure of the Italians at Dongo. The German troops had been permitted to move forward after that stop but were halted again at the bridge at Ponte del Passo pending approval of higher Partisan headquarters for their further movement. While they camped that night they tossed out whatever they thought might be compromising. Some paper money they burned. They

74. Bellini, *Dongo ultima azione*, p. 177. Mussolini is also reported to have told Hofmann at about the same time: "Pay careful attention, Signor Hofmann, I have with me documents of great importance for Italy" (Spampanato, *Contromemoriale* 3:274).

Cf. Saini, *Notte di Dongo*, pp. 140, 142.

75. Bellini, *Dongo ultima azione*, pp. 177–78.

According to Lazzero, "Un passo," August 25, 1968 [p. 43], there was also some poetry in a notebook, a file regarding Pietro Nenni, and a file of correspondence between Churchill and Mussolini. Lazzero's source here, we would guess to be Pier Bellini delle Stelle ("Pedro"), who is listed by Lazzero as one of his collaborators.

This is a puzzle. The crucial participant and witness on this point is Urbano Lazzaro ("Bill"), but Bill was not one of the collaborators consulted by Ricciotti Lazzero. If there was such a Churchill file, why did Bill not mention it in his contemporary manuscript which is given in italics in *Dongo ultima azione*? If Pedro knew of Bill's seizure of the Churchill file at Dongo, why did he not offer some qualification or correction in that book of combined authorship which he published with Bill in 1962? Could Bill have had some motive for not mentioning the Churchill file?

On the other hand Lazzero refers to two other persons who were collaborators in the composing of his article and who, he states, saw the Churchill file, Aldo Castelli ("Pinùn") and Virginio Bertinelli. See note 146 below.

threw the gold into the Mera River. Next morning it was dragged up by a fisherman who turned it over to Hofmann. It was reported to weigh 35.88 kilograms, and when it was spread out on the table in Hofmann's house there were heaps of wedding rings and other jewelry, representing some of the patriotic donations of Italian women for the Abyssinian War. Hofmann also told Bill that one of the Germans turned over to him 33 millions in 1,000 lire notes.[76]

Count Bellini delle Stelle was fully aware of the importance of his prisoner, conscious of the responsibility he bore. After consultation with Buffelli, sergeant of the Finance Guards, he considered that the most secure place for Mussolini would be the barracks of the *Guardia di Finanza* at Germasino. Buffelli along with Bellini escorted Mussolini to this initial place of imprisonment where they arrived at about a quarter to seven. Here Mussolini had a light supper; he wrote out a brief statement that the treatment accorded him was correct; and after quite a conversation with Buffelli undressed for the night. The former Duce apparently expected that he would be tried by some court for he told his custodian: "In any case I shall have much to say at the Tribunal and I shall show that in these 18 months I saved Italy from worse disasters." [77]

Bellini sent some sort of message to Milan stating that Mussolini and most of the ministers of the Republic of Salò had been captured. Somewhat later Lazzaro informed him that Carlo Scappin, sergeant of the Finance Guards of Gera Lario, had telephoned Milan by a private line of an electric company reporting the capture of the former Duce and of some of his chief supporters. Bellini had made up his mind regarding the treatment of his famous prisoner: there would be no summary execution; Mussolini would be turned over to the Italian authorities and in no case would he be surrendered to the Allies. A rather mysterious message came through from Milan that night from some headquarters not clearly identified: to treat Mussolini with every regard; not to touch a hair of his head (this was purely a figure of speech); rather than do violence to him in case of an attempt to escape, to let him flee. Bellini felt assured that his own message had got through to Milan and that his superiors would take the responsibility for Mussolini's fate.[78]

Late during the night of April 27–28 Bellini, for some reason not altogether clear, decided to transfer Mussolini from the barracks of the Finance Guards at Germasino. He would rely, for the protection of his famous prisoner, on secrecy rather than on the strength of the Partisans and the Finance Guard. That force was quite adequate against any possible stroke by Fascist bands, but it would have availed nothing if the U.S.

76. Bellini, *Dongo ultima azione*, pp. 185–87 (from the narrative of Urbano Lazzaro).
77. Bandini, *Ultime 95 ore*, pp. 178–87.
78. Bellini, *Dongo ultima azione*, pp. 205, 226–28. Cf. Saini, *Notte di Dongo*, p. 94.

Fifth Army had demanded Mussolini's person on the basis of the clauses of the Long Terms of the Armistice on September 29, 1943. Luigi Canali ("Neri"), who knew the area well from his Partisan service, suggested the cottage of the De Maria family, a rather isolated dwelling in Giulino di Mezzegra where he had often been sheltered.[79]

Several persons among the followers of Mussolini would have preferred that he be seized by the Anglo-Americans or turned over to them, feeling that he would be judged less harshly by an international tribunal than by his own people. Vittorio Mussolini hoped that his father would be turned over to the Allies.[80] Claretta Petacci pled with Bellini to surrender Mussolini to the Allies. He rejected the plea indignantly, saying:

> I am an Italian, I am a soldier belonging to the Italian Army. I owe an accounting only to my headquarters and to my government. The Allies have no concern with this and I will certainly try to prevent Mussolini from falling into their hands.[81]

Pedro did, however, permit Claretta to join Mussolini in the new hiding place. Sometime after 1:00 A.M. of April 28 Mussolini was awakened and told to dress. He and his escort left Germasino about 1:35 A.M.

79. Bellini, *Dongo ultima azione*, pp. 188–91; Saini, *Notte di Dongo*, pp. 94–95.

Bandini, *Ultime 95 ore*, pp. 216–19, suggests that the decision to transfer Mussolini to some secret place was not "autonomous" on the part of Bellini. The U.S. Fifth Army was in search of Mussolini and American agents were in Como where Virginio Bertinelli had taken over from Celio as prefect. On the morning of April 27 a U.S. Counter Intelligence Corps representative known as "Giuseppe" had appeared in the prefecture and demanded that Bertinelli turn over Mussolini to the U.S. forces on the basis of Article 29 of the Long Terms of Armistice. Bertinelli eluded the demand saying that his writ ran only a few meters beyond the prefecture, but having learned of the capture of Mussolini by a despatch received about 6:30 P.M. he suggested to Bellini that the former Duce be moved to a secret place.

80. This according to Bandini, *Ultime 95 ore*, pp. 281–82. Vittorio himself records that above all else his father wished to avoid falling alive into the hands of the Allies to face the impossible humiliation of a sensational trial, but this is qualified by recording that Mussolini further stated that the Italians fought without cruelty, that there were no war criminals in Italy (*Vita con mio padre*, p. 222).

But Vittorio's own attitudes, or at least his contemporary actions and his later recollections, do not seem to be consistent. On April 26 when Mussolini was attempting to reach the Swiss frontier by way of Grandola and Porlezza, Vittorio was at Como, attempting, along with his cousin Vito, and Vanni Teodorani, to reach an agreement with the leaders of the CLN of Como. The Fascists, it was proposed, would move into a neutral zone in the Valle d'Intelvi where they would await the arrival of the Anglo-American forces. A provision was included that Vanni Teodorani and some spokesmen of the CLN would go to Mussolini and offer to transport him and his followers to that neutral zone to await the Allies. Lazzero, "Un passo," August 25, 1968 [p. 43].

Surely these negotiations were part of that "psychological collapse" so greatly deplored by the neofascist historians.

81. Bellini, *Dongo ultima azione*, p. 205.

They stopped briefly near Dongo to pick up Claretta and more guards, and then started down the road to Giulino di Mezzegra, a small group of buildings outside the town proper. "Lino" (Giuseppe Frangi) and "Sandrino" (G. Cantoni) were left as guards outside the De Maria cottage. Mussolini had lost his precious documents, he had lost the currency and other treasure which he had taken with him on leaving Milan, but he still had his mistress on the last night of his life. It was she who insisted on sharing his fate.[82]

Mussolini's Death: Assassination or Execution? (April 28)

Since the meeting of its representatives with Mussolini on April 25, the CLNAI had done its best to follow the trail of the fleeing former dictator. Late that same day the insurrection was proclaimed and on April 26 the patriots had largely gained control of Milan. The Finance Guards, which represented an effective, disciplined force with a network of stations throughout the North, had on that day come over to the side of the Partisans. The military arm of the CLNAI was the CVL, the Corps of Volunteers of Liberty (*Corpo Volontari della Libertà*), organized, as we have noted, in divisions, brigades, detachments, and squads. But there were very few organized Partisans in Milan on the twenty-sixth.[83]

82. Bandini, *Ultime 95 ore,* states that there was a secret plan to transfer Mussolini to Moltrasio where a boat would pick him up to take him across the lake to a hiding place in a villa near Blevio, a plan worked out between General Cadorna and Gen. Giovanni Sardagna who on April 27 assumed command of the piazza of Como (pp. 222–30). Bellini makes no mention of this plan and Bandini concedes that Count Bellini probably did not know its full scope. The scheme fell through, Bandini explains, either because the boat failed to arrive or because of new orders which cancelled the plan (pp. 237–38).

A second part of the plan is supposed to have been General Cadorna's scheme to transfer Mussolini from Blevio to the airfield of Bresso on the outskirts of Milan, there to be turned over to the Americans (pp. 238, 251). I give no credence to this explanation. It does not accord with the character of Cadorna, a man of integrity. The evidence suggested by Bandini on this point is so thin as to be evanescent. There is no such explanation in Lazzero's article, and Lazzero lists Sardagna as one of his collaborators.

Lazzero's own explanation seems much more probable. The lead car, he states, was driven by "Neri" who reached Moltrasio about 3:00 A.M. on the way to Como to turn over the famous prisoner. Neri halted when he saw lights and heard firing down the lake near Como, for he feared that the party might fall into Fascist hands or get caught in fighting between the Americans and Fascist forces. When Pedro caught up with Neri it was decided to turn back, and Neri then suggested Giulino di Mezzegra as a good hiding place (Un passo," 3, August 25, 1968 [p. 54]).

83. The "Pavia" Division, about one thousand well-armed men, arrived in the afternoon of the twenty-sixth (Delzell, *Mussolini's Enemeies,* p. 528). Bandini (*Ultime 95 ore,* pp. 113–14) emphasizes the key role of the Finance Guards in the seizure of power by the insurrection.

General Headquarters of the CVL was the *Comando Generale*, often designated by the initials CG/CVL, which was headed by Gen. Raffaele Cadorna. A division commander at the time of Italy's surrender in 1943, he remained loyal to the legal government in the South and had been sent into the North by the Allied armies in Italy to coordinate the Partisan struggle with the Allied campaign. He was expected to carry out the directives sent him by AFHQ and at the same time to execute the will of the CLNAI. That political committee emerged from underground on April 26. Next morning General Cadorna moved his headquarters from the convent where he had previously operated to the former Fascist military command post on the via Del Carmine.[84]

Not much information regarding Mussolini's movements reached Milan on April 26. Next day there were first some false rumors and later the definite word of his capture. Not long after 11:00 P.M. of April 27, General Headquarters was notified in detail that Mussolini had been arrested and was being held in the barracks at Germasino.[85]

The Committee of National Liberation of Upper Italy was not the only political body which wished to take over custody of Mussolini and to render justice in one fashion or another. There was the Royal Italian government at Rome[86] against which Mussolini had committed treason and rebellion by setting up the Italian Social Republic. There were also the governments of the United States and of Great Britain to which Italy had formally surrendered in 1943. Clause 29 in the Long Terms of Armistice stipulated the surrender of Mussolini and his chief Fascist associates.[87]

84. Cadorna, *La riscossa,* pp. 254, 257.

85. Bandini, *Ultime 95 ore,* pp. 205–17. Bandini has taken great pains to identify each message and to pinpoint its time of arrival at the CG/CVL.

86. Legitimate, but not very regal by this time, for the head of the state was the Lieutenant General of the Realm, Prince Umberto, and actual governmental authority was exercised by the ministry whose membership was determined by the Roman Committee of National Liberation. Under the terms of the *Decreto Legge Luogotenenziale* 151 of June 25, 1944, the government was pledged to determine the permanent form of government in accordance with the popular wish at the end of the war. See my article, "Italy: From Fascism to the Republic," *Western Political Quarterly* 1, no. 3 (September 1948): pp. 205–22, which includes a translation of the decree-law.

87. See note 23 above, where the exact text of the article is quoted. The Long Terms were still secret in April 1945 but the determination of Roosevelt and Churchill to bring Mussolini to trial was well known. In his speech to the House of Commons on September 21, 1943, Churchill mentioned that "a particular stipulation was made for the surrender of Mussolini" (Great Britain, *Parliamentary Debates* [Commons], 5th ser., 392 [1943]:83). On September 10, 1943 Radio Algiers announced that the transfer of Mussolini was provided for among the terms of armistice (Mussolini, *Il tempo del bastone e della carota,* p. 30). Cf. Amicucci, *600 giorni,* p. 228.

By April 1945, the U.S. Fifth Army with its headquarters at Sienna had an excellent network of clandestine radios in the parts of Italy still held by the German army and the neo-fascist government. That headquarters seems to have learned of Mussolini's arrest as early or even earlier than did the CG/CVL in Milan. As we have already noted, during the morning of April 27 an American C.I.C. agent came to the new prefect of Como (who was being assisted in taking over the job by Celio, the Fascist prefect) and demanded that Mussolini be handed over to him.[88]

A second attempt to take custody of Mussolini was launched about the same time. An Italian officer, Commander (*Capitano di fregata*) Giovanni Dessì, a member naval intelligence (*Servizio Informazioni Segrete della Marina* or S.I.S.) who worked closely with the American OSS and with the British Secret Service arrived in Como and apparently was able to gain assurances from Allied authorities in Switzerland that if Mussolini gave himself up, he would be given a fair trial. Commander Dessì's little expedition, which started on the trail of Mussolini on April 27, did not get very far. The whole situation along the road had radically changed. Partisans halted the expedition. They discovered that one of its members was Franco Colombo, commander of the Muti brigade of Milan. The expedition was turned back to Como without Colombo who was unceremoniously shot.[89]

A third attempt to grab Mussolini was undertaken by Capt. Emilio Daddario, an OSS agent. Daddario took the surrender of Graziani whom he delivered in Milan, but when he headed back for Como and Dongo, Mussolini was already dead.[90]

88. See note 79 above.

89. Saini, *Notte di Dongo*, pp. 8, 42; Bandini, *Ultime 95 ore*, pp. 278–86. Bandini's account of the Allied efforts to take Mussolini is based largely on Italian sources which are to be viewed with a degree of caution. They are, however, nicely complemented by Lazzero's researchers in the Pentagon files. See "Un passo," 3, August 25, 1968 [p. 145], which gives the exact text of the message sent by the U.S. Fifth Army to the clandestine units in the North: "Pursuant to orders from AFHQ it is the desire of allies to take Mussolini alive. These headquarters will be notified and he will be held in security pending the arrival of allied troops."

90. Bandini, *Ultime 95 ore*, pp. 286–90.

Emilio Quincy Daddario was born in Newton Center, Mass., in September 1918; received a B.A. degree from Wesleyan University in Connecticut in 1939; a law degree from the University of Connecticut in 1942 and was admitted to the bar in Connecticut and Massachusetts. He enlisted in the army in 1943 and for his wartime services received the medal of the U.S. Legion of Merit and the Italian *Medaglia d'Argento*. After the war he served as mayor of Middletown (1946–48); was called back into service during the Korean War; was elected to Congress in 1958 and reelected for three successive terms. He was subsequently Democratic candidate for governor of Connecticut.

In 1945 Captain Daddario had but recently been transferred to Lugano to work with Allen Dulles's man Scotti. Scotti did not know of the Sunrise Operation, that is the secret

The CLNAI and General Headquarters in Milan were quite aware of this determination of the Allied armies in Italy to take custody of Mussolini. During the night, April 27–28, Allied Headquarters radioed Milan a couple of times. In the first message, which was received about 6:00 P.M., the Allies asked exactly where Mussolini was, and stated that they were ready to send a plane to accept his transfer. A second message stated that the plane for Mussolini would land at 1800 hours the next day (April 28) at the little airfield of Bresso just outside Milan and ordered that appropriate signals be prepared on the field.[91]

It was the fear that the Allies would take Mussolini and put him on trial that precipitated the decision by some members of the CLNAI and the *Comando Generale* to seize the famous prisoner and execute him forthwith. General Cadorna records that during the night of April 27 the news was received that Mussolini and his entourage had been captured by Partisans north of Como. He goes on to say:

Two communist representatives presented themselves to me, Lampredi and Valerio (the accountant Audisio) and told me that they had received the mandate of the CLNAI to get to the scene with the mission to execute Mussolini. My first thought was that this was some order of an insurrectional Committee and one of the customary coups of the Communists who had constituted that Committee for their own ends, for which it would be better on my part to demand a written communication. I had to consider, however, that the CLNAI, although it had not made a formal decision, had held the need for execution of the principal members of the Fascist Party on simple recognition as something obvious and understood. Furthermore, the points of American armored forces had already passed through Como and there was no doubt that as soon as they learned of his capture, they would demand the transfer to them of war criminal No. 2.[92]

Cadorna felt that he faced an emergency situation. He could not make direct contact with the CLNAI which was not in permanent session. He gave his approval and support to the mission of Colonel "Valerio," acting in accordance with his duty to his country and his views of what would best serve Italy's interest in her future reconstruction. He records:

In no case would I voluntarily have proceeded to bring Mussolini into the hands of the Allies for him to be tried and executed by foreigners. I remembered very well the indignation which was aroused both at home and abroad after the 8th of

negotiations for the surrender of the German forces in Italy. Dulles was chiefly concerned lest Mussolini make a last ditch stand and interfere with an orderly surrender of the German forces (Dulles, *Secret Surrender*, pp. 183, 189–90).

91. Bandini, *Ultime 95 ore*, pp. 246, 249. It is stated that the Italian reply indicated that Mussolini had already been shot (p. 258).

92. Cadorna, *La riscossa*, p. 259.

September by the word that such a transfer by the Italian Government was included in the secret clauses of the armistice.[93]

It definitely was not a plenary session of the CLNAI which decided on Mussolini's execution. Rather it was a kind of *ad hoc* committee composed of the Communist representatives Luigi Longo and Emilio Sereni and the Socialist Sandro Pertini. These three came over to General Cadorna's headquarters at about 11:00 P.M. to discuss launching the special mission.[94] Early in the morning of April 28 Leo Valiani of the Party of Action came to Cadorna, bringing, he said, the order of the CLNAI for Mussolini's execution. In the postliberation polemic it became clear, however, that the committee had not adopted such a motion. Cadorna replied that he had already been informed of the decision.[95] On April 29, after Mussolini was dead, the CLNAI issued a statement that it took full responsibility for his execution.[96] Ferruccio Parri, leader of the Party of Action in the North, later declared that he approved the mission of Valerio and that he particularly wished to prevent Mussolini's falling into the hands of the Allies.[97]

Much to the relief of General Cadorna who on April 26 had very few Partisan troops at hand, during the next day more well-armed men arrived. It is said that in the discussion at General Headquarters a division commander was suggested as head of the mission to seize Mussolini. He declined, saying that such a mission was a police action and he was a soldier. One of the brigade commanders likewise declined. The choice then fell on Colonel "Valerio" (Walter Audisio), an auditor by profession, an ardent Communist and veteran of the Spanish Civil War, and a recent appointee to the *Comando Generale* where he headed the secretarial staff.[98] Valerio said he would need men, credentials, and information regarding Mussolini's place of detention. The credentials which were provided at General Headquarters included a special pass written out in English by Daddario who had brought the Fascist generals Graziani and Bonomi to Milan.[99] The information apparently indicated that Mussolini was to be sought at Dongo.

Twenty persons made up the expedition. "Piero" records that at

93. Ibid., p. 260. I accept Cadorna's words at face value and I reject the interpretation of Bandini (*Ultime 95 ore*, pp. 221, 250–53, 266–67, 272–73) that Cadorna was secretly planning to transfer Mussolini to the Allies. This is almost as if Cadorna were conspiring against himself.

94. Bandini, *Ultime 95 ore*, pp. 253, 256–57. Cf. Saini, *Notte di Dongo*, pp. 38–39.

95. Cadorna, *La riscossa*, p. 260.

96. Ibid., p. 261; Saini, *Notte di Dongo*, p. 40.

97. Saini, *Notte di Dongo*, p. 37.

98. Cadorna, *La riscossa*, p. 254; Bandini, *Ultime 95 ore*, p. 295.

99. Bandini, *Ultime 95 ore*, pp. 257, 266, 297.

about 11:30 P.M. of the twenty-seventh, Colonel Valeri [sic] came in person to the school on viale Romagna where the Crespi brigade had closed for the night. Piero, his companion Albero, and the Zone Inspector "Riccardo" (Riccardo Mordini) picked out fourteen men from the Crespi and Capetini brigades. An automobile and a truck were also made available. Colonel Valerio, "Guido" (Aldo Lampredi), Inspector Riccardo, who served under Valerio as commander of the troop, and the driver rode in the car. In the truck rode the fourteen Partisan troopers, Piero and the driver.[100]

After a drive of about one hour Valerio and his troop reached Como at 8:00 A.M. but there they encountered a series of bureaucratic roadblocks. The newly established authorities of Como expected that Mussolini would be delivered to them for imprisonment. After considerable discussion at the prefecture Valerio agreed to take two men of Como with him, Major De Angelis and Oscar Sforni, the secretary of the CLN of Como. Then at about 11:00 A.M. Valerio got the disconcerting news that Guido, Riccardo, and the driver had taken the car and had headed off for Dongo without him. After pleading for fifteen minutes or so at the prefecture that he be supplied with another auto, Valerio threatened that he would shoot the secretary of Celio, the former prefect, unless he promptly produced a substitute vehicle. After about ten minutes there were provided a Green Cross ambulance and a couple of cars, one of which was used by Sforni and De Angelis. Commander Dessì and a certain "Carletto," also a member of Italian naval intelligence, insisted on going along. The three vehicles drove first to a garage to fill up with gasoline. There at gunpoint Valerio ordered Dessì and his assistant to get out. Their protests and official positions made no impression on Valerio who simply declared that he did not need their services. Valerio did, however, take Dessì's driver, a certain Giovanni Tacchino, whom Dessì himself had commandeered a couple of days before from Buffarini-Guidi along with the car. While on the point of leaving Como, Valerio noticed a big, yellow truck which much better would suit his purpose than the ambulance. The truck was taken and the ambulance abandoned.[101]

Shortly after 2:00 P.M. Valerio and his platoon arrived at Dongo. Pedro had been alerted from Menaggio that a couple of vehicles had sped along the road and had refused to stop. Scarcely had he arrived at the

100. "Deposizioni di Piero delle formazioni Garibaldini dell' Oltrepò Pavese," pp. 83–89 in *Nemesi, Dal 25 al 28 aprile 1945: Documenti e testimonianze sulle ultime ore di Mussolini*, Renato Salvadori (Milan: Baldasare Gnocchi, 1945). Hereafter cited as *Nemesi*. "Piero" is identified only as a militant Communist of ten years standing and a member of the Crespi Brigade. Bandini, *Ultime 95 ore*, p. 308, is apparently in error in stating that there were only twelve Partisan soldiers.

101. Bandini, *Ultime 95 ore*, pp. 311–14; Saini, *Notte di Dongo*, pp. 8–9.

town hall of Dongo when one of his men reported that there were fifteen armed men drawn up in the piazza in a threatening attitude. The leader introduced himself as Colonel Valerio, on special mission from General Headquarters. The men of the fifty-second Garibaldi Brigade were very suspicious; they feared that the newcomers might be Fascists intent on rescuing Mussolini. Pedro had very few men at hand and again sought to stall for time as he had done the day before. He asked if the men from Milan had eaten and invited them into the kitchen of the town hall for a meal. Meanwhile he sent out calls for reinforcements.[102]

Sforni and De Angelis had driven to Dongo in the Aprilia with the royal navy plates, RM (*Regio Marina*) 001, which Dessì had attached to Buffarini-Guidi's car. In their hasty departure from Como, however, they had neglected to bring along either an armed escort or credentials. Valerio insisted that they be locked up as suspicious persons. Pedro complied. Oscar Sforni suffered the additional indignity of sharing a cell with Marcello Petacci (brother of Claretta), from which, not long thereafter, he witnessed the slaughter of the hierarchs.[103]

On the other hand Valerio's credentials were completely in order. "Guido" (Lampredi) was known to "Neri" (Luigi Canali) and Guido guaranteed Valerio. There was no room for doubt that Valerio was Pedro's superior and that he came from General Headquarters. Pedro was stupefied by Valerio's blunt assertion that he had come to shoot Mussolini and the hierarchs, for it ran completely counter to Pedro's own views and preparations. There was nothing he could do, however, to oppose Valerio, and neither Neri nor "Pietro" (Michele Moretti), who had assisted in the transfer of Mussolini to the De Maria cottage during the previous night, could suggest any course other than compliance. Valerio announced also that he would shoot Claretta Petacci because she was a counselor of the Duce. Pedro got nowhere with his protests against such an action. Reluctantly he turned over the list of prisoners and explained where they were being held: Mussolini and Claretta about halfway down the lake; others at Germasino; nine in Dongo itself.[104]

102. Bellini, *Dongo ultima azione*, pp. 251–54; Bandini, *Ultime 95 ore*, pp. 316–18.

According to Lazzero, "Un passo," 3, August 25, 1968 [p. 55], when Valerio arrived at Dongo, he was first locked up in a closet of the town hall but was released when Lampredi intervened and guaranteed him to be a Partisan. This statement is in sharp contrast to the other sources, particularly Bellini's account in his book. If Bellini as collaborator with Lazzero was the source of this statement, one wonders how he could so much have changed his story between writing his book and helping Lazzero. If Bellini was not the source for this episode, one wonders what the basis was for Lazzero's account at this point.

103. Bellini, *Dongo ultima azione*, p. 256; Saini, *Notte di Dongo*, p. 10.

104. Bellini, *Dongo ultima azione*, pp. 256–61. Attilio Tamaro, *Due anni di storia 1943–1945*, (Rome: Tosi editore, 1949–50) 3:630, prints a facsimile of the typewritten list of prisoners with the check marks made by Valerio.

Pedro still tried to stall for time. He proposed to Colonel Valerio that all of the prisoners be brought together at Dongo where he would formally turn them over. He himself offered to bring the prisoners from Germasino and to send Neri and Pietro to fetch Mussolini and his mistress. Instead of this, Valerio took the two as guides for himself and Guido. Those who made the trip were all Communists. The driver of the car, a black 1100 with Roman license plates which was commandeered on the spot, was Giovambattista Geninazza.[105]

The group reached the De Maria cottage in something less than an hour and were recognized by the guards, "Lino" (Giuseppe Frangi) and "Sandrino" (G. Cantoni) who had been left outside the door during the night before. Valerio burst into the room and ordered Mussolini and Claretta to follow him, saying: "I've come to liberate you." The executioners and prisoners climbed into the car, they drove a short distance and then walked perhaps fifty meters to the grilled iron gate of the Villa Belmonte. It was locked. There was no chance for Valerio to use the garden of the estate for his purpose. He posted Guido and Pietro as guards, the one up, the other down the road by several meters, and then lined Mussolini and La Petacci up against the wall. He pronounced the words: "By General Headquarters of the Corps of Volunteers of Liberty I am charged to render justice for the Italian people." Valerio pulled the trigger of his weapon, but it jammed. He then yelled to Pietro, ran halfway to meet him, snatched his submachine gun, and fired a burst of shots. Mussolini and Claretta Petacci crumbled to the ground and Valerio fired a few more rounds. After a short pause the party started back to Dongo, leaving Lino and Sandrino to guard the corpses.[106]

105. Bellini, *Dongo ultima azione*, p. 262, states that he himself suggested that Neri and Pietro bring in Mussolini. Bandini, whose book appeared before that of Bellini, states rather inaccurately that the two Communists under Bellini's command betrayed his confidence by revealing Mussolini's hiding place to Colonel Valerio (*Ultima 95 ore*, pp. 319–20).

106. Valerio (Walter Audisio) published three significant accounts of his shooting of Mussolini: on April 30, 1945; on December 13, 1945; and on March 28, 1947. These are reprinted in Saini, *Notte di Dongo*, pp. 26–29. There are certain discrepancies and inaccuracies in these three accounts yet they cannot, for that reason alone, be disregarded as evidence. In all three Valerio states that he pronounced the sentence. In the second account he states that he borrowed the submachine gun from Bill. Bill was not there. In the third account Valerio writes that when his own submachine gun jammed, he passed it to Guido, and then tried his own pistol but this too misfired. He then called to the commissar of the Fifty-second Brigade from whom he borrowed the submachine gun which fired the fatal shots.

In the accounts of 1945 Valerio was careful not to reveal the presence of Michele Moretti, who was wanted for questioning by General Zingales in the preliminary investigation of the affair of Dongo, that is the disappearance of Mussolini's documents and of the treasure. Valerio's inconsistencies and the ownership of the submachine gun which fired the fatal shots led General Zingales and author Saini after him to state positively that

Pedro had scarcely returned to Dongo from Germasino and as-
sembled the other prisoners when Valerio opened the door and declared:
"Justice is done. Mussolini is dead." Nothing now would deter Valerio
from shooting the rest of the prisoners whose names he had checked off.
The syndic, Rubini, resigned in protest against the violent action. Padre
Accursio Ferrari appeared; he asked to give the condemned men the last
comforts of their religion. Valerio allowed him three minutes for the lot.
The colonel from General Headquarters urged that the firing squad be
mixed, in part men from the Fifty-second Brigade, in part men from
Milan. Pedro at first refused to have any part in the shooting of his prisoners. Valerio, as his superior, then commanded him to supply some
men and Pedro complied, albeit reluctantly. The fifteen prisoners were
lined up in the square and shot in full public view.[107]

Michele Moretti was the real killer of Mussolini and his mistress (Saini, *Notte di Dongo,* pp.
30, 189).

There is no doubt as to the identity of the weapon, a MAS of French manufacture as
Valerio himself wrote on September 11, 1945, to Comrade "Spano," nor that it belonged at
the time to Moretti (Saini, *Notte di Dongo,* p. 22; Bandini, *Ultime 95 ore,* p. 346). But this
does not prove that Moretti pulled the trigger. Moretti himself told Pedro that Valerio
seized his MAS pistol when Valerio's weapon jammed (Bandini, *Ultime 95 ore,* p. 347, fn.
82).

"La fine di Mussolini e di Claretta Petacci," pp. 78–82 in *Nemesi,* appears to be the account of a witness but the author is not identified.

Luigi de Vincentis, *Io sono te . . . ,* 2d ed. (Milan: Cebes, 1946), pp. 159–60, gives an account which it is claimed is based on the testimony of a witness, but that witness is not
identified.

Chapter 37, "Il calvario," pp. 577–624 of Tamaro's *Due anni di storia 1943–1945,* is rich
in detail and in its illustrations; it adopts the view of Zingales that Moretti was the real
killer of Mussolini; the chapter's title indicates the author's point of view.

Bandini, *Ultime 95 ore,* pp. 335–48 gives the most thorough and accurate account and
provides on pp. 338–44 the direct testimony of the chauffeur, Giovambattista Geninazza, an
independent witness who saw and heard the shooting from not too great a distance. Contrary to other testimony, he states that it was Moretti and Lampredi who went into the cottage to fetch Mussolini (p. 339). He could not hear the whole sentence pronounced by
Valerio; he heard him rattle off something and caught the words "Ordine" and "sentenza di
morte" (p. 341).

107. Bellini, *Dongo ultima azione,* pp. 279–82. Saini, *Notte di Dongo,* pp. 9–16, quotes
some testimony of Oscar Sforni, and of the journalist Pellegrini who witnessed the action
from their cells. Bandini, *Ultime 95 ore,* pp. 352–64, emphasizes Valerio's insistence on executing fifteen Fascists in retribution for the fifteen martyrs of the Piazzale Loreto. The syndic Rubini looked at his watch when the shots rang out; the time was 1748 hours (Bandini,
Ultime 95 ore, p. 356). According to "Piero" two men of the Fifty-second Brigade were
provided in order to bring the firing squad to a total of eighteen (*Nemesi,* p. 85).

Those shot at Dongo were: Francesco Maria Barracù, undersecretary of the presidency
of the council; Nicola Bombacci, a one time socialist who became a Republican Fascist; Pietro Calistri, captain in the air force of the Italian Social Republic; Vito Casalinuovo, commandant of the police guard of Mussolini; Goffredo Coppola, rector of the University of

Sometime that evening Sforni and De Angelis were released from their cells; they drove back to Como where they began a vehement protest against the brutality of the men from General Headquarters. Valerio wasted no time. He ordered some sheets from the town hall and had his men load the corpses into the yellow truck which he had commandeered in Como. At quarter past six they started the return trip. There was a brief pause to pick up the corpses of Mussolini and Claretta which were transferred from the automobile into the truck. Lino and Sandrino drove on with the group as far as Como.

Twice Valerio's men were halted at American outposts but they promptly passed through on presentation of the pass signed by Captain Daddario. In Milan it was a different story. A group of Christian Democrat Partisans refused to acknowledge Valerio's credentials; threatened to shoot him and his men; held them up for some hours. Not until 3:00 A.M. of April 29 were the eighteen corpses unloaded at the garage on the Piazzala Loreto where fifteen Partisans had been shot on August 14, 1944, in reprisal for the shooting of two German soldiers. By late morning an enormous crowd had gathered and had whipped itself to a frenzy at the sight of the bodies of Mussolini, of La Petacci and of three others suspended upside down from an iron beam. In the early afternoon the bodies were removed to the mortuary.[108]

What is one to think of this killing of Mussolini and of the seventeen others captured with him? The pro-Fascist historians and journalists call it assassination; the anti-Fascist writers refer to it as execution. Churchill was deeply shocked by Valerio's action and called it murder.[109] But surely the shooting of Mussolini by Italian anti-Fascists and his public branding by Churchill as a war criminal were not unrelated.

The ruthless, brutal efficiency of Valerio stands out. In some ways his actions with his squad were like that of a lynching party which

Bologna; Ernesto Daquanno, director of the Stefani News Agency; Luigi Gatti, personal secretary to Mussolini with the rank of prefect; Augusto Liverani, minister of communications; Fernando Mezzasoma, minister of popular culture; Alessandro Pavolini, minister of popular culture, October 1939– February 1943, secretary of the Republican Fascist party; Paolo Porta, inspector of the Republican Fascist party of Lombardy; Mario Nudi, president of the Fascist Agricultural Confederation; Ruggero Romano, minister of public works; Idreno Utimperghe, commander of a Black Brigade of Pinerolo; Paolo Zerbino, minister of the interior.

Marcello Petacci, brother of Claretta, whom Valerio for a time mistook for Vittorio Mussolini, tried to escape but was caught and shot apart from the main group.

108. Bandini, *Ultime 95 ore*, chap. 12, pp. 349–78; "Deposizione di Piero delle formazioni garibaldini dell'Oltrepò pavese," in *Nemesi*, pp. 85–89.

109. Letter to Field Marshal Alexander, May 10, 1945, Winston S. Churchill, *The Second World War*, vol. 6 *Triumph and Tragedy* (Boston: Houghton Mifflin Co., 1953), p. 528.

sweeps the sheriff aside, takes the prisoner from the jail and hangs him, thus precluding a trial in court. In any case there is no moral defense or political justification for the shooting of Claretta Petacci; it was absurd for Valerio to call her a counselor of the Duce. Likewise Valerio commanded the shooting of Captain Calistri on the mistaken notion that he was Mussolini's personal pilot. The arbitrary selection of fifteen persons to be shot, of whom only eight were responsible leaders in the Italian Social Republic, was crude vengeance comparable to the savage cruelty of the Nazi occupation which the Italian people found so revolting.

The core of the problem, however, is the shooting of Mussolini. In a sense he had forfeited his right to a trial by his flight to Como after his meeting with the resistance leaders in Cardinal Schuster's palace. The CLNAI from that time on considered Mussolini an outlaw. Massimo Salvadori speaks of the "Dongo Executions" as punishment for the twenty-five years of Fascist tyranny which had not hesitated to murder its enemies, even on foreign soil.[110]

What of General Cadorna's vital role in the launching of Valerio's expedition? It would indeed have been a shameful thing for Italians of any stripe to turn Mussolini over to the Allies, to let him be tried by foreigners. The judgments pronounced by Bandini stating or implying that there were possibilities of some regular court action as an alternative to Valerio's direct action fall wide of the mark.[111] The only genuinely judicial procedure for Mussolini and his leading supporters in the Italian Social Republic would have been a trial by the Italian government on charges of treason and rebellion. The Allies, however, would without doubt have claimed him had he been delivered alive into that government's hands. The alternatives which Cadorna actually faced were either to let Audisio try to grab Mussolini and shoot him, or to see him delivered over to the Allies. Accepting for argument's sake the validity of a trial of the vanquished by the victors, it still is hard to imagine what war crimes could have been charged against Mussolini for his actions in World War II.[112] My view is that the summary execution of Mussolini and of several of his leading supporters saved the Allies a great embar-

110. *Labour and the Wounds,* p. 227.

111. *Ultime 95 ore,* p. 274, n. 66; pp. 275, 378.

112. Mussolini's war crimes were against the Ethiopians in 1935–36, particularly the use of poison gas by Badoglio, but such crimes had been forgiven by Britain and France by 1939. The outrages committed by the Ustaše during the Axis occupation of Yugoslavia cannot be attributed directly to the Italians. See the tongue in cheek work by "Cassius" [pseud. for Michael Foot], *The Trial of Mussolini: Being a Verbatim Report of the First Great Trial for War Criminals Held in London Sometime in 1944 or 1945* (London: Victor Gollancz Ltd., 1943).

rassment. As Churchill himself phrased it: "But at least the world was spared an Italian Nuremberg." [113]

One other aspect of Mussolini's inglorious death must not be overlooked. The Communists and the Socialists in the CLNAI used the shooting of Mussolini and the display of his corpse as a triggering incident to set off the new terror, the outburst of killings and acts of personal vengeance before Allied military government could take over the newly liberated territory in the North and restore order. This most certainly was not in General Cadorna's mind when he made the decision to launch Valerio on his mission. Not without personal risk Cadorna saved Graziani from an impromptu execution by excited Partisans in Milan.[114] It was during this reign of terror, anarchy and lawlessness,[115] stimulated by the maneuvers of the Communists, that portions of Mussolini's most prized papers and the Treasure of Dongo disappeared.

The Fate of the Seized Documents; Divergent Accounts
The Treasure of Dongo

What happened to the documents which Mussolini had with him on his final, ill-fated flight? The testimony and other evidence in this regard is spotty, it is far from consistent, and there are several aspects of the story which are obscure. The disappearance, or rather the fate of the private papers selected by Mussolini has remained a "mystery" for the same reason that the disappearance of the Treasure of Dongo has remained a "mystery." There was much gossip and rumor. There was a preliminary, judicial investigation of these matters conducted by Gen. Leone Zingales, *Procuratore Militare*, but he found himself hampered and obstructed at every turn and finally gave up the task in disgust. The explanation is political. The facts revealed in his initial investigations pointed directly to the involvement and responsibility of some leaders of the Communist party in North Italy at a time when that party formed part of the government of Italy.[116] Nevertheless, we can establish some things.

113. *Triumph and Tragedy*, p. 529.

114. Cadorna, *La riscossa*, p. 263; Graziani, *Ho difeso la patria*, pp. 535–37. Cf. Delzell, *Mussolini's Enemies*, pp. 535–36.

115. Some neofascist writers later gave the fantastic figure of 300,000 slaughtered in the insurrectionary period, but the Ministry of the Interior in 1952 gave an official figure of 2,344. Delzell suggests that the correct figure should be somewhere between the official statistic and 40,000 (*Mussolini's Enemies*, pp. 545–46).

116. The Communist party was represented in every Italian ministry from April 1944, when Palmiro Togliatti returned to Italy from Moscow by way of Algiers and took office under Badoglio until May 1947 when Alcide de Gasperi, responsible to the elected Constituent Assembly, determined to govern without the Communists and their Socialist allies.

One of the satchels of documents which Mussolini had with him at the time of his arrest [117] made its way rather promptly into the custody of the Italian government. On May 3, Colonel Malgeri, whose Finance Guards had played a critical role in the seizure of power by the insurrection on April 26, presented himself to General Cadorna. He brought with him a sergeant who stated that at Dongo the Partisans had seized a satchel full of documents which Mussolini had declared were of the greatest importance for the future of Italy. Cadorna asked that the case of documents be brought to him. The sergeant came back after a few days, this time accompanied by Count Bellini delle Stelle who promised to deliver the package of documents. On May 17 the leather case, which had been opened and apparently had been tampered with, was brought to General Cadorna who promptly sent it to the Ministry of War in Rome. [118]

This case must have been the second one, so to speak, the one for which we have no record of contents at the time it was taken from Mussolini. Cadorna examined the papers, had a complete record compiled, and this too he transmitted to Rome. On the basis of his own cursory examination he did not regard these papers as of very great importance. [119]

When General Zingales undertook his preliminary investigation of the affair of Dongo, Count Bellini delle Stelle testified that he personally had taken custody of both cases of documents which had been taken from Mussolini by Lazzaro. They were at first put in a bank along with parts of the treasure, and after a time were removed and hidden in a crypt of the parish church of Gera. A short while later Bellini and Lazzaro decided that the papers ought to be turned over to General Cadorna. But Bellini was ill at the time and entrusted this delivery to a certain Sergeant Scappin. Before consigning the papers to the sergeant, Bellini examined them. There were various files: one of correspondence between Mussolini and Hitler; one on the Verona trials; a file on the private life of Prince Humbert of Savoy; and a group of papers on the expatriation of Mussolini from Switzerland.

Count Bellini delle Stelle further testified that Sergeant Scappin met Michele Moretti at the headquarters of the CVL and was persuaded or compelled to turn the documents over to the Committee of National Liberation of Como. Bellini added that somewhat later he heard that the documents were to be transmitted to the headquarters at Lecco and that Prince Aldrovandi was entrusted with this transfer. It appeared, how-

117. See notes 73, 74, and 75 above.
118. Cadorna, *La riscossa*, p. 270.
119. Ibid.

ever, that Aldrovandi kept the documents which meanwhile had been photographed in Como.[120]

Lazzaro gave a somewhat different account. He stated that Sergeant Scappin telephoned to Bertinelli, the prefect of the province of Como, and asked that he and the provincial chief of police (*Questore*) be present at the opening of the files, but that these officials failed to appear. Lazzaro inferred that five persons, members of the CLN and all belonging to parties of the Left, examined the documents and photographed them. Some other person, unnamed, testified to Zingales that the files were opened by seven persons including Aldrovandi, and that when the seals were broken, everyone wanted some of the documents for himself.[121]

Dr. Guzzi, former president of the A.N.P.I. (National Association of the Italian Partisans) of Como testified that Aldrovandi kept both the originals and copies of the documents of special importance.[122]

Thus there seems to be some real evidence that certain persons in the Partisan movement and closely associated with the capture of Mussolini, took a portion of the documents which he had on his person on the day before he was shot. They seem to have been brought to Como. Some of the personal papers, exactly which it is not stated, were photographed at Como, and it is said that this work was done in the studio called "La Fototechnica" on the via Indipendenza, and at the order of Communist elements of the headquarters of the piazza.[123]

120. Saini, *Notte di Dongo*, p. 139. Bellini's testimony clearly refers only to the first satchel, for his description of the contents tallies closely with that of Lazzaro when he opened that case in the presence of Mussolini. In his testimony Bellini made no mention of the delivery of one of the satchels to General Cadorna. His book, coauthored with Lazzaro (*Dongo ultima azione*), sheds no light on the problem for it terminates with the departure of Colonel Valerio from Dongo on April 28.

121. Saini, *Notte di Dongo*, p. 142. The reference to seals of envelopes suggests that the papers had been repacked, for when the files were first opened at Dongo, they were tied in blue ribbon. Sealing might have been done at the bank.

122. Saini, *Notte di Dongo*, p. 143.

123. Spampanato, *Contromemoriale*, 3:275. Most, but not all of Spampanato's account of the documents appears to be based on the interrogations conducted by General Zingales.

Amicucci, *I 600 giorni di Mussolini*, pp. 286–87, has a somewhat different explanation regarding the correspondence of Hitler and Mussolini. These exchanges, he states, were kept by Mussolini in three sets of copies: (1) the copies in the leather satchel which was seized with the Duce; (2) a set which was entrusted by Mussolini to the Japanese ambassador, Idaka [Hidaka], who returned to Japan by way of Berlin and the USSR; and (3) a set which was given to Biggini, minister of national education. Biggini, it is maintained, had hoped to write a history of the relations of Mussolini with the Germans on the order of his *Storia della conciliazione*. Carlo Alberto Biggini died of cancer in Milan in the summer of 1945 under an assumed name. Some one tipped off the local CLN that the deceased had a file of important documents, and thus this file also ended up in the hands of the CLN.

The one satchel or briefcase of documents taken from Mussolini at Dongo seems not to have been the only group of his private papers which was seized by partisan elements and photographed at Como or possibly at Milan. There was the metal trunk which disappeared between Milan and Como on April 25, and it was said that there was a black leather satchel which Mussolini gave to Donna Rachele at their last meeting. In any event there are traces of a considerably greater quantity of Mussolini's Papers floating around underground in the period right after his death than could possibly have come from the one briefcase.

What of the Treasure of Dongo which disappeared in the same period of confusion which followed the shooting of Mussolini? Some paper money and checks had been in the first of Mussolini's leather cases taken from him at Dongo. Several other suitcases of valuables, gold bullion, and Italian and foreign paper money had been taken further up the road by the German column which tried to get rid of it at Ponte del Passo, but most of this was recovered by the Partisans.[124] This was all brought together in the house of Hofmann, the Swiss associate of the men of the Fifty-second Garibaldi Brigade. There a rather detailed inventory was made which was signed by Pedro, by "Neri" (Luigi Canali) and Giannna (his mistress), by Michele Moretti, and by Pietro Terzi. It was later said that the treasure amounted to some ninety million dollars.[125]

Apparently Count Bellini's intention was to turn this treasure over to the Italian state. When he reported to General Cadorna in May he an-

Amicucci indicates that the file given to Biggini was the source of the copies printed in the *Corriere d'Informazione* and other newspapers.

Amicucci has a very detailed account of the movements of Mussolini and the hierarchs on April 26 (chap. 22, pp. 267–74) and of the capture and shooting of Mussolini (chap. 23, pp. 275–87) but this is not the testimony of an eyewitness. Amicucci was himself arrested on April 26. His account is that of a very well informed journalist who was close to Mussolini in the period of the Republic of Salò.

124. See notes 75 and 76 above.

In 1949 it was estimated that the total value was something more than $66 million. See Edmund L. Palmieri and John Kobler, "What Happened to Mussolini's Millions: A story of a great political scandal; How partisans captured the Duce's vast treasure . . . How two young lovers were slain to hide it . . . How it helps pay the bills of the Communist party," *Life*, January 17, 1949. These authors give the breakdown (p. 78):

Fascist government reserves (gold bullion, gold coin, Italian and foreign currencies)	$61,000,000.00
German Navy, Quartermaster, and Luftwaffe funds	$ 4,000,000.00
Mussolini's personal funds (Swiss francs, French francs, U.S. dollars, British pounds, etc.)	$ 1,210,590.00
Gold wedding rings for the Ethiopian War	$ 49,000.00
	$66,259,590.00

125. Saini, *Notte di Dongo*, p. 97; Delzell, *Mussolini's Enemies*, p. 541.

nounced that he would deliver not only a satchel of documents but also thirty kilograms of bullion and twenty million lire in paper money. This delivery was never made. Cadorna heard nothing further at the time regarding the seized treasure nor did he then imagine that it would later become such a matter of dispute.[126]

It is said that Communist members of the Fifty-second Garibaldi Brigade insisted that the treasure be turned over, not to the Italian government, but to the Communist party. The suitcases with the currency and valuables, some testified, were loaded into an auto which was escorted by a few Garibaldini. During the move they were joined by other Partisans, Communists all, who shot the members of the original escort, making it appear that it was a seizure by unknown persons. General Zingales determined that Gianna personally delivered a box of jewels from the Dongo treasure to Dante Gorreri in Como who, along with Pietro Terzi, seems to have played a big part in the diversion of the treasure to Communist party headquarters in Milan.[127]

Neri and Gianna had objected to the stratagem employed to disguise the diversion of the treasure. Neri, it is said, had looked forward to a democratization of the Italian Communist party. He began making inquiries as to what had become of the treasure and seems to have been led into a trap by Terzi. His body was hauled out of Lake Como. Gianna then began looking for those responsible for her lover's death and she too disappeared.[128]

Possibly Walter Audisio himself narrowly escaped the fate of Neri and Gianna. As his identity emerged he became quite a hero for the Communist press, but he was not a member of the inner circle directing the party, and some said that he knew too much about the disappearance of the documents and the treasure. It was reported that some Communists planned to shoot him when he spoke at the Basilica Massenzio on March 30, 1947, and then for false carabinieri to shoot into the crowd and create a panic, and then to blame the action on neofascists and the carabinieri.[129]

Although General Zingales gave up in his preliminary investigation of the Dongo affair, the rumors persisted that Pietro Terzi had arranged the delivery of the treasure to Dante Gorreri who moved it to Communist headquarters in Milan. But Gorreri had been elected to parliament and thus acquired immunity from arrest. This immunity expired in 1956, and

126. Cadorna, *La riscossa*, pp. 270–71.
127. Saini, *Notte di Dongo*, p. 98.
128. Saini, *Notte di Dongo*, pp. 55, 97–99.
129. Rome telegram no. 683, March 29, 1947 (865.00/3-2947), Central Files, Department of State.

in April 1957 Gorreri and 34 others were brought to trial in the court of Assize of Padua. During the course of the trial Terzi testified that the Fifty-second Brigade had decided to hand the treasure to the Communist party because the Communists had fought harder than any others. Another Partisan testified that five heavy suitcases were loaded onto a Fiat and delivered to Gorreri in Como. Gorreri refused to admit any of these allegations. In August one of the jurors committed suicide, and the presiding judge was forced to declare a mistrial—this after more than a million words of testimony from 381 witnesses.[130]

Publications by *L'Unità* and Others

In the month following the "execution" of Mussolini, on May 24 to be exact, the Milanese edition of *L'Unità*, organ of the Communist party of Italy, began a series of articles entitled: "From the Secret Documents of the Founder of the Empire." This brief series was introduced by the explanation:

Among the documents which Mussolini had with him when he was captured by patriots there was also this letter from Hitler which we are publishing first of all: it was in the original text and also in the Italian translation. We are in possession of the photographic reproduction of both. It was the last letter sent to Mussolini by his accomplice and master *[padrone]*. . . .

The criteria which prevailed in the choice of the documents—there were some 300 which Mussolini intended to carry with him into Switzerland—becomes clear enough at the first examination. They were to have been used, according to his intention, for his own defense. They are, however, without exception, the proof of his guilt and of that of his colleagues.

The series led off with the text in full of Hitler's letter to Mussolini dated December 27, 1944.[131] The series continued on May 25 with two memoranda by Carlo Silvestri to Mussolini dated respectively April 23 and April 24, 1945. On May 28, *L'Unità* of Milan published two more items in the series: A letter by Mussolini to Kesselring, commander of the German forces in Italy, without date but after the Allied conquest of the Apennines and of France, and an incomplete text of a letter of Musso-

---

130. Delzell, *Mussolini's Enemies*, p. 542.

Apparently there was no retrial, nor any publication of testimony rendered during the trial (letter of Dr. Giorgio Rochat, Comité international d'histoire de la deuxième guerre mondiale, Milan, January 15, 1973, to the author in response to questions submitted through Professor Delzell as intermediary).

131. I have followed the lead provided by Re, *Storia di un archivio*, p. 23, and by Spampanato, *Contromemoriale*, 3:246, and checked the files of the Milanese edition of *L'Unità* in the Library of Congress.

lini to Hitler, dated September 27, 1943. Then on June 1, 1945, *L'Unità* published the text of the letter which Carlo Silvestri, on behalf of the Duce, addressed on April 25, 1945, to the Central Committee of the *Partito Socialista Italiano di Unità Proletaria.*[132]

These documents were, of course, the property of the Italian state. Legally the Allies, that is the United States and Great Britain, could have claimed them on the basis of Article 35 of the Long Terms of Armistice of September 29, 1943.[133] In the course of the investigation of the affair of Dongo, General Zingales summoned the editor of *L'Unità* to testify, but he managed to avoid appearing.[134] After a few months there were other letters from the file of correspondence between Mussolini and Hitler which were published in the *Corriere d'Informazione,* the afternoon edition of the famous *Corriere della Sera* of Milan.[135]

On December 10, 1945, the ANSA News Agency put out a flier offering exclusive rights of publication to its member associates "of documents originating in the secret archive of the Palazzo Venezia." It was stated:

There are in all 375 letters, hand written pieces, secret reports, telegrams, many of them autographs, reflecting a particularly hectic *[nevralgico]* period of Italian life in the years 1934–35–36. They are concerned with the preparation and development of the Ethiopian War, with its behind-the-scenes actions, its internal and foreign repercussions, the rivalries among the leaders, the mania of Mussolini for imperial greatness.

In a follow-up circular letter of December 22, 1945, the director of ANSA announced: "Work is proceeding in preparation of the articles obtained from the documents which were recovered in the baggage of a Fascist ex-prefect in the train *[al seguito]* of Mussolini."

In reporting this development, the American embassy mentioned that the head of the police had informed ANSA that publication of the documents would be regarded as an infraction of the public security law, but he had not threatened action, and ANSA planned to go ahead with its distribution. As a measure of precaution the agency had photographed all of the documents in case the originals should be seized, and the photographs were to be ready with the explanatory articles at the end of January 1946. An ANSA official had stated that "the documents were

132. Cf. Deakin, *Brutal Friendship,* pp. 796–98. The series terminates at this point, apparently, without explanation. Cf. Spampanato, *Contromemoriale,* 3:246.

133. This article stipulated: "The Italian Government will supply all information and provide all documents required by the United Nations. There shall be no destruction or concealment of archives, records, plans or any other documents or information."

134. Saini, *Notte di Dongo,* p. 143.

135. Spampanato, *Contromemoriale,* 3:246.

purchased from a Partisan in the North who had taken them from a flee-ing Fascist official." The *Corriere d'Informazione* of Milan had practically concluded a deal for purchase of the documents when ANSA appealed to its members for support in putting in a better bid and was able to get possession of the documents.[136] These facts rather suggest that this par-ticular group of documents came from the zinc chest which disappeared on the road between Milan and Como on April 25, 1945.

In February 1946, the French publishing house, "Éditions du Pa-vois," released a little book, *Les lettres secrètes échangées par Hitler et Mussolini*.[137] It offered French translations of twenty-eight messages ex-changed by Hitler and Mussolini between January 1940 and May 1943. André François-Poncet, who had been French ambassador in Berlin, 1931–38, and in Rome from November 1938 until June 1940, wrote a delightful introduction to the compilation with a finely drawn compari-son of the Latin with the Teutonic dictator. But there is not the remotest suggestion anywhere between the covers of the book regarding the prov-enance of the documents. Somewhat impudently a kind of claim of copy-right is raised regarding these documents of a foreign state.[138]

In June 1946 the Italian publishing house Rizzoli brought out a book entitled: *Hitler e Mussolini: Lettere e documenti*. It presented the texts of sixty-three messages between the two dictators plus four other official Italian documents of July–August 1943.[139] The letters include the Italian originals of the French booklet, plus eighteen letters or messages of the year 1939, and texts of other documents such as Mussolini's report on the meeting with Hitler on June 18, 1940, and the minutes of the meeting of October 15, 1940, when the decision was made to attack Greece. No serious question was raised from any quarter regarding the authenticity of these texts. The circumstances indicate overwhelmingly that the ver-sions as published in the Italian press in 1945, in French translation in Paris, and in the Italian booklet in 1946 were the copies which came from Mussolini's private archives and which fell into Communist-Partisan hands as a result of the capture of Mussolini and his summary shooting.

The Italian book has an introduction by Vittorio Zincone, a distin-

136. Rome despatch no. 2929, January 11, 1946, copies of the flier and letter as enclo-sures (865.918/1-1146), Central Files, Department of State.

Cf. Gaetano Salvemini, *Prelude to World War II* (London: Victor Gollancz, 1953)p. 207, fn. 1, citing the London *Times* January 20, 1945 [1946].

137. "Achevé d'imprimer sur les presses de l'Imprimerie de Sceaux le 25 février 1946 pour les Éditions du Pavois, 51 Avenue Montaigne, Paris."

138. "Tous droits de reproduction, traduction, et adaptation réservé pour tout pays, Paris 1946."

139. These texts are from the documents left behind by Badoglio when he abandoned Rome in September 1943. Cf. note 4 above.

guished Italian journalist, coeditor of the Roman daily, *Il Risorgimento Liberale*, former editor of *Il Resto del Carlino* of Bologna. He provides us with only this teasing suggestion about the acquisition of the documents: "What we now offer (by agreement with an American publisher to whom the texts came by diverse routes) has above all the merit of being the only collection which is almost complete.[140] It is difficult to provide a clean bill of sale with hijacked goods.

This publication of Italian state papers by Rizzoli has an asserted claim of copyright by King Features of New York. What that amounts to or signified I have been unable to determine.[141]

There cannot be the slightest doubt regarding the authenticity of the texts given in *Hitler e Mussolini: Lettere e documenti*. In that great series of documents which is of basic importance regarding the origins and early course of World War II, the *Documents on German Foreign Policy, 1918–1945*, we editors conscientiously strove to provide sound texts of every known significant communication between Hitler and Mussolini.[142] I myself spent many hours comparing the texts of the various copies of Hitler-Mussolini correspondence: that is, the copies in the German Foreign Office archives, in the Italian *Archivio di Gabinetto* as recorded in the films from the Lisbon Papers, and in the published book-

---

140. *Hitlere Mussolini*, p. ix. Zincone doubtless knew something more about the source of the Hitler-Mussolini correspondence than he let his readers know in June 1946. In a signed article in the *Risorgimento Liberale* of April 3, 1947, he referred to Audisio's remarks at the Basilica di Massenzio (cf. note 129 above) and other remarks at other times and places by Communist orators suggesting a new version regarding the disappearance of Mussolini's documents after his capture. Zincone went on to state:

"The Mussolini-Hitler file, to which the Communist orators referred might very well be that which I was personally engaged in editing for the firm of Rizzoli and which was handed over by an American agency. It should be added that the block of material in possession of the American firm was integrated with many letters of other provenance, but all of them were checked as to authenticity of text by persons who previously had been able to know the originals."

141. On April 22, 1966, I called the Register of Copyrights and asked about that book. I was told that that office had no record of registration of this copyright by King Features Syndicate. But it was explained that lack of registration does not necessarily prove that a book was not copyrighted.

On April 25 I wrote to King Features Syndicate about their claim of copyright and about the source of the letters and documents offered to the public. Their reply of May 5, 1966, stated: "These letters constituted an International News Service feature and, undoubtedly, were distributed by us since we were representing the news service at that time in the foreign field. International News Service no longer is in existence. It was merged several years ago with United Press, which is now United Press International. We have been unable to locate any records which would provide answers to your questions."

142. That is excluding such trivia as "Thank you for your last letter," or "I have received your telegram."

let, *Hitler e Mussolini*, which are, beyond all reasonable doubt, the copies from Mussolini's own files. In no case did I encounter anything that looked like a fabrication or forgery. In every case the texts were identical or had only such minor variations of punctuation, paragraphing, spelling and phraseology as to indicate that one copy was probably drawn from a slightly different stage of drafting.[143] As the late Sir Charles Webster so correctly emphasized, it is seldom in the modern era that an important document survives in one form or one version only.

Was There a File of Correspondence with Churchill Which Churchill Retrieved?

Prime Minister Churchill was deeply hurt and bitterly disappointed when the British people, whom he had so magnificently served during the war, turned him and the conservative party out of office in the election of July 1945.[144] For a time he seems to have thought of going to the Riviera, which was under General Eisenhower's command, where he could do some painting, one of his favorite pastimes. He decided, however, in favor of a vacation in North Italy whither he was invited by Field Marshal Alexander, Supreme Allied Commander, Mediterranean. Alexander had prepared a villa for his illustrious guest, a villa sequestered by the Allied armies, located at Moltrasio on the western shore of Lake Como and which was the property of Guido Donegani, and Italian industrialist. Alexander also provided his Dakota plane for the flight from England to Milan on September 2. For a couple of weeks of that month Churchill painted at various points along the shores of Lake Como; he reviewed his wartime minutes to the cabinet and to the chiefs of staff preparatory to writing his memoirs of the war; and the whole party enjoyed themselves in the home of the absent Donegani. Field Marshal Alexander paid his respects on September 7 and 8.[145] There is no doubt that Churchill was on the shores of Lake Como in September 1945, and that while there he did quite a bit of painting.

143. See particularly ser. D, vol. 9, nos. 92 (p. 131); 168 (p. 237); 190 (p. 271); 233 (p. 321).

144. See the comment of Averell Harriman in the book by Gerald Pawle, *The War and Colonel Warden* (London: George G. Harrap & Co., Ltd., 1963), p. 7; see also Charles McMoran Wilson, *Churchill, Taken from the Diaries of Lord Moran: The Struggle for Survival 1940–1945* (Boston: Houghton Mifflin Co., 1966), p. 310 (entry for August 8, 1945).

145. There is an account of Churchill's vacation and a record of some of the persons who called in Wilson, *Churchill* (pp. 313–27). See also Elizabeth Nel, *Mr. Churchills's Secretary* (New York: Coward-McCann, Inc., 1958), pp. 182–84.

Churchill's delightful little essay, *Painting as a Pastime* (1950; reprint ed., New York: Cornerstone Library, 1965) includes eighteen illustrations. Nos. 3, 6, 8, and 17 are on the

Some of his other actions are more problematical. Italian and Swiss journalists were rather quick to suggest that Churchill's real motive in visiting near Como so shortly after the end of hostilities was to regain possession of the Italian copies of his correspondence with Mussolini. Saini notes that "Renzo" (Lorenzo Bianchi) declared that he saw such a file in the leather case which Mussolini turned over to "Bill" at Dongo.[146] *Il Tempo* in a despatch from Milan stated that Churchill had regained his letters to Mussolini. The *Voix Ouvrière* of Geneva in an article of June 8, 1946, gave some details: that Churchill stayed in Moltrasio in the villa of Donegani who, it was said, had fled to Switzerland. Churchill was said to have been seen burning papers. Emilio Re in his book of 1946 expressed disbelief in the story.[147]

When Duilio Susmel, as coauthor of the life of Mussolini, first dealt with the problem in 1955, he, too, felt that the evidence was inadequate

shores of Lake Como or nearby and are dated September 1945. No. 14, "The Mediterranean near Genoa," is also dated September 1945.

The English sources for Churchill's Italian vacation do not identify the villa as that of Guido Donegani but refer to it simply as the property of an Italian steel magnate. Donegani was wanted by the patriots for his role in support of Mussolini. Identification of the owner is from Italian and Swiss sources.

146. Saini, *Notte di Dongo*, p. 143, fn. 40. Saini himself considers this information about a Churchill file to be inadequate and contradictory.

Lazzero, "Un passo," 3, August 25, 1968 [p. 43], states definitely that there was such a Churchill file, but there are certain difficulties about that statement as we have noted above, note 75.

Other references to a Churchill-Mussolini file are to be found in Ruggero Zangrandi, *1943: 25 luglio–8 settembre*, 2d ed. (Milan: Feltrinelli editore, 1964), p. 772; Amicucci, *600 giorni*, p. 286; Spampanato, *Contromemoriale*, 3:275–77; Bandini, *Ultime 95 ore*, pp. 85–86. All of these are secondary.

On the other hand the late Professor Mario Toscano, writing in 1961, referred to the story as "the legend of a Mussolini-Churchill file" which, because of Mussolini's intense resentment toward Great Britain, "should be definitely buried, at least for the period prior to July 25 [1943]." See "Le vicende degli archivi di Palazzo Chigi e dei dairi di prigionia di Mussolini catturati dai nazisti dopo l'armistizio," in *Pagine di storia diplomatica contemporanea*, vol. 2 *Origini e vicende della seconda guerra mondiale* (Milan: Dott. A. Giuffrè editore, 1963), p. 280. Against this argument is Mussolini's curious action on April 23 in drafting a letter intended for Churchill (see note 32 above).

In any case if there had been such a file, it would have been in the first leather case, and not in the one delivered to General Cadorna, for he most certainly would have noted it and recorded it.

147. *Storia di un archivio*, pp. 30–31. I also find the account in the *Voix Ouvrière* very difficult to accept. It gives the time of Churchill's visit as August rather than September, a minor inaccuracy. It then states that English agents tried to interrogate Mussolini when he was first arrested in July 1943, but that he replied that he would state his case only before the international tribunal. How British agents were able at that time to talk to Mussolini when even the Germans could not discover him is not explained.

to support a positive statement regarding a file of letters between Churchill and Mussolini.[148] Susmel, however, was intrigued by the problem; he devoted more time for its research over the succeeding years, and ultimately reached a very different conclusion.[149] Susmel first points out that there was some correspondence between the British statesman and the Italian dictator: Churchill's letter of May 16, 1940, and Mussolini's reply of May 18.[150] This exchange was not all. When the Germans seized the archives of the Palazzo Chigi in September 1943, they shipped forty-one cases of documents to Berlin. Although these papers themselves were lost, the records were studied by officials of the German Foreign Office and some summaries of the studies have survived in the records of the *Auswärtiges Amt* which later were seized and microfilmed by the British and Americans.[151] The German summary report of November 20, 1943, refers to the British efforts at the end of May 1940 to induce Italy to remain neutral and states: "We already know that these last English efforts took in part the form of letters from Churchill to Mussolini." Susmel here correctly finds documentary evidence that Churchill wrote other letters to Mussolini after the one of May 16.[152]

I myself find it temptingly easy to believe that there may have existed a file maintained by Mussolini of correspondence with the British statesman and that Churchill succeeded in retrieving it and destroying it. What of the relations of the two men and of the circumstances? Churchill first met the Duce in 1927 and formed a strong admiration for him. Like most of the Tories, he accepted completely the myth that Mussolini had saved Italy from communism. In a press interview held after that meeting with the Italian dictator, he declared that were he an Italian, he would support Mussolini in his struggle against Leninism. Churchill also clearly indicated his view that Britain's policy during the Ethiopian crisis was a mistaken one.[153] Although Churchill poured out his contempt and

148. Pini and Susmel, *Mussolini, l'uomo e l'opera*, 4:514.

149. Duilio Susmel, "Così Churchill rientro in possesso del carteggio con Mussolini," *Domenica di Corriere* (popular weekly of the *Corriere della Sera*), January 29, 1967, pp. 15–19. Cited hereafter as Susmel, "Così Churchill".

150. Ibid., p. 15. Texts of these messages are printed in full by Churchill himself, *The Second World War*, vol. 2, *Their Finest Hour* (Boston: Houghton Mifflin Co., 1949), pp. 121–22.

151. See the Introduction, note 1 (p. 2) and chap. 1, note 49.

152. Susmel, "Così Churchill," p. 16. The German report of November 20, 1943, is printed in English translation in Deakin, *Brutal Friendship*, pp. 834–37.

Susmel clearly establishes the fact that there was some correspondence between Churchill and Mussolini. This does not prove that Mussolini kept a special file of such exchanges. The few letters that are positively known to have been exchanged may have been filed in some different fashion.

153. *Their Finest Hour*, p. 121.

scorn for Mussolini in his role as Hitler's lackey in World War II, he nevertheless retained to the end a kind of admiration for the man whom he called the great Italian lawgiver.

Furthermore, the circumstances in North Italy in the summer and fall of 1945 would certainly have made it possible for Churchill, or for some British agents serving him, to ferret out a Mussolini-Churchill file once they had picked up its trail. Churchill and Alexander were close friends. Northern Italy remained under Allied Military Government until December 31, 1945.[154] Spampanato suggests that the sudden termination of the publication by L'Unità of some of Mussolini's correspondence may have been because of Allied pressure.[155]

Although Churchill was an accomplished historian,[156] he would have had no scruple about suppressing documents which might have cast shadows on his wartime reputation. Churchill was extraordinarily zealous in defending the reputation of the British royal family, in trying to suppress records which would further damage the public image of the Duke of Windsor.[157]

But possibility, probability, and analogy do not constitute historical proof. How good are the sources? Gravelli, the last chief of staff of the guard, told Spampanato that Mussolini showed him the folder of correspondence with Churchill on April 21, 1945, and exclaimed: "Gravelli, it is necessary to resist for another month; I have enough in my hand to win the peace." [158]

154. C. R. S. Harris, *Allied Administration of Italy 1943–1945* (London: H. M. Stationery Office, 1957), pp. 354, 366.

155. *Contromemoriale*, 3:276. See note 132 above.

156. See the interesting appreciation of Churchill as an historian by J. H. Plumb in *Churchill: Four Faces and the Man*, issued by A. J. P. Taylor et al. (London: Allen Lane—The Penguin Press, 1969).

157. When the Anglo-American teams began the collecting and microfilming of the German Foreign Office documents in 1945 the file on the Duke of Windsor's passage through Spain and Portugal in the summer of 1940 soon came to light. In August of 1945 and earlier the British ambassador in Washington proposed that the file be withdrawn or restricted in circulation. A part of this story is indicated in *Foreign Relations of the United States, 1945* (Washington: U.S. Government Printing Office, 1968), 3:1120–21, Aide Mémoire of the Secretary of State to the British Ambassador, October 11, 1945.

The Tripartite Project for the publication of the *Documents on German Foreign Policy, 1918–1945*, was prevented, by the direct intervention of Churchill, from proceeding with preparation for publication of documents from this file when the Conservatives came back into power. The way was cleared for their publication in ser. D, vol. 10, only after Mr. Attlee had again succeeded Churchill as prime minister.

158. Spampanato, *Contromemoriale*, 3:275. Oscar Sforni also referred to such a file in a letter of September 29, 1945 (See note 165 below).

This is not quite firsthand. The clinching proof that Mussolini maintained a file of correspondence with Churchill would be the listing of such a file in some index of Mussolini's Private Papers.

What happened to the file, or alleged file, beyond Milan? Bandini asserts that when Mussolini last saw his wife at the prefecture in Como, he gave her a black leather folder containing the correspondence with Churchill—this along with other documents and objects of great value. Donna Rachele was staying at that time with the minor children, Romano and Anna Maria, at the Villa Mantero. Mussolini, it is said, told her, in case of threats to her safety, to make contact with the English: that the file of correspondence with Churchill would serve as a kind of safe-conduct.[159]

Of course Donna Rachele's autobiography has serious limitations and omissions. Possibly she did receive the Churchill-Mussolini file from Benito and avoided mention of it. On April 29, she and the children were taken to the police station; on May 2, she was moved to Milan; on May 10, she was transferred to the custody of the British and was held in a camp at Terni; and then, toward the end of July, she was transferred to Ischia.[160] It is not absolutely excluded that British agents were able during this time to take the file from her person, or to learn from her where it had been hidden. But we have no mention of any such thing on her part.

Lazzero, who states definitely that the Churchill file was in the briefcase taken from Mussolini at the town hall of Dongo, has some comments regarding its further vicissitudes. Mussolini's briefcase, he states, was first taken to the Villa Miglio, headquarters of the Fifty-second Partisan Brigade, even before it was deposited in the safe in the bank, identified as the savings bank of Domàso (a small town between Gravedona and Gera Laria). Bill had to be absent on April 28 and removed the case from the bank and turned it over to "Pinùn" (Aldo Castelli), a Partisan who was staying at the inn, "Italia." Castelli opened the briefcase and saw the file of Mussolini-Churchill correspondence, a rather voluminous

159. Bandini, *Ultime 95 ore*, pp. 85–86, fn. 26. See note 50 above.

Here the crucial testimony is missing, that of Donna Rachele herself. See note 49 above. There is no mention in her autobiography, *Vita con Benito*, pp. 267–71, of receiving anything directly from Benito at Como. In the interview which she granted Federico Patellani in April 1947 she mentioned her private correspondence with Benito, the file on Ciano and Buffarini-Guidi, the manuscript for the *Storia di un anno*, and Mussolini's record of imprisonment in the summer of 1943. But she made no mention of a Churchill-Mussolini file. There is no apparent reason for her not mentioning it if she had received it.

In her autobiography Donna Rachele mentions that she and the children decided to notify the CLN of their presence in Como, and that shortly thereafter three men searched the house. They found thirty-one objects of value which were listed officially the next day, April 29, 1945, but here again there is no mention of documents. See note 50 above.

The explanations offered by Bandini about the Churchill-Mussolini file at Como are not convincing.

160. *Vita con Benito*, pp. 274–79.

file, but he did not read it through. A few days later it seems that Bill returned and declared that the Churchill file had been stolen from the headquarters during the night.

According to this explanation it was only then, that is after the disappearance of the Churchill file, that the briefcase was hidden in the crypt of the church at Gera Laria whence it was taken to the prefecture of Como. The disappearance of the Churchill file coincided with the appearance on the scene of a lawyer from Verona and two British counterespionage agents. The new prefect of Como, Virginio Bertinelli, held the Mussolini documents for a time, it is stated, and used the opportunity to read the Churchill file. He remembered a series of letters to Eden and other English politicians regarding use of funds of the British intelligence service for supporting Denikin and Wrangel against the Red Army during the civil war in Russia.

We learn further from Lazzero's article that Churchill demanded the file through the Allied military command and Lord Hamilton, chief of the British information service, but Bertinelli gave only evasive responses. Churchill himself then came to Italy and occupied the villa in Moltrasio belonging to Donegani. Bertinelli hid the Churchill file in a long horse in the gymnasium of Como. One day at dawn a group of British agents broke into the gymnasium, found and seized the file. Churchill himself returned to England a day later.[161]

Susmel has an explanation different both from that of Bandini and from that of Lazzero. The key element in his account is Guido Donegani, owner of the villa where Churchill stayed during his visit to North Italy.[162] Donegani was arrested on April 29 at the order of the new, anti-Fascist prefect, Lombardi, and confined in the San Vittore prison along with Buffarini-Guidi at the beginning of May. A third prisoner in San Vittore was Ignazio Brückner who often heard Donegani and Buffarini-Guidi talk about Mussolini's archives and particularly about the famous file of correspondence between Churchill and Mussolini. According to Susmel, Buffarini-Guidi was interrogated by the American C.I.C. in regard to that file but the leads which he suggested proved false. The British Field Security Service (F.S.S.) interrogated Donegani and on July

161. Lazzero, "Un passo," 3, August 25, 1968 [p. 44]. Pier Bellini delle Stelle, Aldo Castelli, and Virginio Bertinelli are all listed as contributors or collaborators in Lazzero's article which has a certain consistency and considerable credibility. Indeed, it seems a more plausible explanation than that which is offered by Susmel and which is taken up below. Yet it presents some difficulties. If Bellini is one essential source regarding the Churchill file, why did he not mention it in his testimony to General Zingales? Cf. note 120 above.

162. Termed the Villa Apraxin in Moltrasio, a property which had belonged to Donegani since 1926. Susmel, "Così Churchill," p. 18.

14, much to everyone's surprise, Donegani was released. It would seem
that a bargain had been struck between the F.S.S. and Donegani: if he
would lead them to the file he would have his freedom.[163]

Susmel states that there is confirmation from someone else regarding
the bargain and regarding Donegani's role in directing the F.S.S. to the
hiding place of the file, someone who did not wish to be named and is
simply designated "Signor X." Susmel assures us that this Signor X was
quite close to Major Malcolm Smith, the Britisher who in the summer of
1945 dug up the file from its hiding place. Signor X adds the details
regarding the bargain that Donegani would be enabled to retain his real
estate and other properties if he would indicate the place where the
famous file would be found. This he did. The release of Donegani from
his imprisonment excited great indignation, for his support of Mussolini
was notorious. The Italian officials who were involved in the release
were punished. But the British kept their part of the bargain and concealed Donegani while the word was given out that he had escaped to
England.[164]

Donegani directed the F.S.S. to the garden of the Villa Mantero and
there the file was dug up by Major Smith, a trusted friend of Churchill
and of Alexander. Susmel offers no explanation of how Donegani got
control of the file or at what price. This, he states, will always remain a
mystery. Major Smith reported to Field Marshal Alexander, who in turn
promptly notified Churchill in London. When Churchill was settled in at
the Villa Apraxin in early September, he sent his bodyguard, Captain
Johnson, along with Lieutenant Wildmore, to Major Smith who turned
over the documents. Furthermore, according to Signor X, Churchill on
September 13 went to the Villa Venegono, where Donegani was se-
cluded, to thank him personally for the assistance in the recovery of the
Italian copies of the correspondence with Mussolini. Susmel has no positive explanation of how the file got to the garden of the Villa Mantero. He
offers only the suggestion that on April 24 Mussolini entrusted the file to
his secretary, Gatti, who hid the file in the garden of the villa.[165] We can

163. The evidence cited here by Susmel is a letter addressed to him on December 20,
1966, by Ignazio Brückner, confirming earlier conversations, printed in "Così Churchill" p.
17. Brückner is certain of having heard the discussions of Donegani and Buffarini-Guidi,
and inferred the bargain of Donegani with the F.S.S. from a few chance phrases of Donegani and the expression on his face. This sort of evidence is not much more than gossip
and hearsay; but it served Susmel as a lead.

164. Susmel, "Così Churchill," p. 17.

165. Ibid., pp. 18–19. This account cannot be disregarded even though the identity of
Susmel's informant is not revealed. It frequently happens that a journalist gains very accurate information which he is able to publish, yet is professionally obligated not to disclose
his source. Likewise, contemporary historians sometimes use testimony from persons

say that it seems quite possible that Churchill in 1945 got possession of Mussolini's file of their correspondence, that is, the English originals and the Italian carbon copies.

Other writers have suggested or asserted that there were three sets or copies of this correspondence in Italy, or that three duplications were made of the documents in Mussolini's file. According to Dino Campini, Mussolini retained one copy on his person and had it in the leather case which he carried; he entrusted another copy to the Japanese ambassador, Hidaka; and the third copy was entrusted to Carlo Biggini. Biggini had been a Grand Councillor; later he served as minister of education in the Italian Social Republic; he had written a history of the reconciliation with the Church for which Mussolini had supplied him with documents from his private archives. Campini served as private secretary to Biggini and enjoyed his confidence.[166]

Bandini speaks of three sets of photocopies of the Churchill-Mussolini correspondence and states that in 1949 Churchill made another trip to Italy during which he succeeded in recovering two of these sets of copies but not the third.[167] Then in April 1970, Susmel announced at Florence, not without fanfare, that after years of search, he had found that third set of photocopies of the Churchill-Mussolini correspondence.[168] But we still lack positive proof about the file and its retrieval by Churchill, that is, the direct testimony of an eyewitness of the action.

whose anonymity must be protected, or some are permitted, from time to time, to study documents or personal papers but are restrained from citing them. Such restrictions frequently lead to abuse. Some writers spoof the public with references to mysterious, unnamed persons whose existence is shadowy indeed.

It is impossible to go very far with criticism if the critic cannot know the relationship of the testifier to the event described. One cannot determine if Susmel's Signor X was Italian, or British or what. Yet the informer gave specific names, dates and places; the information has something of a ring of authenticity. To use the metaphor of the marketplace: We "buy" that story; but we do not make final payment until the witness is identified and we are shown how he was able to know his facts.

Susmel finds partial confirmation of the facts which he relates in a letter of Oscar Sforni dated September 29, 1945, in which he wrote in part: "There was a personal file between Mussolini and Churchill and between Mussolini and Chamberlain. Now we have the unbelievable news that these documents, of such evident importance for the nation and for history, have been taken by officials of the English Intelligence Service on the occasion of Churchill's visit to Lake Como" (Susmel, "Così Churchill," p. 19).

166. Spampanato, *Contromemoriale*, 3:275–76, citing Campini, *Strano giuoco di Mussolini*. This account of the Churchill file in three copies is very much like Amicucci's story of the Hitler-Mussolini correspondence. See note 123 above.

167. Bandini, *Ultime 95 ore*, p. 85, fn. 26.

168. *Il Messaggero*, April 12, 1970, despatch dated Florence, April 11. Once again Susmel asks his readers to accept his words on faith. He was not able to state where he found

Seizure of the Feltrinelli Archives
and Their Transfer to AFHQ

But it is high time now that we turn to the other side of the picture, and follow the adventures of Mussolini's Private Papers in the hands of the Allies and as recorded in Anglo-American records.

On April 25, the day when Mussolini had been conferring with the Resistance leaders in the archiepiscopal palace of Cardinal Schuster, the Tenth Mountain Division crossed the Po at San Benedetto di Po, with the Tenth Counter Intelligence Corps (C.I.C.) detachment attached. On the twenty-sixth the division entered Mantua and the next day some of its elements reached Lake Garda. That night of April 27, Partisans who had come in a boat from Gargnano stated that they had heard that Mussolini and the ministers of the Fascist republic were packing and were planning to leave Gargnano. This was reported to G-2, and to the divisional commander, Maj. Gen. George P. Hays. It was decided to make a landing across the lake and take Gargnano.

On April 30, troops of the division made an amphibious landing shortly after midnight approximately three kilometers north of Gargnano. The orders were to surround Gargnano in the early morning hours. Special Agent James P. Furniss and Maj. Peter Gordon accompanied the troops. Immediately after the landing they took off for Gargnano, alerted Italian Partisans, and moved into Mussolini's abandoned villa. In the early morning of May 1 they found the former headquarters of the republican Fascist regime. Near Mussolini's office was a small room with partly packed cases of dossiers—Mussolini's personal files.

Major Gordon recalls seeing at the time some letters in Hitler's handwriting, police reports about Badoglio's activities, various materials on Curzio Malaparte and Balbo. General Hays was notified; he came to inspect; the room with the documents was then sealed off and Fifth Army's Document Section was notified.[169]

the documents, he declared, nor to describe their contents because of a precise pledge in this regard. He refers specifically only to the two letters of May 1940 first published by Churchill (see note 150 above) and to the other correspondence immediately prior to Italy's entrance into the war which is mentioned in the German Foreign Office memorandum (See note 152 above).

It is impossible to judge the significance of this discovery, or alleged discovery, on this basis. The secrecy regarding the source and the contents as well, leaves the reader with a degree of skepticism. We end up with the texts of only those two messages which Churchill himself published in 1949.

169. Letter, Major Peter Gordon, AUS (retired) to the author, April 26, 1966. The existence of Mussolini's archive was well known to the Allies. It constituted one of the prime

From the C.I.C. detachment of the Tenth Mountain Division Mussolini's files found at Feltrinelli were forwarded to the Documents Section of G-2, Fifth Army, Maj. Bart Ciforelli. In turn Major Ciforelli sent the collection of documents to the Intelligence Section of Fifteenth Army Group, Lt. Col. F. R. Rawes. Colonel Rawes then moved the documents to G-2, AFHQ.[170]

Four items from a file which Mussolini kept on Dino Grandi were apparently sent to London where for a time it was thought they might be used in charges against Grandi.[171] On May 20, 1945 Ambassador Kirk telegraphed the Department of State:

> G-2 section, A.F.H.Q., has come into possession of 42 large mail pouches containing certain private files of Fascist Party captured from Mussolini's villa in north Italy. A superficial inspection of them reveals a large amount of material which heretofore has not been available to us. Some of the documents·are of historical interest such as letters from d'Annunzio to Mussolini during the period 1919–1921 and letters exchanged between the former Italian Dictator and Hitler. Some files are of immediate use such as dossiers on Fascist organizations at Turin and Milan up to mid-April. There are also included dossiers on certain personalities of the Fascist Party which Mussolini kept personally, and there are included files on people such as Croce, Sforza, Kesselring, Ciano, Archbishop Spellman and members of Mussolini's own family. These files are in the Italian language.
>
> Since we do not have sufficient qualified personnel familiar with the Italian language to go through these documents with a view to picking out what would be of interest to the Department, we will go through as much as possible and will insure that American side of G-2 will make everything available to War Department.[172]

targets of the C.I.C. The Italian Documents Section of P.W.B. had it listed as Target 69. But when the P.W.B. team got there, they found the documents had all been cleaned out. ("Italian Documents Section, P.W.B. Northern Italy Assignment Activity April 27–May 31" p. 21, a report in twenty-eight typewritten pages, signed by Blanchard W. Bates, P.W.B. Unit 12. Copy of the report transmitted to the Department of State by Ambassador Kirk, despatch no. 1866, Rome, July 6, 1945 [865.414/7-645], Central Files, Department of State.)

170. Letter, Major D. E. L. Hayes to AC of S, G-2, AFHQ, 13 November 1945; letter, Colonel C. R. Tuff to Director of Military Intelligence, War Office (M.I.5) London, 20 February 1946, reel 476-A, heading "Mussolini-Grandi," Combined British-American Records of the Mediterranean Theater of Operations in World War II, Record Group 331, NARS.

171. The file on Dino Grandi was taken from what AFHQ designated as Bag no. 1 of the *Segreteria Particolare* of Mussolini. The items were:

(1) A thirteen-page letter ot Grandi to Mussolini, dated at Italian Embassy London, January 30, 1934; (2) Covering letter, one sheet, both sides, Grandi to Ciano, February 2, 1934; (3) An eight-page holograph, Grandi to Mussolini, March 1, 1935; (4) File copy of letter, one page, typed, Mussolini to Grandi, March 8, 1945, Sent to London, July 22, 1945. (Item GBI. 389.601/28, reel 476-A, AFHQ Microfilm Records, NARS.)

172. Caserta telegram no. 2259, (800.414/5-2045), Central Files, Department of State.

Acquisition of Mussolini's Papers Initially Seized by the Partisans: The Work of Translation at AFHQ

Mussolini, as we have noted, had taken a portion of his private archives with him on his final flight and these had been seized by the Partisans at the time of his capture. This part of the Mussolini private archives, or at least a major portion of this part, also came into the custody of the Anglo-American forces. On May 23, Ambassador Kirk notified the Department:

Certain very important documents which were taken from Mussolini on his capture have come into our possession at A.F.H.Q. They were surrendered by three Italian partisan leaders who have been responsible for capturing and executing the Duce and who made an offer to SAC [Supreme Allied Commander] on condition that (A) they would not be used to the future detriment of Italy and (B) that one of the partisans who had been an officer in Italian air force should be sent to England and a second one, a doctor, should be given Brit [ish] nationality and be allowed to live in one of Brit [ish] dominions.

These documents illustrate the international crisis of 1939 the entrance of Italy into the war, the first operations against Egypt, the attack on Greece, the Verona trials and plans for an alpine redoubt early in 1945. They consist mostly of Mussolini's personal copies taken from archives of his personal secretariat. They demonstrate fully official Italian attitude on various proposals mentioned above and illustrate the Italian side of relationship between Germany and Italy. The documents seem to have been picked out of Mussolini's files for purpose of writing a defense of his own position. Some of the papers in question are autographed by King Victor Emmanuel, Mussolini and by other prominent Italians and Fascists.

Pending decision as to final disposition of these documents, we will have photostatic copies made and transmitted to Department as soon as possible. Should the Dept. prefer, we could delay forwarding the documents for a time with a view to doing the best we can in making English translations thereof for the Department's files. What are Department's views? [173]

In the Operations Intelligence (O.I.), Documents Section of G-2, AFHQ, the work of studying and exploiting the Mussolini papers began promptly and was pushed with great energy, and, judging from the output, a considerable staff was employed in the work. Of the two parts of

173. Caserta, telegram no. 2317, (800.414/5-2345), Central Files, Department of State.
Apparently this group of documents was first delivered over to the British embassy, which then transferred it to AFHQ. In report no. 2, Operational Intelligence Section, Assistant Chief of Staff, G-2, AFHQ 29 May 1945, the documents listed in report no. 2 are described as: "Documents in addition to those turned in to the British Embassy in Rome by Italian Partisans and covered in report no. 1." Cf. notes 174 and 175 below.

the Mussolini private archives, those which Mussolini had with him at his death, and which had come into AFHQ's custody slightly later, were definitely the more interesting and thus were given a certain precedence. On May 26, the Document Section G-2, AFHQ, made a preliminary catalogue of these documents: Report no. 1, "List of Contents of 37 Files Formerly in Possession of Mussolini."[174] The other part or group, the papers initially seized in the Feltrinelli villa by the U.S. Fifth Army, were briefly described in report no. 2.[175]

The documents, it appeared after preliminary examination, consisted of bundles of files, most of which were dossiers on both prominent and lesser-known individuals and a few up-to-date situation reports on towns in Northern Italy. A total of 32 bags were listed (numbers 1 to 33 but without any number 25), which, after preliminary examination were divided into 4 groups:

   a. Personalities: Bags 1, 2, 3, 8, 9, 11, 13, 14, 17, 18, 19, 21, 22, 23, 26, 28, 29, 30, 31, 33;
   b. Politics and Government of the Fascist Republic: Bags 5, 7, 10, 16, 20, 24, 27, 32;
   c. Economics: Bags 6, 12;
   d. Publications and Propaganda: Bags 4, 15.

Distributed among the 20 bags listed under "a. Personalities" are a total of 149 numbered files on "Minor Party Members." Otherwise we have only a series of headings listed under each bag as indications of files. There is no immediate explanation of the discrepancy between the "42 large mail pouches" mentioned in Ambassador Kirk's telegram of May 20 (no. 2259) and the total of 32 bags listed.

Report no. 3 of AFHQ, Office of Assistant Chief of Staff, G-2, (Operational Intelligence Section) dated 25 May 1945 entitled "Additional Files from the Villa of Mussolini" lists 9 bundles of additional files received from Fifteenth Army Group. If these 9 "bundles" are equivalent to "bags" then we have in reports 2 and 3 a total of 41 bags, with the discrepancy of only one from the figure of "42 bags" in Ambassador Kirk's telegram.

The Documents Section of G-2, AFHQ proceeded with great energy

174. This report, classified "secret," was mimeographed. Copies were sent both to the War Department and to the Department of State in Washington. The copy sent to the State Department was used extensively in the Division of Foreign Activity Correlation as a check on the microfilming work subsequently performed under its guidance. FC. later transferred it to the German Documents Branch of the Historical Office.

175. Allied Force Headquarters, Office of the Assistant Chief of Staff, G-2 (O.I. Documents Section), report no. 2, "Preliminary Catalogue of Documents found in the Mussolini Villa," 24 May 1945. Seven pages mimeographed, copy from the Central Files, Department of State.

to select individual documents from the files and to make translations of these into English.

We have translations: From report no. 1. (37 files)

File 3	26 Sept.	File 19	9 July
File 5, part 1	5 August	File 20	15 August
File 5, part 2	5 August	File 21, part 1	7 Sept.
File 5, part 3	5 August	File 21, part 2	7 Sept.
File 5, part 4	5 August	File 26	7 June
File 7	19 June	File 28	26 Sept.
File 8	21 June	File 29, part 1	26 July
File 9	15 August	File 29, part 2	26 July
File 10	11 June	File 29, part 3	26 July
File 11	21 June	File 30	26 Sept.
File 13	15 August	File 31	11 June
File 14, part 1	26 Sept.	File 32	19 June
File 14, part 2	26 Sept.	File 33	4 June
File 16	11 June	File 34	7 June
File 18	9 July	File 36	7 June

And we have a series of numbered "extracts," translations of selections from the materials listed in report no. 2:

Extract No. 1 (3 pp.—18 June 1945): "Quarrel between Kailani, President of the Iraqui Council, and the Grand Mufti over the Arab Question" 29 July 1942. From file, Report on Black Market, bag no. 10.

Extract No. 2 (2 pp.—18 June 1945): "From an account of an interview granted by the Duce to Colonel of Carabinieri Luca on his return from Ankara 21 Jan. 1943." From file, Report on the Black Market, bag no. 10.

Extract No. 3 (3 pp.—18 June 1945): "Report on certain cabinet changes, notably the removal of Ciano from the Office of Foreign Secretary" 10 Feb. 1943. From file, Report on Black Market, bag no. 10.

Extract No. 4 (4 pp. & 3 pp. Append.—19 June 1945): "Correspondence and Comments on Italo-Spanish agreement made in 1934" (from subfile on Carpi). From file, Spain, bag no. 10.

Extract No. 5 (2 pp.—2 July 1945): "Letter dated 18 Oct., 1935 from Grandi to Duce reporting a conversation with Ramsay MacDonald." From file, Grandi, bag no. 10.

Extract No. 6 (8 pp.—2 July 1945): "Appendix A—Letter dated 22 March 1939, Grandi to Duce, in which Grandi reports on a letter to Ciano. Appendix B—Letter dated 6 Nov. 1936—Grandi to Ciano (mentioned above)." From file, Grandi, bag no. 1.

Extract No. 7 (5 pp.—2 July 1945): "Documents relating to international conferences, 1931–1932." From file, Grandi, bag no. 1.

Extract No. 8 (1 p.—2 July 1945): "An ordinance of Kesselring regarding jurisdiction in the Rome area" (memorandum for the Minister from Pagnozzi, 30 March 1944). From file, Liaison between Ministry of Interior and Germany, vol. 1 (p. 118), bag no. 16.

Extract No. 9 (7 pp.—13 July 1945): "File letters Grandi to Mussolini and one response by Mussolini—written over a period of years up to 1939." From file, Grandi, bag no. 1.

Extract No. 10 (6 pp.—14 July 1945): "Translation of chapter on Grandi from Mussolini's book *Between the Stick and the Carrot*. From file, Grandi, bag no. 1.

Extract No. 11 (19 pp.—16 July 1945): "Subject: Address by Mussolini to the Fascist Grand Council—7 April 1932." From file, Minutes of Grand Council 1932, bag no. 24.

Extract No. 12 (11 pp.—18 July 1945): "Subject: Address by Mussolini to the Fascist Grand Council—7–8 April 1932" (deals with foreign affairs; follows on extract 11). From file, Minutes of the Grand Council 1932, bag no. 24.[176]

Establishment of the Joint Allied Intelligence Agency

While G-2 of AFHQ was busily engaged in going through the private papers of Mussolini in the summer of 1945, sorting them and selecting the more important documents for translation, both the British Foreign Office and the American State Department were preparing to assert interest and claim to these extraordinary files. In a telegraphic instruction of May 30, the American political adviser at Caserta (Ambassador Kirk) was notified that the Fascist documents captured in North Italy were of great interest to the department, and he was directed to insure that either the originals or reproductions of everything be sent to the War Department in Washington with the stipulation that the Division of Foreign Activity Correlation (FC) in the State Department be notified.[177] The Foreign Office was even quicker in its response. They sent Mr. E. D. Gannon of their research section to Caserta, for the captured archives appeared to have hundreds of dossiers on personalities who might prove to be hostile to the Allies, or in whose records the new anti-Fascist government of Italy might itself be interested. After several dis-

176. For the English translations prepared by G-2 of AFHQ in the summer of 1945 see reel 476-A, heading "Captured Files (Previously) Held by Mussolini" (indicator no. 0100/11S/1513, 1514, and 1515, G.B.I. 389.457/1) and reel 69-K (indicator 613), Combined British-American Records of the Mediterranean Theater of Operations in World War II, Record Group 331, NARS.

177. No. 533 to Caserta, May 30, 1945 (840.414/5-3045), Central Files, Department of State.

cussions in Caserta the proposal was put forward that an Anglo-American integrated team of experts be immediately established for the purpose of microfilming the captured Mussolini Papers. Such a project, it appeared, would require many months and would best be operated under the day-to-day control of the British and American embassies in Rome.[178]

Meanwhile there had been the department's instruction of May 30 asking that either the original documents themselves or reproductions be sent to the War Department. Accordingly on June 16 a batch of microfilms of the documents which had been seized on Mussolini's person was airmailed to the War Department in Washington. English translations were promised later.[179] This seems to have been the extent of microfilming by G-2 of AFHQ of the Mussolini Papers. The package apparently was lost.[180]

In Washington, the Division of Foreign Activity Correlation selected Vincent La Vista to head up the American component of the newly-to-be-constituted combined group of experts for exploitation and filming of the Mussolini archives.[181] La Vista arrived in Rome on July 14. In this period of the summer of 1945, just after the war in Europe had ended,

178. Caserta telegram no. 2591, June 12, 1945 (840.414/6-1245), Central Files, Department of State.

179. Caserta telegram no. 2641, June 16, 1945 (840.414/6-1645), Central Files, Department of State. The package was given the number C-3452 and was addressed to Assistant Chief of Staff, G-2, War Department.

In a subsequent telegram, no. 3135 of July 30 (840.414/7-3045) Kirk referred to the matter and mentioned his assumption that these microfilm copies had been brought to the attention of FC in the Department of State.

180. In a letter dated December 12, 1946, the chief of the Division of Foreign Activity Correlation explained that the microfilms had never been transferred to the State Department and asked the War Department to make a thorough search (letter, Jack D. Neal to Lt. Col. C. B. Smith, Collection Branch, W. D. [840.414/12-1246]).

In an airgram of January 7, 1947 the department notified La Vista that nothing had been found (no. A-7 to Rome for La Vista [800.515/1-647], Central Files, Department of State).

181. Vincent La Vista; born Dobbs Ferry, New York, Jan. 2, 1907; received an A.B. degree from New York University 1925; an L.L.B. from New York Law School 1929; J.D. from Hamilton College of Law 1930; did graduate work in Spanish and Italian at the University of Southern California 1936. Before entering the foreign service he served for six years with the New York Department of Labor, 1930–37, three years as a private investigator, 1937–40. He served as an attaché of the embassy at Madrid 1943 to February 1945 when he resigned. He was reappointed June 8, 1945, as economic analyst and was initially assigned to Ambassador Murphy's staff for work with CIOS (the Combined Intelligence Objectives Subcommittee). On June 23 he was transferred to the American embassy, Rome, for Safehaven work under the guidance of the Division of Foreign Activity Correlation. Deceased.

three or four different organizations, each with its own point of view and interest in these captured Mussolini archives, were involved in their fate.

There was G-2 of AFHQ, a combined Anglo-American headquarters, which had actual custody of the documents, and whose chief interest was in their value for military information. From the point of view of immediate intelligence, the translations which G-2 was preparing were quite as useful as the texts of the documents themselves. The war in Europe was by now over, and political intelligence, as distinguished from strictly military, was perhaps a bit beyond G-2's range. Once the translations were made, G-2 was quite ready to turn the documents back to the Italian government or to hand them on to any other agency with valid claim.

On the opposite side in this parallelogram of forces was the Italian government, which was not happy about the exploitation by foreigners even of Fascist Italian documents, and which wished above all to get its records back into its own control and custody. *Commendatore* Emilio Re, a loyal Italian and dedicated archivist, was the principal proponent of this interest, and at the time he was working closely with the Monuments, Fine Arts, and Archives Subcommission of the Allied Commission.

The subcommission itself constituted a separate and distinct force. Its aim, purpose, and mission was to restore to Italy, as quickly as possible, all of her artistic and literary patrimony that it was possible to rescue and preserve from the ravages of war. The commission had no interest in archives for intelligence purposes: At most it recognized that there might be such an interest by other agencies. Finally there were the Department of State and the Foreign Office, which had a great interest in the exploitation of these Mussolini archives for their political information, a kind of "intelligence" which phased in, where G-2's intelligence phased out.

G-2 was, of course, quite proud of its coup in grabbing the personal files of the Fascist dictator and not averse to a bit of favorable publicity. On July 3 an article appeared in *Stars and Stripes* with a dateline of Caserta, July 2:

Much of the inside story of Benito Mussolini and Fascist Italy is believed to be contained in voluminous personal papers of the ill-fated dictator now being examined under Allied supervision here, it was learned today.

The documents, which recently fell into Allied hands, are considered extremely important and an immediate release for publication is impossible, a spokesman said.

One report said that the papers, some of which were believed to be in

Mussolini's own writing, are in the process of translation under the fullest security measures.

The note promptly caught the eye of the watchful *Commendatore* Re who immediately appealed to his friends on the Monuments, Fine Arts, and Archives Subcommission. A day later Captain McCain, regional archivist of Lombardy, wrote to the director of the commission, referring to the newspaper story as an account which

describes one of the main collections of records that should be returned to the Italian Government. A discussion of the way in which it came into Allied possession would gain nothing. The Allies have the collection. Something should be done about its eventual return to the Italian Government.

In turn on July 12 the Office of the Chief Commissioner wrote to AFHQ:

1. The Commissary of State Archives of Italy (Commendatore Re) has brought to my notice a statement in "Stars and Stripes" of 3rd July that personal papers of Mussolini are at present being examined under Allied supervision at Caserta. These are presumably the records of Mussolini's Segretario Particolare, which I understand were removed from Viale della Vittoria 16, Gargnano, and transferred successively to G-2 Fifth Army, G-2 Fifteenth Army Group and finally G-2 A.F.H.Q.

2. While fully realizing the necessity of intelligence exploitation of these important archives, I am anxious that so far as possible their dispersal be avoided and that, finally, unless there is over-riding military or political objection to this course, they may be handed over to the Italian Government. I need hardly stress the enormous historical significance that these archives will have.

3. In particular I should like to suggest that, as soon as possible, a member of the Italian archives service be allowed access to these papers, and assist in any sorting, or arrangement of them, that may be necessary.

The letter concluded with an expression of the Allied Commission's great interest in all Italian archives seized for intelligence use, and urged that all documents taken for such exploitation pass through G-2 documents section and in no case leave the theater by any other channel, and that all documents removed be registered locally by subordinate G-2 agencies.[182] G-5 (Civil Affairs) of AFHQ however replied: "The disposal

182. Letter, 4 July 1945, sub. "Return of Italian Records of the Italian Government," pp. 418–417, file 20905/A/2 "Archives Policy—Modern Archives—Liaison w. G-2, February 1944–October 1945," 10,000/145/320. Several of the files of the Monuments, Fine Arts, and Archives Commission of the Allied Commission were built up in the field in reverse chronological order, and the page numbers were stamped in later following the chronological order. Thus for several references the numbers run backward. See notes 185, 187, 192, and 196 below. Cf. chap. 3, note 31.

Letter, Brig. Upjohn to G-5 Section, AFHQ, p. 1773, file 20905/C/4/C, "Archives—Rome Central Ministries, Part II" June 1945–February 1946), 10,000/145/329, Records of the Allied Commission, Record Group 331, NARS. Cf. Re, *Storia di un archivio*, pp. 26–27.

of these records is for the decision of the Foreign Office and State Department who are sending out representatives to deal with the question. Therefore your kind offer of an archivist must be refused." [183]

La Vista's opposite number on the British side was Lieutenant Colonel Thomson. [184]

A series of meetings was held in August between FC's man and the Foreign Office's representative which resulted in the setting up of the La Vista-Thomson organization which initially took for itself the title of Joint Allied Intelligence Agency (J.A.I.A.). But the Subcommission on Monuments, Fine Arts, and Archives insisted on its intervention in the discussions and on emphasis of the need for careful handling of the documents; on consideration of the interest of the Italian government in all of the archives of the modern era located in North Italy whose files the Joint Allied Intelligence Agency proposed to examine; and it insisted on constantly reiterating the need for return of all archives to Italian control as quickly as the intelligence requirements of whatever sort were met.

On August 11, Colonel Thomson held a discussion with Maj. H. E. bell of the MFAA Subcommission who reported that "the problems may be stated two ways:

(a) *From Lt. Col. Thomson's point of view* it is a question of maintaining control of those papers already held, and of obtaining control of anything of interest still in the North.

(b) *From the Italian Government's point of view* it is a question of not losing sight of archives of present administrative utility and future historical importance.

7. To attempt to reconcile these points of view, I suggested the establishment of a simple repository to receive archives of the type mentioned in para 5 [archives of purely political significance, and which had already been seized by intelligence agencies and were at Caserta or Rome]; that this repository should be under Allied control, but that archives in it should be open to Allied agencies and the Italian ministries alike, and that an Italian archivist should be on its establishment.

183. Letter, Maj. C. J. Macnamara (for Assistant Chief of Staff, G-5 AFHQ), 23 July 1945, p. 428, file 20905/A/2, "Archives—Policy—Modern Archives, Liaison w. G-2," February 1944–October 1945, 10,000/145/320, Records of the Allied Commission, NARS, Record Group 331, NARS.

184. The lieutenant colonelcy was an assimilated military rank. Robert Currie Thomson, (1886–1967) had been appointed to the Foreign Office in 1906; was promoted to be a staff officer in 1920, to senior translator in 1922. In 1925 he had been attached to the Locarno Conference; in 1939 was assistant in the Librarian's Department of the Foreign Office. In May 1945 he was assigned on special duty in Germany where he headed the British Foreign Office group of investigators and played a very important role in the discovery and collection of the archives of the German Foreign Office. Ambassador Murphy commended him for his effectiveness and for his cooperation with the American investigators on the ambassador's staff.

9. Lt. Colonel Thomson agreed in principle [to] the solution proposed in para 7, explaining that of course he could not commit Mr. La Vista, whom he will see tonight at Caserta.[185]

La Vista strenuously objected to having an Italian archivist working directly in his organization. He was willing, however, to recommend that a representative of the Italian Ministry of Foreign Affairs might be attached to the new agency as a liaison officer.[186]

Colonel Thomson did not actually remain in Italy long enough to work on the organization that came to bear his name in the records of the Monuments, Fine Arts, and Archives Subcommission. He returned to Germany but left Captain Haynes as his delegate. From Major Bell's report of September 3, 1945, we learn about the search for additional documents in the other archival deposits of North Italy and the

modifications necessitated by the requirements of the La Vista-Thomson organization. This was done during the period 21st–30th August, when all concerned proceeded to Milan and thence to the various archive deposits in Lombardy and Venezie.

Broadly speaking there were three parties to the negotiations.

(1) Representatives of the La Vista-Thomson organization (Mr. La Vista, Capt. Ciforelli, Capt. Haynes, Capt. Hall, Capt. Pio);

(2) Representatives of the Italian ministries and High Commissariat of Epuration (listed at Appendix A.);

(3) Local Commissaries of the Italian ministries, who have had control of the great bulk of the archives since the liberation (listed at Appendix A.).

Administration and co-ordination of the work of these three groups was the

185. Memo, Maj. H. E. Bell, A.E.C., Archives Officer to Director, MFAA Subcommission, 11 August 1945, sub. "Exploitation of Italian Archives," pp. 1812–1811, file 20905/C/4/C, "Archives Rome Central Ministries, Part II," 10,000/145/329, Records of the Allied Commission, Record Group 331, NARS.

186. Rome telegram no. 2444, Aug. 24, 1945, (800.515/8-2445), Central Files, Department of State.

FC's instructions of July 28 for La Vista directed that he look particularly for: documents on Fascist organizations and agents, particularly those involving the U.S. and Latin America; for Safehaven matters (commercial and industrial records such as cartel agreements, patents, correspondents with German firms, German governmental agencies, Spanish and Argentine firms, financial records including Italian gold transactions since 1941). He was asked at the same time to state his estimated personnel requirements (no. 1262 [840.414/7-2845]).

These were stated as five investigators, including one with experience in bank or insurance company auditings, all with a reading knowledge of Italian, and three stenographers capable of transcribing Italian. All were to be specifically assigned to Safehaven (Rome telegram no. 2213, August 4, 1945, [840.414/8-445]).

The department's telegraphic instruction no. 1322 of August 9, 1945 commended Thomson for his work in Germany and directed La Vista to contact him (840.414/8-945), Central Files, Department of State.

joint responsibility of: Archives Officers of this Sub-commission, Capt. W. D. McCain and Major H. E. Bell; of Commendatore Re and Dr. L. Sandri of the Italian Archives Service; and of Conte P. M. Annoni di Gussola, Vice-Commissary of the *Presidenza del Consiglio*. In particular, Archives Officers had the somewhat delicate task of attempting to reconcile the needs of the new intelligence agency with those of the Italian ministries.

The report went on to summarize the work done, and the progress made during this period in this fashion:

1. *The La Vista-Thomson Organization*. A series of meetings between the representatives of this organization and Archives Officers was held on 21st and 22nd August.

At these meetings it was found possible, on the basis of reports of Archives Officers, and of Captain Ciforelli, to eliminate many deposits of ministerial archives that clearly held nothing of interest for the organization. Indeed, it became apparent that examination of a comparatively small number of archives was contemplated. It was arranged that this should be carried out during the following week, and that on chests, etc., that it was intended to seize there should be placed a distinguishing mark.

On 23 August members of the intelligence agency left Milan, armed with paint pots, for the examination and marking of archives. They were able to complete this work during the week following. In some cases they actually removed archives, where bulk required was small. This was not within the terms of the original agreement; but since it saved further visits was a common-sense procedure, and unexceptionable since receipts were left. For the rest, documents wanted were marked and put on one side; it will be the responsibility of the La Vista-Thomson organization to collect them before the transfer of the remainder to the Italian ministries commences. Lists of documents taken and earmarked are at Appendix D.

Mr. La Vista expressed himself as very pleased with the work accomplished.

The report went on to emphasize:

It should be stressed that, except for those records seized by Allied Intelligence Agencies, and in the last period by the La Vista-Thomson organization, all ministerial archives now become the responsibility of the Italian Government. . . .

There remains the question of the disposal of archives seized for intelligence exploitation, both in the months immediately subsequent upon liberation and more recently by the La Vista-Thomson organization.

This Sub-Commission welcomes the setting up of that organization since it is understood that in its premises (the old P.W.B. building, Via Vittoria Veneto, Rome) will be housed all documents seized since the occupation of Northern Italy. That concentration is, from a technical archivist's standpoint, most desirable, since most important series of archives (notably Ministry of Popular Culture and Ministry of Foreign Affairs records) are involved.

On the question of final disposition, however, no decision appears yet to have been reached.

This Sub-Commission reiterates strongly the opinion expressed throughout all these negotiations that ultimately Italian archives should be returned to the Italian Government, saving only the very exceptional case where political or military reasons render such return imprudent. These archives record a part of Italy's history, and as such their proper place is in Italy.

It is recommended that representations be made to Higher Authority that, as and when the work of the La Vista-Thomson Organization on separate series of archives is completed, these be returned to the Italian Government.

The report concluded with a recommendation that an Italian archivist be appointed to work within and under the orders of the organization, and that it promptly notify the subcommission of all documents moved out of the country to Washington or London.[187]

By letter of September 20, 1945, from the American embassy in Rome, La Vista gave his assurances to the Civil Affairs Section of Headquarters, Allied Commission that

the archives which we have taken into possession for intelligence investigation will be preserved and returned to the respective ministries with all possible speed. Your letter indicates that we have in our possession the bulk of the archives in question. This is not the fact. Of the several thousand tons of archives in existence we have selected less than twenty tons which in my opinion are less than one-tenth of one per cent of the official Italian State archives. It is definitely not our intention to take or send any official State archives out of Italy. Any which might be so sent would be personal papers belonging to individuals and that would be done only on specific orders from London or Washington.[188]

In a meeting held on October 4, 1945, the La Vista-Thomson Organization, which now designated itself the Joint Diplomatic Research Agency (J.D.R.A.) agreed that the Italian Government might be requested to attach an Italian archivist to the Ministry of Foreign Affairs until such time as it would be found possible to incorporate him directly into the agency. His immediate duties were defined as follows:

(1) to act as a channel for all enquiries and requests regarding archives from individual Italian Ministries;

(2) to arrange for the collection and transfer to the appropriate Ministries of

187. Report, Maj. H. E. Bell to the Vice President, Civil Affairs Section, Allied Commission, 3 September 1945, sub. "Italian Ministerial Archives in Northern Italy," pages 1845–1838, file 20905/C/4/C, "Archives Rome Central Ministries, Part II, June 1945–February 1946," 10,000/145/329, Records of the Allied Commission, Record Group 331, NARS.

188. La Vista to Brigadier Carr, Civil Affairs Section, Hq. Allied Commission, file 20905/J/MFAA "La Vista-Thomson Research Organization, Aug. 1945–March 1946," 10,000/145/355, Records of the Allied Commission, Record Group 331, NARS.

such files as are already available for disposal as of no further importance to the Agency. Some categories of archives are already available for transfer in this way—notably much material of the Ministry of Popular Culture.[189]

The Italian government named *Direttore* Leopoldo Sandri to act as its liaison official between the J.A.I.A. (or J.D.R.A.) and the various Italian ministries.[190]

Difficulties of the J.A.I.A.: Its Work of Microfilming

With the fall season the new Anglo-American group was fully recognized and its work well under way. G-2 of AFHQ turned over the collection of Mussolini's Private Papers to La Vista's agency. In a letter of October 14, 1945, to Brigadier Carr, La Vista listed by provenance his holdings of Italian documents:

1. Ministry of the Interior (Maderno, Lake Garda): 3 mail bags approximately 200 pounds each;
2. Ministry of the Interior, Director General of the Secret Police (Valdagno): 46 cases, approximately 180 pounds each, passport and visa applications;
3. Ministry of Foreign Affairs (Salò, Lake Garda): 2 mailbags containing records, correspondence, and communication between the Ministries of Foreign Affairs and the Budapest consulate; 2 mailbags containing the private files of the Italian undersecretary of state;
4. Ministry of Italian African Colonies, Director of Political Affairs (Pallanzo): 4 mail bags;
5. Ministry of Foreign Exchange (Milan): 12 cases each about 200 pounds;
6. Ministry of Industrial Production (Bergamo): 135 cases each about 150 pounds;
7. Prefect of Realm (Turin): "An assortment of 8 files dealing primarily with political espionage, sabotage, activities of fascist agents in Palestine, Switzerland and Spain";
8. Ministry of the Interior, Director General of Civil Administration (Venice): "32 files dealing primarily with intelligence activities both on behalf of and in opposition to the Fascist Party by the Catholic clergy throughout the world";
9. Ministry of Popular Culture (56 Via Vittorio Veneto, Rome): "All files now in this office";[191]
10. Ministry of Foreign Affairs: 44 selected cases. *From G-2, AFHQ, Caserta;*
11. "Approximately 5 tons of assorted documents which are the remainder after selecting and eliminating all documents of a strict military nature which have already or will be processed by G-2. These are the archives which I believe the Italian authorities are anxious to obtain and for which we have set up a priority for processing";

189. Memo, "Italian Archives held by the Joint Deiplomatic Research Agency," 4 October 1945, p. 1937, file 20905/C/4/C, "Archives, Rome Central Ministries, Part II, June 1945–February 1946," 10,000/145/329, Records of the Allied Commission, Record Group 331, NARS.

190. Letter, Brigadier Carr to Dr. Giorgio Amendola, Undersecretary of State, Presidency of the Council of Ministers, 9 October 1945, p. 4217, file 20905/J/MFAA. "La Vista-Thomson Research Organization, August 1945–March 1946," 10,000/145/355, Records of the Allied Commission, Record Group 331, NARS.

191. Cf. below Microcopy T-586: Analysis of the Collection.

12. "37 files found in a suit case in Mussolini's personal baggage at the time of his capture";

13. "400 files found with Mussolini's private secretary at the time of his capture";

14. "10 mail sacks of private files belonging to Robert Farinacci which will show the original organization of the Fascist Party Secret Political Police";

15. "42 sacks of private and secret files of the Fascist Party taken from the villa of Mussolini." [192]

The first batch of microfilming done by this agency seems to have been some forty-three double reels of 16-mm film, reels which on their transfer to the National Archives were given container numbers 1207–49.[193]

At the end of October, La Vista left Rome for Madrid in connection with other aspects of the Safehaven program; in December he was called back to Washington for consultation; he was then granted a period of

192. Letter, Vincent La Vista to Brigadier M. Carr, V.P.C.A., Hq. Allied Commission, 14 October 1945, stamped pages 989–986, file 20905 s "Allied Commission Hq.—Sub-Comm. for Monuments, Fine Arts, and Archives. Sept. 1945–Oct. 1945," 10,000/145/444, Records of the Allied Commission, Record Group 331, NARS.

It will be noted that items 12 and 15 correspond respectively to those seizures or acquisitions reported by Ambassador Kirk in his telegrams of May 20 (no. 2259) and May 23 (no. 2317).

In a rather curious and highly critical report which Capt. D. E. L. Haynes submitted to Lt. Col. A. B. Ward Perkins, and which found its way into the subcommission's records we find comments on some of the numbered items:

> Item 10. I think this must refer to the 42 cases of Foreign Ministry documents from Cadenabbia. Of these 26 are from the Direzione Italiani all' Estero, 4 from the Sezione Affari Privati and 12 have a miscellaneous content, including typewriters, stationery and a saucepan. Only 8 cases of the 42 appear to us to be worth detailed examination.
>
> Item 11. The 150 sacks are luckily mythical. Perhaps a collection of approximately 150 Gabinetto files of personal records is intended. We received from A.F.H.Q. 20 cases of badly packed documents; 10½ Foreign Ministry, 8½ Ministry of the Interior and 1 Ministry of the Armed Forces. . . .
>
> Item 12. No remarks.
>
> Item 13. See item 15.
>
> Item 14. No remarks.
>
> Item 15. We have 34 sacks of files from Mussolini's Segreteria Particolare which were found at Gargnano, Lake Garda. I think these 34 sacks which equal approximately 400 files must explain items 13 and 15.

Dated 22 Oct. 1945, same file as cited above, stamped p. 990.

193. These containers all hold two reels except for two. This batch seems to correspond with those of AFHQ's report no. 2, of May 24, 1945 for this is the initial frame of reel no. 1207, "Preliminary Catalogue of Documents Found in Mussolini's Villa."

La Vista seems to have sent these films with a covering Safehaven report of October 18, 1945, but I have been unable to locate that report.

In a telegraphic report of about a year later La Vista informed Cummings of FC that his agency did not start using 35-mm film until November 1945. Rome telegram no. 3984, October 9, 1946, (800.515/10-946), Central Files, Department of State.

home leave, and did not return to Rome until March 1946. During his absence Dr. Collins took over his work.[194]

The La Vista-Thomson Agency, as the officials of the Monuments, Fine Arts, and Archives Subcommission insisted on calling it, had its troubles and problems and not only from the subcommission. The Division of Foreign Activity Correlation in Washington tended to view the records seized in Italy, not in terms of their own inherent value or historical interest, but from the Safehaven point of view, looking everywhere for a tie-up with Spain and Latin America. The department's telegraphic instruction of November 30 appeared to request material from the Ministry of Popular Culture. The agency proceeded to make microfilm copies of the reports from the files of the Ministry of Popular Culture which had already been submitted by the Italian Documents Section of P.W.B. The department then instructed Collins that it already had the P.W.B. reports so that it was not necessary to microfilm them further. They had practically all been filmed when this instruction reached Rome.[195]

The agency in fact was caught in a scissors between the Allied Commission's reiterated demands for prompt return of the documents to the Italian government and its own shortage of manpower. In a letter of November 6, 1945, Brigadier Carr on behalf of the chief commissioner stressed the point of view "that, except in individual cases where strong military reasons prevent it, return of the archives to the Italian Government should be effected as rapidly as possible." A few days later the chief commissioner (Rear Adm. Ellery W. Stone, U.S.N.R.) wrote to the British ambassador, urging three things:

(1) An effort to increase the speed of handover to documents from the J.D.R.A. to the Italian government;

(2) Careful arrangement and systematic listing of the residue "so that, upon request from Italian ministries concerned, it [will be] possible to indicate reasonably certainly whether or not a particular class of archives is actually held. At the request of the Allied Commission, outline lists of archives held have, in fact, been supplied by the J.D.R.A. But these do not tally with the details of material that G-2 agents are known to have taken, and the plain fact would seem to be that the J.D.R.A. does not itself know,

194. Ralph S. Collins, born in Grifton, North Carolina, November 1, 1910; received an A.B. degree from the University of North Carolina in 1929; M.A. from the same institution in 1931; studied at the University of Munich 1932–33; and received a Ph.D. degree from Johns Hopkins University in 1938. He had been associate professor of German and French at Maryville College prior to his entrance into the Foreign Service Auxiliary in March 1945 when he was assigned to the Office of the U.S. Political Adviser in German Affairs (Ambassador Murphy). In 1966 he served at the Foreign Service Institute.

195. Telegram no. 2234 to Rome (840.414/11-3045); telegram no. 165, to Rome (for Collins), January 24, 1946 (740.00119 Control [Italy]/1-2446), Central Files, Department of State. Cf. below (Microcopy T-586; Analysis of the Collection).

with even approximate precision, what is held. Six months after seizure, many of the documents remain unexamined."

(3) That the archivist appointed by the Italian government to work with the J.D.R.A. be employed at once in the work of arrangement of the materials. Admiral Stone mentioned his personal opinion that "Having regard to the status of the Italian Government, I cannot feel that security considerations need prevent the immediate employment of an Italian national in this capacity."

The chief commissioner concluded his letter by stressing that his recommendations should not be taken as criticism of the work of the J.D.R.A., and that he recognized its difficulties in the lack of staff and equipment, but insisting that continuation of the present unsatisfactory position would result in serious administrative inconvenience to the Italian government.[196]

It was sheer lack of staff that made progress so slow for the Joint Diplomatic Research Agency. Captain Stevenson was now head of the British element which consisted of himself and three other officers. The four were largely engaged in shifting packing cases around with their own hands, but as a result of Sir Noel Charles's appeals to London following Admiral Stone's letter, more staff members were authorized.[197] On the American side Dr. Collins was quite alone, and it was several months before he was able to return to Germany to work with the captured records of the *Auswärtiges Amt*.[198]

Apparently there was some further gathering of documents by the J.D.R.A. beyond those which were transferred to it by AFHQ or which the agency itself selected during the tour of North Italy in the summer of 1945. After La Vista's return to Italy in the spring of 1946 he reported that in Milan he had located several boxes containing diaries and official papers of Marshal Balbo, and he asked the department for instruction in regard to them.[199]

196. Chief Commissioner Rear Admiral Ellery W. Stone to Sir Noel Charles (with copy to Ambassador Kirk), 10 November 1945, stamped pages 4243–4241, file "20905/J/MFAA La Vista-Thomson Research Organization, Aug. 1945–Mar. 1946," 10,000/145/355, Allied Commission Records, Record Group 331, NARS.

Ambassador Kirk forwarded a summary of the letter to Washington and asked for the department's comments. Rome telegram no. 4022, December 13, 1945 (840.414/12-1345), Central Files, Department of State.

197. Sir Noel Charles to Admiral Stone, 27 November 1945, (293/105/45), stamped page 4244, file 20905/J/MFAA, "La Vista-Thomson Research Organization, Aug. 1945–Mar. 1946," 10,000/145/355, Allied Commission Records, Record Group 331, NARS.

198. Interview with Dr. Collins, April 20, 1966.

199. Rome telegram no. 2588, May 24, 1946 (800.515/5-2446) Central Files, Department of State.

Termination of the Work of the J.D.R.A.:
Return of the Documents to the Italian Government

The work of microfilming Mussolini's Private Papers and ancillary documents was formally concluded on September 1, 1947. The organization which in the records of the Monuments, Fine Arts and Archives Subcommission was always referred to as the La Vista-Thomson Organization, but which initially called itself the Joint Allied Intelligence Agency and somewhat later the Joint Diplomatic Research Agency, was dissolved, at least for the task for which it was originally constituted in the summer of 1945. The last reel, job no. 331, was made on July 26, 1947, and consisted of: "Miscellaneous Papers not previously Microfilmed"; some documents found in the German embassy in Rome; a letter of Giovanni Preziosi; an order of Kesselring of August 22, 1944; and an order issued during the forty-five days of Badoglio for dealing with strikers. This last job was made without numbering of the frames.

Termination of the J.D.R.A. was part of the general process of winding up the various agencies of the Allies which had been set up during the course of the Italian campaign and occupation of Italy. The Treaty of Peace with Italy came into effect on September 15, 1947, and the Italian government regained its full sovereignty. There were, however, several tons of documents which La Vista still had in custody, and there were some projects quite distinct from the Mussolini Papers, which were being considered. In September, La Vista moved out of 56 via Vittorio Veneto and set up shop in the basement of the United States embassy at via Boncompagni 2. He had one microfilming machine, an adequate supply of film, and one assistant. In the final period, La Vista usually used the designation, Joint Diplomatic Research Section, for his project.[200]

What became of the original documents drawn from Mussolini's private archives and other record groups which were microfilmed by the J.D.R.A.? These papers never left Rome once they were gathered together at 56 via Vittorio Veneto. There were the four items which on July 22, 1945, were sent to London,[201] but these were apparently returned to the

200. Memorandum in five pages by La Vista, forwarded to the department in despatch no. 1617, Rome, November 13, 1948, Subject: "Transmitting Report on Status of Safehaven Project," (124.656/11-1348) Central Files, Department of State.

The memorandum itself bears no date but was submitted with a covering memorandum, "Prospective Termination of Archives Exploitation Project," dated October 21, 1948, Rome Mission Files, Record Group 84, Accession no. 56-A-528, box 248, file 841.4 "Italy-Fascist Archives," NARS.

201. See note 171 above.

main body of the collection. Furthermore, from the autumn of 1945 onward, the Italian government had its own liaison officer, Dr. Leopoldo Sandri, attached to the J.D.R.A. and able to report directly on its work. In La Vista's memorandum of October 1948 he reported:

The microfilm work of the Joint Diplomatic Research Section was terminated as previously scheduled on September 1, 1947, and the archives processed and microfilmed by the Section during the period of its existence, returned to the Italian Government as planned. No complications were experienced and the work as organized and executed was completed to the satisfaction of the Department and of the Italian Government.[202]

La Vista's final report states that the agency or section made a total of 421 rolls of film. Only 273 containers were transferred within the department from the Division of Foreign Activity Correlation to the Division of Historical Policy Research. That final report indicates that the agency made biographical summaries of some 75,000 Italians and of 1,711 Germans. These biographical summaries probably account for the discrepancy of 148 rolls between the output in Rome and what was ultimately transferred to the National Archives. Aside from the fact that much biographical data was drawn from Mussolini's Private Papers, the biographical project was quite distinct from that of microfilming the Duce's archives.[203]

It is to be regretted that *Commendatore* Re published his book in November of 1946, quite before the work of microfilming was completed. The effect of the book, if left to stand without correction, is to give the Anglo-American occupying powers a quite undeserved black eye, and to reinforce the so-called "mystery" of the fate of Mussolini's private archives.

Up to this point we have been talking both about the original documents which constituted Mussolini's private archives and about the microfilm copies which were made from them. From now on, as regards this collection, reference is to the films only. As the films were made, copies were sent both to the Department of state (Division of Foreign Activity Correlation) and to the British Foreign Office. The data sheets which were made by the J.A.I.A. were turned out in five copies each: one to the British Foreign Office; one to the Department of State (FC);

202. As cited in note 200 above.
203. La Vista's report states that the 421 reels of film recorded a total of 776,200 selected documents. This figure appears to the author to be a misprint or an absurd exaggeration. An average reel or roll of 35-mm microfilm runs to about 750 or 800 *frames* or pages. The total of 776,200 on 421 reels would mean some 1800 documents per reel. The average document runs over one page. In any case it is the frame which is the unit for measuring microfilm, not document.

one to the British embassy; one to the American embassy; and a file copy.

These data sheets made by the agency were not very detailed or complete. They usually list the time of filming, the provenance of the documents, and the inclusive frame numbers (except for the first part of the first job, and the final reel of July 1947). Possibly it was Dr. Ralph Collins, who was familiar with the data sheets which were being prepared in the filming of the German Foreign Office records, who suggested data sheets and frame enumeration for the work at Rome.

Within the Division of Foreign Activity Correlation in the Department of State, where the films were held for some time, these microfilmed copies of the records were subjected to intensive study. Additional or supplementary data sheets were prepared in FC for a considerable number of the reels, that is for those which seemed to be the most interesting ones.[204]

Both sets of data sheets are at hand in the collection of data sheets at the National Archives and are recorded in the microfilm of the data sheets, roll 1, microcopy T-586.

In England, Frederick William Deakin, in the preliminary work for his study, *The Brutal Friendship*, also made some detailed listings of individual documents within the different jobs or reels, and a microfilm reel of this British catalogue of the Mussolini private papers is also at hand at the National Archives.[205]

204. There were 16 "jobs" for which detailed data sheets were prepared in the Division of Foreign Activity Correlation, as follows:

Job No.	Container No.
1	405
2	406
3	407
105	454
107	454
108	459
109	456
110	457
111	457
112	458
113	458
114	117
115	117
116	117
117	466
120	460

205. At my request this microfilm reel was kindly sent to me by the Honorable Margaret Lambert, the British editor in chief of the *Documents on German Foreign Policy,*

Transfer of the Microfilms to the National Archives

The Division of Foreign Activity Correlation was closed out in 1948 and the Historical Office, then known as the Division of Historical Policy Research, took over a portion of its administrative records and most of its holdings. The German Documents Branch, which was headed at that time by Professor Raymond J. Sontag, had immediate custody of these records transferred from FC. The collection of films of Mussolini's private papers was included. This branch, the unit which was directly concerned with collections of foreign documents and films, now had three significant sets of Italian materials: (1) the Lisbon Papers on film; (2) a microfilm and a "blowup" set of the Ciano Papers: Rose Garden; and (3) the microfilms of the Mussolini Private Papers. The suggestion was made that some expert in modern Italian history be brought in to consider possible publication of selections of these Italian documents.[206]

But the Historical Office was having difficulties enough maintaining an adequate staff for the German Documents Project; the Division of Southern European Affairs did not favor the direct participation of the Department of State in publishing Italian documents, although it had no objection to their being made available to the use of scholars; and thus the suggestion was dropped. The Lisbon Papers were retained in the branch for use in checking against the German Foreign Office copies of Italo-German correspondence. It was decided to pass the microfilms of the Mussolini Papers on to the National Archives.

Dr. James S. Beddie of the German Documents Branch, Historical Office, in January 1950 delivered the films of Mussolini Papers to the National Archives. These were at the time 269 cans or containers, together with the data sheets, both those made in Rome, and those which had been made in Washington by FC. It was thought that there should be 270 containers, but on checking it was discovered that the last reel made in Rome, job 331, was missing.[207] The collection was formally "accessioned" in the National Archives, March 22, 1950.[208]

1918–1945. I then transferred it to the National Archives. (Letter, Lambert to Smyth, February 4, 1964; Smyth to Lambert, April 27, 1964; Lambert to Smyth, May 7, 1964; Lambert to Smyth, May, 13, 1964; Smyth to Lambert, May 27, 1964; receipt by (Mrs.) Patricia G. Dowling, Diplomatic, Legal, and Fiscal Branch, National Archives, June 4, 1964.)

A microfilm copy of Deakin's catalogue was also prepared for the Director of the National Archives in Rome (letter, Lambert to Smyth, February 4, 1964).

206. Memorandum, R. J. Sontag to G. B. Noble, September 3, 1948, files of the German War Documents Branch, Historical Office, Department of State.

207. Receipt by Donald L. Goodwin, representing the National Archives, January 19, 1950, Branch Files, Historical Office, Department of State.

208. Memorandum, Herman G. Goldbeck, National Archives, to H. M. Smyth, Department of State, "Filming of Captured Italian Records," February 21, 1963, Branch Files, Historical Office, Department of State. But the reel itself gives the date of February 28, 1950.

No announcement of the transfer of these microfilms to the National Archives was made at the time because the collection was a *restricted* one. Access was only by permission of the Department of State, that is with the formal authorization through the Advisory and Review Branch of the Division of Historical Policy Research. By request of the Department of State the accession inventory included the statement:

Unless express permission is obtained from the Department of State to use any of these records, regardless of date, they shall be withheld from examination by officials, private individuals, or other persons as provided for by Section 3 of the Act of June 19, 1934, as amended on March 3, 1948 (48 Stat 1122–1124; 62 Stat 58).

The policy of the department was declared to be "to make these records rather freely available to qualified scholars, on clearance of their applications by appropriate officers of the Department.[209] At the National Archives, the data sheets of the collection, which was designated microcopy T-586, were made available to scholars after clearance through the Department of State, and scholars, might make notes or full copies of documents as enlarged on microfilm readers. But there were no arrangements for the sale of duplicates of reels or of "blowups" of selected frames such as was possible with the completely open film collections at the National Archives.

These restrictions remained in force until the spring of 1964. A year earlier, that is in the spring of 1963, the *Newsletter* of the Society for Italian Historical Studies contained the announcement: "The Department of State has released to the National Archives some 400 reels of microfilm of Italian records of the Ministero degli Affari Esteri, 1938–1943." [210] This announcement was incorrect in every respect.[211]

There have been quite a few scholars to make use of the collection of Mussolini's Papers during the period of restricted use. Among them was the late Professor Gaetano Salvemini, and it is a pleasure on my part to record that I was able to facilitate access to, and use of a small fraction of

209. Letter, G. B. Noble, Chief, Division of Historical Policy Research, Department of State, to Wayne C. Grover, Archivist of the United States, May 6, 1949, file copy, Branch Files, Historical Office.

210. No. 1, Spring 1963, p. 6, Society for Italian Historical Studies, 502 Casa Italiana, New York, New York.

211. As to propriety; it pertains to the Department of State to make public announcement of its releases, not to private individuals. There were 316 reels in the collection; not "approximately 400." As to provenance of the documents; the bulk of them came from Mussolini's private archives, and only a small portion, chiefly copies, came from the Italian Ministry of Foreign Affairs. The collection contained papers as early as 1922 and as late as 1944 and 1945; and even a few which antedated World War I.

these filmed records on the part of that great scholar and champion of right (not rightist) causes.[212]

When the work of the German War Documents Branch was closing out with the publication of volume 13 of series D, *Documents on German Foreign Policy 1918–1945*, the final allotment of films of the files of the former German Foreign Office was transferred from the Department of State to the National Archives. It was then discovered in the check which was made at the National Archives that three containers, thought to belong to the German collection (microcopy T-120) had been misclassified. Reels 24, 136, and 721 on inspection proved to be Italian materials, and really formed parts of the collection of Mussolini's Private Papers. The addition of these three reels, plus the final film of that collection (331), thus appeared to bring the total number of reels to 273.[213] On April 14, 1964, Dr. William M. Franklin, director of the Historical Office, Department of State, wrote to the national archivist, Wayne C. Grover, proposing that the earlier restrictions on the use of this collection be abolished.[214] Only after receipt of this letter was the collection made completely free, and reels of film, or "blowups" of documents made available for sale.

Microcopy T-586: Analysis of the Collection

At the National Archives this film collection is designated microcopy T-586. It is described as: "Personal Papers of Benito Mussolini, Together with Some Official Records of the Italian Foreign Office and the Ministry of Culture, 1922–44, Received by the Department of State." As a group of microfilms the collection can be broken down into "jobs," "containers" or boxes, reels or rolls, and "frames." There are certain rather puzzling discontinuities in each of these which need explanation.

Microfilm reels are usually kept in cans or boxes, the containers. There were, as mentioned earlier, 273 containers in the collection, plus the associated reel of data sheets, and the reel of the British catalogue. These containers are numbered, but the numbers are not a sequence.

212. Smyth to Beddie, Feb. 20, 1954; Beddie to Smyth (I was then at Whaddon Hall in England), March 31, 1954; Smyth to Beddie, April 7, 1954; Beddie to Smyth, April 14, 1954, Personal Files.

By a special arrangement and with special restrictions, microfilm copies of certain selections were made available to Professor Salvemini. They were punctiliously restored and now repose in the vault of the Historical Office, Department of State.

213. Memorandum by (Mrs.) Patricia G. Dowling, National Archives, November 15, 1963; Memorandum by H. M. Smyth, January 23, 1964, Branch Files, Historical Office, Department of State.

214. Branch Files, Historical Office, Department of State.

How did this happen? These films were transferred to the National Archives along with other films, chiefly those of the documents of the German Foreign Office (microcopy T-120), and the numbers attached to the boxes were determined in the State Department, which maintained a single list of all transfers.

The films are not of uniform size; there are more reels than there are containers; not every reel has a data sheet (although as noted above some have two); and "jobs" and reels are not coterminous.

The first batch of filming which La Vista and Thomson did in Rome in the early autumn of 1945 was on 16-mm film. There were, apparently, no regular data sheets for these films which were lost for a time. They go 2 in a box. These are in the containers listed as numbers 1207 to 1249. Each of these boxes has 2 of the narrow, 16-mm reels except boxes 1216 and 1244. When FC could not trace these films from Rome to the War Department to the State Department, La Vista was directed to film the documents over again. When he was able to start the work anew he managed to get ahold of some 35-mm film.

This repetition of the original work left some puzzles for later. We do not have data sheets for the 16-mm films and thus, to say the least, they are difficult to use. When Dr. Beddie transferred the microfilm collection of Mussolini's Private Papers to the National Archives on January 19, 1950, a careful count was made of the containers. Instead of the expected 270 there were only 269. This error was duly noted on the receipt.

Another error also developed. It was assumed that these 269 containers meant 269 rolls of film. Later examination of the collection at the National Archives indicated that the 16-mm films had showed up. The containers for these narrow films were recorded as numbers 1207 to 1249 in the list of transfers maintained by the German Documents Branch, Historical Office, Department of State. These cans, which numbered 43, each had 2 reels except for numbers 1216 and 1244. They had but 1 each. Thus there are 41 more reels than containers or boxes in the collection. Two additional reels were made at the National Archives and added to the collection so that microfilm publication T-586 now consists of 318 reels, 277 containers.[215]

Jobs and reels are not coterminous. A "job" is a unit of filming which can be described or comprised under one heading, the data sheet. A reel usually runs to about eight hundred frames or pages. Sometimes a job will comprise 2 or 3 reels, just as a book may have two or three vol-

215. These are designated roll 23 and roll 25. Roll 23 consists of P.W.B. reports 9, 10, 16, 96, 127 and 137, made from the transcripts of documents from the files of the Fascist Ministry of Popular Culture. Roll 25 consists of microfilm copies of the photostats of the original Ciano diaries, that is of the five booklets which were removed to Switzerland.

umes. Sometimes 1 reel will suffice for 2 or more jobs. Thus we have for microfilm publication T-586 a total of 318 reels but only 254 jobs.

What of the duplication or repetition? With the aid of Mrs. Patricia Dowling and of Mr. Harry Rilley I have made several spot checks in the 16-mm films. Each time I came up with duplicates, documents which I recognized as ones that I had already seen or identified on the 35-mm films. I cannot be absolutely certain, however, that the narrow films do not contain some copies of documents not to be found in the main collection, that is in the 35-mm films which have data sheets. The difficulty arises from the fact that when the work was started over again in Rome, the method was somewhat different: the sequence of filming the documents differed, and possibly, with the use of data sheets, the renewed filming was more selective than the original. I judge that it would be a very unrewarding labor to go through all of the 16-mm films in search of documents not recorded in the main collection. In this analysis I have simply considered the narrow films as duplicates and confined my comments to the main collection.

There is a discontinuity in the numbering of the jobs which run from 1 to 54; 101 to 178; and 215 to 331. It looks at first glance that we should have numbers 55 to 100 and 179 to 214. But apparently there were no such jobs as part of the filming of Mussolini's Private Papers because the numbering of the frames is continuous. Job 54 ends with frame 027001. Job 101 begins with frame 027002. Frames 054308 and following jump over the gap between jobs 178 and 215.

The basic unit, is, of course, the microfilm frame, which is almost always one page of document. Microcopy T-586 has approximately 114,000 frames. There are 113,317 frames that are numbered in sequence from the middle of job 1 to the end of job 330. In addition there is the unnumbered part of job 1; the final job, no. 331, which has about 100 frames which are not enumerated; and job 281 (container 1164) is not numbered by frames, although the printed material which it records has its own page numbers. The same is true of job 321-A which consists of pamphlets.

What of the provenance of the documents in this film collection? By far the greatest single group consists of Mussolini's Papers, the *Segreteria Particolare*. We have this breakdown:

Mussolini's Papers	139
P.W.B. Reports	27
Ministry of Foreign Affairs	24 *a*
Japanese embassy-Rome	18
Ministry of the Interior	12
Ministry of Popular Culture	10 *b*

Italian Armistice Commission in France	8
Ministry of Italian Africa	6 a
Miscellaneous	10
Films made in the National Archives	2
	256 [216]

The miscellaneous category includes job no. 118 (frames 032151–242), Graziani's papers, which were taken from him by Captain Daddario in April 1945 and filmed as of May 26, 1946.[217]

The Film Collection in England

The making of this collection was a combined American-British operation. The American Fifth Army seized Mussolini's archives which remained in the Feltrinelli Villa: The British embassy in Rome got a good part, at least, of the documents which Mussolini took with him on leaving Milan. Although the American, La Vista, was a guiding spirit in the work from beginning to end, the initial filming machine was English and for a good part of the time, at least at the start, most of the staff were British.

One complete set of the films was sent to London. From this British set we were able to get a duplicate for job 331, and also to patch up a couple of our reels which got damaged in Washington. As mentioned earlier, the Honorable Margaret Lambert, British editor in chief of the *Documents on German Foreign Policy, 1918–1945,* graciously and speedily responded to each appeal to supply something missing in Washington.

In the old country this collection has been handled on a much more informal basis than on this side of the Atlantic. It is not listed in the *Guide to the Contents of the Public Record Office.*[218]

Soon after the filming had been completed it was used in part by Elizabeth Wiskeman for her *Rome-Berlin Axis.* Sometime later the collection was moved physically to St. Antony's College, Oxford. This is the collection which was the core of the Italian documentary material used by F. W. Deakin for his monumental and exhaustive study, *The Brutal*

216a. Two jobs are counted twice because each has material from the Ministry of Foreign Affairs and from the Ministry of Italian Africa. Thus this breakdown adds up to 256 jobs, two more than the total of 254.

b. Other than those originally comprised in the the the P.W.B. Reports.

In estimating the total collection to have about 114,000 frames I have not counted the two films made in the National Archives.

217. Cf. Graziani, *Ho difeso la patria,* pp. 533–34; Schuster, *Ultimi tempi di un regime,* p. 161.

218. (London: H.M. Stationery Office, 1963, approx. 415 pp.). The edition of 1972 bears the title, *The Second World War: A Guide to Documents in the Public Record Office.*

Friendship: Mussolini, Hitler and the Fall of Italian Fascism. But his description of it (p. 819) is not accurate. He mentions that "An unsolved mystery surrounds the fate of Mussolini's personal archives, which disappeared during the final exodus from Milan in April 1945, though some of the files in this collection, on circumstantial evidence, may come from this source." It is unfortunate that Deakin's references to the unpublished Italian material are so tantalizingly incomplete. The filming by the La Vista-Thomson Organization, with due consideration of the handicaps of the time when it was done, was a good performance. Almost any document can be pinpointed by its job number and frame number. But throughout Deakin's notes (pp. 839–71) there is not a single identification of a file of the original documents, or of job or frame number of the film collection. This is as frustrating and as baffling as a postal address with street number only, and no mention of town, county, or state.

In that great collection of materials on the origin and early course of World War II, the *Documents on German Foreign Policy, 1918–1945,* the Tripartite Project (American-British-French) set a splendid standard of precise reference, identifying each microfilmed document by its serial and frame number, and correlating the serials precisely with the files of the German Foreign Office archives in the appropriate appendix for each volume. Any scholar with access to those documents which are now back in Germany at Bonn, or to the film collections deposited respectively in the National Archives in Washington or in the Public Record Office in London, can quickly get the original text.

Natural scientists proclaim the truth of their discoveries with exact descriptions of their experiments, thus enabling their colleagues to verify their conclusions by duplicating those experiments. Careful scholars show forth the validity of their statements of fact by precise references to the documentary evidence. All writers who expect full concurrence or acceptance of their bits and pieces of historical truth should face the obligation of facilitating easy verification by precise citations. Now that microfilming has come of age, that it has become a basic tool of modern research, it is imperative that this splendid tool be used in proper fashion.

6 / Miscellaneous: Conclusions

Italian Manuscript Materials Held by the Library of Congress

There is a small collection of Italian materials in the Library of Congress, six cartons of miscellaneous records in the custody of the Manuscript Division. Through the kindness of Dr. George O. Kent, who at the time was in the Manuscript Division, I was able on May 23, 1968, to examine these documents. The processing sheets, dated February 15, 1954, indicate that they were all received by the Library of Congress in 1948 and that they came either from the Department of State or from the Washington Document Center.[1]

In the library, the items were given accession numbers, brief descriptions were made on the three processing sheets, and the materials were shelved in labeled containers or cartons. In February 1964, Dr. James E. O'Neill prepared a somewhat fuller description of each item according to the six accession numbers and, for the final number (AC 9098) for its twelve subdivisions. When I examined the materials they were in the six archival storage boxes (blue cardboard boxes, 4½ by 10½ by 15 inches) as follows.

1. The Washington Document Center was set up by the Military Intelligence Division (MID) of the War Department General Staff during World War II. When the German Military Documents Section (GMDS) was established in accordance with the Bissell-Sinclair agreement of May 1945, this section became a part of the Washington Document Center. For the Bissell-Sinclair agreement and GMDS, see chap. 4, note 94. The functions and files of the Washington Document Center were later taken over by the Departmental Records Branch, Administrative Service Division, TAGO. In turn this was succeeded by the Modern Military Records Division, National Archives.

Box 1 consists only of materials of AC 9098, which according to the processing sheet was received on June 15, 1948, from the Washington Document Center. There are four folders of an outline history of the headquarters of the "Cuneo" infantry division (*Diario storico militare-bozza-Comando Divisione Fanteria "Cuneo"*). Folder 1 (June 10, 1940–January 26, 1941); Folder 2 (January 26, 1941–July 14, 1941); Folder 3 (July 15, 1941–June 22, 1942); Folder 4 (June 23, 1942–June 30, 1943).

Box 2 likewise consists exclusively of materials from AC 9098, that is materials transferred from the Washington Document Center. There are nine items:

1. A black, bound account book labeled "Maestro" 1942, of the Society of Friends of Japan.

2. An orange-brown folder of correspondence of the Society of Friends of Japan, 1938–40 with several letters signed by Ezio M. Gray.

3. A folder of correspondence of the *Società amici del Giappone* for the year 1938.

4. Typescript of a manual for disarming mines issued at Verona in 1943.

5. A one-page letter from the clandestine CLN of Capodistria dealing with the events of October 30–31, 1943; a list on 10 pages of 277 Italians murdered by the "Slavo-Communists" during the period of Partisan domination in Istria (September–October 1943), plus a list of names of 53 Italians shot by the Slavs, November 1943 to 1945.

6. Unidentified record of correspondence for 1942 in one volume.

7. Paper folder with typescript on the modifications in Law 1093, the law regarding the status of warrant officers of the Royal Italian Army.

8. Typescript in 40 pages entitled "Le operazioni di sbarco" (debarkation operations), by Lt. Col. Sebastiano Alfieri. No date, but it appears to relate to the period of the Spanish civil war.

9. Two personnel files; the Fascist party record of Francesco Cacciatore; the naval record of Francesco Laitano (1905–42).

Box 3 consists of two parts or items, each from AC 9098:

1. A paper folder with a register of publications of the *Comando Supremo, Ufficio Operazioni* (Operations Office of the Armed Forces General Staff), pertaining to the Western theater and debarkations, a list of 141 entries.

2. Twenty folders of the *Comando Supremo. Ufficio Operazioni,* as follows:

(1) *Comando 1ª squadra aerea* (1939)

(2) *Informazioni del S.I.M.* (Military Intelligence) July 13–26, 1943.

(3) *Messaggi in arrivo giorno 15-7-43* (messages received July 15, 1943) beginning with two notes from the German Liaison Office attached to the *Comando Supremo.*

Folders (4) through (20) are of messages received for July 16 and for each subsequent day of the month with a final folder for August 1, 1943.

Box 4 consists of materials initially given the accession number 8943, received from the Department of State on February 27, 1948. They are twelve logbooks of the S.S. *Confidenza* for the years 1935 and 1936.

Box 5, a continuation from Box 4, consists of logbooks numbered in folders 13 to 22.

Box 6 is a miscellany. First there are folders 23 to 34 of the logbooks of the S.S. *Confidenza*, a continuation from Boxes 4 and 5, and originally labeled AC 8943.

Next comes a folder, "Ordini di pagamento; Deposito 69ª reggimento fanteria "Sirte"—12 typed pages of records of food supplies for the Sixty-ninth Infantry Regiment in 1941 (AC 8950, received from the Department of State, February 27, 1948).

The third item is a booklet entitled, "Quaderno per registrazioni radiogonimetriche," a carbon copy of the record book of radio-direction finding of the S.S. *Confidenza*, July 12, 1937–February 15, 1938 (AC 8944, received from the Department of State, February 27, 1948).

The fourth item is the *Libretto personale* (personnel file) of Mattia Giglio (AC 8946, received from the Department of State, February 27, 1948).

Fifth we have AC 8948, "Moduli per comportamento batterie anodiche," a 12-page record book of battery inspections, 1936–38, of the radio operator of the S.S. *Confidenza*, transferred from the Department of State.

Sixth is an item in 10 typed pages, "Comando deposito 86ª reggimento fanteria 'Sabrata' "—inventory of supplies of the Eighty-sixth Infantry Regiment for July 1942 (AC 8950, transferred from the Department of State).

I am not able to judge the scientific importance of the data of the logbooks and the battery records of the S.S. *Confidenza*. The materials in Box 2, item 5, from the CLN of Capodistria, if not available elsewhere, would be important in the history of the Resistance movement, and of the Italo-Yugoslav conflict over Istria.

With one egregious exception the military records in the holdings of the Library of Congress appear to be of secondary or tertiary importance at the most, significant only for study in detail of certain aspects of the Royal Italian Army in World War II. The twenty folders of documents of the *Comando Supremo* are the exception and are of the greatest historical interest. Here we have the messages which came in to the Operations Office of the Italian Armed Forces General Staff during the military-political crisis which led to the overthrow of Mussolini on July 25, and we have also the incoming messages up to and including August 1, when

the German military occupation of Italy began.[2] These records deserve
the most careful scrutiny by any serious student of Italy's role in World
War II. They should carefully be correlated and compared with the Italian
Military Documents whose vicissitudes and acquisition by the United
States government are described in chapter four.[3]

Regarding Some Other Graziani Papers

Certain of the papers of Marshal Rodolfo Graziani apparently came
into possession of the United States military in the early period of the occupation of Italy. Professor William L. Langer saw some of these and
cited some Italian general staff documents relating to the negotiation of
the armistice with France.[4] These materials seem to be those which were
in four cases and were described in Graziani's letter of May 16, 1946, to
Admiral Stone (head of the Allied Commission in Italy) in which he
asked for their return.[5] These documents are quite distinct from those
which were turned over by Graziani to Captain Daddario on April 29,
1945, immediately after Graziani's surrender in North Italy and which
found their way into the film collection of Mussolini's Private Papers,
microcopy T-586.[6]

In March 1947, the American embassy in Rome was notified that the
Graziani papers which "came into the possession of the U.S. military
during the early period of the occupation of Italy" and which consisted
of "personal correspondence, photographs, pictures, and certain book
materials" were being transmitted under separate cover. They were to be
returned to the Italian government.[7] By despatch no. 1077 of June 24,
1947, the embassy reported that the documents had been returned and
an appropriate receipt had been obtained from the Italian government.[8]

2. See Albert N. Garland and Howard McGaw Smyth, *Sicily and the Surrender of Italy*
(Washington, D.C.: Office of the Chief of Military History, Department of the Army, 1965),
pp. 263–68, 281–99. Would that I had known of these materials when working on that book!

3. Microcopy T-821. For documents of the *Comando Supremo* see the National Archives,
National Archives and Records Service, General Services Administration, *Guide to Records
of the Italian Armed Forces* (Washington, D.C., 1967), pt. 1, pp. 140–41; pt. 2, p. 126; pt. 3, p.
159.

4. *Our Vichy Gamble* (New York: Alfred A. Knopf, 1947), pp. 48–49, fnn. 11, 12, and 13.

5. Rodolfo Graziani, *Ho difeso la patria*, 4th ed. (Milan: Garzanti, 1948), pp. 595–96.

6. See chap. 5 (Microcopy T-586: Analysis of the Collection) and note 217.

7. Instruction no. 1943, March 5, 1947, (865.414/3-547), Central Files, Department of
State. When retired to the National Archives, these files constitute Record Group 59.

8. (865.414/6-2447), Central Files, Department of State.

Mussolini's Writings of the Summer of 1943
Preserved in the German Foreign Office Archives

When Mussolini was arrested at the order of the king, following the vote against him in the Grand Council of Fascism, he was first taken to the *Carabinieri* barracks in Rome. He himself expressed the wish to return to his home at the Rocca delle Caminata; he seems to have hoped that this would be his fate and that he could retire peaceably. But Mussolini was reckoning without Hitler. The Führer could not believe that his friend, the Duce, had resigned willingly, and he promptly formulated plans to occupy Italy and to restore Mussolini and fascism. He seems to have believed that such a stroke would be so great a shock to "the English" as to turn the scales of the war in the Mediterranean. But in order to restore Mussolini, the Germans first had to find him. The Italian secret police quickly became aware of this German interest in Mussolini's whereabouts, and from July 27 to September 12—for more than the whole of Badoglio's forty-five days—there was played out a curious cat and mouse game, with German special forces, led by General Student and *Sturmbannführer* Skorzeny,[9] hot on the trail of Mussolini, and the Italians one step ahead, moving him under guard from one hiding place to another.

Mussolini was first taken by Admiral Maugeri aboard the corvette *Persefone* to the island of Ponza, but this hiding place seems to have become known to the Germans and he was then secretly moved to the little island, La Maddalena, just off Sardinia, an Italian naval base in World War II and famous in the history of the Risorgimento as Garibaldi's retreat. One of Skorzeny's men seems to have spotted Mussolini on Maddalena, but before the *Sturmbannführer* could organize and launch his stroke, the Italians moved the former Duce to the Campo Imperatore, a ski lodge atop the Gran Sasso, highest peak in the Apennines. It was there that that swashbuckler, Otto Skorzeny, "rescued" Mussolini on September 12. He was then flown to Rome in a little *Storch* plane, transferred to a three-motored Heinkel, and flown on to Vienna together with Skorzeny and Police Inspector Gueli, the official in charge of the Italian armed guard on the Gran Sasso.[10]

9. *Sturmbannführer*, a rank in the SS and in the SA equivalent to major in the regular army.
10. There is a good account of this "Exile and Liberation" in Frederick W. Deakin, *The Brutal Friendship: Mussolini, Hitler and the Fall of Italian Fascism* (New York and Evanston: Harper & Row, 1962), pp. 538–47.
Mussolini's own account of his imprisonment is in his *Il tempo del bastone e della carota: storia di un anno (ottobre 1942–settembre 1943)* Supplemento del *Corriere della Sera*, no. 190 del 9-8-1944. Cf. chap. 2 (The Cianos "Escape" to Germany).

In addition to his *Storia di un anno*, Mussolini left two discussions of this period which have come to light; there may possibly have been a third which so far has not been discovered. The first of the two is his narrative of the events of July 25 ("La giornata del 25 luglio"), written at Ponza and dated August 2, 1943. The second in seventy-five numbered paragraphs, is entitled "Pontine and Sardinian Reflections" ("Pensieri pontini e sardi") and was completed as a first notebook on August 20, 1943. Deakin comments that the "Pontine and Sardinian Reflections" are remarkable for their banality.[11] Our problem, however, is not their literary quality nor their historical value but the authenticity of the texts.

There have been three significant discussions of these writings of Mussolini of the summer of 1943: by Edoardo and Duilio Susmel, published in 1961; by Deakin, whose book was issued in 1962; and an article by the late Professor Toscano, whose first printing was in 1961.

Edoardo and Duilio Susmel, those assiduous editors of Mussolini's collected works and worshippers of his memory, provide texts of the Duce's documents of the summer of 1943 and an interesting explanation of their derivation.[12] Mussolini, they narrate, made some intimate notations in two notebooks (*quaderni*) which he called "Pontine and Sardinian Reflections." He made a reference to these in his *Storia di un anno*, where he states that he was allowed to do some writing, to keep a kind of diary, but he regarded it as lost.[13] The truth was, according to these editors, that the diary was not returned to him. Nevertheless, they state, he reported some fragments.[14] The first booklet covered the period August 2 to August 19.

Mussolini had the two booklets with him when he was on the Gran Sasso, the Susmels explain, and turned them over to the police inspector, Giuseppe Gueli. In Vienna, Gueli transferred the notebooks to Skorzeny who turned them over to Himmler, his superior (chief of the *Sicherheitsdienst* or SD).[15] Himmler had the documents of the Duce photographed and translated into German. The originals, we are informed, were con-

11. Deakin, *Brutal Friendship*, p. 540.
12. *Opera omnia di Benito Mussolini* (Florence: La Fenice, 1961) 34:273–99. The "Rapporto sul 25 luglio" is on pp. 273–76, followed immediately by the seventy-five numbered paragraphs. The two documents are treated as one, under the heading "Pensieri pontini e sardi." At the end of paragraph 75 is the line: "Qui finisce il primo quaderno dei *Pensieri pontini e sardi* 19 agosto 1943, ore quindici."
The explanation is provided in the notes, pp. vii–viii.
13. See *Il tempo del bastone e della carota*, p. 22, which states: "Fu concesso a Mussolini di scrivere. Pare abbia fatto delle notazioni quotidiane di carattere filosofico, letterario, politico, ma questa specie di diario non lo si è più trovato."
14. Cf. *Il tempo del bastone e della carota*, p. 33. See notes 29 and 30 below.
15. See chap. 2 (The Cianos "Escape" to Germany) regarding Himmler.

signed to Hitler, and several copies of the translations were distributed. Citing Skorzeny's memoirs, the Susmels explain that he wished to pay a visit to the Duce on the shores of Lake Garda, but only if he could return the notebooks sequestered from Gueli. The German minister of foreign affairs, Von Ribbentrop, interfered, however, because he did not know how the delay in restitution could be explained to Mussolini.

One copy of the German translation of Mussolini's writings was sent to an office set up in the monastery of Kreismünster, near Linz, and which was under the command of Kaltenbrunner. Shortly before the German surrender the office was dissolved and the order was issued to destroy all documents lest they fall into the hands of the Russians. An SS officer saw this copy. Recognizing its importance he saved it from the flames and kept it hidden for years. In 1950 this German translation was published in the *Salzburger Nachrichten*. The text offered in the *Opera Omnia* is a retranslation back into the Italian, a text for the first booklet only. About the same time as the Susmels published their version, these writings appeared in Italy elsewhere. No one knows, the editors conclude, where the original notebooks are, but they express the hope that some day they may be tracked down.

Deakin's discussion is in the form of an appendix to his chapter on "Exile and Liberation" which is entitled, "The Memoirs of the Duce written in Exile." [16] He uses the German translations or Italian retranslations as texts and gives substantially the same account of the movement of the Duce's papers to Austria as is provided by the Susmels. However, he adds some detail regarding the treatment of the documents by the Germans in the spring of 1944, citing three documents from the "German Collection," that is, the microfilm records of the former German Foreign Office made by the Tripartite (American-British-French) German War Documents Project and designated microcopy T-120 at the National Archives. These three documents are: (1) telegram of the German Foreign Office dated January 27, 1944, asking the views of Rahn, their plenipotentiary in Italy, regarding restitution of the Duce's writings; (2) Rahn's reply of February 2, recommending postponement; and (3) a Foreign Office memorandum of April 9, 1944, which recorded that the originals had been destroyed in an air raid on Berlin, and proposed that photostatic copies of the papers be returned to Mussolini with an explanation of what had happened.[17] He adds that only Mussolini's account of the

16. *Brutal Friendship*, pp. 547–48.
17. It is practically impossible to determine which copies of these documents were seen by Deakin or in which files. Here, as throughout his book, the messages have date, sender, and recipient only; but no number, no reference to the file, no designation of serial and frame numbers in the film collection.

events of July 25 is to be found in the "German Collection." For the
"Pensieri" he cites to the text in the book of Walter Hagen who, apparently, is the SS officer who rescued the precious document from the
flames and published it in 1950.[18]

Deakin adduces no further evidence but infers that the photostatic
copies were delivered to Mussolini because internal evidence indicates
that he used them in his *Storia di un anno*. Deakin's analysis of the
"Reflections" leads him to conclude that they were composed on La
Maddalena between August 8 and 28.

A far more penetrating discussion of the German treatment of Mussolini's writings of the summer of 1943 is by Mario Toscano who conducted a considerable research in the microfilm records of the former
German Foreign Office.[19] Toscano first covers the same ground as did
Deakin regarding the problem of the return of the Duce's papers as it
was developed in the *Auswärtiges Amt* in the spring of 1944. The memorandum of April 9, however, was by no means the final word. Skorzeny
at long last did visit Mussolini on June 26–27, 1944, and at the time discussed the matter of restitution of the documents with Rahn and with
Obergruppenführer [20] Wolff. By this time it appeared that the originals
might not have been destroyed by the Allied air raid after all. They had
been placed in a metal safe which got covered with rubble but the fire
had been brought under control. Skorzeny told the Duce that if the
papers were found, they would be returned to him. Skorzeny's memorandum, which reached the Foreign Office on December 4, 1944, records
the June visit, and the concurrence of both Himmler and of Ribbentrop
in his renewed plea to be permitted to return Mussolini's papers to their
author. Sometime in January of 1945 Skorzeny transmitted the original
papers to Wolff who delivered them, apparently in a sealed envelope, to
Mussolini. Ribbentrop retained only photostatic copies of the papers.[21]

Toscano points precisely to the documents whose copies were re-

18. [Pseud. for Wilhelm Hoettl], *Die geheime Front: Organisation, Personen und Aktionen des deutschen Geheimdienstes*, 2d ed. (Linz and Vienna: Nibelungen-Verlag, 1950), pp. 410–32. English translation from the German in *The Secret Front: The Story of Nazi Political Espionage*, 2d ed. (London: Weidenfeld & Nicolson, 1954), chap. 14, "Musings of a Dictator," pp. 234–64.

19. "Le vicende degli archivi di Palazzo Chigi e dei diari di prigionia di Mussolini catturati dai nazisti dopo l'armistizio," chap. 9, pp. 249–81 of the book, *Pagine di storia diplomatica contemporanea*, vol. 2, *Origini e vicende della seconda guerra mondiale* (Milan: A.
Giuffrè Editore, 1963). The chapter was initially published in the *Nuova Antologia* of March
1961. The discussion of Mussolini's "diaries" is confined to the final sections of the article
7, 8 and 9, pp. 269–81.

20. SS rank equivalent to lieutenant general.

21. Toscano, *Pagine di storia*, pp. 274–77.

tained by the German Foreign Minister: (a) the "diary" and personal notations of the Duce; and (b) reports of one "G. Giuli" to Mussolini, which he suggests is probably a German misreading of Gueli.[22] Interestingly enough, Toscano did not have any text at hand when he wrote. He cites to none in his original article in the *Nuova Antologia* of 1961 or in the reissue in book form in 1963. But he had a very clear conception that the "diary" of Mussolini had to be such as his jailers permitted him to keep; that it was written during his period of imprisonment; that its contents were of human interest but of no great political or historical importance. Furthermore, inasmuch as the papers were restored to Mussolini only in January 1945, they could not have been used by him in writing his *Storia di un anno* which was composed in 1944.[23]

Let me at this point add some of my own findings. There are two files in the *Auswärtiges Amt* archives with two corresponding serials in the microfilm collection T-120 at the National Archives, one of which serves to put at rest some of the problems regarding the German treatment of Mussolini's papers, and the other to provide the original texts.[24]

In a letter of October 19, 1943, the *Sicherheitsdienst* forwarded to the Foreign Office the four documents taken by Skorzeny from Inspector Queli *[sic]* with the request that they be returned to Mussolini.[25] The proposal was a sure indication that the papers were not regarded by the Germans as of much significance. *Referent* [26] Geiger in the Foreign Office on October 25 ordered three photocopies of the papers to be made, and that the customary stamp indicating copying be omitted. Next day he ordered translations of each of the four plus two carbon copies of the translations in preparation for presentation of the matter to the foreign minister.[27]

What were these papers? The index prepared in the Foreign Ministry lists five items:

1) Typewritten memorandum of the Duce entitled "La giornata des *[sic]* 25 luglio," dated August 2, 1943, with the appended;

22. Ibid., p. 277.
23. Ibid., pp. 270–71.
24. File "Inland II g, Geheime Reichssachen 1944, Vol. XV (Box 3)" Seriel 712, frames 262328 to 262765 and a package or file marked "Duce Dokumente" Serial 715, frames 263604–817. Citations to the films will be by the serial number, an oblique stroke, and the frame number.
25. Received October 20. The incoming message, on being logged into the AA records, was given the filing number Inl. II 450 gRs. (712/262582).
26. A term meaning in general expert or specialist: in the *Auswärtiges Amt* it meant an official corresponding to the desk officer in the Department of State.
27. 712/262585 and 262584.

2) Handwritten memorandum of the Duce in pencil in a notebook with some added loose sheets;

3) One small map of Sicily;

4) A letter of Giuseppe Giuli [sic] to Mussolini dated Vienna, September 14, 1943;

5) Letter of Giuseppe Giuli (again) to the Duce dated Vienna, September 23, 1943.[28]

These are the documents which Skorzeny took. If there was another notebook, a second *quaderno*, it was never in the possession of the Germans; it did not leave Italy. We can exclude the idea that the SD withheld any paper of the Duce, for in such a case Skorzeny would have noticed and protested or at least would have made inquiries.

In the file "Duce Dokumente" (Serial 715) we have eleven items as follows:

1) Film of the German photostats of Mussolini's typewritten account of the events of July 25, four pages entitled, "La giornata del 25 luglio" (263605–8);

2) German translation of no. 1 (263609–16);

3) Film of the photostatic copy of the "Pontine and Sardinian Reflections" in Mussolini's handwriting (263617–705);

4) Typewritten copy of no. 3 (263706–33);

5) German translation of no. 3 (263734–58);

6) Film of the photostatic copy of Giuseppe Gueli's letter of September 14, 1943 (263759–79);

7) Typewritten copy of no. 6 (263780–92);

8) German translation of no. 6 (263793–814);

9) Film of photostatic copy of Gueli's letter of September 23, transmitting to Mussolini the longer letter of September 14 no. 6 (263815);

10) Typewritten copy of no. 9 (263816);

11) German translation of no. 9 (263817).

Thus we have available in Washington the authentic texts of the two known documents written by Mussolini in the summer of 1943. The typed copy prepared by the Germans (no. 4 above) is not very accurate. Gueli's name is rendered "Giuli"; there are several corrections in ink over the typewritten words; and blank spaces appear now and then where the words in Mussolini's pencil handwriting could not be read. Possibly it was a rush job to get ready for the presentation to the Foreign Minister. Walter Hagen's German text appears to be that which was prepared in the *Auswärtiges Amt*.

Was there a second notebook? There is some evidence that something of the sort may once have existed even though the Germans never had it. The concluding line of the "Pensieri" states: "here is finished the first booklet." This seems to imply that there was, or would be, a second. In the *Storia di un anno* the Duce mentions: "In a kind of diary which Mussolini wrote on Maddalena, there stands written [here follow four

28. Zu Inl. II 450 gRs, n.d. (712/262586).

passages which mention a return of fascism: Napoleon's mistaken judgment in counting on British chivalry when his cycle was ended; the significance of the Napoleonic era for France; and finally the need of suffering by the Italians in order to achieve redemption]." [29] These passages are not to be found in the "Pontine and Sardinian Reflections." In any case, as Toscano pointed out, the "Pensieri" were not restored to Mussolini until after the composition of his *Storia di un anno*. But, so far, there appears to be no definite trace of a second booklet of the summer of 1943.[30]

Conclusions

These six, discussed in as many chapters, are the documentary collections with their secrets of the Fascist era, which are now available in Washington. My stated purpose in describing each group of materials was to explain how they got here, to discuss the *vicende* of the collections, their adventures, voyages and vicissitudes, matters strictly of external criticism. Each has its own interesting history of how it came to be seized or otherwise acquired, where it was transported, how the microfilming or other reproduction was done. Ours is the age of tape recorders, of microfilm, and of Xerox reproduction of documents enabling institutions and scholars (and thieves and spies as well) to save enormously in time and effort in the collection of materials.

It was only a generation or so ago that microphotography began to make its way hesitatingly into the working methods of scholars.[31] Before then the researcher was obliged to make his journey to the archival deposit (and if the archive was in Europe, this meant a sea voyage of many days) and painfully to make his notes or transcriptions in longhand. The accuracy of copying tended to decline toward the end of the day. In few archives or libraries was the typewriter permitted because of disturbance to others. Longhand transcriptions were the rule. It was a method essentially like that of the medieval monks who painstakingly and often very beautifully copied out the works of their scholarly predecessors and contemporaries and thus handed down the literary legacy of the past. But these monks inevitably made mistakes, and what a problem it is for criti-

29. *Il tempo del bastone e della carota*, p. 33.

30. See chap. 5, notes 49 and 50. for the assertion that Donna Rachele at Como on the night of April 25–26 received from Mussolini "the record of imprisonment on Maddalena." The citation is to Franco Bandini, *Le ultime 95 ore di Mussolini*, 3d ed. (Milan: Sugar Editore, 1963) pp. 97–98. These words might just as easily refer to what is already known as to a second booklet. In any case the evidence for the assertion is rather thin.

31. See "New Tools for Men of Letters," pp. 179–97 in *Selected Papers of Robert C. Binkley*, ed. Max H. Fisch, Foreword by Luther H. Evans (Cambridge: Harvard University Press, 1948), reprinted from the *Yale Review*, Spring 1935.

cal scholars to reconstruct an initial text when only copies survive! Automatic duplication is superior to longhand transcription in every way save one: the time-consuming making of notes or copying out of material does impress the matter on the mind of the researcher in a way which photography does not.

Although ours is the age of the mechanization of literary reproduction, some of the stories of the men and women involved in securing, transporting, and in copying out the papers of the Fascist era—in other words the adventures of the documents in surviving—are not, in essence, unlike those of the texts of the Greek philosophers of antiquity when they made their way over the Arabian civilization back to the West in the movement which Charles Homer Haskins so aptly called *The Renaissance of the Twelfth Century*. (Cambridge: Harvard University Press, 1928). The forms and techniques of copying, of communication, and of travel have changed enormously since medieval times, but the human stories, which constitute the substance of history, remain much the same.

The Lisbon Papers were got safely out of Rome by the Italians in August 1943; they made the aerial trip from the Italian capital to Lisbon where they remained in seeming safety for over two years. Then Uncle Sam intervened. American intelligence officers learned of the documents, the Department of State demanded their surrender, and thus they came by pouch to Washington. The department microfilmed the Lisbon Papers and, after restoring the originals to the Italian government, it transferred the collection of films to the National Archives by way of the Historical Office. Uncle Sam's various agencies were essential in the discovery of these documents, in their filming, and in making them available to the scholarly public.

Count Ciano's diaries and the supporting papers relating to them—those which he himself selected—made several moves into hiding in Italy, and then each went northward over the Alps by separate paths. The diaries crossed into neutral Switzerland around the belly of Countess Edda; the supporting documents traveled to Berlin under official protection. The Italian originals of the supporting papers were consumed in the holocaust of records which Hitler ordered in April 1945, but the German translations survived by going underground, literally, in the rose garden of Frau Beetz. Here again the role of Uncle Sam was crucial. It was Allen Dulles, chief OSS representative in Switzerland, who got Ciano's diaries for the United States government, who enabled Paul Ghali to arrange for their publication. Furthermore it was OSS agents, men of the Counter Intelligence Corps, who got the Rose Garden papers. The State Department transferred them to the National Archives.

The enormous task of screening and then of transcribing wholesale the top level documents of the Fascist Ministry of Popular Culture, which was successfully undertaken by the Psychological Warfare Branch, was also a job that could have been performed only by a governmental agency. Furthermore P.W.B. played a most important role in surveying and in making copies of documents of the Italian Social Republic. Whereas at the suggestion of the Italian government we passed copies of the Lisbon Papers to the British, and we voluntarily gave London a copy of the Rose Garden papers, the Psychological Warfare Branch was a combined Anglo-American organ and the fruits of its labors were automatically shared.

With the Italian military documents we encounter a very different story. It was the Germans, Italy's erstwhile allies, who first seized the records of the Italian armed forces, who assembled them, and who made the initial catalogue. The seizure of the *Aktensammelstelle Süd* was a purely American operation, yet we must note that the only initial report about that Document Center which survived, was by a Britisher. The subsequent storing, sorting, screening, filming, and indexing of these papers were purly American undertakings, paid for completely by funds from the federal government. The travels of these documents were complicated: over the Alps to Germany; over the ocean to the U.S.A.; from Camp Ritchie to the Pentagon; then to the old Torpedo Factory in Alexandria; and finally back to the Italian homeland.

Mussolini's Private Papers were grabbed by various agencies and shifted from place to place, but, in contrast to the military documents, they did not leave Italy. All of their movements were within the Italian peninsula. As with the case of P.W.B., the work of the Joint Diplomatic Research Agency in filming these documents in Rome was an Anglo-American operation. The films were shipped back both to Washington and to London, but the handling of the film collections at the National Archives has made the documents available to all scholars on an equal basis whereas use of the films in England appears to have been restricted to a few.

The little collection at the Library of Congress is noted because of a few documents of crucial importance for the Italian crisis of 1943. The other Graziani papers are mentioned lest some scholar pick up the trail in the footnotes and go looking for something that is not here. I myself once tried to track down these documents, believing them to be in Washington. I made a phone call to an appropriate office. After two or three weeks I had the amusing experience of getting my own inquiry back; it had gone around to half a dozen or more stops in various offices of the federal bureaucracy. The microfilms of the German foreign office documents are again shown to shed light on the story of Mussolini.

It must be emphasized that the gathering of each of these collections of top-level documents of Mussolini's period was the work of Uncle Sam. Not only that, but the microfilming of these documents, the systematic indexing of a great many of them, and their publication in the general sense of the term, that is making them public in the National Archives, was the work of the federal government. These are days of vigorous discussion over executive privilege, these are times of bitter criticism, particularly in academic circles, of the system of security classification which appears to hide so many of our own government's papers from public view. In the midst of all these suspicions and accusations, it is well for the public, and for the academic community especially, to remember the superb service of Uncle Sam in respect of the documentary records embodying the secrets of the Fascist era.

Appendix
Bibliography
Index

Appendix

Concordance of Documents Printed in *L'Europa verso la catastrofe* and on Microfilm in the Lisbon Papers [1]

1936

Date	Book (Page)	Lisbon Papers (Reel, file, and page)
1. Colloquio con l'incaricato d'affari di Francia		
June 12, 1936	20	2196-C, p. 1
2. Colloquio con l'ambasciatore di Turchia		
June 15, 1936	21	2196-C, p. 4
3. Colloquio con l'ambasciatore di Argentina		
June 15, 1936	21	2196-C, p. 2
4. Colloquio con l'ambasciatore di Gran Bretagna		
June 16, 1936	23	2196-C, p. 7
5. Colloquio con l'ambasciatore di Germania		
June 18, 1936	23	2196-C, p. 8
6. Colloquio con l'ambasciatore di Francia		
June 24, 1936	24	2196-C, p. 10
7. Colloquio col ministro di Haiti		
June 25, 1936	26	2196-C, p. 13
8. Colloquio con l'ambasciatore di Polonia		
June 27, 1936	26	2196-C, p. 14
9. Colloquio con l'ambasciatore di Francia (annex) *		
June 29, 1936	27	2196-C, p. 15
10. Colloquio con l'ambasciatore di Germania		
June 29, 1936	28	2196-C, p. 21
11. Colloquio con l'ambasciatore di Gran Bretagna (2 annexes) *		
June 30, 1936	29	2196-C, p. 24
12. Colloquio col ministro d'Austria *		
July 2, 1936	30	2196-C, p. 35
13. Colloquio con l'ambasciatore di Francia		
July 4, 1936	31	2196-C, p. 39
14. Colloquio col ministro di Romania *		
July 4, 1936	32	2196-C, p. 41
15. Colloquio col ministro del Messico		
July 4, 1936	32	2196-C, p. 43
16. Colloquio con l'ambasciatore di Francia		
July 9, 1936	33	2196-C, p. 44

1. An asterisk indicates that the printed text is incomplete or imperfect.

1936

Date	Book (Page)	Lisbon Papers (Reel, file, and page)
17. Colloquio con l'ambasciatore di Francia		
July 11, 1936	35	2196-C, p. 47
18. Colloquio col ministro di Romania		
July 11, 1936	36	2196-C, p. 49
19. Colloquio con l'ambasciatore di Gran Bretagna		
July 11, 1936	37	2196-C, p. 51
20. Colloquio con l'ambasciatore di Spagna		
July 22, 1936	39	2196-C, p. 54
21. Colloquio con l'ambasciatore di Francia e gli incaricati d'affari di Gran Bretagna e del Belgio		
July 24, 1936	41	2196-C, p. 56
22. Colloquio con l'ambasciatore di Germania		
July 25, 1936	42	2196-C, p. 58
23. Colloquio con l'ambasciatore di Francia		
July 29, 1936	44	2196-C, p. 61
24. Colloquio con l'ambasciatore di Germania		
July 30, 1936	45	2196-C, p. 63
25. Colloquio con l'incaricato d'affari della Gran Bretagna		
July 30, 1936	46	2196-C, p. 65
26. Colloquio con il ministro di Romania		
July 30, 1936	47	2196-C, p. 67
27. Colloquio con l'ambasciatore di Francia		
August 3, 1936	50	2196-C, p. 69
28. Colloquio con l'ambasciatore di Francia		
August 5, 1936	51	2196-C, p. 71
29. Colloquio con l'incaricato d'affari di Gran Bretagna		
August 6, 1936	52	2196-C, p. 73
30. Colloquio con l'ambasciatore di Francia		
August 7, 1936	54	2196-C, p. 77
31. Colloquio con l'ambasciatore di Francia		
August 10, 1936	55	2196-C, p. 81
32. Colloquio con l'ambasciatore di Francia		
August 14, 1936	56	2196-C, p. 83
33. Colloquio con l'ambasciatore di Francia		
August 17, 1936	57	2196-C, p. 85
34. Colloquio con l'incaricato d'affari di Gran Bretagna (aide memoire *)		
August 17, 1936	58	2196-C, p. 87
35. Colloquio col signor Avenol *		
September 7, 1936	60	2196-C, p. 96
36. Colloquio col ministro di Ungheria		
September 7, 1936	63	2196-C, p. 91

1937

1937

Date	Book (Page)	Lisbon Papers (Reel, file, and page)

8. Colloquio del Duce col ministro degli esteri del Reich Von Neurath
   May 3, 1937   175   2196-C, p. 238
9. Colloqui con il presidente del consiglio d'Ungheria Darányi e il ministro
   degli esteri Kánya
   May 19–22, 1937   178   2196-C, p. 242
10. Colloquio con l'ambasciatore di Turchia
    June 2, 1937   185   2196-C, p. 250
11. Colloquio con l'ambasciatore di Germania
    June 14, 1937   186   2196-D, p. 1
12. Telegramma dell'ambasciatore d'Italia a Berlino
    [June 14, 1937]   188   2196-D, p. 5
13. Colloquio con l'ambasciatore di Germania
    June 16, 1937   189   2196-D, p. 4
14. Colloquio con l'ambasciatore di Gran Bretagna
    June 19, 1937   190   2196-D, p. 7
15. Colloquio con l'ambasciatore di Gran Bretagna
    June 25, 1937   192   2196-D, p. 11
16. Colloquio con l'ambasciatore di Germania
    June 26, 1937   193   2196-D, p. 13
17. Colloquio con l'ambasciatore di Germania
    June 26, 1937   195   2196-D, p. 18
18. Colloquio con l'ambasciatore del Giappone
    July 19, 1937   198   2196-D, p. 20
19. Colloquio con l'ambasciatore del Giappone
    July 31, 1937   199   2196-D, p. 23
20. Colloquio con l'incaricato d'affari di Gran Bretagna
    August 16, 1937   202   2196-D, p. 28
21. Colloquio con l'ambasciatore di Spagna
    August 19, 1937   205   2196-D, p. 31
22. Colloquio con l'incaricato d'affari di Gran Bretagna
    August 23, 1937   206   2196-D, p. 33
23. Colloquio con l'incaricato di affari della Gran Bretagna (aide memoire *)
    August 27, 1937   208   2196-D, p. 39
24. Colloquio con l'ambasciatore di Gran Bretagna (aide memoire *)
    October 2, 1937   210   2196-D, p. 43
25. Colloqui con l'ambasciatore del Giappone e con l'ambasciatore di Germania
    October 20, 1937   213   2196-D, p. 52
26. Colloquio col ministro degli affari esteri del Reich Von Ribbentrop
    October 22, 1937   214   2196-D, p. 159
27. Colloquio del Duce col ministro degli affari esteri del Reich Von Ribbentrop
    October 22, 1937   216   2196-D, p. 161

1938

1938

Date	Book (Page)	Lisbon Papers (Reel, file, and page)
12. Colloquio con l'ambasciatore degli Stati Uniti		
March 24, 1938	296	2196-D, p. 111
13. Colloquio con l'ambasciatore di Gran Bretagna (annex 2 *)		
March 26, 1938	297	2196-D, p. 113
14. Colloquio col ministro di Jugoslavia		
April 15, 1938	301	2196-D, p. 126
15. Colloquio con l'ambasciatore di Germania		
April 24, 1938	303	2196-D, p. 126
16. Appunto per il Duce: Resoconto del viaggio in Albania per il matrimonio di re Zog		
May 2, 1938	305	2196-D, p. 179 2196-B, p. 1
17. Colloquio con l'ambasciatore di Gran Bretagna		
May 18, 1938	318	2196-D, p. 132
18. Colloquio con l'ambasciatore di Gran Bretagna (appunto *)		
May 21, 1938	321	2197A-X, p. 1 2196-D, p. 136
19. Colloquio con l'ambasciatore di Gran Bretagna		
May 22, 1938	322	2196-D, p. 140 2197A-X, p. 5
20. Colloquio con l'ambasciatore di Gran Bretagna		
June 3, 1938	325	2196-D, p. 143
21. Colloquio col presidente del consiglio di Jugoslavia Stoiadinovic		
June 18, 1938	328	2196-G, p. 126
22. Colloquio con l'ambasciatore di Gran Bretagna		
June 20, 1938	333	2196-G, p. 28
23. Colloquio con l'ambasciatore di Turchia		
June 23, 1938	338	2196-G, p. 74
24. Colloquio con l'ambasciatore di Gran Bretagna		
June 28, 1938	339	2196-G, p. 45
25. Appunto del governo italiano in risposta alla nota del governo britannico del 20 giugno 1938		
July 1, 1938	341	2196-G, p. 53
26. Colloquio con l'ambasciatore di Gran Bretagna		
July 2, 1938	343	2196-G, p. 49
27. Colloquio con l'incaricato di affari di Francia		
July 6, 1938	345	2196-G, p. 3
28. Colloquio con l'ambasciatore di Gran Bretagna		
July 11, 1938	347	2196-G, p. 56
29. Colloquio del Duce con il presidente del Consiglio d'Ungheria Imrédy e il ministro degli esteri Kánya presente il conte Ciano		
July 18, 1938	351	2196-G, p. 153

1939

1939

Date	Book (Page)	Lisbon Papers (Reel, file, and page)

4. Resoconto del viaggio in Jugoslavia e colloquio col presidente del consiglio Stoiadinovic
   January 18–23, 1939   405   2196-G, p. 135
5. Relazione sul viaggio in Polonia e colloquio con il presidente del consiglio Beck
   February 25–March 3, 1939   414   2196-G, p. 148
6. Colloquio con l'ambasciatore di Germania
   March 17, 1939   418   2196-G, p. 17
7. Colloquio con l'ambasciatore di Germania
   March 20, 1939   419   2196-G, p. 20
8. Lettera del ministro degli esteri del Reich Von Ribbentrop al conte Ciano
   March 20, 1939   420   2196-G, p. 166
9. Lettera al ministro degli esteri del Reich Von Ribbentrop
   March 24, 1939   422   2196-G, p. 170
10. Colloquio col ministro di Jugoslavia
    April 7, 1939   423   2196-G, p. 25
11. Colloquio col ministro degli affari esteri del Reich Von Ribbentrop
    May 6–7, 1939   428   2196-G, p. 100
12. Telegramma al ministro a Sofia, Talamo
    May 30, 1939   434   2196-G, p. 1
13. Lettera all'ambasciatore al Berlino Attolico
    July 2, 1939   435   2196-E, p. 162
14. Colloquio col generalissimo Franco
    July 19, 1939   439   2196-E, p. 133
15. Colloquio col ministro degli esteri del Reich Von Ribbentrop (signed copy dated August 12) *
    August 11, 1939   449   2196-E, p. 13
         2197-H, p. 14
16. Primo colloquio col Führer
    August 12, 1939   453   2197-H, p. 20
         2196-E, p. 20
17. Secondo colloquio col Führer
    August 13, 1939   458   2197-H, p. 28
         2196-E, p. 29
18. Lettera al ministro degli affari esteri di Gran Bretagna Lord Halifax
    September 14, 1939   461   2196-G, p. 153
         2196-E, p. 172
19. Colloquio con l'ambasciatore di Francia
    September 16, 1939   462   2196-E, p. 1
20. Colloquio col Führer
    October 1, 1939   466   2196-G, p. 177
         2196-E, p. 32

1940

1940

Date	Book (Page)	Lisbon Papers (Reel, file, and page)
12. Lettera al ministro degli interni Serrano Suñer, Madrid		
June 8, 1940	559	2196-F, p. 153
13. Colloquio con il ministro degli esteri del Reich Von Ribbentrop		
June 19, 1940	562	2196-F, p. 1
14. Colloquio del conte Ciano col Führer		
July 7, 1940	566	2196-F, p. 8
15. Colloquio col Führer		
July 20, 1940	574	2196-F, p. 18
16. Colloquio del Duce con il capo del governo romano Gigurtu presente il conte Ciano		
July 27, 1940	576	2196-F, p. 100
17. Lettera al ministro degli interni Serrano Suñer, Madrid		
August 7, 1940	579	2196-F, p. 156
18. Lettera al luogotenente generale in Albania, Jacomoni		
August 22, 1940	580	2196-F, p. 131
19. Colloquio col Führer		
August 29, 1940	581	2196-F, p. 21
20. Lettera al reggente d'Ungheria Horthy		
September 9, 1940	583	2196-F, p. 168
21. Colloquio del Duce con il ministro degli esteri del Reich Von Ribbentrop, presente il conte Ciano e gli ambasciatore Alfieri e Von Mackensen		
September 19, 1940	586	2196-F, p. 24
22. Colloquio del Duce con il ministro degli esteri spagnolo Serrano Suñer presente il conte Ciano *		
October 1, 1940	592	2196-F, p. 105
23. Colloquio del Duce con il Führer alla presenza del ministro degli esteri del Reich Von Ribbentrop e del conte Ciano		
October 4, 1940	594	2196-F, p. 33
24. Colloquio con l'incaricato di affari di Germania		
October 20, 1940	600	2196-F, p. 130
25. Colloquio del Duce col Führer, presenti i ministri degli esteri Ciano e Von Ribbentrop		
October 28, 1940	601	2196-F, p. 43
26. Colloquio col ministro degli esteri del Reich Von Ribbentrop		
November 4, 1940	608	2196-F, p. 55
27. Colloquio con il Führer, presente il ministro degli esteri del Reich Von Ribbentrop		
November 18, 1940	612	2196-F, p. 61
28. Lettera all'ambasciatore a Berlino, Alfieri		
December 16, 1940	617	2196-F, p. 141
29. Lettera all'ambasciatore a Berlino, Alfieri		
December 17, 1940	618	2196-F, p. 143

1941

Date	Book (Page)	Lisbon Papers (Reel, file, and page)
1. Colloquio con il ministro degli esteri del Reich Von Ribbentrop		
January 19, 1941	625	2196-F, p. 69
2. Colloquio del Duce con il Führer, presenti i ministri degli esteri Von Ribbentrop e Ciano		
January 19, 1941	628	2196-F, p. 73
3. Lettera al ministro degli interni Serrano Suñer, Madrid		
January 22, 1941	629	2196-F, p. 158
4. Lettera al ministro degli esteri Von Ribbentrop, Berlino		
January 22, 1941	630	2196-F, p. 150
5. Colloquio del Duce con il Caudillo e il ministro degli esteri spagnolo Serrano Suñer		
February 12, 1941	631	2196-F, p. 108
6. Colloquio con il Führer		
March 25, 1941	645	2196-F, p. 75
7. Colloquio con il Führer		
April 20, 1941	649	2196-F, p. 81
8. Colloquio con il ministro degli esteri del Reich Von Ribbentrop		
April 21, 1941	652	2196-F, p. 86
9. Colloquio con il ministro degli esteri del Reich Von Ribbentrop		
April 22, 1941	654	2196-F, p. 90
10. Lettera al Poglavnik di Croazia, Pavelic, Zagrabia		
April 30, 1941	656	2196-F, p. 135
11. Lettera al ministro degli esteri di Spagna Serrano Suñer, Madrid		
May 4, 1941	658	2196-F, p. 161
12. Colloquio col ministro degli esteri del Reich Von Ribbentrop		
June 2, 1941	660	2196-F, p. 94
13. Lettera al ministro degli esteri di Spagna Serrano Suñer, Madrid		
June 3, 1941	663	2196-F, p. 164
14. Colloquio col ministro degli esteri del Reich Von Ribbentrop		
June 15, 1941	665	2196-A, p. 15
15. Colloquio del Duce col Führer		
August 25, 1941	669	2196-A, p. 20
16. Secondo colloquio del Duce col Führer		
August 25, 1941	672	2196-A, p. 25
17. Lettera al ministro degli esteri del Reich Von Ribbentrop, Berlino		
September 28, 1941	676	2196-A, p. 83
18. Lettera all'ambasciatore a Berlino, Alfieri		
October 6, 1941	677	2196-A, p. 85
19. Colloquio con il Führer		
October 25, 1941	678	2196-A, p. 32
20. Colloquio con il Führer		
October 26, 1941	679	2196-A, p. 34

1941

Date	Book (Page)	Lisbon Papers (Reel, file, and page)

21. Colloquio del conte Ciano col Führer, col maresciallo Göring e col ministro degli affari esteri Von Ribbentrop
    November 24–27, 1941   686   2196-A, p. 47

22. Colloquio del Duce con l'ambasciatore del Giappone alle presenza del conte Ciano
    December 3, 1941   694   2196-A, p. 76

23. Colloquio con l'ammiraglio Darlan
    December 10, 1941   698   2196-A, p. 7

24. Colloquio del conte Ciano col Poglavnik di Croazia, Pavelic
    December 16, 1941   703   2196-A, p. 1

1942

Date	Book (Page)	Lisbon Papers (Reel, file, and page)

1. Colloqui con il reggente Horthy, il presidente del consiglio Bárdossy e altre personalità politiche ungheresi
   January 15–18, 1942   709   2196-G, p. 161
       2196-A, p. 68

2. Lettera al presidente del consiglio Bárdossy, Budapest
   February 17, 1942   713   2196-A, p. 93

3. Colloquio con il ministro degli esteri Von Ribbentrop
   April 29–30, 1942   715   2196-A, p. 60

Bibliography

BIBLIOGRAPHIES, GUIDES

The American Historical Association, Committee for the Study of War Documents (Howard M. Ehrmann, Director of the Project). *A Catalogue of Files and Microfilms of the German Foreign Ministry Archives, 1867–1920.* Oxford: Oxford University Press, 1959.

Great Britain, Public Record Office. *Guide to the Contents of the Public Record Office.* London: H.M. Stationery Office, 1963.

Great Britain, Public Record Office (Public Record Office Handbooks No. 15). *The Second World War: A Guide to Documents in the Public Record Office.* London: H.M. Stationery Office, 1972.

Kent, George O., comp. and ed. *A Catalog of Files and Microfilms of the German Foreign Ministry Archives 1920–1945.* Vols. 1–4. Stanford University, Cal.: Hoover Institution Press, 1962–1972. Published as a joint project of the United States Department of State and the Hoover Institution on War, Revolution, and Peace.

Munden, Kenneth W. *Analytical Guide to the Combined British-American Records of the Mediterranean Theater of Operations in World War II.* Headquarters Military Liquidating Agency, Allied Force Records Administration: Rome, 1948. 290 pages, mimeographed. Pt. 7 (pp. 236–90) includes some records of Allied military government, of the Allied Commission (Italy), and other Allied Control Commissions.

National Archives and Records Service (General Services Administration), National Archives. *Federal Records of World War II.* Vol. 1, *Civilian Agencies;* vol. 2 *Military Agencies.* Washington: U.S. Government Printing Office, 1950, 1951. National Archives Publication, nos. 51-7, 51-8.

National Archives and Records Service (NARS). *Catalogue of the Combined British-American Records of the Mediterranean Theater of Operations in World War II* (exclusive of the Records of the Allied Commission for Italy). Compiled by Archives Division, Allied Force Records Administration. 3 vols. Rome, 1948 (typewritten). For use of the NARS staff only.

National Archives, National Archives and Records Service, General Services Administration. *Guide to Records of the Italian Armed Forces.* Pts. 1, 2, and 3. Washington, 1967.

National Archives, National Archives and Records Service, General Services Administration. *Guides to German Records Microfilmed at Alexandria, Va.* Washington, 1958–. No. 66 was issued in 1972. No. 12, *Records of Headquarters of the German Army High Command.* Pt. 1 (a guide to microcopy T-78). Washington, 1959.

(TAGO) The Adjutant General's Office, Departmental Records Branch, Administrative Services Division. *Guide to Seized Records: Reference Aid Nr. 17.* Edited by Philip P. Brower, Archivist. Washington, 1957.

ARCHIVES, UNPUBLISHED DOCUMENTS

Records of the Allied Commission (Italy), formerly Departmental Records Branch, Record Group 946, now comprised in NARS Record Group 331, "Allied Operational and Occupational Headquarters of World War II." Monuments, Fine Arts, and Archives Subcommission Catalogue reference 10,000/145.

Department of State, Central Files. When retired to the National Archives these files constitute Record Group 59.

Personal file of Allen W. Dulles, marked "Edda Ciano Diaries", a manila folder 15 by 8½ inches. The left side, a series of copies of telegrams and official correspondence in reverse chronological order, 62 items from July 14, 1945 to December 26, 1944. The right side, a series of memoranda, letters, etc., 71 items. *Pucci Report,* a letter or report, 17 typewritten pages, double spaced, legal size, dated May 24, 1945, signed by Emilio Pucci di Barsento. Item 18R in File "Edda Ciano Diaries."

Historical Office, Department of State, files.

German Documents Branch, (former), Historical Office, Department of State, files.

National Archives. Administrative files.

National Archives. Miscellaneous Reports of Hq. U.S. Seventh Army.

Office of the Chief of Military History (OCMH), Department of the Army, files. (Initially Historical Office, War Department.)

Personal file of E. Ralph Perkins (former editor-in-chief, *Foreign Relations of the United States*). A file regarding the search for Nazi German civil records, 1944–45.

Archival Microfilm Collections Held by the National Archives and Records Service (NARS)

Combined British-American Records of the Mediterranean Theater of Operations in World War II: A collection of 1648 rolls of microfilm; the original documents were transferred in 1947–48 to the Historical Section of the British

Cabinet in London. NARS, Record Group 331. "Psychological Warfare in the Mediterranean Theater" mimeographed, Naples, Italy, August 31, 1945. Reel 554-A.

Records of Headquarters of the German Army High Command. Microcopy T-78.

Files of the German Foreign Ministry (*Auswärtiges Amt*). Microcopy T-120.

Records of the Italian Armed Forces. Microcopy T-821.

The Lisbon Papers. Microcopy T-816.

Mussolini's Private Papers. Microcopy T-586. "Segreteria Particolare del Capo del Governo—Administration of Mussolini's Secretariat." Job 154, frames 045272–400.

PUBLISHED DOCUMENTS

Akten zur Deutschen Auswärtigen Politik, 1918–1945. Vols. 1–7, series D (1937–41) were issued by the Tripartite (American-British-French) Project, 1950–56, and were printed at the Imprimerie Nationale, Baden-Baden. Vols. 8–13 of that series were issued by the Quadripartite Project (American-British-French-German) with German editorial responsibility, 1961–70, and with various printers. The Quadripartite Project plans to cover the whole period, 1918–45, and has so far issued five vols. in series B (1925–33), one vol. in series C (1933–37), and two vols. in series E (1941–45), all printed by Vandenboeck & Rupprecht in Göttingen, 1966–72.

Il processo Carboni-Roatta: L'armistizio e la difesa di Roma nella sentenza del tribunale militare. Estratto dalla "Rivista Penale," maggio–giugno 1949, fasc. 5–6. Rome: Società Editrice "Temi," n.d.

The War Speeches of the Rt Hon Winston S. Churchill. Compiled by Charles Eade. 3 vols. London: Cassell & Company, Ltd., 1952. Vol. 2.

Ciano, Galeazzo. *L'Europa verso la catastrofe:* 184 colloqui con Mussolini, Hitler, Franco, Chamberlain, Sumner Welles, Rustu Aras, Stoiadinovic, Göring, Zog, François Poncet ecc. Verbalizzati da Galeazzo Ciano con 40 documenti diplomatici inediti. Milan: Arnoldo Mondadori, 1948.

———. *Ciano's Diplomatic Papers*. Edited by Malcolm Muggeridge, translated by Stuart Hood. London: Odhams Press [1948].

———. *Les archives secrètes du comte Ciano 1936–1941*. Traduction de Maurice Vaussard. Paris: Librairie Plon, 1948.

Department of State, *Consultation among the American Republics with Respect to the Argentine Situation*. Memorandum of the United States Government, Washington, D.C., February 1946. Washington: U.S. Government Printing Office, 1946.

Department of State (and the British Foreign Office). *Documents on German Foreign Policy 1918–1945*. Vols. 1–13, series D. (1937–41). Washington and London, 1949–64, Vols. 1–5, series C (1933–37). Washington and London: 1957–66. As of this date, vol. 6, which will complete the series, is still in preparation. These are English translations of the *Akten zur Deutschen Auswärtigen Politik 1918–1945*.

Department of State, *Foreign Relations of the United States 1945*. Vol. 3, *European Advisory Commission: Austria; Germany*. Washington: U.S. Government Printing Office, 1968.

Department of State, Transfer of Archives, Agreement between the United States of American and the Federal Republic of Germany, effected by exchange of letters signed at Bonn and Bonn/Bad Godesberg, March 14 and April 18, 1956. *Treaties and Other International Acts Series 3613*.

Germany, Auswärtiges Amt, 1939/41 Nr. 6. *Die Geheimakten des französischen Generalstabes*. Berlin: Zentral-Verlag der NSDAP. Franz Eher Nachf. GMBH., 1941.

Graziani, Rodolfo. *Processo*. 3 vols. Rome: Ruffolo, 1948–50. Vol. 3, *Il testimoniale e gli incidenti procedurali*.

Great Britain. *Parliamentary Debates*, (Commons), 5th ser., 392 (1943).

Hitler, Adolf. *Hitler e Mussolini: Lettere e documenti*. Introduction and notes by Vittorio Zincone. Copyright by King Features Syndicate, New York, 1946. Milan: Rizzoli, 1946.

———. *Les lettres secrètes échangées par Hitler e Mussolini*. Introduction de André François-Poncet. Paris: Éditions du Pavois, 1946.

———. *Hitler's Secret Book*. Translated by Salvator Attanasio. Introduction by Telford Taylor. New York: Grove Press, Inc., 1961.

International Military Tribunal. *Trial of the Major War Criminals before the International Military Tribunal, Nuremberg, 14 November 1945–1 October 1946*. 42 vols. Nuremberg, Germany 1947–49. Official text in the English language.

Italy, Consiglio di Stato, Sezione speciale per l'epurazione. *Documenti prodotti a corredo della memoria del Consigliere di Legazione Blasco Lanza d'Ajeta*. Rome: Tipografia Ferraiolo, 1946.

———. *Memoria a svolgimento del ricorso del Consigliere di Legazione Blasco Lanza d'Ajeta contro la decisione della Commissione per l'epurazione del personale dipendente dal Ministero degli Affari Esteri*. Rome: Tipografia Ferraiolo, 1946.

Italy, Ministero degli Affari Esteri, Commissione per la pubblicazione dei documenti diplomatici. *I documenti diplomatici italiani*. (Projected in nine series to cover the period 1861 to 1943). Rome: Libreria dello Stato, 1952–. 8th ser., vol. 13, Rome, 1953.

Jenkinson, Hilary, and Bell, H. E. *Italian Archives During the War and at its Close.* London: H. M. Stationery Office, 1947. Issued by the British Committee on the preservation and restitution of works of art, archives and other material in enemy hands. Based on the final report on Italian archives presented to the Allied Commission.

Mussolini, Benito, *Opera omnia di Benito Mussolini.* Edited by Edoardo and Duilio Susmel. 35 vols. Florence: La Fenice, 1951–62. Vols. 34 and 35.

Salvadori, Renato, ed. *Nemesi: Dal 25 al 28 aprile 1943:* Milan: Baldassarre Gnocchi, 1945. *Documenti e testimonianze sulle ultime ore di Mussolini.*

Schramm, Percy Ernst, and Greiner, Helmuth, eds. *Kriegstagebuch des Oberkommandos der Wehrmacht (Wehrmachtführungsstab).* 4 vols. in 7 pts. Frankfurt am Main: Bernard & Graefe Verlag für Wehrwesen, 1961–65. With a Supplement, edited by Andreas Hillgruber, *Der Krieg in Finnland, Norwegen und Dänemark vom 1. Januar–31 März 1944* (1969).

MEMOIRS

Acheson, Dean. *Present at the Creation: My Years in the State Department.* New York: W. W. Norton & Co., 1969.

Alfieri, Dino. *Due dittatori di fronte.* Milan: Rizzoli, 1948.

Badoglio, Pietro. *L'Italia nella seconda guerra mondiale: Memorie e documenti.* Milan: Arnoldo Mondadori, 1946.

Basso, Antonio, Gen. *L'armistizio del settembre 1943 in Sardegna.* Naples: Rispoli, 1947.

Bellini delle Stelle, Pier Luigi ("Pedro"), and Lazzaro, Urbano ("Bill"). *Dongo ultima azione.* Milan: Arnoldo Mondadori, 1962.

Benini, Zenone. *Vigilia a Verona.* Milan: Garzanti, 1949.

Bottai, Giuseppe. *Vent'anni e un giorno (24 luglio 1943).* Milan: Garzanti, 1949.

Cadorna, Raffaele. *La riscossa: Dal 25 luglio alla liberazione.* Milan: Rizzoli, 1948.

Caracciolo di Feroleto, Mario. *"E Poi?": La tragedia dell'esercito italiano.* Rome: Casa editrice Libraria Corso, 1946.

Carroll, Wallace. *Persuade or Perish.* Boston: Houghton Mifflin Co., 1948.

Churchill, Winston S. *The Second World War.* 6 vols. (Boston: Houghton Mifflin Co., 1948–53). Vol. 2, *Their Finest Hour* (1949); vol. 6, *Triumph and Tragedy* (1953).

Ciano, Galeazzo. *Diario.* 2 vols. Milan and Rome; Rizzoli, 1946.

———. *The Ciano Diaries 1939–1943: The Complete, Unabridged Diaries of Count Galeazzo Ciano, Italian Minister for Foreign Affairs, 1936–1943.* Edited by Hugh

Gibson. Introduction by Sumner Welles. Garden City, New York: Doubleday & Co., 1946.

———. *1937–1938 Diario*. Bologna: Cappelli, 1948.

———. *Journal politique 1939–1943*. Traduction française intégrale d'après l'original italien par S. et S. Stelling-Michaud. 2 vols. Neuchatel: Éditions de la Baconnière; Paris: La Press Française et Étrangère [1948].

———. *Ciano's Hidden Diary 1937–1938*. Translation and notes by Andreas Mayor. Introduction by Malcolm Muggeridge. New York: E. P. Dutton & Co., 1953.

Dolfin, Giovanni. *Con Mussolini nella tragedia: Diario del Capo della Segreteria Particolare del Duce 1943–1944*. Milan: Garzanti, 1949.

Dulles, Allen *The Secret Surrender*. New York, Evanston, and London: Harper & Row, 1966.

Eden, Anthony (Earl of Avon). *The Eden Memoirs: Facing the Dictators*. London: Cassell & Co.,Ltd., 1962; Boston: Houghton Mifflin Co., 1962.

Goebbels, Paul Josef. *The Goebbels Diaries 1942–1943*. Edited, translated and with an Introduction by Louis P. Lochner. Garden City, N.Y.: Doubleday & Co., 1948.

Graziani, Rodolfo. *Ho difeso la patria*. 4th ed. Milan: Garzanti, 1948.

Guariglia, Raffaele. *Ricordi 1922–1946*. Naples: Edizioni Scientifiche Italiane, 1950.

Hagen, Walter [pseud. for Wilhelm Hoettl]. *Die geheime Front: Organisation, Personen und Aktionen des deutschen Geheimdienstes*. 2d ed. Linz and Vienna: Nibelungen-Verlag, 1950.

Hoettl, Wilhelm. *The Secret Front: The Story of Nazi Political Espionage*. 2d ed. London: Weidenfeld & Nicolson, 1954.

Mussolini, Benito. *Il tempo del bastone e della carota: Storia di un anno (ottobre 1942–settembre 1943)*. Supplemento del "Corriere della Sera," no. 190 del 9-8-1944—XXII.

———. *The Fall of Mussolini: His Own Story by Benito Mussolini*. Edited by Max Ascoli. New York: Farrar, Strauss and Co., 1948.

———. *Benito Mussolini: Memoirs 1942–1943 with Documents Relating to the Period*. Edited by Raymond Klibansky, translated by Frances Lobb, Introduction by Cecil Sprigge. London: George Weidenfeld & Nicolson, Ltd., 1949.

Mussolini, Rachele. *La mia vita con Benito*. Milan: Arnoldo Mondadori, 1948.

Mussolini, Vittorio. *Vita con mio padre*. Milan: Arnold Mondadori, 1957.

Navarra, Quinto. *Memorie del cameriere di Mussolini*. Milan: Longanesi & C., 1946.

Nel, Elizabeth *[née Layton]. Mr. Churchill's Secretary.* New York: Coward-Mc-Cann, Inc., 1958.

Pawle, Gerald. *The War and Colonel Warden.* (Based on the recollections of Commander C. R. Thompson C.M.G., O.B.E., R.N. *[ret.].)* With a foreword by W. Averell Harriman. London: George G. Harrap & Co., Ltd. 1963.

Rossi, Francesco. *Come arrivammo all'armistizio.* Milan: Garzanti, 1946.

Salvadori, Massimo. *The Labour and the Wounds: A Personal Chronicle of One Man's Fight for Freedom.* London: Pall Mall Press, 1958.

Schellenberg, Walter. *The Labyrinth: Memoirs of Walter Schellenberg.* Translated by Louis Hagen, Introduction by Alan Bullock. New York: Harper & Brothers, 1956.

Schuster, Cardinal Ildefonso (Archbishop of Milan). *Gli ultimi tempi di un regime.* Milan: "La Via," 1946.

Tompkins, Peter. *A Spy in Rome.* New York: Published by arrangement with Simon and Schuster, Inc., 1962.

Von Rintelen, Enno. *Mussolini als Bundesgenosse: Erinnerungen des deutschen Militärattachés in Rom, 1936–1943.* Tübingen: R. Wunderlich, 1951.

Wilson, Sir Charles (Lord Moran). *Churchill: Taken from the Diaries of Lord Moran—The Struggle for Survival, 1940–1965.* Boston: Houghton Mifflin Co., 1966.

SECONDARY WORKS

History of AFHQ (History of Allied Force Headquarters and Headquarters NATOUSA): A History of Command, Administration and Organization at the Headquarters Level. Pts. 1–3 with pts. 2 and 3 each in four separate sections. Allied Force Headquarters, Caserta, 1945. Pt. 4, *Draft History of AFHQ* (November 1946).

Amicucci, Ermanno. *I 600 giorni di Mussolini.* Rome: Editrice "Faro," 1948.

Bandini, Franco. *Le ultime 95 ore di Mussolini.* 3d ed. Milan: Sugar Editore, September 1963.

Binkley, Robert C. *Selected Papers of Robert C. Binkley.* Edited by Max H. Fisch, Foreword by Luther H. Evans. Cambridge: Harvard University Press, 1948.

Cassels, Alan. *Mussolini's Early Diplomacy.* Princeton: Princeton University Press, 1970.

Cersosimo, Vincenzo. *Dall'instruttoria alla fucilazione: storia del processo di Verona.* Milan: Garzanti, 1949.

Churchill, Winston S. *Painting as a Pastime*. 1950. Reprint. New York: Cornerstone Library, 1965.

Craig, Gordon A., and Gilbert, Felix, eds. *The Diplomats*. H. Stuart Hughes, "The Early Diplomacy of Italian Fascism," chap. 7, pp. 210–33; Felix Gilbert, "Ciano and his Ambassadors," chap. 16, pp. 512–36. Princeton: Princeton University Press, 1953.

Davidson, Eugene. *The Trial of the Germans: An Account of the Twenty-two Defendants before the International Military Tribunal at Nuremberg*. New York: The Macmillan Co., 1966.

Deakin, Frederick W. *The Brutal Friendship: Mussolini, Hitler and the Fall of Italian Fascism*. New York and Evanston: Harper & Row, 1962.

Delzell, Charles F. *Mussolini's Enemies: The Italian Anti-Fascist Resistance*. Princeton: Princeton University Press, 1961.

Detwiler, Donald S. *Hitler, Franco und Gibraltar: Die Frage des spanischen Eintritts in den zweiten Weltkriege*. Wiesbaden: Franz Steiner Verlag, 1962.

Dombrowski, Roman. *Mussolini: Twilight and Fall*. Translated with a Preface by H. C. Stevens. New York: Roy Publishers, 1956.

Ebenstein, William. *Fascist Italy*. New York, Chicago, Cincinnati, Boston, Atlanta, Dallas, and San Francisco: American Book Company, 1939.

Ferraris, Luigi Vittorio. *L'amministrazione centrale del Ministero degli Esteri italiano nel suo svilupo storico (1848–1954)*. Florence: Poligrafico Toscano, 1955.

Cassius [pseud. for Michael Foot]. *The Trial of Mussolini: Being a Verbatim Report of the First Great Trial for War Criminals Held in London Sometime in 1944 or 1945*. London: Victor Gollancz Ltd., 1943.

Garland, Albert N., and Smyth, Howard McGaw. *Sicily and the Surrender of Italy*. Washington, D.C.: Office of the Chief of Military History, Department of the Army, 1965.

Giannuzzi, Col. Gaetano. *L'esercito vittima dell'armistizio*. Turin: P. Castello, 1946.

Harris, C. R. S. *Allied Military Administration of Italy 1943–1945*. London: H.M. Stationery Office, 1957.

Harrison, Gordon A. *Cross-Channel Attack*. Washington, D.C.: Office of the Chief of Military History, Department of the Army, 1951.

Haskins, Charles Homer. *The Renaissance of the Twelfth Century*. Cambridge: Harvard University Press, 1928.

Howe, George F. *Northwest Africa: Seizing the Initiative in the West*. Washington, D.C.: Office of the Chief of Military History, Department of the Army, 1957.

Kirkpatrick, Ivone. *Mussolini: A Study in Power.* New York: Hawthorne Books, Inc., 1964.

Langer, William L. *Our Vichy Gamble.* New York: Alfred A. Knopf, 1947.

Monelli, Paolo. *Roma 1943.* 3d ed. Rome: Migliaresi, September 1945.

Namier, Lewis Bernstein. *Diplomatic Prelude, 1938–1939.* London: Macmillan & Co., 1948.

Page, Bruce; Leitch, David; and Knightly, Philip. *The Philby Conspiracy.* Garden City, New York: Doubleday & Company, Inc., 1968.

Pini, Giorgio, and Susmel, Duilio. *Mussolini, l'uomo e l'opera.* 4 vols. Florence: La Fenice, 1953–55.

Pogue, Forrest C. *The Supreme Command.* Washington, D.C.: Office of the Chief of Military History, Department of the Army, 1954.

Re, Emilio. *Storia di un archivio: le carte di Mussolini.* Milan: Edizioni del Milione, 1946.

Saini, Ezio. *La notte di Dongo.* Rome: Casa Editrice Libraria Corso, 1950.

Salvemini, Gaetano. *Prelude to World War II.* London: Victor Gollancz, 1953.

Scholz, Richard, ed. *Marsilius von Padua: Defensor Pacis.* pts. 1 and 2. Hanover: Hahnsche Buchhandlung, 1932–33.

Settimelli, Emilio. *Edda contro Benito: Indagine sulla personalità del Duce attraverso un memoriale autografo di Edda Ciano Mussolini, qui riprodotto.* Rome: Corso, 1952.

Silvestri, Carlo. *Mussolini, Graziani e l'antifascismo.* Milan: Longanesi, 1949.

Silvestri, Giuseppe. *Albergo agli Scalzi.* Milan: Garzanti, 1946.

Spampanto, Bruno. *Contromemoriale.* Vol. 3, *Il segreto del nord* (con un' appendice storica, una foto-documentazione, e i "discorsi" di Mussolini). Rome: Edizione di "Illustrato," 1952.

Susmel, Duilio. *Vita sbagliata di Galeazzo Ciano.* Milan: Aldo Palazzi, 1962.

Tamaro, Attilio. *Due anni di storia 1943–1945.* 3 vols. Rome: Tosi, 1948–50.

Taylor, A. J. P., et al. *Churchill: Four Faces and the Man.* London: Allen Lane, Penguin Press, 1969.

Toscano, Mario. *The History of Treaties and International Politics.* Pt. 1. *An Introduction to the History of Treaties and International Politics: The Documentary and Memoir Sources.* Baltimore: The Johns Hopkins Press, 1966.

Toscano, Mario. *Pagine di storia diplomatica contemporanea.* 2 vols. Milan: A. Giuffrè, 1963. Vol. 2, *Origini e vicende della seconda guerra mondiale.* "Le vicende degli archivi di Palazzo Chigi e dei diari di prigionia di Mussolini catturati dai nazisti dopo l'armistizio," pp. 249–81.)

United Nations War Crimes Commission. *History of the United Nations War Crimes Commission and the Development of the Laws of War.* London: H.M. Stationery Office, 1948.

Vincentis, Luigi de. *Io son te.* . . . 2d ed. Milan: Cebes, 1946.

Zangrandi, Ruggero. *1943: 25 luglio–8 settembre.* 2d ed. Milan: Feltrinelli, 1964.

PERIODICAL AND OTHER ARTICLES

American Historical Association. *Newsletter 7,* no. 5 (June 1969).

Bush-Fekete, Laszlo. "The Last Four Days of Mussolini," *Life,* 12 January 1948.

Department of State, Historical Office. "Public Availability of Diplomatic Archives," May 1968. 25 pages, mimeographed.

Grandi, Dino. "Count Dino Grandi Explains," *Life,* 26 February 1945.

Kotze, Hildegard v. "Hitlers Sicherheitsdienst im Ausland," *Die politische Meinung,* August 1963.

Lazzero, Ricciotti. "Un passo verso la verità sulla morte di Mussolini: Dongo," *Epoca,* 11, 18, 25 August 1968.

Niccoletti, Andrea. "The Decline and Fall of Edda Ciano," *Colliers,* 20, 27 April 1946.

Palmieri, Edmund L., and Kobler, John. "What Happened to Mussolini's Millions: A story of a great political scandal; How partisans captured the Duce's vast treasure . . . How two young lovers were slain to hide it . . . How it helps pay the bills of the Communist Party," *Life,* 17 January 1949.

Pancino, Don Giusto. "Tentai di riconciliare Edda Ciano e Mussolini," *Oggi* 22 September 1954.

Pensotti, Anita. "Edda Ciano parla per la prima volta: Conversazioni di Anita Pensotti con Edda Ciano," *Oggi* (article in four pts.), 3, 10, 17, 25 September 1959.

Posner, Ernst. "The Administration of Current Records in Italian Public Agencies," The National Archives, *Records Administration Circular,* no. 5, November 1943.

Smyth, Howard McGaw. "Italy: From Fascism to the Republic," *The Western Political Quarterly* 1, no. 3 (1948), pp. 205–22.

———. "The Command of Italian Armed Forces in World War II," *Military Affairs* 15, no. 1 (Spring 1951), pp. 38–52.

———. "Italian Civil and Military Records on Microfilm." Paper delivered at the Conference on Captured German and Related Records held at the National Archives, November 13, 1968.

———. "Gli archivi civili e militari italiani conservati in microfilm a Washington," *Storia contemporanea* 3, no. 4 (1972) pp. 969–87 (Italian translation of the above).

Society for Italian Historical Studies. *Newsletter*, no. 1 (Spring 1963).

Susmel, Duilio. "Così Churchill rientro in possesso del carteggio con Mussolini," *Domenica di Corriere* (popular weekly of the *Corriere della Sera*), 29 January 1967, pp. 15–19.

Watt, Donald C. "United States Documentary Resources for the Study of British Foreign Policy, 1919–1939," *International Affairs* 38, no. 1 (1962) pp. 63–72.

———. "Restrictions on Research: The Fifty-Year Rule and British Foreign Policy," *International Affairs* 41, no. 1 (1965), pp. 89–95.

NEWSPAPERS

Christian Science Monitor (Boston), 27 May 1943. Despatch dated Washington, D.C.

Corriere della Sera (Milan), 15 December 1946. Unsigned article with heading: "Gli archivi segreti di Mussolini nelle mani della Commissione alleata" (based on a report prepared by Emilio Re).

Allen W. Dulles, personal file marked "IV. Lanfranchi-Mussolini." A series of newspaper and periodical cuttings, American, French, and Italian; 45 different items, some of them in several parts.

Il Giornale del Mattino (Rome), 21 September 1945. Despatch dated Lipari, September 20, "Sono stato a Lipari e ho parlate con Edda," signed Jader Jacobelli.

Giornale di Sicilia (Palermo), 6–22 September 1945. A series of signed articles entitled "Le memorie del marchese Pucci," (identical with the series printed in the *Libera Stampa*).

Libera Stampa (Rome). 6–16 September 1945. A series of signed articles under the title "Relazione Pucci," or "Il marchese Pucci racconta."

Il Messaggero (Rome), 12 April 1970. Despatch dated Florence, April 11 entitled "Trovato il carteggio Churchill-Mussolini? Lo studioso Duilio Susmel afferma di essere entrato in possesso di parte delle lettere in fotocopia di enorme interesse storico e politico."

Neue Zürcher Zeitung 13 March 1947. Despatch dated Milan, March 12 entitled "Der Befehl zur Erschiessung Mussolinis."

New York *Times*, 30 July 1944, 2 July 1946.

Risorgimento Liberale (Rome), 18–28 July 1944. A series of articles signed 'Porfirio' and entitled "Il diario di Ciano."

————, 14 March 1947. Unsigned article with the heading "Dichiarazioni di Togliatti sull'esecuzione di Mussolini."

————, 1 April 1947. Signed article by Vittorio Gorresio entitled "Il sensazionale atto d'accusa del colonello Valerio nel comizio di domenica alla Basilica di Massenzio."

————, 3 April 1947. Signed article by Vittorio Zincone entitled "Chi prese le carte di Mussolini? I fascicoli sui Savoja scomparvero dopo il 25 luglio—I documenti di Dongo furono fotografati dai comunisti."

L'Unità (Milan edition), May–June 1945.

Voix Ouvrière (Geneva), 8 June 1946. Article initialed "p.n." and headed "Les documents de Mussolini disparaissent et M. Churchill apparaît."

Washington *Post*, 25 February 1967.

MISCELLANEOUS

Interviews

Andrew H. Berding, 28 November 1967 at 1630 Crescent Place, N.W., Washington, D.C.

Philip P. Brower, Deputy Director, Archival Projects Division, NARS, 3 March 1965 at King and Union Streets, Alexandria, Virginia.

Dr. Ralph S. Collins, 20 April 1966 in the Executive Dining Room, Department of State.

Herbert J. Cummungs, 4 June 1964 in room 1314 Commerce Building.

Allen W. Dulles, 17 January 1966 and 19 June 1968 at his home in Georgetown, 2723 Q Street, N.W.

Paul Ghali, 18 June 1969, Hotel Jefferson, Washington, D.C.

Miss Lisa Sergio, 10 July and 10 December 1969, luncheon discussions.

Letters

Blanchard W. Bates, professor at Princeton University, member of the OSS during World War II, 22 February 1970.

James Stuart Beddie, assoc. ed., *Documents on German Foreign Policy, 1918–1945*, February–April 1954.

Philip P. Brower, deputy director, Archival Projects Division, NARS, 5 August 1965.

George A. Carbone, professor of history, Portland State University (then in Rome), April–July 1967.

Charles F. Delzell, professor of history, Vanderbilt University, 22 November 1972.

(Mrs.) Patricia G. Dowling, Diplomatic, Legal, and Fiscal Branch, National Archives, 1964–68.

Maj. Peter Gordon AUS (retired), 26 April 1966.

King Features Syndicate, 5 May 1966.

Hans Kohn, then visiting professor of history, University of Texas, 27 April 1967.

Margaret Lambert, British editor in chief, *Documents on German Foreign Policy, 1918–1945*, 1964–70.

William L. Langer, professor emeritus, Harvard University, wartime head of the Research and Analysis Branch, OSS, 15 August 1966.

(Mrs.) Florence W. Lehman, alumni director, Reed College, 17 February 1970.

John Marshall, Rockefeller Foundation, then in Bellagio, Italy, January–February 1968.

Brian Melland, Cabinet Office, Historical Section, London, October–December 1955 and June–September 1968.

Wilbur J. Nigh, chief, World War II Reference Branch, NARS, 13 May 1966.

Raymond Rocca, member of the OSS during World War II, February 1969.

Dr. Giorgio Rochat, Comité internationale d'histoire de la deuxième guerre mondiale, Milan, 15 January 1973.

Raymond J. Sontag, initial U.S. editor in chief of the *Documents on German Foreign Policy, 1918–1945*, 21 August 1964.

Peter Tompkins, free-lance writer, member of the OSS during World War II, 12 July 1967.

Arnold J. Toynbee, Royal Institute of International Affairs, Chatham House, 7 November 1966.

Hugh Trevor-Roper, professor at Oxford University, 18 July and 28 August 1968.

Robert Wolfe, specialist for Modern European History, National Archives, 1966–72.

Reference Works

Almanach de Gotha (1943): annuaire genealogique, diplomatique et statistique. Gotha: J. Perthes, 1944.

Chi È? Dizionario degli Italiani d'oggi 1940. 4th ed. Rome, 1940.

Codignola, Arturo, ed. *L'Italia e gli italiani di oggi.* Genoa: Il Nuovo Mondo, 1947.

The Columbia Encyclopedia. 3d ed. New York and London: Columbia University Press, 1963.

Department of State. *Foreign Service List.* Washington: U.S. Government Printing Office, issued periodically.

Enciclopedia italiana di scienze, lettere ed arti. 35 vols. Copyright by Giovanni Treccani, 1929–37. Vol. 36, Indici (1939); Appendice 1 (1938); Appendice 2 for the period 1938–48 in 2 vols. (1948); Appendice 3 for the period 1949–60 in 2 vols. (1961).

Italy, Ministero degli Affari Esteri. *Elenchi del personale.* Rome: Tiografia riservata del Ministero degli Affari Esteri, issued periodically.

Index